LAWYERS AND LEGAL CULTURE IN BRITISH NORTH AMERICA

Beamish Murdoch of Halifax

PATRONS OF THE SOCIETY

Blake, Cassels & Graydon LLP

Gowlings

Lax O'Sullivan Scott Lisus LLP

McCarthy Tétrault LLP

Osler, Hoskin & Harcourt LLP

Paliare Roland Rosenberg Rothstein LLP

Torkin Manes LLP

Torys LLP

WeirFoulds LLP

The Osgoode Society is supported by a grant from
The Law Foundation of Ontario.

The Law Foundation of Ontario
Building a better foundation for justice in Ontario

The Society also thanks The Law Society of Upper Canada
for its continuing support.

LAWYERS AND LEGAL CULTURE IN BRITISH NORTH AMERICA

Beamish Murdoch of Halifax

PHILIP GIRARD

Published for The Osgoode Society for Canadian Legal History by
University of Toronto Press
Toronto Buffalo London

ISBN 978-1-4426-4410-6

Library and Archives Canada Cataloguing in Publication

Girard, Philip
Lawyers and legal culture in British North America :
Beamish Murdoch of Halifax / Philip Girard.

Includes bibliographical references and index.
ISBN 978-1-4426-4410-6

1. Murdoch, Beamish, 1800–1876.   2. Lawyers – Nova Scotia – Biography.
3. Practice of law – Nova Scotia – History – 19th century.
I. Osgoode Society for Canadian Legal History.   II. Title.

KE411.M86G57 2011   340.092   C2011-903380-1
KF345.Z9M86G57 2011

University of Toronto Press acknowledges the financial assistance to its
publishing program of the Canada Council for the Arts and the
Ontario Arts Council.

 Canada Council   Conseil des Arts   ONTARIO ARTS COUNCIL
for the Arts   du Canada   CONSEIL DES ARTS DE L'ONTARIO

University of Toronto Press acknowledges the financial support of the
Government of Canada through the Canada Book Fund for its
publishing activities.

To Sheila

Contents

Foreword

Philip Girard is well known to Osgoode Society readers as the author of an award-winning biography of Bora Laskin. Girard's *Lawyers and Legal Culture in British North America: Beamish Murdoch of Halifax* is much more than a biography of Nova Scotia's best-known nineteenth-century lawyer and legal author. It is also a first-class account of an everyday lawyer's practice in the first half of the nineteenth century and has a great deal to say about the British North American legal profession and legal culture. Girard places Murdoch and the legal profession in one colony in the broader context of what we know about the international history of the legal profession at the time, and he also draws interesting links between Murdoch's legal practice and legal ideas and the politics of the period, especially arguments over responsible government.

The purpose of the Osgoode Society for Canadian Legal History is to encourage research and writing in the history of Canadian law. The Society, which was incorporated in 1979 and is registered as a charity, was founded at the initiative of the Honourable R. Roy McMurtry, formerly attorney general for Ontario and chief justice of the province, and officials of the Law Society of Upper Canada. The Society seeks to stimulate the study of legal history in Canada by supporting researchers, collecting oral histories, and publishing volumes that contribute to legal-historical scholarship in Canada. It has published eighty-four books on the courts, the judiciary, and the legal profession, as well as on the history of crime and punishment, women and law, law and economy, the legal treatment of ethnic minorities, and famous cases and significant trials in all areas of the law.

Current directors of the Osgoode Society for Canadian Legal History are Robert Armstrong, Christopher Bentley, Kenneth Binks, Patrick Brode, Brian Bucknall, David Chernos, Kirby Chown, J. Douglas Ewart, Martin Friedland, John Honsberger, Horace Krever, C. Ian Kyer, Virginia MacLean, Patricia McMahon, R. Roy McMurtry, Laurie Pawlitza, Jim Phillips, Paul Reinhardt, Joel Richler, William Ross, Paul Schabas, Robert Sharpe, James Spence, Richard Tinsley, and Michael Tulloch.

The annual report and information about membership may be obtained by writing to the Osgoode Society for Canadian Legal History, Osgoode Hall, 130 Queen Street West, Toronto, Ontario, M5H 2N6. Telephone: 416-947-3321. E-mail: mmacfarl@lsuc.on.ca. Website: www. osgoodesociety.ca.

R. Roy McMurtry
President

Jim Phillips
Editor-in-Chief

Acknowledgments

This book began as a doctoral thesis in history at Dalhousie University, and I would like to thank my supervisor, David Sutherland, and committee members Michael Cross and Judith Fingard for their advice and critique along the way. After its completion in 1998, I decided to put it away for a while – a decade, as it turned out – while I pursued other projects. When I returned to it in 2008, it was clear that there had to be at least one new chapter (chapter eight), significant revisions to the others, and a completely new introduction and conclusion. In that process I have accumulated more debts, especially to research assistants Jeffrey Haylock and Daniel Huffaker and to Jim Phillips for encouragement and feedback throughout the rewriting process. Conversations with Richard Devlin about contemporary issues facing the legal profession have also stimulated my thinking.

The librarians and staff at the Sir James Dunn Law Library at the Schulich School of Law and the Killam Library at Dalhousie have been unfailingly helpful, as have the archivists and staff at the Public Archives of Nova Scotia. I am grateful for the insightful comments of the Osgoode Society's anonymous reviewers and for funding from the Social Sciences and Humanities Research Council of Canada. The Centre for Criminology and Sociolegal Studies at the University of Toronto provided a congenial home where I completed the final revisions to the manuscript while on sabbatical leave. Len Husband and Curtis Fahey at the University of Toronto Press were a pleasure to work with, as was Marilyn MacFarlane at the Osgoode Society.

Beamish Murdoch
(Courtesy of Nova Scotia Archives and Records Management)

LAWYERS AND LEGAL CULTURE IN BRITISH NORTH AMERICA

Beamish Murdoch of Halifax

1

Introduction

Beamish Murdoch (1800–76) was, in the economical language of the *Dictionary of Canadian Biography*, a Nova Scotian 'writer, lawyer, and politician.'[1] By examining and contextualizing his life and career, this book aims to explore the role of lawyers and the development of legal culture in a particular settler society, British North America, from roughly 1800 to 1867.

The reader may well ask whether we need more work on pre-Confederation lawyers in British North America. There are excellent studies of Ontario lawyers and of the Law Society of Upper Canada, of early Montreal law firms, and of lawyers and legal education in New Brunswick and Quebec, in addition to work placing lawyers in the larger context of their regional legal cultures.[2] We have learned much about the contours of old-style gentlemanly professionalism and its adaptation to an early colonial society with a more fluid social structure, more widespread landholding, and a more scattered population than the mother country. We know about the importance of the education and socialization of lawyers through long apprenticeships, eventually leading to university legal education beginning with McGill University in 1848. We have studied the drive of lawyers to organize themselves in ways distinct from both England and the United States, first with the statutory creation of the Law Society of Upper Canada in 1797, then with similar bodies in Quebec in the 1840s, and with a mix of voluntary associations and statutory measures in the Maritimes before they too created robust statutory bodies in the post-Confederation period to which all lawyers had to belong. We are familiar with lawyers as ideological entrepreneurs, both upholding the 'mixed and balanced' constitution present in each of the colonies and developing arguments against it during the campaign for responsible government.[3] We are interested in the relationship between lawyers and business and lawyers and the state, though, aside from the work of G. Blaine Baker, we do not yet know much about this in the pre-Confederation period.[4]

We could of course stand to learn more about all these things, but this book seeks to do something different. It aims, first, to examine in detail the professional life of a single nineteenth-century lawyer, thus permitting a new, more grass-roots perspective on the work and role of colonial lawyers. Second, it posits that nineteenth-century lawyers shared a British North American experience. While the empirical focus of the book is Nova Scotia, the existing literature from the other colonies is regularly invoked to show how, well before Confederation, and in spite of minimal formal, personal, or commercial contacts between the Maritimes and Upper and Lower Canada, British North American lawyers shared a similar *mentalité*, made similar choices about what lawyers should or should not do, and played similar roles in their communities and their societies. Comparisons with lawyers in England and the United States will further highlight this account of the British North American lawyer. These will be pursued especially in chapter 4 and in the Conclusion, where I analyse the Canadian example with the aid of Michael Burrage's work on the impact of national revolutions on the legal profession.[5]

I approach my subject through the lens of cultural history. As described by David Sugarman and Wesley Pue, one of the main preoccupations of this perspective is 'to describe and analyse the production, transmission and reception of the ideas and practices of lawyers in society over time: of how differing fractions within and beyond the legal community consume the practices and ideas of lawyers and their larger significance ... A cultural approach to lawyers in history would also critically describe and assess the role of lawyers as potentially important actors in the complex process by which notions of national distinctiveness and personal identity were imaginatively constructed.'[6] But a legal-cultural approach is not restricted to the study of ideas, as Sugarman and Pue make clear: 'What lawyers did, how they earned their bread and butter, their practices and ideas, how they dealt with clients ... the reputation of lawyers, and the extent to which there was access to legal advice and assistance (as well as alternatives to lawyers and litigation)' are also essential parts of the enterprise.[7]

Nor is legal culture restricted to legal institutions or to ideas and practices within the legal profession. Lawrence Friedman has described legal culture as 'ideas, values, expectations and attitudes towards law and legal institutions, which some public or some part of the public holds,'[8] and, even though the concept has been criticized, it remains an important tool in socio-legal and legal-historical work.[9] Legal culture as used in this book follows the further development of Friedman's idea by Michael Grossberg and Ann Fidler as well as Sugarman and Pue. Legal culture should be understood as having a lived or behavioural component as well as an intellectual one, and I follow Grossberg in understanding legal culture as 'an arena of conflict occupied by a myriad of sub-cultures capable of influencing law, and in turn, being influenced by it.'[10] In other words, legal culture is not monolithic in any given society and it is always dynamic. Legal culture in British North America, as we shall see, was a terrain on which a variety of subcultures interacted within the matrix of an inherited tradition of English common law.

An advantage of the cultural approach is its ability to straddle disciplinary frontiers that often isolate bodies of scholarship from one another. Ideally, this book will appeal not just to legal historians but to social, economic, intellectual, political, and urban historians, comparative law scholars, scholars of the contemporary legal profession, and historically oriented sociologists. Lawyers are specialists in the law, but law touches on virtually every aspect of life; in the colonial period, this was especially so, since specialization within legal practice was almost unknown. The myriad involvements of colonial lawyers thus call for an open-ended historical approach that triangulates what lawyers did, what they said and thought, and what others said about them.

This examination of the legal career of Halifax native Beamish Murdoch will focus on three main themes: the lawyer as professional, as contributor to intellectual and cultural life, and as economic actor. Murdoch's life, his writings, and the surviving sources from his law practice permit a more detailed analysis of these themes than would be possible for most other lawyers of this period. Although biographical in form, this is not a traditional biography. It does not examine to any great extent the psychological development of its subject, and it is more a 'career of' Beamish Murdoch than a 'life.' The book proceeds mostly in chronological sequence (chapters 2, 3, 5, 6, and 8), but chapters 7 and

9 are thematic accounts covering Murdoch's political and cultural contributions respectively, while chapter 4 departs from the biographical format to consider trends in the growth, mobility, and organization of the Nova Scotia bar to which Murdoch belonged.

One feature that makes lawyers difficult to study is the seemingly protean nature of their involvements. In addition to mastering their chosen profession, lawyers often played important roles in politics and contributed to the development of political ideas, worked as officeholders or civil servants, served as leaders of voluntary societies and reform movements, appeared in religious controversies, contributed to literature and journalism, acted as spokespersons for various economic interests, and became directly involved in business enterprises outside their law practices. Not all lawyers did all these things, but a surprising number of colonial lawyers functioned in many of these capacities over the course of a lifetime. Beamish Murdoch, for example, participated in all of the above activities except the last, and his identity as a professional lawyer – 'one of the fraternity,' in the contemporary phrase – both subsumed and was a function of all of them.

It has been suggested in the context of the early-twentieth-century Montreal bar that the wide range of lawyers' non-legal activities was an important factor in defining their professional identity.[11] One of the goals of this study is to examine the life of a lawyer who came before the public eye in many capacities, but not primarily as a politician or a judge, in order to better understand the synergies created by these many roles. In spite of the seeming prevalence of anti-lawyer sentiment in British North America, the colonial population needed and expected lawyers to assume a variety of leadership roles, and not just those in the political or judicial sphere. In the colonial period, the role of lawyer included ideals of statesmanship, scholarship, and gentlemanly behaviour. At some level most colonial lawyers tried to include all three as part of their professional 'image.' This theme is integrated into the entire book, although it features most prominently in chapters 3, 6, 8, and 9. The formative influence of his Anglo-Irish Uniacke patrons on the young Murdoch is explored in chapter 3. Murdoch's political ideas as an opponent of responsible government are explored in chapter 7. The fact that his stance would appear to have been contrary to his material interests directs us to the role of ideas in political debate, and more generally in colonial society as a whole. It is argued that Murdoch's aversion to political reform was rooted in his convictions about the transcendent rightness of traditional British ideas about the constitution, and his belief that civic virtue could never flourish under a party system. Yet Murdoch adapted to the new order in the urban sphere by serving as recorder of the city of Halifax from 1850 to 1860 (see chapter 8), when city politics were arguably more democratic and responsive than provincial politics; and in his *History of Nova-Scotia, or Acadie,* written in the 1860s, he effectively recanted his earlier views and came to accept not just the legitimacy but the desirability of popular sovereignty as the fundamental basis of the political order.

Chapter 9 is a study of Murdoch's contribution to literature, legal letters, and provincial history. His four-volume *Epitome of the Laws of Nova-Scotia* (1832–3), described by David Bell as 'the apogee for the whole nineteenth century [of] lawyerly literary achievement in the Maritimes,'[12] provides a uniquely comprehensive overview of the substantive law, legal institutions, and legal culture of the colonial legal order on the eve of the achievement of responsible government.[13] In the days before law reporting and legal periodicals, both of which effectively began in British North America only in the 1850s, uncovering evidence of how lawyers thought about their profession and about the law is a difficult task. They accepted the law as a kind of cultural given, upon which it was not necessary to elaborate. When rhetorical emphasis was required, as in legislative debates, lawyers' views tended to be hidden behind stock phrases such as 'the rights of Englishmen' and 'British justice.'[14] It is mainly in private papers that one gets the occasional glimpse of their opinions on these subjects. The *Epitome,* as a statement of one lawyer's reflections on the organization of the substantive law, the relationship of colonial law to English law, the position of indigenous peoples, and many other topics, is thus a document of some significance.

Uniting all aspects of Murdoch's cultural endeavours were two principal aims: his concern with 'improvement' and his desire to delineate a Nova Scotian identity. For Murdoch, the former meant both self-improvement through constant self-education and self-discipline, and self-exertion in concert with others to improve one's society.[15] Through his journalism, literary efforts, political contributions at the provincial and city level, law-reform activities, leadership of temperance societies, and involvement in philanthropic activities and voluntary associations, Murdoch was a veritable whirlwind of improving activity, unusual perhaps in its breadth and assiduity among the British North American lawyers of his day, but not in its basic thrust.

With regard to his second aim, Murdoch's attempt in the *Epitome* to uncover a Nova Scotian identity secreted in the interstices of the colony's laws and legal institutions 'ranks with Judge Haliburton's literary effusions,' according to one commentator, 'as impressive evidence of emergent self-confidence in the region.'[16] It is worth adding that Murdoch's views on the Nova Scotian identity as expressed in the *Epitome* are much fresher and more nuanced than those that can be inferred from his *History of Nova-Scotia, or Acadie*, published over thirty years later. And even though Murdoch was concerned only with the question of a Nova Scotian identity, his description of provincial law as 'simple, elegant, and free' would probably have struck a chord in the other British North American colonies, even in Quebec after the mid-century transformations leading to the abolition of seigneurial tenure (1854) and the codification of private law (1866).[17] In his redrafting of the charter of the city of Halifax in the 1850s, Murdoch tried to practise what he had preached in the 1830s, as will be seen in chapter 8.

The historical value of the *Epitome* would be much lessened if its author had been a theoretical lawyer with limited knowledge of the law's practical side. On the contrary, he was a typical lawyer of his day, neither the most nor the least successful of his peers. While he was eventually recognized as a leader of the bar, Murdoch's account books reveal the painstaking process of building up a clientele as a sole practitioner, the long steady climb to financial independence for those young entrants of the 1820s and 1830s who had no ready-made network of business contacts through kin or social position, and the final solidification of a reputation and a reasonably lucrative practice by the 1840s.

The primary sources documenting Murdoch's professional career are, while not unique, certainly far from common for this early period, and they are supplemented by the legal papers and/or correspondence of his Nova Scotian contemporaries William Young (1799–1887), Harry King (1807–65), and William Blowers Bliss (1795–1874).[18] Murdoch's papers include the commonplace book he kept during his apprenticeship from 1814 to 1820, letter books for the 1820s, and account books from the 1820s to 1850s. Chapters 5 and 6 use these sources to develop the third theme of this study, the lawyer as economic actor, by means of a detailed analysis of the growth of Murdoch's clientele (both numerically and in terms of gender and social status), the changing variety of services he provided, and his professional income over the first two decades of his professional career. The prevalence of 'small' clients, mainly artisans and small tradesmen and their widows, in the early years of Murdoch's career, and their continuing presence thereafter, offers a fuller picture of the role of lawyers in their communities than has hitherto been available. Lawyers provided a range of services to all but the very poor and the lowest echelon of day labourers, not just to the amply propertied.

Murdoch had very few corporate clients and, outside the rapidly growing centres of Toronto and Montreal, neither did many other pre-Confederation British North American lawyers. Important work has been done, especially by G. Blaine Baker, on the role of a small group of Montreal lawyers who played an active role in the emergence of early transportation, banking, and manufacturing companies in Quebec in the 1830s–1860s.[19] In the generation after Murdoch's death, Halifax lawyers would become active in the creation and promotion of large financial corporations. But in the period covered in this book, virtually all of the hundreds of lawyers in British North America advised individuals rather than business corporations, and they did so as sole practitioners or in two-man partnerships rather than as members of law firms.

The career of a single lawyer in any historical period needs to be assessed with reference to the activities of his or her peers. Thus, the lens broadens in chapter 4 to examine trends in the legal profession at large, quantitative, geographic, and organizational. First I provide a detailed quantitative study of lawyers in nineteenth-century Nova Scotia, with particular reference to the first half of the century and to lawyerly mobility. During the second quarter of the century, the bar moved beyond its urban base in Halifax and spread out to virtually every settlement of any size in the province. It is generally known that these two decades witnessed an exponential increase in the numbers of lawyers and in their geographic mobility, but there has been no detailed study of the latter phenomenon.[20] It will be argued that the blanketing of the British North American countryside with lawyers provides important evidence of the economic role of lawyers and of their integration within colonial society. There follows a study of how Nova Scotia lawyers tried to organize themselves through the creation of a voluntary society, set within the context of developments elsewhere in British North America and the United States. Analysis of these collective actions by lawyers complements the more individualistic focus of the main narrative, and allows for some generalizations about lawyers and the legal profession in Nova Scotia and British North America.

This portrait of a nineteenth-century lawyer and his ambient legal culture paints a less colourful picture than the bold tones found in the anti-lawyer polemics (and some histories) of the colonial period, and a less bland one than that found in an earlier hagiographic literature. It is less concerned with labelling lawyers than with reconstituting their lived experience, individually and collectively: in discovering who their clients were, what they read, where they lived, what their incomes were, what kinds of contributions they made to their society, how they interacted with other lawyers, and so on. Lawyers were powerful figures in colonial society, but they were certainly not equally powerful, and the nature of their power has often been misunderstood. Some attained official power as statesmen or judges but many more wielded an authority one might better call cultural, in that it flowed from the cultural capital they possessed. It also flowed from the demand for their services, which was growing rapidly in the middle decades of the century and made the small-town lawyer as familiar as the local clergyman in most parts of British North America. Few could depend on a small number of wealthy individual or institutional clients; most were constantly seeking new clients and new means of exposure to secure them. The independence of the lawyer was a necessity as much as a reality in an age when virtually all clients were individuals rather than corporations, and that independence was in turn part of the cultural capital that distinguished lawyers even as it made some people resent their dependence on them.[21]

Well before the rise of corporations, however, the colonial bar was moving away from the robust notion of independence that characterized the English bar. By the nineteenth century, English barristers had totally insulated themselves from clients by means of their relationship with solicitors and thus, to a large extent, from business and commercial interests. British North American lawyers, working within a fused profession, did not have this option. They lived among their clients and had to understand and embrace their concerns if they were to prosper. They were, in a word, more responsive than their English counterparts, and this responsiveness helped secure their place in colonial society while also contributing to a more supple and pragmatic notion of independence.

Finally, a word about periodization. This study ends around 1867, not because Canadian Confederation is itself a watershed in the history of the legal profession (which it is not), but for two other reasons. The first is simply that Beamish Murdoch's career came to an end around this time. The third volume of his *History of Nova-Scotia, or Acadie* appeared in 1867; he wound up his law practice shortly thereafter and retired to Lunenburg on the province's South Shore in 1872. The more substantive reason is that the years around Confederation represent a rough divide between an older type of legal professionalism centred on the independent gentleman-universal scholar-statesman, of whom Murdoch himself was such an exemplar, and the new professionalism of the later nineteenth century, centred on university-derived expertise and a modified version of independence more suitable for the emergent corporate world.[22] In the Conclusion I will attempt to link the world of the pre-Confederation lawyer with the 'new professionalism' that arose in the following generation, arguing for an essential continuity bridging the two.

2

Antecedents

Beamish Murdoch was born at Halifax on 1 August 1800.[1] He had deep roots in Nova Scotia: not only had both parents been born in the province, but also his grandmothers. Amelia (Mason) Ott Beamish and Abigail (Salter) Murdoch were both born at Halifax in the 1750s, less than a decade after the town's foundation in 1749. Murdoch was raised by his grandmother Beamish after the early death of his mother, and it was she and her daughters who inspired his attachment to his birthplace and his interest in its history. In a society where kinship counted for so much, a study of Beamish Murdoch's ancestry is necessary to set the successes and failures of his later career in context. Murdoch's attempt to use but also to transcend the ties of kinship, and to link his public persona to representation of a recognizably middle-class interest, is a central theme in his life.

Despite the relative depth of Murdoch's New World roots, the Old World was equally important to his identity, especially in his early years. Both his grandfathers had emigrated from Ireland to Nova Scotia in the 1760s, and his Irish ethnicity was an important feature of his public persona until roughly 1830, when he began to assert a more 'Nova Scotian' identity. For Beamish Murdoch, Nova Scotia provided an environment where the ethno-religious enmities of the Old World might be transcended, and religious tolerance was a principal ingredient of the Nova Scotian identity that he sought to fashion and proclaim.

   Benjamin Salter Beamish Murdoch, to give him his full name, was the only child of Elizabeth Ott Beamish and Andrew Murdoch, who married at St Paul's Cathedral in Halifax on 29 October 1799.[2] Their union would have been an unusual one in the Ireland from which their fathers had come: Elizabeth's father belonged to an Anglo-Irish family from County Cork which adhered to the Church of Ireland, while Andrew was the son of a Scots-Irish minister of the Secession Church from County Donegal. Although differing in their religious loyalties, the Beamishes and the Murdochs shared a common experience as colonizers of Ireland. Both families had been established in Ireland for about a century and a half before emigrating to Nova Scotia. Both suffered during Ireland's tumultuous seventeenth century but survived and prospered in the eighteenth.

   The emigration of the Beamish and Murdoch families was not, so far as is known, propelled by any dire economic circumstances at home. In this they represented an entirely new phenomenon in the history of European emigration, beginning in the 1760s. Emigration became less a collective response to intolerable conditions at home by dissenters, alienated groups, and the poor, and more an act of choice by an increasingly mobile and skilled population moving within an Atlantic economy.[3] This seems an apt characterization of the actions of both Murdoch's grandfathers. James Murdoch came to Nova Scotia as a missionary in response to appeals from leaderless Presbyterian congregations, but his arrival was really part of a larger economic strategy which would see his father sell his farm in Ireland and attempt to reestablish the family in agriculture in Nova Scotia. Thomas Beamish had the status of 'gentleman' in Ireland, and emigrated shortly after the sale of family lands provided him with some capital. He chose to come to Halifax, when he might have gone to England, to the West Indies, or to some other North American colony.

   The experiences of Beamish Murdoch's grandfathers in Nova Scotia were also quite similar. Both emigrated in the 1760s as young men in their early twenties, married women who were the daughters of locally prominent men, and had very large families. After a period of initial success in their new environment, both suffered severe financial setbacks which created serious strains for them and for their families. By the late 1780s, both had been compelled to surrender to creditors the premises upon which they had established themselves, and to move to more marginal locations. Lack of business acumen, the demands of raising large families, an extremely creditor-oriented debt law, and the strains imposed on the provincial economy after the end of the war in 1783, all conspired to bring these men and their families close to complete financial ruin. It would be left to the generations of their children and grandchildren to try and re-establish their fortunes on a more secure basis, and in this they were generally successful.

The Murdoch Family

James Murdoch was born about 1745 at Gillie Gordon (present-day Killygordon) in County Donegal, the only son of a prosperous flax grower and linen producer. The family, originally Scottish, had emigrated to Ulster by the early seventeenth century, where they were staunch supporters of the Protestant cause.[4] James went to the University of Edinburgh to study theology in 1759,[5] then attended a theological hall run by the Anti-Burgher wing of the Secession Church – the most anti-authoritarian and evangelical of all the factions that had developed out of the Church of Scotland during various theological controversies.[6] By the time he returned to Ireland, he had become interested in emigrating to North America, though probably not as a missionary to the Mi'kmaq, as recounted in family tradition. In September 1766 James Murdoch was ordained a minister by the presbytery of Newton Limavady (Ulster) 'for the Province of Nova Scotia or any other part of the American continent where God in his Providence might call him.'[7]

Murdoch arrived in Nova Scotia by early 1767 and by 1769 had secured a grant of 500 acres of land in Horton Township, including some marsh land on the Grand Pré which had been set aside for the first minister to settle in the township. These fertile lands in the Annapolis valley, cleared and made productive by the Acadians whom the British had deported in 1755, had by this point been resettled by migrants from New England now known as the Planters. Murdoch's parents came out to Nova Scotia at this time with daughter Elizabeth (James's sister) and her fiancé, Matthew Frame.[8] The family bought more land and soon expanded with James Murdoch's 1771 marriage to Abigail Salter, daughter of prominent New England merchant and assemblyman Malachi Salter. Between 1772 and 1796 they had eleven children, of whom Beamish Murdoch's father, Andrew, was the fourth, born in 1777.[9]

Murdoch's relations with his mainly New England Congregationalist flock began well, but within a few years he was embroiled in disputes over finances, politics, and theology, possibly exacerbated by rumours of a ministerial problem with alcohol. The Alline Revolution and the American Revolution soon followed each other in quick succession, turning Murdoch's world upside-down. Henry Alline (1748–84), who had arrived in Nova Scotia as part of the Planter migration, rejected the Calvinism of his Puritan forebears and began preaching a brand of evangelical pietism based on the possibility of salvation for all. His 'existential mysticism' led to a type of Nova Scotian Great Awakening among his 'New Light' followers that greatly unsettled the clergy of the traditional churches.[10] A product of the scholarly and classical traditions of the Scottish ministry, Murdoch was aghast at the displays of religious enthusiasm now erupting throughout the Planter townships. He could not stand aside; he publicly 'exhort[ed] [the] father of the New Lights to give up his idle and fanatical notions' and warned his parishioners repeatedly against Alline's 'dangerous soul-destroying delusion.'[11] Adding to Murdoch's problems was Malachi Salter's arraignment on charges of sedition; he died in 1781 in financial distress, ending his customary support of his daughter and son-in-law's household.[12]

All these difficulties came to a head in the early 1780s, when Murdoch and his congregation came to a parting of the ways.[13] By 1789, James and Abigail had lost all their holdings to creditors, joining the ranks of many smallholders squeezed out as the lands of Horton Township quickly accumulated in the hands of an ever-diminishing circle of owners.[14] Left with virtually nothing, Murdoch moved to Musquodoboit in 1791 to look after a small congregation of Loyalists. He continued to minister to families and small groups as far away as the New Brunswick border, travelling by foot, horse, and canoe in all seasons under punishing conditions.[15] His struggle ended on 21 November 1799 when his body was found at the edge of the Musquodoboit River, not far from his home. Some accounts suggest that he drowned after an epileptic fit, others that he died of exposure after suffering a seizure.[16] Any suggestion of suicide would have been suppressed by contemporaries, but, whatever his cause of death, the Reverend James Murdoch came to a tragic end.[17]

Murdoch's eldest son, Andrew, was twelve years of age when the family lands at Horton were surrendered. He was then sent to the Halifax home of Abigail's brother Benjamin Salter, who ran a ship's chandlery and marine insurance business. Given the wreck of the Murdoch family fortunes, young Andrew and his siblings would have to make their own way in the world with some assistance from their extended family. Benjamin Salter trained Andrew in his business, and by the time of Andrew's marriage to Elizabeth Ott Beamish in 1799, he had been taken on as a partner.[18] Planter diarist Simeon Perkins obtained insurance a number of times 'in Mr. Salter's office, by giving a Memdm to Andrew Murdoch.'[19] On 27 April 1799 he noted that 'Mr. Murdoch' and others had come from Halifax to speculate in a prize ship which had been awarded to Perkins.[20]

Andrew Murdoch's problems may be traced to the untimely death of his uncle on 25 March 1800. Benjamin Salter died intestate, leaving his affairs in some disorder.[21] His widow, Susannah, petitioned the court that Murdoch and her two brothers be appointed as co-administrators to assist her in administering the estate. They were sued by the London mercantile firm of Brook Watson and Company for the sum of £4,365 allegedly due on Salter's accounts. When Salter's assets proved insufficient to satisfy this huge judgment, the firm sued Andrew Murdoch as the 'surviving partner of Benjamin Salter, late of Halifax.' Judgment was entered against him on 2 July 1802 for £3,000.[22]

A year of negotiations followed during which Murdoch desperately tried to recover debts owing to him, arranging for the commitment of one of his own debtors to jail in the process.[23] It was all to no avail. A writ of execution issued on 25 October 1803, which sheriff Lewis M. Wilkins endorsed on 10 December with the curt notation: 'I could find no goods and Chattels Land or Tenements of the within named Andrew Murdoch whereon to levy this Writ. I have therefore taken the Body of the said Andrew Murdoch and committed him to Jail.'[24] Compounding Andrew's misfortune was the death of his wife about this time. Elizabeth Ott Murdoch is usually said to have died in childbirth, but in fact she survived her son's birth by over three years, dying in late 1803 or early 1804. With her death, Andrew lost not only his wife but his son, as the homeless Beamish was taken in by his maternal grandmother. For his part, young Beamish would be left with only fleeting memories of a mother who shared the fate of many others in an era of high maternal mortality. The loss of his mother, a literate woman who would no doubt have taken great interest in her son's education, was probably at least as great a misfortune to Beamish Murdoch as the financial ruin of his father.

Andrew Murdoch would remain in the squalid Halifax jail for at least the next four years. The experience of imprisonment for debt was not uncommon, but Murdoch's length of stay in prison was unusual.[25] Under a Nova Scotia law, insolvent debtors could be released if they were prepared to make an inventory of all their property and assign it to their creditors, even though the value of that property was not enough to satisfy the full debt. This law reflected the prevailing belief that it was better to have debtors engaged in useful work than languishing in prison if they genuinely did not have sufficient assets to cover their debts. Provincial law did not recognize bankruptcy as such, but the insolvent debtors' law went some way in that direction. Unfortunately for Murdoch, relief was available only to debtors whose debts totalled less than £100. There remained only two possible avenues of release: mercy by the creditor, or a special relief act passed by the House of Assembly.[26]

Murdoch's December 1805 petition to the House of Assembly makes for grim reading in spite of its eloquent, learned, and forceful expression, testimony to the superior education that James and Abigail Murdoch had been able to provide to their children. The petition did not ask for Murdoch's release, merely for better conditions for imprisoned debtors. Only fuel and water were supplied in jail, and Murdoch alleged that creditors seldom arranged to supply to their debtors the eight pounds of bread per week that they were obliged by law to provide. Debtors thrown on their own resources would have perished had other prisoners not shared their food with them. Murdoch also complained that the absence of prison yards for air and exercise was 'far from [demonstrating] that Humanity, Benevolence and Attention which so eminently distinguishes the British character in Europe above all the civilized Nations of the World.' This invocation of the British national character may have provoked the desired result: in January 1806 the Assembly voted £50 for the relief of distressed debtors.

Two bills in 1807, reacting to a second petition by Murdoch in November 1806, would have allowed him to take advantage of the insolvent debtors' law in spite of his large debts. The first was rejected by the Council on 8 January, while the next passed second reading in the Assembly on 19 December but ultimately did not become law.[27] There is no record of a provincial act in Murdoch's favour, but he appears to have been released in 1808, possibly as an act of grace by the estate of Sir Brook Watson, who died in October 1807.[28]

Upon his release, Andrew Murdoch sought to support himself as a teacher, though he continued to style himself 'gentleman' in legal documents. For the rest of his life he eked out an existence in the settlements scattered around the eastern part of the Bay of Fundy, following literally in his father's footsteps. Thomas Chandler Haliburton's 1849 account of the life of a colonial schoolteacher might have been written with Andrew in mind: 'When a man fails in his trade, or is too lazy to work, he [re]sorts to teaching as a livelihood, and the school-house, like the asylum for the poor, receives all those who are, from misfortune or incapacity, unable to provide for themselves. The wretched teacher has no home; he ... resides, a stipulated number of days, in every house – too short a time for his own comfort, and too long for that of the family.'[29] Murdoch was paid £50 to teach at the village school in Parrsboro in 1811–12, and he received a licence to keep a school at Noel in Hants County in 1816.[30] This wage of £1 per week was about that of a day labourer, and was not far above the minimum required to keep body and soul together in colonial British North America.

Yet Andrew Murdoch was not entirely dependent on his teaching wage. Through all his travails he had managed to keep his interest in certain property which had come to him through his wife's estate. Elizabeth Ott Murdoch had inherited an interest in various Halifax properties, including a valuable wharf, under the will of her mother Amelia's stepfather, Frederick Ott. The wharf was the subject of lengthy litigation between the Cochran and Beamish families beginning in 1802. Thomas Beamish held the wharf in trust for his children under Ott's will, but, being heavily indebted to the Cochrans, he had conveyed the wharf to them in 1787, having received authorization from the Court of Chancery to do so. The Cochrans, one of the most powerful mercantile and political families in the provinces, alleged that this transfer was in full settlement of his debts to them; while the Beamishes alleged that it was intended merely as a mortgage, with the wharf to be reconveyed to them when Thomas's debts were repaid. It was not until 1820 that the claims of the Beamish family were finally upheld after an appeal to the Privy Council in England, and the Cochrans were compelled to return the wharf to its rightful owners.[31] This litigation was a pivotal event in the fortunes of the Beamish family in general, and of Beamish Murdoch in particular; had they lost, it is unlikely Murdoch would have had the financial security to undertake a career at the bar or contemplate any public or political involvements.

Had Elizabeth Ott Murdoch been alive, she would have been entitled to a share in the wharf property in common with her siblings. Upon her death, her share descended to her son Beamish, subject to a life interest in her husband, known to the common law as an estate by the curtesy. In order to avoid this encumbrance, the family entered an arrangement

in 1825 whereby Andrew gave up his life interest in a number of properties, in return for ownership of a one-fifth interest in two tenements
near the Market Wharf.[32]

Land ownership was a mixed blessing for Andrew Murdoch in that
it gave him a source of credit which encouraged him to live beyond
his means. He mortgaged his lands twice and within a decade was in
default. His son came to the rescue, paying off the mortgages and arranging for a sale of Andrew's interest.[33] Now nearly seventy, Andrew
Murdoch faced the prospect of total destitution at the end of his working life. Without savings or property of any kind, it was up to his son to
support him if he was not to be left to the ministrations of the overseers
of the poor. For the last decade of his father's life, Beamish Murdoch
paid £26 annually to one Robert Dewis of Fort Belcher for Andrew's
board, lodging, and washing.[34]

In economic terms, Andrew Murdoch's story is a simple one. He was
a poor manager of money in a society which provided little relief for
those so afflicted. His first failure in business was probably precipitated
by being thrown in over his head upon the early death of his uncle;
his later failures were mostly his own. At a psychological level, the
story is more complex. The relationship between Andrew and Beamish
Murdoch is usually characterized as one of estrangement, yet that term
does not fully capture their lives. Beamish Murdoch did not have the
luxury of being totally 'estranged' from his father – they remained in
contact throughout Andrew Murdoch's long life, and Beamish fulfilled
his filial duties to the end.

The nature of their emotional relationship is a puzzle. Beamish Murdoch could probably have forgiven his father's poverty but Andrew's
lack of respectability must have been more problematic. His great-niece
Susan Stairs records in her memoir that 'all his life his habits and character were a constant source of grief and mortification to his sisters,'
but, with typical Victorian reticence, she omits to specify what his failings were.[35] Certainly, Andrew's financial woes were enough to justify
familial and societal disapproval, but more is hinted at in this phrase.
Sexual irregularity or intemperance or both are the most likely causes
of this 'grief and mortification.' The latter is suggested by Stairs's ellip-
tical reference to Andrew's time in prison where, she states, he beguiled
his time 'in posting books for merchants and in the more questionable
pursuits practised in this Marshalsea.'[36] Alcohol was freely available to
those inmates of the prison who could pay for it, although there were
periodic attempts to suppress the activity of the jailer in supplying in-

toxicants. It would not be surprising if Andrew had turned to drink during his long stay in jail.

The failed father hovered like a doppelgänger over the son. The hereditary principle was fundamental to colonial society, and it was assumed that well-placed fathers would assist their sons to replicate their own status. Andrew Murdoch would never be able to make the connections that might ease his son's entry into the colonial elite. Ill luck or even incapacity in money matters would probably have been easier to bear than Andrew's moral unworthiness, which was a constant liability for his son. The only way Beamish Murdoch could escape this *damnosa hereditas* was to fashion an identity that emphasized sobriety, thrift, temperance, civility, and, above all, hard work. For every paternal vice, he would find the corresponding virtue. Where Andrew Murdoch was mobile, shiftless, and defied the expectations of his family and peers, his son became a pillar of Victorian stability, rectitude, and respectability.

Galvanized perhaps by the spectacle of their brother's failure, all of Andrew Murdoch's siblings managed to avoid his fate. Unfortunately for Beamish Murdoch, however, none of his Murdoch uncles was able to serve as a substitute paternal figure. Three of Andrew's brothers were sacrificed to the sea at an early age, while Andrew's youngest brother, Benjamin, only four years older than Beamish Murdoch, apparently emigrated to the United States and nothing more is known of him.[37]

Andrew's sisters fared rather better. In particular, his eldest sister, Susannah, married Scottish immigrant William Duffus, who became a successful Halifax merchant. Their children, Beamish Murdoch's cousins, penetrated to the highest levels of the Halifax elite. Daughter Susan married shipping magnate Samuel Cunard, her sister Elizabeth his brother Henry; Mary Ann married merchant John Morrow and became the mother-in-law of the Honourable W.J. Stairs, one of Nova Scotia's most successful finance capitalists. Margaret married lawyer William Sutherland, with whom Beamish Murdoch would have some professional dealings later in life. Beamish Murdoch appears to have been almost completely estranged from these paternal relatives. If Andrew was a source of 'grief and mortification' for his sisters, they were unlikely to have much to do with his son, for fear of bringing shame on their husband's houses.

The Salter connection did not provide much assistance to Beamish Murdoch either, confounding his parents' expectations. By christening their son Benjamin Salter Beamish Murdoch after his recently deceased great-uncle, Andrew and Elizabeth demonstrated their gratitude and loyalty to the relative who had taken in Andrew as a child. Murdoch was known in his youth as 'Salter' rather than 'Beamish,' even by his Beamish relatives, until about the time of his majority.[38] However, Murdoch appears to have had little to do with the Salters. By the time he reached early manhood, his absorption into his maternal family, symbolized by his selection of the Christian name of Beamish, was complete.

The Beamish Family

The surname Beamish is said to derive from the place name Beaumais-sur-Dive in France, but the English branch of the family had been long settled in the western counties by Elizabeth's time. A family member settled near Bandonbridge (or Bandon) in what later became County Cork in the wake of the Munster rebellion of 1579, and his descendants became part of the Protestant establishment over the next two centuries.[39] In the eighteenth century, Cork prospered as a port of call for transatlantic shipping. Prevented by British tariffs from producing wool or grain, area landowners turned their lands to the production of meat, hides, and dairy products. Vast amounts of foodstuffs left the port for the continent, North America, and the West Indies. By 1760, the population of Cork was 60,000, twice the size of Glasgow, Liverpool, or Birmingham.[40]

Thomas Beamish was raised in Bandon but he and his brother Richard both removed to nearby Cork to enter trade. Cork's very success in the export trade made it vulnerable to embargoes imposed during wartime by the British government. A series of such restrictions during the war with France caused many failures among the provision merchants, and this experience may well have led the Beamish brothers to consider emigration.[41]

Cork's close economic ties with the eastern colonies of North America meant that Thomas Beamish would probably have been reasonably familiar with the conditions prevailing at Halifax, where he arrived about 1765.[42] He set himself up as a merchant and soon had formed an association with Frederick Ott, whose fifteen-year-old stepdaughter, Amelia, he married in 1770. Ott was a highly successful victualler in early Halifax: a 1776 survey showed him as one of the largest landowners in the town.[43] Beamish's relationship with Ott, cemented by the marital tie, initially allowed him to establish a secure place within colonial society. In 1781 he was considered able and loyal enough to be appointed warden of the port of Halifax, responsible for verifying the status of all incoming vessels during the Revolutionary War. The bubble burst in 1783, when the death of Frederick Ott, the end of the war, and the influx of the Loyalists gave rise to an entirely new situation. Reduced British spending, a fall in commodity prices from inflated wartime levels, and the sudden appearance of a whole troop of competitors gave a sharp shock to the Halifax mercantile community, and the Beamish fortunes suffered accordingly. Ott left his substantial estate to Thomas and Amelia in trust for their children, born and to be born, so that they were not able to use his assets as security.[44] The net result was increasing indebtedness which led to Thomas Beamish being committed to debtors' prison by 1787 – at the suit of the same English creditor, Brook Watson, who would render Andrew Murdoch a similar favour sixteen years later. Beamish's release was secured only by conveying to his creditors a valuable wharf property belonging to the Ott estate, but he was now 'a broken man on a Halifax pier.' The family removed to Cole Harbour, and Thomas Beamish disappeared in 1792, never to return.

It was Amelia Ott Beamish who was crucial to the restoration of the Beamish family fortunes over the next two decades. She was determined to regain the wharf and her decades-long legal struggle finally succeeded in 1820, as noted earlier. In addition, after the early deaths of two of her daughters, Amelia took in two grandsons, Beamish Murdoch and Thomas Beamish Akins, and raised them as her own with the assistance of her three unmarried daughters, Sarah, Maria, and Harriette. Rounding out the household was Thomas Beamish's unmarried sister, Elizabeth.

This bevy of Beamish women shaped Beamish Murdoch's youth and adolescence. On the intellectual plane, they inspired his interest in history and literature. Amelia had practically been born with the town and was the custodian of a long family memory. Sarah was said to have tasted the wine raised from the ships wrecked in the Duc d'Anville's ill-fated expedition of 1746.[45] Maria worked for some years at the Royal Acadian School as 'female superintendant,' while great-aunt Elizabeth Beamish ran her own school.[46] All these women were highly literate and valued education enough to arrange for Beamish to attend the Halifax Grammar School before he began his apprenticeship as an attorney. On the financial plane, the Beamish women fought along with their male kin for the restoration of the inheritance wrongfully wrested from them in the 1780s. Their eventual success secured for Beamish Murdoch a measure of economic security which would enable him to aspire to an important role on the provincial stage.

On the psychological plane, the influence of the Beamish women is more difficult to judge. They may have intensified the alienation that existed between father and son in their efforts to ensure that Beamish did not follow Andrew's example. They raised him as an Anglican, ignoring Andrew's Presbyterianism, and sought to remake him as a member of the Beamish family. Contemporaries would no doubt have seen these measures as entirely appropriate, but they probably exacted a psychological toll on young Beamish which cannot be precisely defined. And, in spite of the valuable assistance they provided, the Beamish ladies were women in a society where authority was expected to be, and largely was, exercised by men. There were male corridors of power they would never enter, male conversations over port and cigars into which they would never be able to inject their nephew's name, the way a well-placed male relative might have done.

For someone who would later be labelled 'Nova Scotia's Blackstone,' the parallels with William Blackstone's own family are instructive. Where Murdoch was effectively orphaned at an early age, Blackstone was actually an orphan, his father having died before his birth and his mother when he was twelve. Blackstone's father, a textile merchant, died heavily in debt with his affairs in some disarray, and Blackstone, like Murdoch, would have almost no contact with his paternal family during his life. Mary Blackstone tried to run the business with the aid of a partner, but when she died a dozen years later there were still substantial debts owing; she generously left £1,000 from her own estate to the creditors of her late husband. The crucial difference between the two life stories was that Mary had two brothers who took an interest in their nephew's welfare and were well placed to do so. Thomas Bigg, who became Blackstone's guardian after his sister's death, was assistant surgeon at a London hospital and saw to young William's early education at Charterhouse school. Another uncle, an attorney who lived not far from Oxford, encouraged his nephew's entry into the law and helped him financially during his studies at Oxford and his early years at the bar.[47] Murdoch's Beamish uncles took some interest in him but had neither the money nor the social, cultural, or political connections to promote him in the higher echelons of colonial society.

Though very much part of the Beamish family in his private life and in public perception, Beamish Murdoch ultimately sought to transcend the heritage of both his Beamish and his Murdoch kin. The unhappy fates of his grandfathers and his parents meant that Murdoch did not have a secure place within the colony's political or social elites. He could not expect the deference accorded members of those elites in what was still a very hierarchical society modelled on, though less rigid than, class-divided Britain. If he were to achieve any notice in colonial society, it would have to be through his own efforts. In time, then, he would turn to the most communicative professions: law and journalism. Yet recognition presumes an audience. Murdoch's initial constituency would be neither the elites nor the unpropertied labourers at the bottom of the social hierarchy but everyone in between, from tradesmen and artisans to smallholders and shopkeepers to other professionals and the middling ranks of merchants: in short, those literate citizens, whether in Halifax or in rural Nova Scotia, who were in the process of coalescing into a 'public' thanks to the proliferation of newspapers.

3

Apprenticeship

What John Adams had observed as a law student in Boston in 1756 was just as true in Regency Halifax. To get ahead in the law, one needed not only knowledge, time, and a large collection of books but, most important, 'the Friendship and Patronage of the great Masters in the Profession.' Knowledge and time Murdoch possessed, and he was in the process of acquiring a large library. When he began his five-year apprenticeship as an attorney on 11 November 1814 with Crofton Uniacke, the second of Attorney General Richard John Uniacke's five lawyer sons, it seemed that he had found the best patron Nova Scotia had to offer. The Uniacke law office was in a sense the nerve centre of the Nova Scotian legal profession in the first third of the nineteenth century. Although the principal role of a patron is to advance the material interests of the client, another role can be that of intellectual mentor. This chapter considers the Uniackes' 'patronage' of Murdoch in the latter sense. It is based on the premise that apprenticeship was not just the means of reproducing the legal profession but a vehicle for the transmission of a legal culture. As U.S. scholar Ann Fidler observes, 'the days spent reading law transformed laymen into lawyers. The ordering of their identity as lawyers began in an environment filled with ink-splattered commonplace books and dog-eared copies of Blackstone. Through a range of encounters, law students developed beliefs about the nature of law, its applications and their responsibilities to community, country and each other.'[1]

The legal culture being transmitted in Murdoch's case was Anglo-Irish, via Richard John Uniacke's experience qualifying as an attorney in Dublin; hence part of this chapter will be devoted to an examination of that culture in Ireland itself in the eighteenth century.[2] Before proceeding, however, some understanding of the development of the distinct legal professions of barrister and attorney in England, Ireland, and colonial America is required. Nova Scotia, like other British North American colonies, took elements of all these traditions in order to shape its own legal profession.

The Legal Professions in England: Entry and Governance

The essential distinctiveness of the North American legal profession lay in its decision to fuse what in England and Ireland were two separate professions, the barrister and the attorney/solicitor. In England prior to 1700, 'legal training had revolved around two powerful traditions, one vocational, the other more self-consciously liberal and academic.'[3] The former related to attorneys and solicitors, whose training by apprenticeship meant that they shared a form of education with many other occupations from grocers to silversmiths. Preparation for the bar, in contrast, was the responsibility of the inns of court, and by 1591 a call to the bar of one of them was recognized as the sole qualification for pleading before the royal courts. In the early modern period, the inns provided an extensive educational program of lectures and moots, although by the early seventeenth century students increasingly sought out a pupillage with a barrister or apprenticeship with an attorney to round out their education.

By the 1680s, the inns had ceased to provide any real educational offerings and the resort to pupillage or apprenticeship for would-be barristers became virtually universal though not formally required. It was partly in an attempt to counter this trend that William Blackstone gave the first set of university lectures on the common law at Oxford in 1753, subsequently published as his *Commentaries on the Laws of England* (1765–9).[4] Blackstone was fiercely critical of apprenticeship and strongly urged a return to a more liberal and academic education for barristers, whom he regarded as England's true leadership class. He had no immediate successor, however, and when university education in the common law did begin to develop later in the nineteenth century, the organized bar remained uninterested in it and the inns of court went on to develop their own law school.[5]

Meanwhile, the office of attorney was clearly gaining in prestige, marked by increased recruitment among younger sons of the lesser gentry and enhanced statutory regulation that aimed to control admissions and prohibit unlicensed practitioners.[6] This period also saw the emergence of voluntary professional associations of attorneys in both England (by 1739) and Ireland (by 1753).[7] An English statute of 1729 required an aspiring attorney to serve an apprenticeship of five years with an attorney 'duly sworn and admitted,' who was not to take more than two apprentices at any one time;[8] an Irish statute of 1773 had similar terms except that an attorney might take three apprentices.[9] Every candidate in England would have to take an oath and be examined by the judges on his 'fitness and capacity to act as an attorney' before being admitted and enrolled in any court, while in Ireland the judges of each court were to appoint as examiners 'four of the most reputable practising attornies' of that court. The Irish statute also imposed a requirement on all attorneys to attend one of the Four Courts in Dublin for two terms at least in each of the last three years of their apprenticeship: a requirement, as we shall see, that was replicated in Nova Scotia (1811) and later in Upper Canada (1828).

To the extent that the English bar could be said to be governed at all in the period under review, the inns of court officially exercised that role. In fact, during the three hundred years after the Glorious Revolution, the bar enjoyed an unprecedented autonomy; as Michael Burrage observes, during this time 'no monarch, no parliament, no judge, no state agency ever interfered in the affairs of the inns on the matter of king's counsel or anything else. They were seldom even mentioned in the law, and then only incidentally.'[10] The inns themselves, however, exercised almost no control over individual barristers. The real governance of the bar resided in the code of etiquette observed by all barristers. The main thrust of this code was to ensure the protection of the barristers' chosen jurisdiction – pleading in the higher courts – from encroachment by solicitors. Far from using their expansive autonomy to increase their field of endeavour, the bar in the eighteenth and nineteenth centuries chose to restrict it, abandoning to attorneys and solicitors 'the miscellaneous managerial and clerical activities of their seventeenth, sixteenth and fifteenth century predecessors.'[11] They also abandoned offering their services publicly to the market, relying on contacts with solicitors to bring in a clientele. There were obvious economic risks to this strategy, but, as Burrage concludes, 'over the long run, status considerations evidently outweighed ... other concerns, and sharp separation [from solicitors] gradually obtained the consent and support of the entire bar.' Very few barristers sought to challenge this practice, 'despite the fact that a good number of them were, in the mid-nineteenth century, chronically underemployed or unemployed.' Thus, the bar 'ceded total economic dependence to maintain status distance.'[12]

Attorneys also sought increased honour and status but had to rely on the state to achieve it. The act of 1729 protected the attorneys' jurisdiction by providing penal sanctions for unauthorized practice. In 1760 a court victory over the Scriveners' Company of the city of London gave the attorneys a monopoly over the drawing of deeds, while in 1804 they and the solicitors gained a statutory monopoly over conveyancing. In 1824 attorneys and solicitors purchased a hall which would function as their own inn of court; this led to the creation of the Incorporated Law Society, which received a royal charter in 1831, at which time the Society of Gentlemen Practisers wound up their organization. While membership was not obligatory, gradually all attorneys and solicitors acquiesced in its authority.[13]

With regard to entry, during the period under review, both branches of the profession continued to rely on informal but effective means of controlling entry, and neither had any reason to be interested in university education in law. The prerequisites for call to the bar were caricatured as signing one's name and eating a certain number of dinners, but the need to support oneself during the five long years of pupillage and the early barren years at the bar ensured that only the sons of the propertied, who had normally received a gentlemanly education, could consider entering the profession. In addition, success at the bar would depend on contacts with practising barristers and attorneys, and this meant that recruitment to the profession was skewed to the sons of existing members of the professions.[14] Meanwhile, attorneys (after 1875 known as solicitors) continued to rely on service under articles as the principal mode of entry into the profession until late in the twentieth century, though a practitioner-administered set of preliminary, intermediate, and final exams was gradually grafted onto the apprenticeship during the nineteenth century.

In England and Ireland, then, professional legal culture was bifurcated, much of it driven by ideas of class and gentlemanly status that led barristers to insulate themselves more and more from clients and solicitors, while the latter played a perpetual game of catch-up. Barristers were in effect judges in training, while solicitors could never aspire to the bench nor to higher legal offices such as that of attorney general. The kind of success enjoyed in the New World by Richard John Uniacke, a 'mere' attorney, could never have been replicated in the Old.

The Legal Profession in North America: Entry and Governance

In the Thirteen Colonies before the Revolution, the establishment of local inns of court did not seem either feasible or desirable. During the seventeenth century, the colonies seemed bent on suppressing the legal profession altogether, rather than providing for its education. Admission to plead before a court was normally within the discretion of the judges of that court, and little standardization in the requirements of professional entry occurred before the Revolution. 'Attorneys in fact,' lay persons appointed by litigants to act for them, long competed with regularly sworn attorneys. The courts were loath to bar them, and no professional organizations that might have disputed their claims arose until late in the colonial period.[15] Lawyers were generally styled 'attorneys,' with the appellation 'barrister' reserved as a courtesy for those who had been called to the bar in England or Ireland. Some colonies instituted licensing by the governor or other authority as a prerequisite to legal practice, but this was unusual. During the colonial period, the requirements for entry to the legal profession remained largely within the purview of the courts, assisted by bar associations, and generally required some period of apprenticeship plus the demonstration of good character.[16]

By the middle of the eighteenth century, the anglicization of colonial legal culture resulted in increased concern over the educational attainments of lawyers and in attempts to institute a formally bifurcated profession.[17] In Massachusetts, Chief Justice Thomas Hutchinson introduced the rank of barrister in 1762. The Suffolk County bar then resolved that it would not recommend anyone to the court for admission as a barrister unless he had pursued two years of legal study, two of practice as an attorney in the lower courts, and two in the superior courts. This represented not so much a 'divided' as a 'graded' profession, since barristers were not precluded from practising as attorneys. The future Loyalist and chief justice of Nova Scotia, Sampson Salter Blowers, was admitted as a barrister before the Superior Court of Massachusetts under this dispensation on 3 October 1770, he 'having studied and practiced the usual time.'[18] The next year, the Suffolk County bar resolved that no candidate would be recommended without a university education or its equivalent. These practices did not have legislative force, however, and the courts could reject candidates approved by the bar. In Virginia too, there were efforts to create a truly divided bar distinguished from the body of attorneys.[19] Even had the Revolution not intervened, however, these efforts were unlikely to have succeeded in replicating the English division between barrister and solicitor in a systemic fashion. The vast majority of lawyers practised as both barristers and solicitors for the simple reason that the economy of the eighteenth-century American colonies could not support a barrister-like caste on the English model, as Thomas Jefferson found to his chagrin when he tried to practise in such a fashion.[20] Likewise in Upper Canada, when the Law Society of Upper Canada was created by statute in 1797, it did not, as one might have expected in that Loyalist bastion, seek to recreate barristers and attorneys as two distinct professions. The statute recognized the functional distinction but then proclaimed that all lawyers would be admitted as both barristers and attorneys.[21]

Apprenticeship and Cultural Transmission in Nova Scotia: Murdoch and the Uniackes

The legal profession Murdoch was attempting to enter was a fused one that sought to combine the gentlemanly and scholarly standards of the bar with the more utilitarian training and practical knowledge of the attorney.[22] His principal's father, Richard John Uniacke, Sr, exemplified this fusion. Although admitted only as an attorney in Ireland and Nova Scotia, he had acquired a magnificent library and held successively the posts of both solicitor general and attorney general in the colony. Uniacke had proved that one could uphold the standards of the English bar without ever having attended the inns of court, and while his powerful connections in Britain were essential to the advancement of his career in Nova Scotia, there is no doubt that he also possessed much innate ability.

An obvious question presents itself: How was it that Murdoch came to be taken on as an apprentice to Nova Scotia's first family of the law? Murdoch's existence would have become known to Richard John Uniacke through the latter's representation of the Cochrans in the long-running Beamish-Cochran litigation (mentioned in the previous chapter), which was entering the final stage of its Nova Scotian phase in 1814. At the time Murdoch entered the Uniacke office, the outcome of the suit was by no means certain. The Uniackes must have been extraordinarily impressed with the probity of this young man, whose family was in an adversarial relationship with a Uniacke client, to invite him to apprentice with them. Likewise, Murdoch would have learned early in his career the ability to place personal and professional concerns in totally separate compartments.

There were two probable reasons why the Uniackes offered this opportunity to the young Murdoch. Gordon Wood has noted how the colonial New England gentry would recruit new blood by seeking out quick young lads of lower status and raising them up through a process of clientage or informal adoption.[23] All elites must do this to some extent if they are concerned with preserving social stability. To this general consideration one may add a key connection between Murdoch and the Uniackes: their common Irish heritage. The Anglo-Irish roots of the Beamish family in County Cork have been noted earlier. Richard John Uniacke came from an old Anglo-Norman family in the same county, one that had conformed to the Church of Ireland and become part of the Protestant Ascendancy in the eighteenth century. Both the Uniackes and the senior branch of the Beamish family formed part of the landed gentry of County Cork, and both sent MPs to the Irish Parliament. The ties of ethnicity, religion, and region all reinforced each other in this case.[24] The sorry plight of Murdoch's parents and the absence of any well-connected male relative on his part also lent an air of noblesse oblige to the Uniackes' gesture.

As it turned out, Beamish Murdoch worked with almost every one of the Uniacke lawyers. When Crofton was appointed judge of the Vice-Admiralty Court in October 1817, the remainder of Murdoch's term was assigned to the attorney general himself. During this time Murdoch would have worked alongside Crofton's younger brothers. Called to the bar in 1810, Richard John, Jr spent a few years as attorney general of Cape Breton Island, which remained a separate colony until 1820, before returning to Halifax to practise law about 1816. James Boyle and Robert Fitzgerald would both begin their apprenticeships in 1818 after graduating from King's College. James Boyle Uniacke would be called to the bar the year after Murdoch, in 1823, but then proceeded to study at the inns of court before returning to Halifax. Robert Fitzgerald Uniacke experienced a conversion and abandoned his legal career to prepare for receiving holy orders in the Anglican Church. Only the oldest and youngest Uniacke brothers would not have been in the office during Murdoch's apprenticeship. Andrew Mitchell Uniacke, the late child of the attorney general's second marriage, was much younger than Murdoch and would not begin his apprenticeship until 1828. The eldest son, Norman Fitzgerald Uniacke, had trained in his father's office and been admitted to the Nova Scotia bar in 1798 before proceeding to England, where he was admitted to the bar of Lincoln's Inn in 1805. After some years as attorney general of Quebec, in 1819 he returned to Halifax for a two-year period of leave. It may be that Murdoch's lifelong interest in the law and culture of Quebec and France was stimulated by Norman's presence and experiences.[25]

Examining Murdoch's apprenticeship experience obliges us to confront a certain stereotype prevalent in both the legal and the historical literatures. There is a frequent assumption that apprenticeship was a form of professional education inherently inferior to that provided by university education. Once university legal education had been established as the ideal form of education for the bar, there was a good deal of retrospective denigration of the practice of apprenticeship, both from those with vested interests in the perpetuation of university legal education and from legal historians.[26] The quality of the articling experience remained variable, but the circulation of ambitious reading programs, the availability of a variety of advice literature, and the tendency of young students-at-law to form self-improvement societies ensured that an intelligent and energetic apprentice could learn a lot on his own even if his principal was less than fully engaged.

David Bell has shown that, in the case of the first two generations of Loyalist lawyers in New Brunswick (c. 1784–1825), apprenticeship comprised much more than the standard copying of pleadings and low-grade clerical functions. It included a demanding reading program that began with English history, classical, English, and French literature, and legal philosophy, gradually introduced general legal works such as Blackstone's *Commentaries* and Hale's *History of the Common Law*, and ended with the more specialized tomes on civil procedure, evidence, and land law. When carried out under the supervision of an engaged principal and with access to an adequate library, apprenticeship could be an entirely appropriate form of preparation for the legal profession. Admittedly, neither of these desiderata was a given. At its best, however, apprenticeship involved not just the transmission of legal knowledge and conventions but also exposure to a broader set of values which can best be called legal culture.

Legal culture involves an appreciation of how law relates to other dominant discourses such as religion, philosophy, politics, and history, and an understanding of the values that a particular set of legal arrangements seeks to foster and protect. When the dominant ideals of the legal profession were those of the lawyer-statesman and the gentleman-scholar, a broad approach to legal culture and to legal formation was obligatory. Laymen, too, had absorbed this understanding of the legal profession, as revealed by the advice given to future U.S. Chief Justice Salmon P. Chase by his non-lawyer brother. When Chase was contemplating entering the legal profession in 1825, his brother advised that 'to become a good Lawyer it is requisite that you should not only be master of all ... the technical jargon and elegant obscurity of centuries long past ... but that you should have a competent knowledge of all the other sciences, of the arts, and a thorough acquaintance with ancient and modern History – In fine you must become an universal scholar.'[27] A similarly broad approach to preparation for the law is clearly seen in the early New Brunswick lawyers, and also in the apprenticeship of Murdoch's contemporary William Young, who articled with the second-generation Loyalist lawyers Charles and Samuel Fairbanks in Halifax.[28] And, while G. Blaine Baker's account of Upper Canadian legal education does not provide the content of reading programs as such, the seriousness with which the Law Society treated both entrance requirements and the legal education of aspirant lawyers suggests parallel trends there.[29]

New Brunswick's Loyalist legal culture was much more unitary in its founding era than Nova Scotia's. Nova Scotia was influenced by several legal cultures, corresponding to the different populations who had come to inhabit the province. Acadians, Planters, and Loyalists had brought their traditions with them, as had the 'Foreign Protestants' and the Irish.[30] Some educated Scots possibly brought with them a familiarity with the natural law traditions of the Scottish Enlightenment.[31] Prior to the arrival of the Loyalists, a common law legal culture with an Anglo-Irish inflection was dominant, thanks to the presence of certain key figures in the legal hierarchy. Chief Justice Jonathan Belcher (1754–76) was raised in Massachusetts but came to Halifax after twelve years at the bar in Dublin, where he had co-edited an enormous and scholarly *Abridgment of the Statutes of Ireland*, published in the Irish capital in 1754. Dubliner Richard Bulkeley, although not a lawyer, was in a position to influence the development of legal institutions through his role as provincial secretary (1766–92) and master of the rolls in the Court of Chancery (1782–1800). Chief Justice Bryan Finucane (1776–85) also hailed from Ireland, and was instrumental in having his countryman Richard John Uniacke appointed solicitor general of Nova Scotia only four years after he had been arrested on suspicion of treason for his role in the Cumberland rebellion of 1776.[32] Another Irishman, John Parr, was governor (1782–6) and lieutenant governor (1786–91). It was during his tenure that the Irish form of foreclosure and sale was adopted in the Court of Chancery. This process was quite different from the English and survives to this day in Nova Scotia.[33]

Richard John Uniacke was the most conspicuous representative of Anglo-Irish legal culture in Nova Scotia after the death of Chief Justice Bryan Finucane. Uniacke spent most of his adult life in Nova Scotia but he had first trained as an attorney in Dublin in the 1770s, at a particularly agitated time in Irish legal and constitutional history. Some attempt to understand his early legal career in Ireland is required to appreciate his contribution to Murdoch's formation and, more generally, to provincial legal culture.[34] This can be done by setting the few known facts about Uniacke's Irish career in the context of developments within Irish law and the Irish legal profession in the last third of the eighteenth century.

Uniacke acquired his legal training at a time when serious efforts were being made to raise the professional standards of attorneys and the educational attainments of barristers.[35] Those same years in Dublin saw the rapid growth of an unprecedented liberal nationalist (Whig) movement within a segment of the Protestant Ascendancy, culminating in the recognition by Westminster of the legislative supremacy of the Irish Parliament in 1782.[36] In this agitation, which included a campaign to remove or at least reduce the effect of the pernicious penal laws aimed at Catholics, lawyers played no small part. Even if Uniacke's political views later took a more conservative turn, his legal world view remained permeated by the Enlightenment values he had absorbed in those days in Dublin before the French Revolution. The Uniackes would become champions of Catholic relief and liberalization of the debt laws, and unalterably opposed to slavery.

It is not known why Uniacke's father apprenticed him to Dublin attorney Thomas Garde in 1769, rather than launching him on a course for the more prestigious call to the bar. What is known is that father and son were already at loggerheads. It may be that Norman Uniacke could countenance his headstrong son's presence under some type of supervision in Dublin, when he could not tolerate his being at large in London for the period of attendance at the inns of court then required of would-be Irish barristers. Garde came from a gentry background similar to that of the Uniackes in County Cork.[37] By indenture dated 4 October 1769, Uniacke 'put himself an apprentice to the said Thomas

Garde with him to live and dwell as an Attorney's clarke or apprentice for the term of five years.' Father Norman Uniacke paid £115 to
Garde, and Garde undertook to 'provide competent and necessary dyet
and lodging during the said term.' The agreement contained the usual
prohibition on matrimony without the master's consent,[38] but also en-
joined the frequenting of taverns or ale houses and playing at cards or
dice. Unlike later Nova Scotia indentures, which contain explicit covenants relating to instruction in the business of an attorney, this one is
virtually silent on professional education. Garde merely obliged himself 'at the expiration of the five years to use his utmost endeavours to
procure the said Richard John Uniacke ... to be admitted and sworn
one of the Attorneys.'[39] Uniacke served his apprenticeship in two parts:
from 1769 to 1773, when he fled to the New World after a quarrel with
his father; and for a year at some point between his return to Ireland in
the fall of 1777 and June 1779.

Legal life in Dublin revolved around the Four Courts: King's Bench,
Common Pleas, Exchequer, and Chancery. Uniacke was admitted as
an attorney of the Court of Exchequer and a member of the Society of
King's Inns, thus becoming one of the over 700 attorneys in the capital.[40] When added to the approximately 280 barristers present in Dublin in that year, the legal needs of the residents of Dublin would appear
to have been amply filled. However, Dublin was not only one of the
largest cities in the Empire, with some 125,000 souls in 1775, but also
the capital of a kingdom of some 4,000,000. Some of the city's legal
personnel held government offices, while many lived by servicing the
needs of county landowners and merchants or English owners of Irish
estates.

A glimpse of the kind of relationship that might exist between an attorney and a county landowner is provided by the Anglo-Irish writer
Elizabeth Bowen in *Bowen's Court*, a history of her family's ancestral
home in County Cork. In the 1760s the attorney, Mr Chester, 'bought
wine for Henry [Bowen] in Dublin, checked over books Henry ordered
and had them despatched, bought horses (he showed a good deal of
knowledge and attended the sales), bought clothes for the Bowen ladies when he was in London, visited Henry's daughters at their Dublin
school, chose Henry a fishing rod, saw through some business about
some sheep and, last but not least, tried to find the Bowens a cook.'[41]
Attorneys were clearly expected to provide advice on a wide variety of
matters besides business and property, and in this case the relationship
took on an almost familial cast. Such examples go some way to balance

the many examples of anti-attorney sentiment found in the written record of the mid-eighteenth century.

Much of young Uniacke's day-to-day work with Garde would have consisted of the traditional copying of pleadings and precedents, leavened perhaps by the occasional quest for a fishing rod. Whether Garde subjected his apprentice to any more ambitious program of reading or instruction is not known, and no inventories of the libraries of eighteenth-century attorneys appear to have survived.[42] Uniacke could not have failed to be aware, however, of an important reform movement within the Irish legal profession and, particularly upon his return to Ireland in 1777, of dramatic events upon the stage of Irish politics and constitutional history. These matters would have given him a broader view of the role of lawyers and the law within the social fabric than the rather crabbed perspective from the apprentice's desk.

With regard to the Irish legal profession, the efforts of the reforming attorney and scholar Gorges Edmond Howard (1715–86) finally came to fruition during the period of Uniacke's apprenticeship.[43] Howard was the first writer to devote any sustained attention to Irish law[44] and authored a series of works impressive for their scope, length, and learning. Two of these, *A Compendious Treatise of the Rules and Practice of the Pleas Side of the Exchequer in Ireland* (2 vols., Dublin, 1759) and *A Treatise of the Exchequer and Revenue of Ireland* (2 vols., Dublin, 1776), Uniacke thought sufficiently important to bring with him to Nova Scotia,[45] where they remained in his library until his death.[46] In 1773, largely as a result of Howard's efforts, the Irish Parliament passed a bill aimed at the admission and regulation of attorneys, which, as we have seen, imposed a pre-admission examination requirement as well as mandating the keeping of terms at the Four Courts during apprenticeship.[47] With regard to the Irish constitution, the late 1770s saw a remarkable upsurge in liberal sentiment which led to a relaxation of the 'popery' laws and a realignment of the constitutional relationship with England, resulting in the removal of restrictions on the powers of the Irish Parliament in 1782.[48]

Upon his return to Ireland in 1777, Richard John Uniacke thus found the entrance requirements for his chosen profession considerably altered, although he was probably admitted under the earlier rules. There is no evidence that Uniacke actually practised his profession in Dublin – his name does not appear in the annual list of Dublin attorneys from 1779 to 1782 – and once admitted, his focus shifted to laying a foundation for his New World career. He travelled to England in 1780 to lobby for the attorney generalship of Nova Scotia, returned to Nova Scotia in early 1781, and found himself named solicitor general by the end of the year. He attained the office of attorney general in 1797 against the wishes of Loyalist governor Wentworth by appealing over his head to his patrons in England, and from that point until his death in 1830 he remained at the summit of the legal profession in Nova Scotia.

A commonplace book kept by Murdoch during the years 1816–21 does not supply much direct evidence of any transmission of Anglo-Irish legal culture, but it does provide a unique window on an early-nineteenth-century apprenticeship.[49] It appears to have begun as a precedent book of the traditional kind kept by apprentice attorneys, but later became a sounding board for Murdoch's reflections and observations on various topics, both professional and non-professional. The manuscript volume contains draft letters, original songs, poems and hymns, drawings, and jottings on various topics. Except for occasional excerpts from Blackstone, it does not contain indications of any reading program in which Murdoch might have been engaged. Nonetheless, in various ways it permits us to see how Murdoch's views were being shaped. His notations on some precedents suggest that the copying exercise could have a critical component. On a precedent for a covenant for the production of deeds, he noted that 'the Registry Act of this Prov. 32 G. 2 c. 2 seems to make this covenant altogether useless. The best conveyancers here make no use of it.'[50] On a precedent for 'General Words for a Manor,' obviously copied out of some English text, Murdoch protested, 'There are no manors in N.S.'[51] Various parts of a precedent for covenants for title of freeholds are underlined with the observation 'not used here.'[52] From his earliest exposure to the law, then, Murdoch was obliged to think in terms of a distinction between 'here' and 'there,' between English precedents and their applicability or otherwise in Nova Scotia. In his *Epitome of the Laws of Nova-Scotia* he would lament that, 'having access only to works written expressly for English students, much of our time has hitherto been wasted in obtaining, by long and tedious research, an intimacy with the general character of the Provincial usages and statutes.'[53] In that same work, he would make the case for a Nova Scotian legal culture, one that shared much with English legal culture but was ultimately distinct from it.

The learning process sometimes took the form of questions and answers. Murdoch would write down a question followed by his principal's opinion. A master wanted an opinion as to what he might do with an unruly, disobedient, dishonest apprentice. How far was he bound to keep him and what legal steps should he take to procure his dismissal? Crofton Uniacke's answer shows how even a relatively simple legal question can lead to larger issues. Uniacke advised that, under provincial law, the master's only recourse was to make a complaint before two justices of the peace, who could commit the apprentice to the Bridewell for a punishment proportioned to his offence. He was adamant that the master could not discharge the apprentice: 'If the Indenture is in the usual form you must have entered into Covenants for the performance of which you have bound yourself. It therefore lies on you as a duty to fulfil them and you cannot discharge him until you have.'[54] The sanctity of contract was here invoked even where it involved the protection of a possibly dishonest apprentice. In 1819 a question of more constitutional importance was asked: 'If King G. 3 dies, and GPR [George the Prince Regent] abdicates, is the Princess of Wales to be considered as Queen?'[55] No answer is recorded. There are not many of these interchanges, but it is unlikely that Murdoch would have troubled to write down all of them when they occurred.

Murdoch was not critical of apprenticeship itself, or even of starting it at an early age, but rather wished it to be seen as only one step in preparation for the legal profession. He strongly urged aspirant lawyers to acquire a liberal education, something he had not been able to do, at least at the university level.[56] In fact, his inability to attend King's College, the self-proclaimed training ground for the provincial elite, probably left him with some sense of inadequacy. In his *Epitome of the Laws of Nova-Scotia*, Murdoch specifically addressed himself to 'those who enter upon the study [of law] without the benefit of a college education … It is then incumbent on [them] to allow no occasion when they may add to their limited stock of learning, to pass by unimproved.' He recommended the best writers of English literature and history and the acquisition of Latin and French, while warning that 'the orations of Demosthenes, Chatham, Walpole, Fox, Burke, Sheridan, Canning, Curran, and Erskine, should not escape [the apprentice's] vigilance.'[57] Writing to a local newspaper under a pseudonym in 1820, Murdoch exhorted Nova Scotians to hold learning in the same high esteem as it was held in Europe, and lamented that so many parents restricted their children's education 'to writing reading and arithmetic, because every other science is trifling compared with the Science of multiplying Dollars.'[58]

The attainments of 'an universal scholar' were essential, but they were not enough, Murdoch reflected in the *Epitome*. However idealistic he may have been in his youth, by the time he had spent a decade in practice he knew the ways of the world: 'The young collegian is not to expect, that any precocity of genius evinced in scholastic pursuits, will in the world be accepted in lieu of the habits and acquirements of a man of business, such as a colonial lawyer may emphatically be called ... Let him not in the pride of classic lore, undervalue the most minute or humble departments of his profession. While his learning may be an ornament, and perhaps give grace and intensity to his eloquence, yet it is rather a holiday garb; while method and accuracy in things which appear trivial are essential and indispensable, to success in any profession.'[59]

While we do not know the exact content of Murdoch's reading program during his apprenticeship, likely it was similar to the program he himself recommended in the *Epitome* some fifteen years later. He listed some twenty legal titles to be read over the course of five years, beginning with Blackstone, two books on procedure and one on evidence in the first year, books on equity, bailments, and property in the second year, the classics Doctor and Student and Coke on Littleton in the third year, works on contracts, fraud, libel, shipping, crown law, and criminal law in the fourth year, and Browne's *Civil and Admiralty Law*, to which we will have occasion to return below, in the final year. In addition to this program, Murdoch recommended David Hoffman's *Course of Legal Study, Respectfully Addressed to the Students of Law in the United States* (1817) as the best overall introductory treatise on law. One may doubt whether many Nova Scotian students-at-law persevered with this demanding, idealistic, and earnest volume, but the rest of Murdoch's program was similar to the one followed by his contemporary William Young in the 1820s, as recorded in his journal.[60] Contrary to the order followed by David Bell's Loyalist lawyers, Murdoch advised that those training for entry into the legal profession start with some works on attorneys' practice before delving into the more philosophical and speculative works on law.[61]

The reader may wonder at this point about the role of Blackstone in the formation of Murdoch and other British North American lawyers. Blackstone's influence is a favourite theme of legal historians in the United States, where the *Commentaries* have been called 'the urtext of antebellum law students.' Blackstone 'served as a catalyst of professional identity [and] functioned as a site of social and cultural communion for [U.S.] law students,' according to Ann Fidler, but evidence of his influence is harder to come by among British North American lawyers.[62] Murdoch does recommend perusal of Blackstone in the first year of one's apprenticeship as well as 'a 2d and 3d reading of Blackstone's Commentaries, at intervals of one or two years, – the second time referring to, and reading the chief acts of the province, as they bear upon the subjects in the Commentaries, – the third time reading the leading cases referred to.'[63] Clearly, he found Blackstone useful, and of course used the format of the *Commentaries* for his own treatise, but he provides no praise of Blackstone's work, as he does for Hoffman's *Course of Legal Study*; moreover, at various points in the *Epitome* he is critical of Blackstone. Murdoch's contemporary William Young, by contrast, hit it off with Blackstone right away; he was 'wonderfully pleased' after a week and even read the *Commentaries* 'while walking into town from home.'[64] It must be said that Young's encomium finds few echoes in the writings of his contemporaries. John Beverley Robinson seemed annoyed with the *Commentaries* – 'Master Blackstone steps in now and then with his doctrine of entails' – while Christopher Moore's richly detailed account of early Ontario lawyers provides no contemporary references to Blackstone at all.[65]

It is worth pausing to consider the apparently paradoxical contrast of the enthusiastic embrace of the Tory Blackstone in the early revolutionary United States with his more muted reception in loyal British North America. This phenomenon arguably provides an important insight into early divergences in the legal cultures of the two nations. In the early United States, lawyers and aspirant lawyers cast about for some shared legal foundation for the new republic, some way of finding unity in the diversity of state laws. This was especially important since there was much more interstate mobility of lawyers than was the case in British North America. Before the publication of James Kent's *Commentaries on American Law* in the 1820s, Blackstone provided a kind of common law constitution to mirror the national constitution; he allowed lawyers to see the principles that underlay the multiple variations of state laws, and to feel that they moved in a shared legal space. The diffusion of Blackstone's ideas was assisted enormously by the domestication of the *Commentaries* in the form of annotated editions providing U.S. references and critical commentary, beginning with St George Tucker's edition in 1803. As M.H. Hoeflich has noted, these editors played a role similar to that of the medieval glossators in adapting Justinian's *Digest* for use in a very different society.[66]

In British North America, each colony was almost a sovereign entity, with rather little in the way of personal or commercial intercourse with the others. The important ties were vertical, with Britain, rather than horizontal, with other colonies. Lawyers, if they left their home province before about 1850, were as likely to go to England as to another colony, and if they did go to another colony, they could assume the presence of a familiar common law. No one prior to Confederation thought to undertake an annotated version of Blackstone for local consumption, and when Alexander Leith of Upper Canada did so in 1864, it was only the *Commentaries'* section on real property that he reproduced; Blackstone was here reduced to the utilitarian role of aiding conveyancers, not providing an overview of the foundations and rationale of English law.[67] In this context, Blackstone was more like wallpaper – pleasant enough, but taken for granted and not necessary to be remarked upon.

Turning to other key texts, it was noted above that Murdoch recommended Arthur Browne's *Civil and Admiralty Law* in the final year of apprenticeship. His interest in the civil law would have received a powerful stimulus from Crofton Uniacke, who was an enthusiastic proponent of the civil (Roman) law and later, in England, an active advocate of the codification of English law. As an advocate in vice-admiralty in the 1810s, Crofton would have had to acquire a knowledge of the civil law which was employed in that court.[68] His father's library contained a copy of Arthur Browne's *A Compendious View of the Civil Law and of the Law of Admiralty*, published in two volumes at Dublin in 1797–9, which was the first treatise to deal comprehensively with admiralty law in the English language.[69] Browne's accessible and sympathetic overview of the civil law provided an important source for Beamish Murdoch in his turn, as revealed in his *Epitome of the Laws of Nova-Scotia*.[70]

It was Crofton's subsequent career as a barrister and would-be law reformer in London in the 1820s, however, that revealed most clearly his intellectual ambition and commitment to the civil law. His project was nothing less than the codification of English law along the lines of Jean Domat's famous text on the civil law *Les loix civiles dans leur ordre naturel* (1688).[71] In 1825 he published in London *A Letter to the Lord Chancellor, on the Necessity and Practicability of Forming a Code of the Laws of England*, a forceful and elegant plea in favour of a more scientific arrangement of English law. To it he annexed a sample redrafting of the whole of the bankruptcy law in one clear, simple, and well-organized statute, very much along civilian lines, as proof of what might be done. This was followed by a similar exercise on the jury law, and yet another, written by Crofton's protégé Samuel Bealey Harrison, on the law of evidence.[72] These attempts at codification arguably influenced Murdoch's own drafting style when he took in hand the redrafting of the Halifax city charter in the 1850s.[73]

Uniacke's efforts attracted more favourable notice in the United States (his *Letter to the Lord Chancellor* was republished at Boston in 1827[74]) than in England. The resistance of English lawyers to codification has always been strong, and while English law would undergo significant reform after 1830, that reform would never embrace the wholesale codification advocated by Uniacke. Crofton gave vent to some bitterness on this score in a barb he included in the preface to Harrison's treatise on evidence. His only wish, wrote Uniacke, was 'to see method given to the laws of my country which are now in deplorable condition; and legislative sanction afforded to some system, worthy of a great and enlightened nation. [For that, he was] willing to endure the ignominy which attaches to the … names of Blackstone and [William] Jones and to the memory of every *intellectual* lawyer this empire has ever produced.'[75] In his appreciation of the civil law, and his concern to portray the law as a rigorous intellectual system rather than 'merely an unconnected series of decrees and ordinances,' Crofton Uniacke did indeed run counter to a strong anti-intellectual tradition within the legal profession in the common law world.[76] Beamish Murdoch would emulate him in this respect and he too would run the risk, not so much of ignominy, as of the incomprehension that accompanied his own efforts to be an 'intellectual lawyer' in the New World.[77]

When trying to identify the substantive aspects of the Uniacke legacy, specifically the Anglo-Irish aspects of that legacy, it is necessary to look beyond Murdoch's apprenticeship to his political career and his *Epitome of the Laws of Nova-Scotia*. On three major issues, Murdoch's views coincided perfectly with those of the Uniackes: the civil equality of blacks and whites, Catholic relief, and liberalization of the debt laws. In all three areas, the views of the Uniackes and Murdoch were guided by an enlightened Christian humanism. This fact is worth stressing since in recent years Richard John Uniacke has been portrayed, largely on the evidence of his preface to the edition of Nova Scotia statutes published under his name in 1805, as an implacable conservative and foe of any kind of innovation.[78] It is true that the 1805 preface can be interpreted in that way, but Uniacke was certainly not the only public figure to rediscover the virtues of the status quo in the wake of the French Revolution. Some Uniackes had been murdered in Ireland in the 1798 uprising which had led to the Union of 1800, and these dramatic events in his homeland may well have caused Uniacke to reflect with some anguish on his earlier commitment to a more liberal world view.

The 1805 preface is only one piece of evidence from a very long life. Taken as a whole, the record of the Uniacke family is characterized more by independence than by uncritical acceptance of the old regime.[79] The Uniackes were confident enough to be critical of the established order even as they benefited from it. Crofton's radical law-reform views have been noted. With the Whigs, he supported the queen in the divorce crisis of 1820–1 and even wrote a series of letters to the London newspapers highly critical of the king's conduct.[80] Norman Fitzgerald was a noted supporter of the French cause in Quebec, which won him few friends there. Most of the Uniackes left St Paul's Cathedral in Halifax after the row over the crown's right to appoint the new rector after the promotion of the incumbent in 1824, considered in chapter 5. James Boyle Uniacke became the first premier under responsible government, but Crofton and Norman were also enthusiastic converts, in marked contrast to many representatives of old regime families who left the province after 1850. Only their younger brother Andrew Mitchell joined the Tories. The Uniackes in the House of Assembly supported law reform in a number of important areas, of which three can be considered here.

The Uniacke-Murdoch positions on civil equality of the races, Catholic relief, and the debt laws have been chosen because these were also the three issues where a contrast with the Planter/Loyalist legal culture was most evident. The example of New Brunswick shows that a Loyalist legal culture was receptive to the claims of slaveowners.[81] In Nova Scotia their claims were consistently resisted by the courts, in part, arguably, because a more liberal Anglo-Irish ethic was dominant at the bar.[82] In his private capacity, Richard John Uniacke acted as counsel for blacks in a number of cases where their legal status (slave or free) was in question.[83] In his *Epitome of the Laws of Nova-Scotia*, Murdoch interpreted early court decisions to mean that from about 1800 'slaves brought into this country became free ipso facto upon landing.'[84]

With regard to Catholic relief, the aggressively Protestant New England legal culture from which the Planters emerged was not noted for its acceptance of Catholic claims for equal civil rights.[85] It is true that once in Nova Scotia, the Planters and the Loyalists after them became more accommodating in their views when forced to confront a larger Catholic population in the province than they had known south of the border.[86] Nonetheless, leadership on this issue was important and the

Uniackes largely provided it. When the attorney general agreed to accept Laurence O'Connor Doyle as an apprentice in 1823, Catholics were indirectly prevented from becoming attorneys because of the obligation to swear the oath of supremacy and allegiance before admission. Uniacke must already have been contemplating the change in the law which would come about in 1827.

On the issue of debt, the Uniackes and Murdoch consistently supported the abolition of imprisonment for debt and reform of the laws relating to bankruptcy and insolvency. Nova Scotia's law of debtor and creditor was even more creditor-oriented than most, and subject to the kinds of abuse that Murdoch had witnessed personally in the case of his own father. The Uniackes' involvement with this issue seems to have grown out of their general concern about the advancement of civil rights and personal liberty, rather than considerations of economic efficiency, which would become a stimulus to reform later in the century. On this issue, the Planter/Loyalist group won hands down. Halifax merchants were prepared to accept a bankruptcy law and abolish imprisonment for at least small debts, but in the rest of the province the state of debtor-creditor law was seen as an important tool of social control, not to be surrendered lightly.[87]

Murdoch's apprenticeship with the Uniackes represented the old regime at its best. Willing student met inspiring principal, and Murdoch was set on his lifelong course. While he was clearly of a scholarly bent even before he entered the Uniackes' employ, his association with them only confirmed his respect for learning. Access to Richard John Uniacke's magnificent and wide-ranging library, exposure to Crofton Uniacke's civilian learning and to the family's experiences of legal traditions in Ireland, England, Quebec, and Cape Breton, and contact with the wide variety of legal matters within the attorney general's purview, all provided the young Beamish Murdoch with an irreplaceable intellectual stimulus. His *Epitome of the Laws of Nova-Scotia*, with its tolerant Enlightenment humanism, would reveal the extent to which Murdoch's apprenticeship had marked him as the intellectual heir of the Uniackes. With its openness to American law, civil law, and international law, even as it insisted on the autonomy of Nova Scotian law vis-à-vis English law, the *Epitome* also provides eloquent testimony to the role of legal pluralism in British North American law.

Yet, for all this emphasis on scholarship and statesmanship, we should not forget Murdoch's own assertion that the colonial lawyer was 'emphatically ... a man of business.' The North American lawyer was obliged to combine two roles that were ensconced in different professions in England: the solicitor's practical learning and involvement in the local economy with the barrister's higher learning and independence from business interests and local pressures. As Murdoch began his law practice after his admission as an attorney in 1821, he would experience first-hand how to negotiate these two poles of lawyerly endeavour.

4

The Legal Profession in Nova Scotia: Organization and Mobility

When Beamish Murdoch began his apprenticeship as an attorney in 1814, entry to the legal profession had recently been regulated by provincial statute for the first time since the founding of Halifax. An act of 1811 set the period of service at five years after which the candidate was entitled to be admitted as an attorney of the Supreme Court provided he had attained his majority, passed an oral examination administered by the judges, and taken the attorney's oath. He had to spend a further quasi-probationary period of one year before final admission as a barrister, except that graduates of King's College, Windsor, were exempted from this requirement and could be called to the bar of the Supreme Court immediately. During this year, the candidate had no contractual obligations to a principal and could perform unaided the functions of an attorney (if he had any clients), but was obliged to 'attend the terms of the Supreme Court at its regular sittings at Halifax, for at least three terms after his admission as an Attorney.'[1]

It is hard to overstate the importance of the act of 1811 in transforming a small and somewhat disparate collection of law-workers into a distinct and respectable profession. Like the 1785 ordinance regulating the professions of advocate and notary in Quebec, the 1797 statute creating the Law Society of Upper Canada, and the 1823 New Brunswick Rule of Court formalizing the requirements for admission as attorneys and barristers, the 1811 act sought to accomplish at least three of the four goals that Michael Burrage has suggested are characteristic of lawyers' collective action: 1) controlling entrance to the profession by specifying the necessary educational and/or practical attainments; 2) defending a particular area of work and preventing others from doing it; 3) regulating each other's behaviour; and 4) protecting and enhancing corporate honour and status.[2]

This chapter shifts the focus away from the individual lawyer in order to look at the legal profession as a whole, in both its institutional and its spatial contexts. After briefly considering the origins and impact of the Nova Scotia act of 1811, we will examine the emergence of the Society of Nova Scotia Barristers in 1825 and its development down to Confederation. Finally, we will consider the geographic diffusion of lawyers throughout the province during the nineteenth century. We will then be in a position to analyse how the 1811 act, to a lesser extent the Barristers' Society, and the actions of individual lawyers themselves helped to further Burrage's professional goals and solidified the role of the legal profession as a force to be reckoned with in colonial society.

Preparation for the Legal Profession

The legal profession did not emerge in Nova Scotia as the product of any grand attempt to create a class of colonial leaders, as arguably occurred in Upper Canada.[3] Nor was it the product of a particular founding moment or group, as was the case with the Loyalist bar of New Brunswick.[4] Nova Scotia was not founded on any utopian vision and there was no hostility to lawyers as such, as there had been in New France and in some of the New England colonies.[5] Rather, the origins of the Nova Scotia bar were much more utilitarian. Lawyers were needed to carry out a variety of tasks for both official and private purposes, and hence some means of admitting them to practice was needed. The Court of Chancery had admitted solicitors since its inception in 1751, and the Supreme Court began to admit attorneys to practice after its establishment in 1754.[6] In practice, however, there was no distinction between the two groups. More important, there was no distinction between the roles of barrister and attorney/solicitor, as we saw in chapter 3. Attorneys or solicitors once admitted were able to do everything that barristers could do in England except use the name: as in the other North American colonies, there were initially no 'barristers' in Nova Scotia except by courtesy.

Entry to the profession required an apprenticeship, but that was about all that could be said. Beamish Murdoch thought that a minimum period of three years' service had been required before a rule of the Supreme Court set it at four years in 1799. This may be correct since eighteenth-century indentures set terms of apprenticeship varying from three to seven years.[7] Most lawyers in the eighteenth century came to Nova Scotia 'ready-made,' at first from England and Ireland, then as part of the Loyalist immigration of 1783–4. Their disparate experiences made for a rather heterogeneous legal profession, which the act of 1811 aimed to mould into a more unified bar.

The Act of 1811

The Nova Scotia act of 1811 was a bold attempt, similar to those undertaken in the other colonies, to standardize the formation of young lawyers, to raise the profile of the profession, and to ensure that locally called lawyers would not rank inferior in precedence to any English barristers who might come to the colony. Indeed, the act was inspired by the controversy that arose when just such a barrister arrived in the province and tried to claim precedence ahead of all local lawyers including the attorney general, who, as we have seen, was a 'mere' attorney.[8] The act provided for a uniform five-year period of apprenticeship and imposed a statutory obligation on the judges to 'examine and enquire, by such ways and means as they shall think proper, touching [a candidate's] fitness and capacity to act as an Attorney.' They were to admit him only if 'satisfied that such person is duly qualified to be admitted to act as an Attorney ... and not otherwise.' Any person acting 'for, or in expectation of, any gain, fee or reward' in any of the courts of the province without being admitted as an attorney was liable to forfeit £10 to the prosecutor for every such offence. No attorney was permitted to take more than two apprentices at any one time. Admission as a barrister or advocate required a further year (three terms) of attendance at the Supreme Court, as noted earlier. This requirement was probably derived from the Irish statute of 1773 noted in chapter 3 and was a way of trying to ensure some uniform measure of legal socialization among nascent lawyers. Upper Canada adopted a similar measure in 1828 which required residence at Osgoode Hall for the requisite number of terms, initially four (until 1857) and later two (until 1871).[9] Graduates of King's College, Windsor, and barristers already called in England or Ireland were spared this year and could be admitted as barristers immediately after being admitted and enrolled as attorneys. The act also gave a monopoly on both initiating actions and pleading 'in expectation of any gain, fee or reward' in the Court of Sessions, the Inferior Court of Common Pleas, and the courts of Admiralty, Probate, and Chancery to regularly admitted attorneys, ensuring that no class of lay pleaders would emerge in the lower courts. The act did not, however, replicate the statutory monopoly over conveyancing given to English solicitors by an act of 1804, and lawyers in Nova Scotia and across British North America long had to compete with the justices of the peace and lay conveyancers who offered these kinds of services.[10]

The act had its defects. It provided no direction to the judges regarding the test they were to administer, nor any quality control of the apprenticeship experience. With regard to the first requirement, it may be that the test was rather perfunctory. A young William Blowers Bliss reported to his brother in 1818 apropos of his own experience that 'on Wednesday I had the honour of breakfasting with Mr. Justice Stewart, and going through a legal examination, such for instance as where I intended to open shop and retail law, and divers other pertinent questions from my Lord Coke, and such old friends I was next day sworn in.'[11] Bliss may be downplaying the extent of questioning but the breakfast-room ambience does not seem very threatening. Among gentlemen, anything more rigorous would have been unseemly.

It was clearly expected that the bar itself would be responsible for providing an adequate educational experience, a challenge that it met in a somewhat haphazard fashion as seen in chapter 3. In none of the Atlantic provinces did one find the significant amount of corporate attention devoted to legal education that characterized the Law Society of Upper Canada. However, the act was crucial in articulating the identity of the legal profession as a separate and distinct professional grouping. It went some considerable distance towards realizing the goals set out by Burrage as characteristic of lawyers' collective action. In conferring a statutory imprimatur on apprenticeship, the act gave existing members of the bar the right to control entry and education; the final examination administered by the court was largely a formality and left the real power over recruitment to the bar with the profession itself. It recognized a particular area of work as a monopoly of the legal profession: only properly admitted attorneys could practise as such for reward.[12] The blurred line between attorney-in-fact and attorney-at-law that had so marked the experience of the Thirteen Colonies before the Revolution was now precisely delineated. And, even though the act did not create a body corporate or contemplate a voluntary society of lawyers, it clearly aimed, by endowing provincial lawyers with the title of barrister, to protect and enhance the corporate honour of the bar. The unique process of qualification as a barrister also set apart the legal profession from others which relied only on apprenticeship. The act was thus adopted not to distinguish *between* classes of lawyer but rather to raise the collective status of *all* lawyers in the eyes of the public.

It is worth pausing to emphasize this point. One might have thought that if anyone would want to replicate the English distinction between barrister and attorney, it would have been the Loyalist lawyers of New Brunswick and Nova Scotia. The Loyalist lawyers of New Brunswick were heirs to the 'advanced professional cultures [of] colonial America,' while the Nova Scotian Sampson Salter Blowers was, as we have seen, one of the few lawyers in pre-Revolutionary Massachusetts actually to attain the distinction of barrister. As chief justice of the province, he would have presided over the Legislative Council when the act of 1811 was passed. If he had found it outrageous or inadvisable, he could and would have said so. But in fact Chief Justice Blowers agreed that the pretensions of English barristers were inadmissible; they had to take their place within the colonial legal profession, not recreate it in their own image. The act clearly stated in section 16 that anyone called to the bar of England or Ireland had to be admitted locally as an attorney of the Supreme Court (though this was pro forma if the candidate could produce a certificate from their home jurisdiction proving their call to the bar) and then could immediately be called as a barrister. This meant that English barristers took precedence only as of the date of their local admission and could not demand any special treatment. A similar desire to put English barristers on a level playing field with local lawyers has also been suggested as one of the main motivating factors behind the creation of the Law Society of Upper Canada.[13]

With his usual sharp eye, Thomas Chandler Haliburton aimed his satiric pen at the novel phenomenon of colonial 'barristers.' In *The Old Judge* (1849), his fictional layman Stephen Richardson lamented: 'They have got so infernal genteel, they have altered their name and very nature ... Formerly they were styled lawyers, but now nothing but bannisters will do, and nice bannisters they are for a feller to lean on that's going down-stairs to the devil.'[14] The very fact that Haliburton chose the pretensions of the bar as an object of satire only confirms the success of the professionalization project undertaken in 1811. The one respect in which the act did not conform to Burrage's scheme was its failure to address the issue of lawyers' discipline. As we shall see, however, informal mechanisms were sufficient to deal with this problem until the creation of a Barristers' Society in 1825 attempted to provide another avenue to address such concerns.

The North American tradition of a unified profession was confirmed by the act of 1811, but the two branches were married by the expedient of defining the attorney as a stage in the progression towards the degree of barrister, rather than as a distinct branch of the legal profession. Although a handful of men did practise as attorneys in Nova Scotia after the act of 1811 without ever proceeding to the final stage of being called to the bar, they were clearly anomalous; it was assumed that all attorneys would become barristers in due course.[15] The situation in Upper Canada was rather different for much of the nineteenth century. In an effort to maintain what Burrage calls 'status distance,' the benchers decided to exclude attorneys from the Law Society of Upper Canada in 1822 and focus on the training and regulation of barristers only (though barristers could continue to practise as attorneys if they chose, several attempts to prevent them from doing so having failed in the 1830s). By 1840, 40 per cent of all legal practitioners in the colony were attorneys only and hence beyond the control of the benchers, but they attracted an increasingly lucrative part of legal business.[16] Gradually, the benchers saw the error of their ways: in 1857 an act was passed requiring all articled clerks to pass an examination before being allowed to practise, and by 1876 they had been fully reintegrated into the Law Society.

In Nova Scotia neither economics nor ideology supported the idea of a distinct caste of barristers superior to the 'low attorney.' Or perhaps it would be more accurate to say that, even though ideology would have supported a divided profession, economics cast the deciding vote, as it did in Upper Canada after some hesitation. When Nova Scotia lawyers banded together to form a Barristers' Society in 1825, our friend William Blowers Bliss observed: 'We are endeavouring to establish our Bar into some kind of an Institution for the better regulating it and keeping up its respectability if it has any. There are so many in it who ought never to have been admitted that it will be a difficult task to keep them in order.' The logical outcome of this kind of caste mentality, which Bliss absorbed with his own elite upbringing and during his years at the Inner Temple, would have been to keep those 'who ought never to have been admitted' relegated to the role of attorney and out of the bar. Bliss knew this was not feasible in economic terms, as he observed to his brother two years earlier with regard to his own efforts to establish himself at the Nova Scotia bar: 'I shall never feel inclined to kill myself with scribbling [a derogatory term for attorneys' work] – and no one here pays for anything else.'[17] When the Barristers' Society was established, as we shall see, virtually every lawyer in the province signed its roll in March 1825.

The success of the professional project begun with the act of 1811 was apparent by the mid-1830s and possibly earlier. One example of this success was the willingness of *Belcher's Farmers' Almanack* to organize its listing of lawyers according to professional desires rather than consumer convenience. Prior to 1835, *Belcher's* listed lawyers by community: the name of each town was followed by a list of the lawyers resident there, without any further notation. In 1835 *Belcher's* adopted a new means of organization. Lawyers' names were now presented in tabular form, in order of seniority, followed by the respective dates of their admissions as attorney and barrister, and finally their place of residence. Those lawyers who were admitted only as attorneys, or who were not admitted in Nova Scotia at all (such as the occasional immigrant lawyer), were exposed as such; their seniority, however, was determined by *Belcher's* according to the date of their entry into practice. A further change came in the 1850s, when such 'irregular' practitioners were demoted to the bottom of the list, precedence now being determined formally only by call to the bar.

The success of the act of 1811 may also be deduced from the statute that replaced it in 1836.[18] The existing system was retained almost intact, with changes restricted mainly to improved recordkeeping. The new geographic reach of the bar was reflected in the decision to abandon the requirement of keeping terms at the Supreme Court in the year prior to call to the bar. Attorneys who were not university graduates still had to wait the year before final call as a barrister, but they no longer had to spend it in Halifax. The examination of candidates for admission was now to be conducted by a judge of the Supreme Court and two senior barristers appointed for that purpose by the court. Finally, the ability of a duly admitted barrister to plead before all the courts of the province, 'without any other or particular admission,' was guaranteed.[19]

The Society of Nova Scotia Barristers: Origins and Impact

There is little solid evidence as to why the Society of Nova Scotia Barristers came into existence in 1825. It is tempting to see the substantial growth in the profession in the preceding few years as having played some role in its foundation. As will be examined in more detail later in this chapter, recruitment to the bar took a great leap forward in the 1820s. During the decade 1811–1820, only nineteen men had been called to the bar, but in the next decade that number rose by over 300 per cent, to sixty, twenty-nine of them being called in 1821–5 alone. But, as will be seen with the U.S. example, rapid growth could end in the dismantling of bar associations, not in their creation. It is clearly not growth alone, but the meaning attributed to it by contemporaries, that is the key variable. In British North America, it was not growth as such but rather the class background of those attempting to enter the profession that exercised the leaders of the bar. In the Maritimes and Upper Canada, the elite of the bar felt obliged to take steps to maintain the gentlemanly character of the profession. In Upper Canada this took the form of the exclusion of the attorneys from the Law Society in 1822. In both New Brunswick and Nova Scotia, it resulted in the creation of barristers' societies in 1825, while in Montreal the elite of the bar gathered in 1828 to form two new associations, the Société de la Bibliothèque/Advocates' Library and the Brothers-in-Law Club. In New Brunswick, the coming into being of the Law Society arguably represented a shift 'from family connexion to peer control' in the face of increased recruitment to the bar from non-elite classes.[20] In Montreal, it was largely the elite of the anglophone bar who founded both societies; membership in the Advocates' Library was obtained by a two-thirds vote of existing members, and the initial subscription fee of £10 would have been prohibitively expensive for many younger lawyers.[21]

In Nova Scotia, contemporaries reported that 'the chief objects of the institution ... are to advance the respectability of the profession, and to gather funds for an increase to the Law Library.'[22] Young lawyer William Blowers Bliss agreed, as we have just seen, and so did Beamish Murdoch. In his *Epitome of the Laws of Nova-Scotia*, Murdoch wrote that 'the members of the bar form a society, governed by very strict regulations, for the purpose of keeping up their honor and character as a body. [Their] valuable library at Halifax ... will probably contribute more than any other circumstance to raise the profession to the station it deserves to fill in an enlightened community.'[23] For Bliss, class background as such was the passport to respectability, while for Murdoch it had more to do with attainment, with intellectual capacity and exertion. The membership rules reflected an uneasy compromise between these versions of respectability. All existing barristers were grandfathered as members of the 'senior class of benchers' of the society provided they 'subscribe[d] the Rules' within one year of the organization's founding, and virtually every barrister in the province had done so by signing the society's roll in March 1825.[24] Members of the 'junior class' were those called after 1825, who had to apply for membership and be approved by at least two-thirds of those voting at the general meeting wherein their candidacy was proposed; after five years as members, they were automatically promoted to the senior class.

It was in the attempt to police the class background of those entering the profession in the future that the agenda of the founders of the Society of Nova Scotia Barristers was most clearly revealed. Rules 25 and 26 of the society's rules are worth quoting in full:

XXV. Before any member of the Society receives a Student into articles, he shall give notice in writing to the Committee, of the name of the proposed Student, his age and place of birth and residence, his father's name, quality and residence, or late residence if dead; and the Committee shall thereupon forthwith require by examination, or otherwise in their discretion, into the qualification of such proposed Student as respects his education, moral character, &c., and if it shall be found that he is so deficient in these qualifications, that the Committee shall think it advisable for the credit of the Profession that he shall not be received by any member of the Society, they shall in a written certificate submit the case to the Benchers who may thereupon if they approve the judgment of the Committee, order that no Member of the Society shall receive such person into his office, until in the opinion of the Committee or Benchers the objection shall be removed. And no member of the Society shall receive a student into articles, without a certificate from the Committee approving of his qualifications in conformity to the requisitions of this rule; every notice and a duplicate original of every certificate, whether of approbation or the reverse, given in compliance with this rule, shall be carefully preserved by the Secretary among the papers of the Society and be accessible to the members.

XXVI. Every member immediately upon receiving into articles any Student agreeably to the foregoing Rule, shall transmit to the Secretary in writing the date and time of the actual execution of such articles; and the Secretary having first received the directions of the Committee, shall enter on a Student's Roll to be kept by him for that purpose, the name of such Student and of the member with whom he is articled, and the date of the commencement of his Clerkship; and also the circumstances required to be detailed in the notice in the 25th article; and so long as any of the regulations required in this and the foregoing Rule, or any other Rule, of the Society respecting Students, shall not be fully complied with to the satisfaction of the Committee, in the case of any student, or students he or they shall not be entitled to any of the privileges to which the Students of members are or may be entitled.

The goal of these rules is crystal clear: the maintenance of a gentlemanly, and preferably quasi-hereditary, legal profession. In a New World society where status was more fluid and the influence of gentlemanly codes less pervasive, however, it proved impossible for the dreams of the society's founders to be realized.

Tracing the subsequent history of the society is no easy task. No continuous series of internal records exists until the mid-1890s, and references to its activities in the newspapers are scarce. Some statements of account from the mid-1830s show that the society was still functioning and paying its secretary £40 per annum, but it had only twenty-seven dues-paying members, in contrast to the charter group of sixty-six in 1825.[25] Not only had most of the original members effectively dropped out, but the society had also been unsuccessful in attracting more than a small fraction, one-sixth to be precise, of the seventy-three new lawyers called to the bar from 1826 to the end of 1836. Even Beamish Murdoch, who was the society's vice-president in 1827, is not shown as a dues-paying member in 1836. And the twelve new lawyers who joined were almost to a man from old elite Anglican families. The voting procedure for new members may have intimidated those who were not absolutely sure of their social status – and was probably designed to do so. Or perhaps the decline in membership was also a manifestation of the 'free rider' problem, where the intangible benefits of the society's existence were seen to accrue to all lawyers, whether members of the society or not. By 1860, things had not changed substantially; a mere twenty-nine lawyers belonged to the society in that year, an even smaller proportion of the bar than in 1836.

Aside from looking after the Barristers' Library and arranging dinners, it is difficult to discover what the society actually did. The most evident group ritual engaged in by the collective bar was their meeting to mourn publicly the death of the attorney general, as they did on the death of R.J. Uniacke in 1830, or the passing of one of the senior judges, as they did after the deaths of Justice James Stewart in 1830, Justice R.J. Uniacke, Jr in 1834, Master of the Rolls S.G.W. Archibald in 1846, and justices Lewis Wilkins and William Hill in 1848.[26] They usually resolved to send condolences to the family of the deceased, attend his funeral as a group, wear mourning crêpe on their hats for a month, and close their offices on the day of the funeral. Sometimes these meetings are referred to as those of the society, and at other times simply of 'the bar.' It is difficult to know whether the latter were in fact meetings called by the society but not reported as such. Beyond these ceremonial occasions, no society activities are evident.[27] It does not appear to have lobbied for statutory recognition except once in 1844, when its petition for incorporation failed in the Assembly – in spite of the large number of lawyers sitting in that body.[28] In New Brunswick, by contrast, incorporation was achieved in 1846. There, the act gave the Barristers' Society authority to create rules for examining both candidates wishing to become students-at-law and apprentices desiring admission as attorneys, and to administer the exams, in spite of the fact that membership in the society itself remained voluntary.[29]

Notwithstanding the less than robust condition of the Society of Nova Scotia Barristers, the bar at large retained some capacity for collective action. On two occasions when matters of professional honour were at stake in the 1830s and 1840s, effective action was taken not by the society but simply by 'the bar.' The first of these occurred in 1837–8, as will be seen in more detail in chapter 6, when the cantankerous judge of vice-admiralty, Charles Fairbanks, prohibited lawyer William Sutherland from practising in his court, then fined and jailed him for an alleged act of contempt. Beamish Murdoch successfully represented Sutherland on a writ of habeas corpus before the Supreme Court, and upon his release a 'Committee of the Bar' undertook to review the whole episode and in effect censured Judge Fairbanks for his high-handed behaviour. Sutherland was not listed as a member of the Society of Nova Scotia Barristers in 1836, so perhaps it is not surprising that no mention of the society as such was made in the report, which was authored by up-and-coming barrister William Young.[30]

Young also featured in the next incident to be considered, though in a more controversial role. On this occasion the bar was galvanized by some critical remarks by Young apropos of the judiciary. The 1830s and 1840s had seen the judges embroiled in numerous controversies, including those over commutation of the judges' fees, the setting of judicial salaries, and the role of the chief justice on the Legislative Council. The emergent Reform party,[31] with Young as one of its leaders, had used these issues to discredit the old regime. It was in this context that Young, sitting as speaker of the House of Assembly, was reported to have remarked in the House that 'a widespread feeling against the Courts existed throughout the Country,' and that he had no confidence in the Court of Chancery headed by Master of the Rolls Alexander

Stewart.[32] This was enough to cause over forty members of the bar to gather in order to dissociate themselves from these criticisms of the courts. Thus, it appears that the bar as a whole retained some capacity for collective action but chose not to channel it through the Barristers' Society except perhaps on ceremonial occasions. Such capacity for informal solidarity was more reactive than proactive, and hence of limited utility in any attempt to reform professional education or advance the interests of the bar in a programmatic way.

Any aspirations of lawyers for collective action were further threatened by gusts of radical populism that accompanied the reform movement in British North America. An important ideological strand in this mid-century moment was anti-monopoly sentiment, and here reformers sought to breach the very heart of the lawyers' citadel: their monopoly on pleading for reward in the superior courts. In Canada West, several bills were introduced in the early 1850s to throw open the courts to anyone who wished to practise in them, and to create 'conciliation courts' in which the common law would be replaced by broad principles of common sense and fairness.[33] In 1850 in Nova Scotia, Joseph Howe successfully promoted a bill allowing any citizen who had voted or paid poor rates to 'Plead and Reason in Her Majesty's Courts ... enjoying all rights and privileges therein, in as full and ample a manner as there are now enjoyed by Barristers, Proctors and Advocates.'[34] The bills in Canada West failed, however, and in Nova Scotia there was no great rush by laymen to push open the door unlocked for them by Howe's bill; in the 1864 statutory revision, the provision was quietly dropped.[35] And, while no attempts to permit laymen to compete with lawyers in the courts seem to have been made in New Brunswick, 'on a number of points [in the 1860s] the provincial legislature took the unprecedented step of curbing the bar's power over professional entry ... [based on] the perceived need to curb the profession's abuse of its *de facto* monopoly over admissions [in order to] make law more accessible to those clamouring for a ticket into the middle class.'[36] In particular, the New Brunswick House of Assembly in 1863 reduced the articling period from four years to three for those with college degrees (and from five years to four for those without) – without consulting the Barristers' Society – and in 1867 substantially reduced the sums levied by the society for enrolment as students and admission as attorneys. In the 1863 debates, there was even some support for doing away with articling altogether based on the American example. In mid-century England too, there was considerable public discontent with various restrictive practices of the legal professions, particularly with the requirement to pay both a solicitor and a barrister when conducting litigation, but aside from solicitors achieving rights of audience in the new county courts, little real change was accomplished.[37]

In Canada West the threat posed by mid-century radicalism was fairly easily rebuffed. One reason was simply the fact that barristers were required to be members of the Law Society of Upper Canada if they wished to practise law in the colony. After some growing pains, the society had become a force to be reckoned with, its power symbolized by its impressive headquarters at Osgoode Hall. Completed in 1832 but constantly expanded, the building was 'the finest and best-situated public edifice in Toronto' according to an 1845 observer.[38] Osgoode Hall and the institution of the Law Society fused in an almost mystical entity vested with considerable cultural authority as well as legal power. Taking on the lawyers meant taking on a statutory body with province-wide authority whose benchers were drawn from the highest echelons of the provincial elite. The anti-lawyer measures proposed at mid-century were championed by a rehabilitated William Lyon Mackenzie, but they were no more successful than his uprising of 1837 had been.

The challenge posed by mid-century radicalism was less easily repulsed in the Maritimes, where the law societies were mere voluntary associations. While the bar expanded with considerable success in the second quarter of the nineteenth century, nowhere in the Maritimes had it created impressive physical headquarters or an institution with the aura of the Law Society of Upper Canada. In both New Brunswick and Nova Scotia, the societies founded with such high hopes in 1825 were coping not only with challenges to their authority by populist legislators but with widespread disaffection among their own potential members. In Nova Scotia, as we have seen, only a small minority of lawyers even belonged to the Barristers' Society by 1860, while its New Brunswick counterpart was derided by one of its own leaders as a 'miserably conducted institution – its most important duties neglected, resulting in sad mischiefs to the great injury of the Bench, the Bar and the People.'[39] Bar associations may not have dissolved in the Maritimes, but they were not in a healthy state at mid-century, and the 1850s also saw a noticeable drop in calls to the bar.

By the late 1850s, however, there are signs of renewed efforts at collective professional action. In 1858 the Society of Nova Scotia Barristers sought and received a corporate charter and changed its name to the one it bears today, the Nova Scotia Barristers' Society.[40] A new constitution and set of rules adopted in 1860 allows us to infer a good deal about the decline and revival of the Barristers' Society between the 1830s and 1860s.[41] Membership had continued to decline: by 1860, only twenty-nine members (aside from the judges, who were honorary members) are listed, representing fewer than one in five of all lawyers then practising in the province. All but one of the twenty-nine, Silas Morse of Bridgetown, resided in Halifax, and, even there, less than half (45 per cent) of the lawyers were members of the society and they tended to be disproportionately old, Anglican, and Tory.[42] So far we have the classic picture of a social club with an aging and dwindling membership unable to attract new members.

As part of its efforts at self-renewal, the society made its governance more democratic in 1860. The 1825 rules stated only that 'there shall be a standing Committee of three Benchers, appointed annually at the general meeting after Michaelmas Term, in whom shall be vested the general management of the affairs of the Society,' without indicating how the selection of these benchers was to occur. The 1860 rules, by contrast, clearly stated that the council of president, vice-president, and five barristers would be 'elected annually at the general meeting' by ballot. The society also sought and achieved a more formal role in recruitment to the profession. In May 1860 the Supreme Court ordered that no person should be received as an articled clerk by any barrister 'until he shall have undergone an Examination at Halifax, before one of the Judges and two of the Office-bearers of the Barristers' Society, as to his educational qualifications, such qualifications to comprehend a knowledge of Geography and of the leading events of English History' and of the Latin classics. The examination was to be oral or in writing or both but a written component seems to have become standard early on. Thus, both entrance and exit exams were now required for those wanting to complete a legal apprenticeship.

The 1860 rules appear to have been requested by the Barristers' Society itself and to have been part of an attempt to reinvigorate the association. On 4 February 1860 an editorialist in the *Acadian Recorder* called attention to an upcoming special meeting of the Barristers' Society. The society, he observed, 'is in progress of organization out of the old "Bar Society" ... It is certainly high time for the Barristers of Nova Scotia to take their own case in hand. Rules are required and pretty stringent ones too if the profession is to be expected to maintain the high position in the community which is its proper place.'[43] The notice of meeting in question, signed by R.G. Haliburton, secretary of the society, stated that the selection of officers would take place and 'a Constitution and Rules will be then be adopted, and among other subjects the necessity for the preliminary examination of law students will then be considered.' No account of the actual meeting has been found, but presumably the Supreme Court's rule of May 1860 represented a ratification of what the society had approved three months earlier; the court's imprimatur was needed to ensure that all prospective lawyers, and not just those wishing to become members of the society, were subjected to the new regime; in the statutory revision of 1864, the legislature in turn confirmed the court's power to make such rules.[44]

The wording of the 1860 rules and usage of the term 'constitution' suggest that those at the meeting on 15 February 1860 saw themselves as creating a new society rather than simply adopting additional rules for an existing one. The second by-law declared that 'all members of the Bar of Nova Scotia not in arrears to the Bar Society may become members of this Society,' and then set out how 'any Barrister desiring to become a member' could apply. It appears that members were not simply continued but had to reapply to the new 'Nova Scotia Barristers' Society,' the name under which it had been incorporated in 1858. While this was in some ways a distinction in form, not substance, the founding of the new society does seem to represent an acknowledgment of past difficulties and a renewed commitment to a spirit of corporate improvement.

In a number of other respects, the rules remained the same. The clauses setting out the power of the council to investigate complaints against barristers or breaches of the rules were similar, as were the detailed rules about library usage. And membership in the society was still obtained by vote, with a two-thirds majority of those present required for admission. Members were to demand a fee of £100 from each articling student (as opposed to 100 guineas in 1825), though they could still take students without fee. The 1825 rules had been silent on the question of whether articling students could be paid, but the 1860 rules forbade the payment of any salary to them. With regard to meetings, the 1860 rules were less demanding on members and much more realistic: where the 1825 rules had mandated three general meetings a year plus two annual dinners, with special meetings called as needed by the governing committee, the 1860 rules referred only to one annual meeting and made no express reference to an annual dinner.

The biggest change between the rules of 1825 and 1860 was that regarding the policing of the class credentials of articling students. We have seen how the 1825 rules were very concerned to ensure that only the sons of gentlemen were admitted. By 1860, the very idea of any formal class-based rule was impossible. The 1860 rules contain nothing comparable to articles 25 and 26 of the old rules, and as a result of the Supreme Court's order the basis of the preliminary examination had shifted to specific educational attainments. A knowledge of Latin might function as a proxy for class but it was not an insuperable obstacle, as shown by the number of lawyers of humble birth who entered the profession later in the nineteenth century. The forces of reform running through British North America in the 1830s and 1840s, leading to elective city government in Halifax (1841) and responsible government provincially (1848), had broken down the elitism underlying the 1825 rules. They looked back to the hierarchical, aristocratic world of the eighteenth century; the 1860 rules and the Supreme Court's order look resolutely forward, to democracy and meritocracy within a world striving for equality and careers open to talents.

It is unfortunate that we have no record of the motivations of those behind the 1860 initiative. The only one who can be safely identified is the secretary of the new society, R.G. Haliburton, the son of Thomas Chandler Haliburton and a man of wide interests and considerable energy and talent. Only twenty-nine years old in 1860, he served as leading counsel for the proprietors during the Prince Edward Island Land Commission hearings held that year. A fervent believer in science and technology and in provincial, national, and imperial progress, Haliburton's devotion to 'improvement' suggests that he was a prime mover of the society's renovation. It is likely that Adams G. Archibald, who became attorney general in William Young's administration in February 1860, supported the initiative even if he was not one of its main proponents; his familiarity with the issue would prove useful a decade later when he became lieutenant governor of the new province of Manitoba, as we shall see later in this chapter.[45]

To sum up, then, after a period of torpor and decline, the Society of Nova Scotia Barristers reinvented itself as the Nova Scotia Barristers' Society in the period 1858–60. It responded to new socio-political developments by adopting at least the forms of democracy in its own governance and seeking out a key role in managing recruitment to the profession through the intercession of the Supreme Court.[46] It also no longer stood in the way, as the 1825 rules had attempted to do, of young men from the wrong side of town who might want to enter the profession. If they could demonstrate basic linguistic competence and cultural literacy, and were known to be of good character, they could sign up as apprentice lawyers. When, in 1864, a year was shaved off the lengthy period of apprenticeship by allowing attorneys to be called immediately as barristers instead of waiting a year, a small step was taken towards making the bar more accessible, but the radical U.S. approach of abolishing or drastically reducing the apprenticeship period was never seriously considered. We will now supplement our attention to institutional matters with some quantitative analysis of the professional lives of lawyers, in particular their mobility patterns – a key factor in the success story of the bar.

The Legal Profession: Growth and Mobility, 1800–1900

The legal profession benefited from a favourable legislative environment – the act of 1811 and its successors – and by 1825 it had established a voluntary association, albeit a somewhat ineffective one, to further its collective goals. The success or failure of the bar would depend largely, however, on its ability to provide services for which there was a demand. In this respect, the third and fourth decades of the nineteenth century were crucial chapters in the success story of the bar. Between 1820 and 1840, as we have seen, the size of the profession trebled, and the ratio of lawyers to population grew from approximately 1:2600 to 1:1800.[47] This enhanced availability of lawyers was most noticeable outside Halifax. While no more than a dozen lawyers were located outside the capital in 1820, more than six dozen were in business two decades later (Table 1). Whereas in 1820 two-thirds of all provincial lawyers resided in Halifax, by 1830 this had dropped to 42 per cent and by 1840 to 36 per cent; for the next century, Halifax's proportion of the province's lawyers remained remarkably stable, always between 36 per cent and 43 per cent. The decades of the 1820s and 1830s thus marked the point when the bar became effectively a provincial institution, serving the needs of a wide array of citizens, not simply an offshoot of the official establishment at Halifax.[48]

In 1800 there were at most twenty lawyers practising in the province, with only a handful of these serving communities outside Halifax. Recruitment to the bar had been sluggish in the eighteenth century, and complaints were heard about the unavailability of lawyers. In 1766

Table 1
Distribution of lawyers in Nova Scotia, 1820–1901

Year & Total Lawyers	Halifax Lawyers (% of prov. total)	Non-Halifax Lawyers (% of prov. total)	Communities outside Halifax with Resident Lawyers
1820 N = 38	25 (65.7%)	13 (34.3%)	10
1830 N = 73	31 (42.4%)	42 (57.6%)	16
1840 N = 117	42 (35.8%)	75 (64.2%)	19
1851 N = 150	55 (36.0%)	95 (64.0%)	21
1861 N = 158	64 (40.5%)	94 (60.5%)	23
1871 N = 198	86 (43.4%)	112 (56.6%)	26
1881 N = 235	98 (41.7%)	137 (58.3%)	26
1891 N = 283	104 (36.7%)	179 (63.3%)	28
1901 N = 361	133 (36.8%)	230 (63.2%)	32

Source: Belcher's Farmers' Almanack (1830–1901); Ward's Almanack (1820)

residents of Horton and Cornwallis townships petitioned the Council regarding the difficulty of suing for debts when attorneys could be had only at Halifax.[49] The arrival en bloc of a dozen or so Loyalist lawyers in 1783–4 eased this situation somewhat, and indeed may have led to an oversupply of lawyers, but only on a temporary and local basis. They tended to prefer the capital to the countryside, and a number of them did not actively pursue their profession. In most areas of the province, the dearth of lawyers did not abate. Decades later, even murder trials might go on outside Halifax with no lawyer appointed to represent the crown. In 1816 a woman was indicted for murder at Liverpool. She had counsel, but attorney Robert Bolman appeared for the crown only because he 'was induced by the repeated solicitation of Gentlemen residing at Liverpool to conduct the prosecution.' He later petitioned the Assembly for compensation and was granted £11. A murder trial at Guysborough had gone on in 1812 without a lawyer on either side. The clerk of the peace represented the accused, while the prosecution was conducted by none other than the deputy clerk of the peace, neither being a trained lawyer.[50]

In the absence of lawyers, legal services of a civil nature were provided by a variety of lay personnel, among whom justices of the peace and notaries public played major roles. The justices usually had no formal legal training, but they had a familiarity with the law sufficient to satisfy most of the population's legal needs, and an air of authority that allowed them to function as community arbiters. Some were respected, others held in awe. The Acadians of Pubnico, reported a visitor, feared their local justice of the peace, Benoni d'Entremont, 'as much as they feared the King of England.'[51] Eighteenth-century almanacs listed the justices by county immediately after the judges of the Supreme Court, and did not list lawyers at all.[52]

By 1820, this picture had not changed dramatically, with some thirty-eight lawyers in the province (including one in newly annexed Cape Breton). Twenty-five of these were located in Halifax, while the remaining thirteen were scattered in ten other communities across the province. Only Annapolis and Pictou could boast more than one lawyer. Virtually all the Halifax lawyers were connected to the official establishment or mercantile elite through birth or marriage, and either held office or would soon become officeholders of one kind or another. The situation was a little more fluid outside Halifax, where the occasional attorney existed on the margins of the local notability, but such examples were rare.[53]

This situation began to change quickly in the 1820s. Recruitment to the bar had been depressed during the long war with France, as it usually is during wartime. The entire decade 1811–20 had seen only nineteen men called to the bar, and four of these were no longer in the province by 1821. With the return of peace in 1815, the young men of the province began to turn their minds to suitable civilian careers, and the law ranked fairly high among them. A sense of the opportunities available outside Halifax may be glimpsed in the bargain that William Young struck with his principals, the Fairbanks brothers, in 1820. They were to pay him £30 salary in the first year of his apprenticeship (highly unusual at the time) and to charge him no fee for acting as principals. Young recorded in his diary that, if during the second year he proved himself 'competent and willing to practice in one of the country towns, they have engaged to allow me one half of the net profits arising out of the business there.'[54]

The long apprenticeship period meant that the post-1815 cohort would not appear at the bar until the 1820s. The years 1821–5 alone saw twenty-nine further calls to the bar, and the second half of the decade (1826–30) thirty-one more. The year 1822 saw nine admissions to the bar, unprecedented in provincial history except for the unique Loyalist influx of 1783–4. By 1830, the number of practising lawyers had doubled, rising to seventy-five, and by 1840 there were 117, for a rate of increase of 56 per cent over that decade. Between 1820 and 1839, a total of 153 men can be identified as practising law in Nova Scotia for at least a year, of whom 122 were new entrants during that period.

Who were these new entrants, and where did they all go? By and large, they remained the sons of prominent figures in the Halifax official or mercantile elite or its local counterparts, but perhaps a half-dozen (at most) of the fifty-seven 1820s entrants were not so favoured. They were not from labouring or even artisanal families but nonetheless came from a background considered less than sterling by the elite. The origins of Alexander Stewart (1822) and William Delaney (1823) are obscure, while Laurence O'Connor Doyle (1829) was the first Catholic at the bar in Nova Scotia. Beamish Murdoch himself possessed a somewhat chequered history, as we have seen.

Taking the whole population of 153 practising lawyers, one feature definitely stands out. This was overwhelmingly a native-born group, who became even more indigenous over the period as the original Loyalist lawyers and a few British and Irish immigrants died off. Even in 1820, only three practising lawyers were not native-born (8 per cent). The last Loyalist lawyer, Nicholas Purdue Olding of Pictou, would retire before the end of the decade. The two immigrants were Robert Hatton, an Irish attorney who arrived at Pictou in 1813 and practised there until his death about 1826, and James Buchanan, a Scottish-trained solicitor who died in that year. During the next twenty years (1820–40), only six new entrants (5 per cent) were not native-born. Five hailed from Scotland, and of these only one came (probably) with prior legal qualifications: James Turnbull, who practised at Arichat between 1831 and 1847. The others came as boys or young men, served a regular apprenticeship in Nova Scotia, and thus should be classified as indigenous lawyers. The non-Scot was James R. Smith, who was born in England and spent some time in the Caribbean before arriving in the province in 1833.[55] Nova Scotia was considerably less attractive to English emigrants than Upper Canada, which even in the second half of the nineteenth century counted 39 per cent of its lawyers as British-born.[56]

The cohort of the 1820s had little choice but to fan out across the province, since the capital would absorb only nine of them by 1830. Halifax was like mayonnaise, able to absorb olive oil only one drop at a time. Among Beamish Murdoch's 'class' of nine in 1822, only he remained in Halifax. The number of communities in which a lawyer could be found rose from eleven in 1820 to eighteen eight years later, as lawyers settled in Antigonish, Arichat, Horton (now Kentville), and Liverpool in 1823,

Guysborough in 1824, Newport in 1826, and Bridgetown and Chester in 1828. Some of these communities had had a resident lawyer intermittently before these dates, but after the 1820s there would always be at least one lawyer present. By 1830, only Cape Breton and the Eastern Shore could be regarded as still underserviced by lawyers in any absolute sense. William F. Desbarres held sway at Guysborough as the only lawyer between Halifax and the Strait of Canso on the mainland, admittedly a thinly populated area even by Nova Scotia standards, while Cape Breton could count only two lawyers in Sydney and one at Arichat.

Certainly, the doubling of the provincial population created a demand for more lawyers. Some communities that could not have supported a lawyer in earlier times now passed a critical threshold. Bridgetown had only eight houses in 1823, but Beamish Murdoch noted that by 1824 'quite a town had sprung up' since his last visit in 1822; by 1827, it could boast two lawyers, Stephen Bromley and James A. Dennison. Taking the period 1820–1840 as a whole, however, the population barely doubled while the number of lawyers in practice trebled. Analysing this trend in supply and demand terms, either the market for legal services was increasing significantly or lawyers' incomes were static or declining as more competitors entered the market.

It is probable that both trends were occurring, for different subgroups within the lawyer population. On the positive side, the return of prosperity after the slump of the early 1820s meant that the services of a lawyer were within the grasp of a larger proportion of the population. A large majority of Beamish Murdoch's clients in the 1820s were artisans, keepers of small shops, or smallholders, as will be seen in the next chapter. This is not to say that these groups previously lacked all legal services, since they may well have used the services of lay legal workers such as justices of the peace, arbitrators, or conveyancers. The more affluent sectors of the population may well have needed more frequent or more complex legal services as the provincial economy diversified, and all sectors of the population may have been more willing to seek legal services from qualified lawyers rather than laymen. The greater physical accessibility of lawyers would have stimulated demand for their services, creating markets where none existed before. On the negative side, more lawyers meant more competition, and inevitably not all would survive in the new environment.

It is true that many lawyers came from relatively affluent family backgrounds or married into money, and were not dependent solely on

Table 2
Lawyer mobility, 1820s–1840s

George R. Grassie	1825–8, Annapolis; 1828–9, Halifax; absent until 1832; 1832–3, Halifax; 1833–43, Truro
Stephen Bromley	1825–6, Windsor; 1826–8, Annapolis; 1828–34, Bridgetown
William Greaves	1825–6, Kentville; 1826–7, Truro; 1827–8, Halifax; 1828–34, Chester
Robert B. Dickson	1826–7, Truro; 1827–30, Pictou; absent 1831–2; 1833–5, Parrsboro; 1835–43, Truro
C.W.H. Harris	1828–30, Lunenburg; 1830–9, Halifax; 1839–43, Wolfville
James A. Dennison	1827–8, Annapolis; 1828–9, Bridgetown; 1829–30, Kentville; 1830–42, Annapolis; 1842–3, Digby

their professional earnings for their livelihood, but the evidence shows that no more than a few lawyers lived on family wealth as genteel dilettantes. The mobility patterns of the 1820s cohort suggest that many new entrants were trying to maximize income by moving to areas with better market opportunities.[57] Not only did newly minted lawyers move increasingly to communities outside Halifax, but they might move a number of times. This is especially noticeable with entrants in the later 1820s. Of thirty-six entrants in the years 1825–9, fifteen had practised in two or more centres within ten years of their call to the bar, and three more moved out of the province after practising for some period in Nova Scotia. This gives a 'mobility rate' of exactly 50 per cent, which can be compared with a rate of 28.5 per cent for the years 1820–4.[58] Table 2 gives an impression of the movements of the most mobile of the group from the later 1820s.

Some of this movement may have resulted from personal or family preferences, but, seen on such a scale, the pursuit of better economic opportunities must have been the more important motive. Another indication of such motives is the frequency with which the death of a lawyer, his departure from a particular community, or his promotion to the bench was followed by the appearance of a new lawyer there in the next year. When Yarmouth's sole lawyer, John Forman, died in 1832, newly called lawyer William Keating (1829) immediately replaced him. Parrsboro had a succession of lawyers in the 1830s and 1840s, each of whom practised there for a few years, but never more than one at a time. A whole chain of moves might be set off by a promotion. When

W.H.O. Haliburton of Windsor was appointed as first justice of the Inferior Court of Common Pleas in 1824, Lewis M. Wilkins soon moved from Kentville to replace him, while the vacant situation in Kentville was attractive to new recruit William Greaves (1825).

The correspondence of Harry King (1829) of Windsor with his fiancée, Margaret Halliburton Fraser ('Halli'), provides a unique window on the building up of the county bars during the years 1829–31.[59] King was the son of the Reverend William Colsel King, rector of Windsor from 1813 to 1843, who was probably the most well-off inhabitant of the village after the Haliburtons. Harry graduated from King's College in 1822, articled in Halifax, was called to the bar in 1829, and returned to Windsor to practise law. In addition to King's family ties there, Windsor was attractive because senior lawyer William P.G. Fraser had just died in 1828. King nonetheless began his career in the summer of 1829 with some trepidation. Lewis Wilkins, Jr was already established in Windsor, as was a young lawyer named George Emerson (1828). King was affected by the 'pitiable description of himself and his little family' that Emerson poured out to him. His confidant raised troubling feelings in King: 'Altho' opposed to him professionally still can I, could any man hear a man of Equal standing & older than himself declare his own misery without feeling deeply? True he has by imprudent and wasteful Expenditure reduced himself to his present state & Equally true it is that my competition has partly contributed to this Consequence – but my competition has been fair & open. I have no reproach from it. Yet it does not diminish my feeling of regret.'[60] Within a few months of King's arrival, 'poor Emerson' followed his brother Hugh (1824) to Newfoundland, discouraged by his poor pecuniary prospects in Windsor after nearly two years there.[61]

In addition to Emerson's tale of ill omen, King was troubled by another event on the horizon. Windsor's venerable W.H.O Haliburton was seriously ill, raising the prospect of Thomas Chandler Haliburton's return from Annapolis to his ancestral seat upon the death of his father. As King reflected later, 'Supposing ... that he [T.C.H.] had come here to practice, of course both Lewis & myself must have been more or less injured, and he would have transacted all his own Law business.'[62] Fortunately for King, matters worked out much better than he had feared. Thomas Chandler Haliburton did return to Windsor after the death of his father in July 1829 but soon succeeded to his position as first justice of the Inferior Court of Common Pleas (Middle Division). As this position statutorily precluded him from practising law, Haliburton then directed all his legal business to King, his second cousin, in preference to Wilkins.[63] The benefits of patronage were obvious to King, and perhaps account for some of his guilt in witnessing Emerson's plight. Haliburton's action, wrote King, was 'likely to be a very great advantage to me bringing me into the Knowledge of an Extensive circle of people who unless thus necessarily brought into collision with me might not have known [of me] for Years to come.'[64] Also for reasons of exposure, it was 'worth the Experiment' to accompany Haliburton to Horton where he was to try a criminal matter on a special commission, on the chance that he (King) might be appointed as defence counsel. 'Tis not the fees,' he explained to Halli, 'but the more we are before the public the More We become Known, and the more we are Known, the more likely we are to succeed in our profession.'[65]

Mere publicity was not sufficient – one also had to be available, which could impose a considerable burden on a sole practitioner such as King, with his 'office Crowded from Morning till night & no one here to whom I could Entrust my business.'[66] Like most young lawyers, King had no clerk or office assistance of any kind. In March he lamented that he did not know when he could steal a few days to visit Halli in the capital. 'I am obliged to Keep my office all & Every day. People are Constantly Calling & if I am not at home they will push down to Lewis Wilkins & that is a dead loss.'[67] The demands of local clients and the circuits meant that King managed only two flying visits to Halifax between Christmas 1830 and the fall of 1831. In April he was with the Inferior Court of Common Pleas in Lunenburg, returned with it to Windsor in May, and spent June in Horton for the sitting of the Supreme Court. Even so well-connected a lawyer as Harry King was constantly seeking exposure and new business, and working to maintain his competitive position.

King, Emerson, and Wilkins were part of the shift to the countryside characteristic of the new entrants of the 1820s. The cohort of the 1830s saw a continuation of that trend. The Halifax legal community continued to grow modestly, at the rate of about one lawyer per year (net) to a total of forty-two lawyers in 1840, but the principal growth occurred in the rest of the province. There were by then seventy-five lawyers outside Halifax, for a total of 117 in the province, compared to thirty-four non-Halifax lawyers only a decade earlier. By 1830, there were few communities of any size without a lawyer, so that the number of communities being served for the first time in the 1830s was necessarily small. Parrsboro and Port Hood (Cape Breton) each welcomed a resident lawyer for the first time in 1833, and Wolfville joined them in 1839. No community lost its sole lawyer during the period,[68] while some hosted substantial numbers of the fraternity by 1840: Amherst featured eleven, Pictou eight, and Annapolis six, while Truro, Kentville, Windsor, Antigonish, Lunenburg, and Sydney had five each.

The mobility characteristic of the entrants of the later 1820s declined with the 1830s cohort. Of sixty-five entrants in the decade 1830–9, only 27.6 per cent had practised in more than one community in the ten years after their call to the bar, compared to 50 per cent in the 1825–9 group. In other words, the 1830s cohort returned to the pattern of the early 1820s. This was perhaps to be expected, now that the bar was growing no faster than the rate of increase in the general population.[69] The relative professional longevity and stability of a large majority of the entrants over the two decades 1820–40 suggest two things: first, that the legal profession was not overstaffed, in spite of a lawyer-population ratio considerably higher than that in Upper Canada; and second, that the services of lawyers were becoming indispensable in a way they had not been before 1820.

Mobility patterns after 1840 remained similar to those of the 1830s. Lawyers continued to move around and to service new communities as they reached a 'critical mass' of population capable of supporting a lawyer. The number of communities served outside Halifax gradually doubled over the course of the nineteenth century, from sixteen in 1830 to thirty-two in 1901 (Table 1). Few lawyers moved into or out of the province until the latter part of the century, when there was a sudden exodus of mostly young lawyers seeking better opportunities, both in the United States and elsewhere in Canada. *Belcher's* helpfully kept track of the destinations of lawyers who had been called to the bar locally and then emigrated, listing only four such men in 1880 but twenty-eight in 1890 and fifty-six in 1900. Only a handful of these were men like Zebulon Lash, the Toronto litigator who had been called to the bar in Nova Scotia presumably in order to argue an important case there and then returned home to Ontario. The vast majority of the non-residents were Nova Scotians who had been called to the bar in the province and then departed. The bar was growing much faster by the end of the century (27 per cent over the 1890s) than the province's population (a feeble 2 per cent over the same decade), leading to significant out-migration by lawyers. But until the 1880s recruitment to the legal profession had remained roughly proportional to increases in popula-

Table 3
Lawyer-population ratio, 1820–1901

Year	Province	Halifax
1820	1:2631	1:480
1830	1:1989	1:467
1840	1:1829	1:357
1851	1:1845	1:348
1861	1:2094	1:391
1871	1:1958	1:369
1881	1:1874	1:406
1891	1:1591	1:429
1901	1:1273	1:343

tion, such that the lawyer-population ratio had remained reasonably stable, both in Halifax and outside it (Table 3).

By the time of Confederation, then, the legal professions in the four founding colonies all possessed a similar structure and the authority of the bar (and in the case of Quebec, the notariat as well) rested on legislation or rules of court or a combination of both. The Law Society of Upper Canada had been first off the mark with its statutory creation in 1797; it was no mere voluntary association, and all lawyers had to become members if they wished to practise law. The incorporating act of the Barristers' Society of New Brunswick, passed as we have seen in 1846, substituted the society for the Supreme Court as 'the primary gatekeeper for the profession' even though membership in the society remained voluntary.[70] In 1847 an act of the Parliament of Canada created three chambers of notaries in Montreal, Quebec, and Trois-Rivières, corporate entities with extensive powers over admission and discipline funded by an obligatory levy on each notary.[71] In 1849 it was the turn of the bar of Lower Canada to be incorporated with similar powers, with three 'sections' in the same three cities, each with its own bâtonnier and elected council.[72] In 1857 the Law Society of Upper Canada resumed its jurisdiction over attorneys, and in 1860 the Nova Scotia Barristers' Society reinvented itself and enhanced its role in controlling access to the profession.

The extent to which it had become simply 'common sense' in British North America that the bar should govern itself and control entrance to and exit from apprenticeship can be seen when the question arose in the new province of Manitoba. Anyone could choose to call himself a lawyer and appear before the courts of the predecessor colony of Assiniboia, but there seems to have been no thought of preserving this state of affairs. One of the early acts of the new province was the 1871 Act to Regulate Admission to the Study and Practice of Law in Manitoba. It specified that 'as soon as ten persons had been admitted to the Bar they could "constitute themselves a Bar Society" and, subject to cabinet approval, make rules to regulate future admissions to the study and practice of law.'[73] By December of that year, fifteen lawyers had been admitted to practice and on 30 December they promptly took up the statutory invitation and formed a Bar Society, incorporated in 1877 as the Law Society of Manitoba.[74] The lieutenant governor since August 1870 had been none other than Adams G. Archibald, who effectively acted as premier until 1872. In the winter of 1871, he put forward thirty-one pieces of legislation based on his Nova Scotia experience, including an act regulating admission to the study and practice of law; he successfully fought off the proposal of his attorney general to have that officer approve all admissions to the provincial bar, thus preserving for the bar itself control over recruitment.[75]

British Columbia's mainland and Vancouver Island were separate colonies until united in 1866. All the mainland colony's early lawyers were imports, and an 1858 order of the Supreme Court permitted barristers to practise as attorneys and vice versa, while an 1863 order permitted lawyers from other Canadian colonies to be called to the bar. Vancouver Island at first adopted the same policy but in 1860 the Executive Council decided that the presence of five barristers and three solicitors was sufficient to order the division of the professions, and did so – to the consternation of local public opinion. The divided profession was short-lived: after union, the mainland practice was imposed on the Island.[76] Thirteen lawyers (both barristers and attorneys) gathered at Victoria on 12 July 1869 and

constitute[d] themselves into a society to be called 'The Law Society of British Columbia' ... having for its objects
1. The formation of a Law Library
2. The publication of Legal decisions
3. The regulation of the call to the Bar and admission on the Rolls of attorneys of persons desirous of practising in the Supreme Courts of the Colony
4. The furtherance and protection of the interests of the legal professions.

In 1874 the Legal Profession Act provided for the incorporation of the Law Society and gave its benchers 'authority to educate, call and admit students and full disciplinary powers over the profession.'[77]

British North American lawyers had the state on their side, but that was not a sufficient or even a necessary condition for their success. Unlike certain European jurisdictions, where the state decreed the number of lawyers who could practise in a given area, the supply of lawyers in British North America was not subject to direct state control. Lawyers flourished by seeking out new markets for their services, locating their practices in previously underserviced areas, finding more clients in their existing locales, or providing more valuable services to their existing client pool. The analysis of Murdoch's practice in subsequent chapters will show him engaged in the latter two strategies, while this chapter focuses on the first: geographic dispersal. Until the end of the century, when the supply of lawyers increased sharply across British North America, supply and demand existed in a rough balance. But the difficulties of transportation before the creation of a railway network meant that lawyers had to be willing to settle where a clientele existed, and this they did with some alacrity. Those who could not make a living in one location moved on, either – unusually – out of the province altogether, like Harry King's competitor George Emerson, or to another settlement where prospects looked brighter.

We may note in concluding this chapter that, in spite of a certain temporary waning of lawyerly esprit de corps in the mid-century Maritimes, the essential hallmark of the story of the development of the legal profession in British North America is continuity: continuity in the efforts of lawyers to regulate their own affairs, to control entrance to the profession, and to enhance the corporate status of the bar, to take three of Burrage's indicia of lawyers' collective action.[78] The British North American bars were able to accomplish these goals because their relationship with their respective provincial legislatures was, in general, cooperative rather than conflictual. The legislative assault on lawyers' corporate privileges, the dissolution of bar associations, and the effective abolition of apprenticeship that occurred in the antebellum United States have, with the exception of some fairly easily repulsed attacks at mid-century, no counterpart in the British North American story. In their efforts to maintain their corporate autonomy and honour, the bars of the Canadian provinces had more in common with the English legal professions although, crucially, they rejected the English model of a divided profession. Meanwhile, in their spatial diffusion, the nature of their day-to-day work, and their responsiveness to market signals, the Canadian bars had much more in common with their American cousins.

5

The Making of a Colonial Lawyer, 1822–7

Whether in pre-Confederation British North America or the antebellum United States, lawyers have seldom been studied *as* lawyers. Their prominence as political leaders, judges, officeholders, or businessmen has interested historians more than the day-to-day business of their legal careers. In 1991 Richard Scott Eckert observed in the context of colonial America that there had been no 'detailed treatment of the legal career of a representative member of the legal profession in either colonial Massachusetts or one of the other colonies,' and his observation remains largely true even for the antebellum United States.[1] Historians of colonial America have been most interested in lawyer officeholders and in lawyers who were active in the Revolutionary movement,[2] while historians of the nineteenth-century United States have been obsessed with the question of how lawyers became the 'American aristocracy.'[3] In British North America, historians have been concerned to examine the role of lawyers as architects of the new Loyalist societies which were being established in Upper Canada and New Brunswick, although two works on the Ontario bar have sought to combine a consideration of lawyers' day-to-day work with larger questions of professional organization and political involvement.[4] In Quebec, meanwhile, Jean-Philippe Garneau has begun to look at the daily work of lawyers in order to understand how a 'culture de l'amalgame' evolved through the interaction of English and French lawyers in a polyjural legal environment.[5]

Certainly their political role was important, but lawyers were often leaders of colonial society even when they did not wield direct political power. While better-than-average education fitted them for a leadership role, their prominence was also a function of the ubiquity of the law in colonial society. Citizens high and low regularly came into contact with the law, mainly in the form of civil rather than criminal justice. They depended on it in a much more direct way – principally, but certainly not exclusively, to enforce debt obligations – than citizens do in the twentieth century. The administration of criminal law was important as spectacle and morality tale, but it unfolded almost entirely with lay rather than professional participation except for the most serious offences. It was for ordinary matters of civil law – debt, conveyancing, succession, marital matters, business transactions – that people sought out lawyers, and it was their constant reliance on lawyers that allowed the latter to assume their unique role in colonial society.

This chapter and the next will look at Beamish Murdoch's law practice during its first three decades.[6] By analysing the nature of his clientele in terms of social position, gender, ethnicity, and volume, and examining the variety of services performed for these clients and Murdoch's professional income, it will be possible to understand better the roles that lawyers played in the lives of their clients and in the broader community. This micro-historical approach is also connected to the larger questions of legal culture and professionalism addressed in this book, particularly through the concept of independence. We will see in chapter 7 the role of independence in Murdoch's political career, but in this and the next chapter we will see it in a distinct but related context: the independence of the bar. Just as independence in the political context meant an absence of dependence on the wealth or power of others, so in the professional context it meant that the advocate was not to be swayed by the fact that the defence or promotion of a client's interests might antagonize the powerful or even public opinion itself. The English bar was able to proclaim its independence from the state, public opinion, and the wealthy because of the convention that no barrister could refuse a brief, no matter how unpopular, and because the division of labour with solicitors meant that barristers were insulated from direct involvement in business matters. In North America the situation was more problematic, as the fused profession continued to proclaim its independence even as it was drawn ever more deeply into the business world through its counselling and solicitorial functions. Until the growth of railways and business corporations in the second half of the nineteenth century, however, these tensions did not become acute.[7]

A study of this kind is possible because a good collection of Murdoch's letter books, account books, and day books has survived. His 'non-Halifax' letter book for the years 1823–9 contains copies of (most of?) the letters he wrote on behalf of clients, whether from Halifax or not, to parties who lived outside Halifax County, and a number of letters written to clients in the United States and the United Kingdom.[8] Several account books have also survived, covering the periods 1827– 30, 1825–51, 1831–7, and 1846–56, along with a day book for January 1834 to August 1836 (which appears to contain a complete listing of his clients over this period), a ledger book covering the period 1845–57, and a small booklet entitled 'Halifax Conveyancing' which covers the years 1850–5.[9] When supplemented by newspaper accounts and cross-checked against surviving court records, Murdoch's business papers permit the reconstruction of an early-nineteenth-century law practice in often surprising detail.

Entering Practice

As noted earlier, Murdoch's five years of apprenticeship to the Uni-ackes ended on 23 November 1819. He had to wait eighteen months until he was old enough to be admitted an attorney of the Supreme Court of Nova Scotia. The following year, Murdoch spent the requisite three terms in attendance at the Supreme Court before his call to the bar, and probably spent much of his time reading at the Barristers' Library. He also acquired new domestic responsibilities in addition to supervising the education of his motherless twelve-year-old cousin Thomas Beamish Akins. In early 1821 Murdoch invited another cousin, Charles Ott Beamish, also aged twelve, to live with him in Halifax after the death of the latter's father, Murdoch's uncle Frederick Ott Beamish of Blandford. Murdoch's assumption of parental authority over Charles created a close bond between the two that would endure for the rest of their lives.

The happy day finally arrived on 14 July 1822, when Murdoch was called to the bar of the Supreme Court and signed the barristers' roll.[10] Mere admission did not guarantee a clientele, and the early years no doubt saw few clients. William Johnstone Ritchie related in later life that it took six months after he opened his office in Saint John, New Brunswick, in 1837 before he welcomed his first client, and that his second year of practice netted him only £5.[11] Unlike the agonizing wait for briefs of the novice English barrister, however, North American lawyers could bring in some income via solicitorial work even if they were not immediately hired to plead cases in court. Fortunately too, Murdoch's professional launch occurred about the same time that a long-running legal dispute over a Beamish family inheritance was resolved in his favour.[12] As part-owner of a valuable Halifax wharf and other real estate, Murdoch had acquired some status as a gentleman of property as well as a private income to support himself during the lean years of early practice. The significance of this legal victory was far more than financial for Murdoch. When the Nova Scotia Court of Chancery decided the case in favour of the Beamishes in 1814 (confirmed by the Privy Council in 1820), even though their adversaries were among the most powerful figures in the province, the result provided for the budding lawyer a potent illustration of the independence of the Nova Scotia judiciary and a confirmation of the essential justice of English law.

Murdoch was well aware of the effort required to create a niche for himself, as he later warned prospective law students in his *Epitome of the Laws of Nova-Scotia* in terms that would warm the heart of any Victorian: 'In the race of competition the lover of his own ease must be left far behind – among the number who press eagerly forward, he who loiters on the way and wastes the precious moments he should devote to self improvement, cannot expect to bear away a prize.'[13] Increasing numbers were indeed pressing 'eagerly forward' just as Murdoch began his career. Halifax was supplied with twenty-five lawyers for a population of some 12,000 in 1821. A further three were called to the bar in that year, and Murdoch was part of a 'class' of an unprecedented nine young men in 1822; a further six were called to the bar in 1823. The capital thus offered a competitive market with no parallel elsewhere in the province. Seven county towns counted no more than one lawyer each, though Pictou boasted three and Annapolis two.[14] Given that 1822 represented the nadir of the post-war slump in Halifax's fortunes, the town simply could not absorb eighteen newly minted barristers. Only five of this group remained in Halifax, while the rest spread out across the province.[15]

Most Halifax lawyers were already well connected to the political, legal, ecclesiastical, military, or mercantile elites. Murdoch began his career without such advantages. His apprenticeship with Uniacke provided him with some cachet, but it could not guarantee access to the kind of connections that Uniacke deployed so assiduously for the ben-

efit of his own sons. Some assistance from family or patron was crucial
in the early years after admission to the bar precisely because of the
time it took to build up a clientele.[16] A government post with some
income, even if modest, could greatly assist a man during those lean
years. Murdoch's friend James Scott Tremain, called to the bar in 1823,
was the son of powerful merchant Richard Tremain. In 1825 this fledg-
ling lawyer had already been appointed deputy registrar to the Court
of Vice-Admiralty, an office that carried handsome fees. His brother
John Lewis Tremain married the daughter of the former chief justice of
Cape Breton in 1822 and was promptly named judge of probate, registrar of deeds, and prothonotary (registrar) of the Supreme Court for the
Inverness County – and he was not even a lawyer. The fact that similar
rewards eluded unconnected men such as Beamish Murdoch allowed
him to insist on his independence even more since he could not be seen
to be in the pocket of government.

Lawyers and Debt Collection

Fortunately, Murdoch began his practice when the demand for legal
services from the non-elite section of the population was reasonably
strong. Artisans, proprietors of small businesses, shopkeepers, small
landowners, mariners – that large group of urban society between the
wage labourers and the small professional, mercantile, and officeholding elite – depended on the law for a whole host of services, but particularly on the law of creditor and debtor.[17] With debt collection such an
important part of all lawyers' work in this period, some brief account of
legal representation in debt matters in the various courts is necessary.

   Lawyers were not necessary for the recovery of small sums because
claims for debts of less than £5 could be brought before two justices of
the peace, and lawyers were not usually involved at this level.[18] Debts
between £5 and £10 could be sued for in either the Inferior Court of
Common Pleas or the Supreme Court, the latter court being authorized
to try such cases in summary fashion (i.e., without a jury) in an effort
to reduce costs. Legal representation for plaintiffs was almost invari-
able in the Supreme Court, but for defendants much less so; one study,
which covers the years 1830 and 1831, shows only 4 per cent of plaintiffs unrepresented, while 40 per cent of defendants had no lawyer; another for 1827 shows 65 per cent of defendants with no lawyer.[19] In the
Inferior Court of Common Pleas, plaintiffs were invariably represented
by lawyers from at least the 1770s, while defendants seldom appeared

with counsel until about 1820, when lawyers began to represent them more frequently.[20] Once the Commissioners' Court was created at Halifax in 1817, it rapidly became the forum of choice for the recovery of medium-sized debts (those between £5 and £10), favoured because of its summary procedure and low costs.[21] Its records have not survived, but the pattern of legal representation there is likely to have been broadly similar to that in the Inferior Court of Common Pleas, although the proportion of plaintiffs with lawyers was probably lower.

Murdoch's account books show a sprinkling of entries for appearances in both these inferior courts in the 1820s and 1830s, with no more than a half-dozen for the Commissioners' Court. The bulk of Murdoch's debt collection took place in the Supreme Court. Already in 1823, Murdoch filed eleven claims in the Supreme Court, for sums ranging from just over £10 to £174.[22] In several of these, his clients were merchants or suppliers, but he also represented Daniel Grant, Jr, tailor, in his claim against George Creelman, yeoman, for £12. In 1824 Murdoch filed thirty-three claims in the Supreme Court, almost all for debt, then twenty-three in 1825 and thirty-two in 1826, falling to fourteen in 1827. A Supreme Court practice, comprising mainly debt collection, was an essential part of Murdoch's practice in the early years. Some of his contemporaries featured even more prominently in debt litigation: William Young and James Stewart Clarke, both called to the bar in 1826, filed fifty-four and fifty-seven claims in the Supreme Court in 1827. Young's extensive mercantile connections would have aided him, while Clarke's father, David Shaw Clarke, was clerk of the peace, Halifax's senior judicial administrator.

A unique overview of the development of a young lawyer's practice in the 1820s can be found in Murdoch's first letter book, covering the period 1823–9,[23] supplemented by his account books and court records for the same period. The letter book contains eighty-four documents, of which eighty are letters, three are petitions, and one is a draft partnership indenture. Of the letters, fully seventy-six relate to debt collection or the drafting of mortgages, although a few also contain advice on property management. The most common addressee of these letters (thirty-four) is the sheriff of a particular county, who had the responsibility for serving summonses, seizing property under writs of execution and attachment, and imprisoning debtors under writs of capias. Since this letter book contains only correspondence relating either to clients resident outside Halifax or to Halifax clients with claims outside Halifax County, it probably overstates the proportion of Murdoch's practice devoted to debt matters, but not dramatically. There is very little in it regarding conveyancing or the settlement of deceased's estates, for example, services that Murdoch performed for his Halifax clientele, albeit infrequently, in the 1820s.

Long-distance debt collection was often tedious and required considerable persistence. On 12 May 1824 Murdoch wrote to the sheriff of Cumberland County, enclosing a writ against a carpenter 'named Turpel,' with the unhelpful observation that he was 'settled somewhere in Cumberland.' Unsurprisingly, the sheriff could not find Mr Turpel, and three months later Murdoch wrote to the sheriff of Kings County with the slightly more helpful advice that Turpel was now believed to be living somewhere near Parrsboro.[24] He eluded detection for another year, until finally run to earth in Halifax: on 15 September 1825 Murdoch obtained a writ of capias against William Turpel on behalf of his client, William Wells, for a debt of £10.[25] The slowness of travel and communication, and difficulties involved in securing accurate information about personal names and residences, meant that the expenses involved in debt collection could easily mount.[26]

Once the debtor had been impleaded in the right court, the law afforded a whole arsenal of weapons to the creditor. In particular, imprisonment for debt, or the threat of it, was a routine feature of the debt-collection process. Murdoch's familial history made him an uneasy participant in this process, as he revealed in his *Essay on the Mischievous Tendency of Imprisoning for Debt and in Other Civil Cases*.[27] His letters show that he sought imprisonment only as a last resort, and usually with an expression of regret. Murdoch felt sorry that a debtor at Annapolis should be detained for a small sum, 'but as he has not made any offer of arrangement it is the only course I have to pursue.'[28] The sheriff played a key role in negotiating with debtors in this regard, especially out-of-town debtors whom neither Murdoch nor his client could meet face-to-face. When Murdoch obtained a writ of capias for his clients, Halifax merchants John Starr and Son, against one James Johnson, he asked the sheriff of Sydney County to enforce it immediately and then gave further instructions. The object of the plaintiffs, he said, 'is to obtain security for their debt, not to distress the defendant, but as they think themselves unfairly dealt with by him they wish his arrest, to bring him to terms.' Starr was prepared to give Johnson up to a year to pay provided he would sign a promissory note for the debt. Murdoch simply asked Sheriff McDonald to use his discretion in this regard.[29]

Imprisonment for debt was not used just by wealthy merchants. In fact, they could afford to forgo it if they thought there was any prospect of repayment. Poorer creditors could not always be so generous. In 1828 Murdoch wrote to lawyer Henry Blackadar at Pictou for some assistance in enforcing three writs of execution, for three different creditors, against one Lowden. Two of them, Murdoch's uncle Thomas Ott Beamish and tailor William Hesson, did not insist on Lowden's imprisonment and were resigned to him taking the benefit of the Insolvent Debtors' Act.[30] Under this act, a debtor whose total debts amounted to less than £100 could escape imprisonment by assigning all his assets (saving some personal items) to his creditors and swearing that he had not concealed any other assets. However, the third creditor, Thomas Marvin, whose claim was for a small sum of wages, would 'not agree to his being discharged and in the event of his taking the oath wishes him to be supplied with bread according to the act of the Province.'[31] Until an 1832 amendment to the act abolished the privilege, a creditor possessed a veto over the release of any otherwise eligible debtor, provided he supplied 'the full quantity of eight pounds of good and wholesome biscuit bread per week unto the said prisoner.' If the debt were small, however, presumably the creditor would not wish it to be literally eaten up by feeding the prisoner over an extended period. Creditors bargained that the debtor's friends or family would come to his aid by paying the debt and securing his release.

As has been noted, the sheriff was a key figure in the debt-collection apparatus. What recourse existed if one suspected that the sheriff himself was acting improperly? Murdoch was faced with this problem early in his career. In trying to realize a claim by the powerful Ratchford brothers of Parrsboro against a debtor in Annapolis County, Murdoch came to believe that Sheriff William Winniett was keeping the debtor's seized goods for his own use. He tried to sue Winniett on his sheriff's bond in 1824, but various technical defences were raised. In 1826 Murdoch finally wrote to the newly appointed master of the rolls, Simon Bradstreet Robie, to obtain authorization to carry on the suit in the name of the crown. Previous complaints about Winniett had resulted in petitions to the governor and the chief justice, but local lawyers had thrown up their hands when his commission was always renewed. Whether the Ratchfords obtained monetary satisfaction is unclear, but Winniett died about this time and Murdoch tried to continue the action against his estate.[32] His perseverance in pursuing an allegedly corrupt official shows him exercising the independence that was supposed to be the hallmark of the bar. In time the unaccountability of officials such as the sheriff helped to fuel the movement for responsible government.

Debtors employed legal counsel much less frequently than creditors, either out of poverty or because in many cases they knew that no valid legal defence existed. Murdoch did occasionally represent a debtor, in which case he would deploy his best persuasive efforts to secure a delay in the collection of the creditor's due. He put the claims of the Reverend Archibald McQueen, who had just confessed a judgment for £12, to the creditor's lawyer Alexander Stewart in the following terms:

If you could delay adding expence or trouble to it for some time he is striving very hard to maintain a wife and large family. The Rev. Mr. Uniacke has just appointed him teacher of the school in Dutch town to which £50 was given last session but of course he cannot receive his salary till he has earned it by the quarter of year's services. I know him to be a worthy man though unfortunate and if without deviating from what you should do for your client you could extend some indulgence to him in the collection of the demand I should take it as a personal favor. He is willing to give up 300 acres of land in Cumberland if he could liquidate the demand in that way.[33]

Stewart was known to be a hard bargainer; whether he acceded to Murdoch's request may be doubted.

Murdoch's account books and the Supreme Court records supplement the picture derived from the letter book. While debt collection retained its predominant role in his law practice throughout the 1820s, it is impossible to quantify that role any more precisely. The most common entry in the account books is for a 'letter' written for a named client to a named party. The contents of the letters are not specified, and although most of them no doubt contained demands for the payment of debts, letters would sometimes have been written for other purposes. The account books provide some 120 entries for the years 1823 through 1826 inclusive, but there are over 120 entries for the year 1827 alone, covering a range of services for some seventy-five clients. Aside from debt collection and drafting letters, these services fall into five broad categories: drafting documents for private parties; drafting petitions to the governor or the Assembly on behalf of individuals; providing advice; arranging property matters, including inter vivos conveyancing and the transmission of assets on death; and attending at court on matters other than routine debt enforcement. Each of these will be examined in turn.

Advising Small Business and Families

The documents that parties were most likely to ask the young Murdoch to draft between 1823 and 1827 related to partnerships, powers of attorney, and arbitration bonds, with the last appearing most frequently. Very few other documents such as ordinary contracts or leases are apparent. In 1823 Murdoch drafted a partnership indenture between two Halifax tailors, Daniel Grant, Jr and John Fraser, containing detailed provisions about the respective contributions of each party, the location of the business, and so on.[34] In 1827 he drafted a deed of dissolution of partnership between Alexander Gordon and Hector McLennan but was compelled to threaten a suit in Chancery when the latter refused either to settle the accounts with his erstwhile partner or to refer the matter to arbitration.[35] Numerous entries for 'arbitration bonds' provide no further details. Such bonds commonly specified that the parties should each name an 'indifferent person' resident in Halifax, with these two naming a third who would act as umpire in case they could not agree.[36] The parties obliged themselves to observe the terms of the award and not to commence suits at law or equity on pain of forfeiting a stated sum of money. In this way the parties tried to preserve some control over the dispute-resolution process, which they had ample incentive to do since the Court of Chancery, with its higher fee structure, was the normal forum for litigating partnership disputes.[37]

Murdoch's entries regarding 'advice' do not always indicate the subject of the client's problem. He seems to have reserved the label for those cases where some reflection was required beyond a simple letter, such as one demanding the payment of a debt. For example, he charged Mrs Mary McPherson 11s 8d for a 'letter to Mr. Clarke & advice re overholding tenant' on 11 November 1826.[38] Murdoch's normal fee for a letter was 6s 8d, suggesting that he had done more than just send a notice to quit to the tenant. He also provided advice regarding a promissory note and another troublesome tenant in 1827, but one can only speculate what the 'advice re Brig Feronia' involved, which he supplied to merchant James Forman, Jr. Fees of 5s for advice on relatively simple matters and 10s for more complex opinions may appear high in comparison to the wages of skilled craftsmen (4s/day until at least mid-century), but they seem to have been remarkably stable over time. Such sums were identical to those charged by Boston lawyer Richard Dana during the early years of his practice nearly a century earlier, in the 1730s and 1740s.[39] They were also identical to those charged by Murdoch's contemporary William Young.[40]

These early years saw Murdoch involved in some conveyancing and estate work, but in modest quantities. Occasional entries for 'searches at Registry' indicate title searches for either prospective purchasers or mortgagees, but between 1822 and 1827 he appears to have drafted only one mortgage, one assignment of mortgage, and one memorandum of lease. Murdoch petitioned the governor-in-council for letters of administration in four cases of intestacy but did not draft his first will until 1829.

The courts in which Murdoch did not appear are as significant as those in which he did. With the exception of his first Chancery case in 1827, the more lucrative pay scales of the Court of Chancery, the Court of Marriage and Divorce, and particularly the Vice-Admiralty Court would elude him until the 1830s. Murdoch nonetheless appeared in several significant Supreme Court cases during this period. The earliest was *Robertson v. Phillips*, which he argued in the fall of 1824. Mrs Robertson was a widow who had cohabited with Halifax grocer Samuel Phillips for some years and borne him three children. When they parted he agreed to pay a weekly sum for maintenance of the children. Upon his default, Murdoch succeeded in obtaining a substantial jury award on her behalf.[41] The press coverage that this case received no doubt assisted Murdoch greatly in the early days of his career, and it will be examined more closely in that light below. A case of less general interest but more legal significance was *Knodel et al. v. Little*, which Murdoch argued and won in 1826. This was an action in partition where all but one of several tenants in common agreed that the land in question should be divided. There were no provincial precedents relevant to a contested partition action, and the application of English precedents was unclear. Murdoch argued that the defendant's technical objection was invalid, and successfully moved for confirmation of the writ of partition.[42]

In the mid-1820s Murdoch was admitted as a solicitor and counsel (the equivalents of attorney and barrister) to the Court of Chancery, which was put on a more professional footing with the appointment of prominent lawyer Simon Bradstreet Robie as master of the rolls in 1826.[43] Murdoch's first case was a simple uncontested foreclosure action. He represented carpenter James Dechman, Jr, who had loaned £130 at 6 per cent interest to Robert Knox, a ministerial assistant at St Matthew's Church. The amount was secured by a mortgage dated 17 May 1823 on which the full principal was due in two years. In June 1825 Knox died intestate, leaving as his only heir his mother, the impugnant (defendant) Jane Knox. She maintained the interest payments but could not pay the principal and agreed to a foreclosure in November 1827; the final order for sale of the property issued in January 1829.[44]

Defining a Clientele

The ethnic, gender, and class identity of Murdoch's clientele during these early years is of some interest, as a way of judging the extent of access to legal services and ultimately to justice. Names are the only indication of ethnic identity, making it the hardest variable to quantify. All that can usefully be said is that only 11 of approximately 153 clients (1823–7 both inclusive), or about 13 per cent, have names that can be identified with some confidence as Irish, when the Irish made up close to one-quarter of the city's population. Murdoch certainly publicized his Irish ties, joining the Charitable Irish Society in 1823 and serving as its vice-president in 1824. On St Patrick's Day, 1825, he and five other men patronized the Irish community to the tune of some £50 which they spent on a lavish meal for a large number of guests.[45] If the proportion of his Irish clients is significantly lower than that of the town's population, the simple explanation is that the immigrant Catholic Irish occupied the second lowest rung in Halifax society, just above the Afro-Nova Scotians. Their marginal economic power was reflected in reduced access to lawyers' services. The Irish retained some access to courts; however, as the 'humorous' newspaper coverage of their presence in the Commissioners' Court demonstrates, the quality of the justice they received is less certain.[46]

No other ethnic or racial groups appear prominently in Murdoch's records for this period. It is unknown whether he had any Afro-Nova Scotian clients, but his friend William Young had several in the 1830s.[47] One Acadian appears: Christian Tybo was a Halifax landlord who consulted Murdoch about a claim against Cape Breton Justice of the Peace William Watts.[48] At least 12 per cent of Murdoch's clientele were women,[49] virtually all of them widows. Widows needed the same assistance collecting debts and dealing with tenants and other property matters as men did, and they were not afraid to pursue their remedies at law even though they seldom resorted to imprisonment for debt. It is not possible to tell if Murdoch's female clients carried on businesses, as some women did in Halifax at this time. A number of them consulted him with regard to property matters, suggesting the traditional roles of landlady or provider of lodging. Their claims were not necessarily small. Margaret Hogg claimed £248 from 'gentlemen' James, Peter, and

William Donaldson in October 1824,[50] while Mrs Ann Hinshelwood, widow of a Council member and a resident of New York City, owned a substantial property on Argyle Street about which she sought advice from Murdoch on numerous occasions.[51]

The vast majority of Murdoch's clientele during this early period came from a modest class background. He was usually careful to note those of his clients who warranted the appellation 'Esquire' (four), three more can be identified as 'gentlemen' from court records, and another client was Murdoch's own physician. Another three clients, all non-residents, might be thought to possess high social status – Mrs Hinshelwood, as an officer's widow, an army captain from Wales, and a London clergyman. No more than 7 per cent (11/153) of his clientele came from the elite. A further group comprised a few reasonably successful merchants, although none of the city's most prominent. About 90 per cent of his business thus came from the smaller merchants and 'mechanics,' leavened by a few farmers and mariners and their widows. Occupations have been identified for eighty of his non-elite clients, and of these twenty-seven were traders of some sort, ranging from small grocers to large wholesale merchants.[52] Artisans and skilled craftsmen were the next most numerous group at nineteen, including a tinsmith, a portrait painter, two confectioners, brewer Alexander Keith, several tailors and carpenters, two cabinetmakers, a brass founder, a saddler, a baker, a butcher, and a shoemaker. A few fell into a miscellaneous category: schoolteacher William Barry, auctioneer Richard Bulger, veteran Anthony Beecham, truckman Edward Warren, and pedlar Patrick Brown. It is probable that more of those with unidentified occupations were artisans than merchants, since merchants can usually be traced through newspaper advertisements and artisans often cannot. Merchants and 'mechanics' and their widows probably made up similar proportions of Murdoch's client base, about 40 per cent each. Their legal needs were relatively simple, relating to debtor-creditor matters rather than the more lucrative conveyancing and estates work that would occupy Murdoch in later years.

Professional Income

What income did Murdoch's law practice generate? It is clear from his account books that he handled a lot of money, but less clear how much of it he retained. When a client lost a suit and paid Murdoch a sum for 'costs,' it is often not possible to distinguish how much of this sum was profit over and above the court fees which he had already paid on the client's behalf. Fortunately, Murdoch tried to calculate his earnings for 1827 and the first five months of 1828. He showed his gross income for the calendar year 1827 as £101 12s 9d, from which he deducted 'charges of business' in the amount of £4 12 1, for a total of £97 0s 8d net income.[53] The rent on his combined residence/office at 32 Barrington Street was £90 per annum, so Murdoch had to depend on his private means to cover anything more than his basic expenses.[54] Yet an annual income of £100 was respectable for a young man of his profession. It was much less than the £600 salary accorded the assistant judges of the Supreme Court in 1822, but twice the wages of a labourer, who typically earned £1 per week or less.

If Murdoch's professional income was satisfactory in 1827, it be-came even more so in 1828. His tally for the first five months of 1828 showed a gross income of nearly £150, almost three times the £56 he had grossed in the same period in 1827. The 'charges of business' are not listed for 1828, but if they represented the same proportion of total income as in 1827, Murdoch would still have substantially augmented his income over the previous year. The 'unusual brisk trade' that Mur-doch referred to in a letter to a client in 1828, as well as his own growing reputation, had an encouraging effect on his professional income.[55]

If Murdoch's income was respectable in the early years, it is also clear that others were much more financially successful than he was. In his first full year of practice (1826), William Young netted more than twice what Murdoch had, £233, while a year later he had more than doubled that amount, earning £504 from his practice.[56] In part, Young's success could be attributed to his more extensive connections with the mercan-tile community, but he also profited from travelling the circuit. Mur-doch did not travel the circuit, probably for reasons of health, with the result that he missed the opportunity to enhance his profile in distant areas of the province. Circuit business was not invariably profitable in and of itself, but it had the potential to create useful connections and to develop a lawyer's reputation with his peers and government of-ficials as well as with the public. William Blowers Bliss was constantly lamenting in the early 1820s that 'the circuit empties the purse rather than replenishing it.'[57] By 1829, however, he was reporting proudly to his brother that he had 'performed nine indictments for [the crown] and conducted six Trials – Rape, Larceny, Burgling and Murder' – on the western circuit at Annapolis, and was now 'what would be called in England, a leader – that is I am the leader of our circuit, and generally get a fee of some kind in most of the causes which are tried.'[58] Even so, his income was comparable to Murdoch's, about £250 per year, largely because he did little attorney work and tried to earn his living solely from advocacy in the style of an English barrister.

Murdoch's absence from the circuit may also have subtly undermined his professional reputation with his peers. Immersion in the dining and social life of the circuit could be crucial in maintaining a sense of professional camaraderie.[59] An important part of that sociability lay in its masculine character, and the importance of the rituals of the circuit in reaffirming the essentially male nature of the legal profession has been explored by other scholars.[60] This missed opportunity, Murdoch's increasing involvement in the temperance movement in the 1830s and 1840s, and his lifelong cohabitation with his unmarried aunt Harriette, all contributed to the difficulties Murdoch sometimes encountered in presenting an appropriately authoritative male image to the world. Given the strong association between independence, citizenship, and masculinity, these problems may also have undermined to some extent the image upon which Murdoch wished to base his political career.[61]

In these early years at least, Murdoch was prepared to do almost all his business on credit. He seldom asked for retainers or for court costs to be paid 'up front' and indeed advanced money to his clients on the anticipated success of their lawsuits. In a society chronically short of specie and without savings banks, most suppliers of goods and services were obliged to provide them on credit. Predictably, Murdoch suffered his share of bad debts. An account he prepared at the end of 1830 showed an outstanding balance of £291 owed him, of which, he noted, £34 were 'very doubtful balances.' If we assume these to be uncollectable, they would represent a default rate of 11 per cent, which was probably optimistic. Clients often took years to pay and were not usually charged interest. A few entries showing Murdoch himself as the debtor reveal that he, too, sometimes took years to settle his accounts with others.

One example of this delay also demonstrates Murdoch's willingness to accept payment in kind. His medical bills with Dr Joseph Prescott for services provided to himself and his aunt Harriette amounted to some £9 over the period 1826–30. Murdoch had provided legal services to Prescott over the same period, and finally deducted the amount from the bill he prepared in 1830. In later years he would deduct from his account with West India merchants Saltus and Wainwright the cost of a 'barrel of Canada flour' and 'one Bermuda plait for H. Beamish.'

William Donaldson of Sherwood was given credit for 'lodging etc. last summer' in 1830, while Robert Geddes acquitted part of his bill by supplying twenty-five pounds of butter. Such entries were unusual: the vast bulk of Murdoch's accounts were ultimately settled in cash.

The organization of Murdoch's law practice remained very simple. His cousin Thomas Beamish Akins began assisting him in 1823 at the age of fourteen and would complete his articles with Murdoch in 1830.[62] There is only one indication that Murdoch contemplated taking on another lawyer in some form of association. Two letters dated August and October 1827 are recorded in Murdoch's letter book as signed by himself and Thomas Forman, who had been called to the bar on 10 October 1827. Perhaps the extra time needed for his political duties after his election to the House of Assembly in September 1826 suggested to Murdoch the need for extra help in his law practice. If so, the experiment was not continued or repeated. Forman left the province in 1828 and is reported to have died at Sydney, Australia, in October 1831.[63]

Murdoch remained a sole practitioner for the rest of his long career. This was virtually the only form of law practice known in the Maritimes – or anywhere else in North America – before 1850.[64] Aside from familial configurations, even the two-man partnership was rarely encountered before 1850 in Nova Scotia. One or two can be identified in the eighteenth century, and a few at most in the first half of the nineteenth. Familial groupings were only an apparent exception, since they did not possess a principal feature of modern partnerships: indefinite duration. Though father-son partnerships were fairly common, they were transitional in nature, destined to advance the career of the son who would in due course become a sole practitioner. The Uniacke brothers, for example, did not function as a modern 'firm.' They shared their father's magnificent library and perhaps the labour of current apprentices, but they operated essentially as sole practitioners. This form of business organization reflected a deeply felt conviction that the lawyer's independence was best guaranteed by providing legal services on an individual basis.

Lawyers and Leadership in Colonial Society

By 1827, Beamish Murdoch had already established himself in the eyes of both the public and his peers as a well-known member of the profession. He drew his clientele mostly from the middling and humbler classes of Halifax society, who had shown their trust by electing him to the House of Assembly in the fall of 1826, but he was also beginning to serve a few of the more substantial merchants and rentiers.[65] He had managed to carve out a better niche for himself than some of his peers.[66] How, precisely, had he done this? Talent, persistence, and a capacity for hard work he had in ample measure, but presumably others did too. What, then, went into the 'making' of this colonial lawyer?

Three factors were key: the rise of journalism, the changing nature of the market that Murdoch served, and the efflorescence of voluntary associations which Murdoch avidly joined. Murdoch's entry into practice coincided with the rapid expansion of journalism in his native Halifax. Newspaper accounts assisted him in becoming better known among the city's increasing numbers of artisans, shopkeepers, and minor merchants, who were growing more affluent as trade recovered after the initial peacetime slump of 1815–22. His activities in court, in municipal affairs, and in provincial politics, his involvement in church controversies, and his literary, philanthropic, and cultural endeavours were fully chronicled by the numerous weekly newspapers circulating in Halifax in the second quarter of the nineteenth century. Murdoch himself participated in this journalistic frenzy through his editorial work for the *Acadian Recorder* in 1824–6, to which he would return a decade later. It is almost impossible to find a period of more than a few months in the second half of the 1820s that does not carry some reference to Murdoch in the newspapers.

In the press Murdoch was portrayed as independent, in the eighteenth-century sense of that word. In the political, legal, and ecclesiastical spheres, he appeared to act on his own beliefs, without fear of reprisal or hope of reward from the powerful. A few examples of his appearances demonstrate the kind of image that grew up around Murdoch, and why it might have been attractive to his nascent clientele. His role as counsel for the plaintiff in the case of *Robertson v. Phillips* in the fall of 1824 has already been mentioned. The case did not look particularly bright for Murdoch. His client was a 'fallen woman,' a widow who had had three children out of wedlock with Mr Phillips. He had orally agreed to support them at a rate of 7s 6d per week, plus clothes and schooling, while she retained custody. Mrs Robertson had brought one of the children back to Phillips at one point, then thought the better of it and clandestinely removed the child from his home. The law allowed an agreement for the support of illegitimate children to be rescinded at any time, which made Mrs Robertson's position rather tenuous.

Phillips was represented by J.W. Johnston, nearly a decade senior to Murdoch and already possessed of a large practice. Johnston tried to argue that Robertson was jealous of 'a new, and a laudable connexion' that Phillips had formed with another, 'virtuous female' and was thus motivated by simple malice in pursuing her claim. Murdoch neatly turned the tables by painting a tragic picture of Robertson as a wronged woman 'struggling in widowhood and poverty with that energy of mind which could only inspire a mother,' who had managed to support her children alone for sixty-eight weeks. He urged the jury not to judge her too harshly for taking back her child, since 'it would be sinning against the best feelings of human nature to condemn her for this – it might be a misfortune, but certainly it was not a crime.' Judge Lewis M. Wilkins recommended £19 compensation, but the jury awarded £22.

The *Novascotian* gave full rein to Murdoch's panegyric to wounded maternity.[67] It gave equal coverage to Johnston, but his arguments sounded stiff and technical in contrast to Murdoch's heartfelt appeal. At a time when the parties to an action were disabled from giving evidence on the ground of their interest in the outcome, there was no chance for the jury to judge their credibility.[68] Everything depended on the lawyer's skill in painting a credible portrait of his client. Murdoch's ability to portray Mrs Robertson in a favourable light not only swayed the jury but was conveyed to a wide public through detailed newspaper coverage. Of course, Murdoch was in the process of creating an image for himself as well: as the man who speaks truth to power, who is not afraid to champion the claims of a poor woman against a more respectable male antagonist with an elite lawyer. The image of power being constrained by law was as old as the common law itself, but in the Halifax of the 1820s there was a new, political edge to it. As the shopkeepers and mechanics of the capital began to question the political order, Murdoch's upset victory over the more genteel Johnston could be read as an omen of things to come.

Murdoch again appeared in the press as the champion of the common man and woman during the dispute surrounding the choice of a new rector at Halifax's Anglican cathedral in 1824–5. The dispute arose when John Inglis, the rector of St Paul's, was promoted to the bishopric in the fall of 1824 and the crown named as his successor the archdeacon of New Brunswick, the Reverend Robert Willis. A large body of the congregation preferred the more evangelical curate, the Reverend John Thomas Twining.[69] The dispute was rapidly framed in legal and constitutional terms. Letters to the editor discussed whether crown prerogative could prevail over the 1759 provincial statute expressly vesting the right of presentation in the congregation, and whether the crown's claim rested on provisions of ecclesiastical law which arguably had not been received into the colony.[70] The matter was also framed in terms of freedom of conscience, with the choice put starkly: the dissenters 'must either submit and sit down contented under the ministry of a gentleman who is forced upon them contrary to their sentiments; or they must nobly assert their independence ... [out of] a just regard for their political and spiritual welfare.'[71]

The secretary of state would not turn back, but neither would the dissenters. A day-long public meeting, which Murdoch and others addressed, resulted in a vote of fifty-seven in favour of the right of the parish and seventeen against.[72] One group of seceders ultimately founded the Granville Street Baptist Church while another took refuge at St George's Anglican, the 'round church' which had been erected in the year of Murdoch's birth. Along with Thomas Chandler Haliburton and Richard John Uniacke, Jr, Murdoch joined the St George's group, abandoning the prestige that accompanied attendance at the cathedral in the name of freedom of conscience. Haliburton's and Uniacke's connections were such that their stand did not harm them – within a few years each had been promoted to the bench, as had William Blowers Bliss, who conspicuously supported Bishop Inglis during the controversy. Just as Twining was consigned to the margins of Halifax Anglicanism, Murdoch, too, was vulnerable, perhaps more vulnerable than he realized. His outspoken opposition to the bishop gave another reason to the Halifax elite to distrust him.[73] Murdoch's public opposition to what was widely regarded as an arbitrary act of royal prerogative was, however, more favourably regarded in those groups from whom he drew his clientele, who continued to vote for him in the 1830 election (which he lost). It rested squarely within the traditions of the Glorious Revolution of 1688 which were a staple of Maritime political discourse in the nineteenth century.[74]

Murdoch's client base was also a key factor in his success. The role played by craftsmen and small merchants in sustaining his practice in the early years could probably only have occurred in the 1820s. By this point, Halifax had a population sufficiently large, prosperous, and economically diversified to support the services of a lawyer like Murdoch, who could not depend on government appointments or the legal business of the mercantile elite. In the 1826 election, which resulted in his upset victory over the well-known merchant John Albro, Murdoch received his principal support from smallholders, shopkeepers, and artisans precisely because of his independence from both the official party and the influence of the major merchants. This election has been interpreted as the first in Nova Scotia in which a recognizable middle-class interest sought to achieve political expression, with Beamish Murdoch as its exemplar.[75]

In addition to the press and personal contacts, voluntary societies were also a means of meeting clients, developing a profile in the community, and gaining leadership experience. Numerous new societies were founded in the second quarter of the nineteenth century, and their membership surged as middle-class residents of Halifax sought stability and meaning against a backdrop of mass immigration, ethno-religious diversity, and a fickle economy.[76] In addition to his membership in the Charitable Irish Society (one of the older societies in the capital), Murdoch also joined a number of others in the 1820s, including the newly formed Society of Nova Scotia Barristers and the Halifax Poor Man's Friend Society. His role in the latter once again provided him with a platform to address his fellow citizens.

The society had commenced activity in 1820 with the aim of relieving distress among the Halifax poor in the winter season. With the reduction in wages and general decline in trade that followed the end of the war in 1815, the plight of the poor in Halifax had become more acute and more evident, especially in winter. The society claimed to help 1,380 persons each year (over 10 per cent of the town's population), mainly by providing wood and operating a soup kitchen. Its budget of some £400 was raised mostly by subscription. A series of letters in the *Novascotian* by 'Malthus,' beginning in January 1825, attacked the society for dispensing charity indiscriminately and encouraging profligacy and immorality. The society was thrown on the defensive and compelled to articulate its mission, one it had assumed to be universally accepted.[77]

Rising to the challenge, Murdoch accused 'Malthus' of being 'led astray by the cries of a cold calculating spirit.' He had once acted as a visitor to the society and had 'found greater poverty than he could imagine, even in a respectable ward.'[78] The society ultimately failed in its attempt to remedy the seasonal employment problem afflicting the labouring classes, but it must have been some comfort for the latter to know that Murdoch could articulate their basic needs in a convincing manner and fend off attacks based on fashionable new theories of political economy.

Deciding when Murdoch could be said to have passed the threshold from being a 'novice' to an 'established' lawyer is of necessity a somewhat arbitrary exercise. But by the end of 1827 Beamish Murdoch had good reason to believe that his career had been well and truly launched. He had not just survived the early years but prospered in every sense. His income was adequate and respectable, if not spectacular, and would grow appreciably in 1828 and later years. He had achieved considerable local prominence through participation in voluntary societies, philanthropic work, and religious affairs, and also through the beginnings of his own literary[79] and journalistic endeavours, all of which had culminated in his election to the House of Assembly in 1826. When named vice-president of the newly established Society of Nova Scotia Barristers in 1827, Murdoch secured recognition within his chosen profession at an unusually early age. Having accomplished so much in such a short period, he no doubt looked forward to even more successes in the future. His professional career would continue to flourish, but in other fields, particularly the political, he would find serious challenges in the years to come.[80] It was perhaps no coincidence that in retirement he ended his *History of Nova-Scotia, or Acadie* with the year 1827. For him, 1827 would always remain the golden year, the high point of Fortuna's wheel, before the descent into the turbulent waters ahead.

6

The Maturing of a Colonial Lawyer, 1828–50

The busy pace Murdoch had set for himself in his law practice and his community, political, and cultural involvements did not slacken in the years after 1827. His law practice continued to grow not only in volume, which probably doubled by the mid-1830s, but also in the variety and complexity of work performed and the amount of remuneration per client. The proportion of his practice devoted to debt collection remained important but declined overall as Murdoch spent more time on other types of work, such as admiralty law, conveyancing, and the settlement of estates. Some tasks developed naturally from transactions he had engaged in during the 1820s: from drafting arbitration bonds, he went on to appear before arbitrators fairly frequently and to sit as an arbitrator himself by the 1840s. He also began to engage in new areas of professional endeavour: insurance, patents, and work related to business corporations. Other horizons opened for him when he was admitted to practice before the Court of Marriage and Divorce and the Court of Vice-Admiralty in the 1830s, and his Chancery practice grew considerably.

Professional growth in the 1830s and 1840s was matched by political defeat. In 1830 the province was convulsed by the 'Brandy Dispute' which became an issue in the election of that year. The dispute arose when the Assembly tried to correct an error in a duty it had imposed on brandy in 1826; instead of a duty of 2s 4d per gallon, the actual amount imposed was only 2d per gallon. The Council twice rejected a bill designed to impose the original amount, leading to charges that it was interfering with the Assembly's right to originate all revenue bills free from amendment. The impasse led to loss of the appropriation bill and the drying up of road money normally distributed throughout the province, which in turn inflamed the populace. At this point the death of King George IV dissolved the Assembly, necessitating an election. All candidates who opposed the Council's actions were returned – except for Murdoch, who lost to the ardently pro-Council Stephen Deblois, the son of Loyalist immigrants. In the heat of the contest, Murdoch unwisely assailed the Loyalists as the 'scum of the United States' who only pretended allegiance to the crown and had fled the republic to escape debts. Behind the scenes the city's merchant oligarchy orchestrated the defeat of this young reformer, who had become something of a thorn in their side.[1]

The changing political landscape of the 1830s was very stressful for Murdoch. One of reform leader Joseph Howe's most prominent supporters at his famous libel trial in 1835, the next year Murdoch opposed him on the hustings, unable to support the nascent movement for colonial autonomy.[2] Again he tasted defeat when he ran in the election of 1840, and afterwards gave up his aspirations to rejoin the Assembly. Labelled a Tory and turncoat, Murdoch turned to the municipal politics which emerged after the incorporation of the city of Halifax in 1841. Here he achieved some success, serving as city recorder for the entire decade of the 1850s.

By 1840, Murdoch also began to achieve modest official recognition in the form of appointments as deputy judge in vice-admiralty (1838), master in chancery (1840), and secretary and commissioner to the newly created Central Board of Education (1841–5). Compared to many lawyers of the period, Murdoch's officeholding began late and confined itself to positions of lesser status. What one may presume to be his ambitions for the provincial bench would never be realized.

In addition to his political activity, Murdoch remained in the public eye in the 1830s through his literary and community involvements. His four-volume *Epitome of the Laws of Nova-Scotia*, modelled on Blackstone and on James Kent's *Commentaries on American Law* (1826), appeared in 1832–3. Although it did not provide its author with the recognition he sought in the legal world, it was a substantial cultural achievement.[3] Murdoch retained membership in a number of fraternal societies but devoted his efforts principally to the Halifax Temperance Society, founded in 1831. He became its president in 1837, and when he retired from that office nine years later, his colleagues noted that he had 'been oftener before the public than any other man resident among us (clergymen excepted). His unaffected kindness and gentleness of manners ... and the language and temper with which he generally addressed himself to the very numerous audiences that he has frequently spoke [*sic*] to, have made him well and acceptably known to almost every inhabitant of the City.'[4] In short, Murdoch's lack of sympathy with Joseph Howe's political goals did not represent a rejection of the whole spectrum of reform sentiments animating early Victorian British North America. Moral, educational, and social and urban reform would occupy him for the middle decades of the century, as a part-time bureaucrat and leader of the Halifax temperance movement. Marginalized in the political realm, he remained in the vanguard of the middle-class reformism that shaped mid-Victorian British North America. Evangelical, philanthropically inclined, and eminently respectable, Murdoch was a veritable icon of the early Victorian middle class.

The organization of Murdoch's law practice remained unchanged during this period, and indeed until his retirement. One might have expected him to go into partnership with his cousin Thomas Beamish Akins. The two men followed very similar life courses, as bachelors who combined law practice with historical research and scholarship. Yet, when Akins was called to the bar in 1831, he soon established his own practice in an office on Granville Street. His separate establishment reflected the widespread assumption that a sole practice was the natural way for a lawyer to offer his services. In the absence of large corporate clients, there was no particular incentive for lawyers to organize their practices any differently, although those lawyers who followed the circuit sometimes found it beneficial to have a partner who could handle business on the home front during the absences required by circuit life. Thus, William Young, who travelled the circuit until well into the 1850s, had a succession of partners over most of his career, while the less itinerant Murdoch could afford to remain a sole practitioner.[5]

Akins's departure would nonetheless have posed a labour problem for Murdoch. Virtually all legal documents, whether pleadings for litigation or private instruments such as mortgages, wills, and deeds, were drawn up individually for each occasion, standard printed forms not being in use until some time after mid-century. Unlike in England, where scriveners or law-writers were employed by the piece, the labour required for all this copying was supplied principally by articled clerks.

As was common during this heyday of 'family capitalism' in North America, family members often pitched in. Murdoch's cousin Charles Beamish appears to have helped in the office after Akins's departure, although he ultimately became a businessman rather than a lawyer. Another younger cousin, Francis Stephen Beamish (b. 1821), the son of Murdoch's uncle Thomas Ott Beamish, articled with Murdoch from about 1842 until his call to the bar in 1847 and may have assisted him in earlier years. Murdoch never married, so he was unable to avail himself of the kind of unpaid labour that some other lawyers drew upon: it was apparently not unknown for the wives, daughters, and mothers of lawyers to put pen to parchment on their behalf. Shortly after beginning his practice at Windsor in 1829, Harry King thought his fiancée, 'Halli' Fraser, would 'have some pleasure in Knowing that it will not be at all mal-Etiquette to have a lady's [hand] Exhibited in Court – Mrs. [W.P.G.] Fraser's delicate & beautiful hand has numberless places assigned to it & I believe the whole family of [Judge Lewis M.] Wilkins assisted [him] when Younger.' King put Halli on notice that 'you will be able to assist vastly by Your rapid hand.'[6]

A Shifting Clientele

After the early 1830s it became increasingly rare for Murdoch to write a letter or two for a client whom he would not see again, although the 'small' clients never entirely disappeared. His practice slowly shifted from one where he offered a few relatively simple services to a large number of 'small' clients to one in which he provided a wider range of services to a more affluent and more regular clientele. Murdoch's clients were virtually all individuals: he continued to provide almost no legal services to government, the military, or the churches, and he had only one ongoing corporate client, Aetna Insurance of Hartford, Connecticut.[7] His practice involved private law almost entirely and he very seldom represented clients in criminal proceedings.[8] The range and sophistication of legal services performed by Murdoch provides evidence of both his widening reputation and his enhanced experience, skills, and knowledge. More prominent clients came to him partly because they perceived that he was capable of doing more for them.

Over the years 1828–42 Murdoch represented Halifax merchant Benjamin Wier, a scion of the New England Planter elite and future Canadian senator. Murdoch appeared for Wier in fourteen lawsuits, including two actions by Wier for defamation; advised him on his interest under a will; searched the title for properties on which Wier wished to take a mortgage; prepared mortgages and a variety of bonds; and provided advice on customs fees regarding the import of sealskins. For West India merchants Saltus and Wainwright, he drafted agreements, protested bills of exchange regarding shipments from Trinidad, Puerto Rico, and St Vincent, provided advice on bottomry with regard to a schooner out of Antigua, and drafted a deed and will for Wainwright.[9] For Benjamin Wier's son-in-law Dunbar Douglass Stewart, Murdoch provided constant conveyancing services and advice connected to moneylending through the 1830s. In 1839 Murdoch represented capitalist Enos Collins in an ejectment action to establish his client's title to land at Windsor and in 1842 he appeared before the new Halifax City Council to object to the assessments levied on Collins's properties for municipal tax purposes.

This shift in the nature of Murdoch's practice is reflected in the class composition of his clientele as of 1834–6, although not noticeably in the gender or ethnicity of his clients, which remained steady at about 10 per cent female and 10 per cent Irish. It should be noted that some of the Irish population were quite upwardly mobile during this period, with the result that Irish ethnicity is not as reliable a proxy for disadvantage as it was a decade earlier. The legal acculturation of Irish Catholics in Halifax would also have been facilitated by the appearance of Roman Catholic lawyers such as Laurence O'Connor Doyle, who was called to the bar in 1829.[10]

Murdoch's clientele underwent an almost complete turnover between the 1823–7 period and 1834–6. Only eleven clients from the earlier period, or about 7 per cent of the total, appear again in Murdoch's day book of 1834–6. This change coincided with a clear decline in the number of artisans in Murdoch's clientele. Only five artisans or their wives can be positively identified in the day book: carpenter James Dechman, Jr, who had been Murdoch's client from an early date; cabinetmaker James Scott, also an old client; Mrs Catherine Laffin, for whom Murdoch successfully obtained a judicial separation from her 'brushmaker' husband; John Robinson, hatter; and Samuel Cowan, furrier, who sought help regarding a troublesome apprentice, among other matters. Undoubtedly there were more who cannot now be identified, but the nature of the services performed by Murdoch for a large majority of the clients in the day book makes it clear that they could only have been merchants or persons of substantial property. Small merchants and widows still made up a significant proportion of Murdoch's clientele in 1834–6, but the artisans showed a substantial decline.

It is unclear whether these artisans sought out other counsel, whether Murdoch discouraged them from continuing as clients, or whether legal services were becoming too expensive for them. Two facts taken together suggest a subtle but visible reorientation of Murdoch's public profile. Aside from giving a very occasional lecture, he was not active in the Mechanics' Institute (founded in 1832), a notable absence given his numerous community commitments. As well, the temperance cause, with which Murdoch was so actively engaged, was regarded with some suspicion by many artisans. Whatever the reasons, Murdoch's client base was decidedly less oriented to manual and skilled labour in the mid-1830s than in the mid-1820s.

This change in clientele provided Murdoch with a higher professional income. He recorded his net income for the fifteen-month period May 1835–July 1836 as £349, or £280 for the year May 1835–April 1836.[11] The near trebling of his income since 1827 was a direct result of a more affluent clientele requiring more complex services for which Murdoch could charge higher fees. Murdoch did not charge more for the same services because of his greater experience; his standard fee for a letter, for example, remained at 6s 8d from 1823 until the end of his practice in the 1860s. The basis for calculation of fees was transaction-based throughout his professional life, although the idea of fees as remuneration for professional time appeared here and there in his records. Occasionally Murdoch charged a higher than usual fee for a particular service for 'extra trouble,' which must reflect some sense that he had to spend more time than usual on the matter. 'Just price' rather than market value long remained the basis for lawyers' fees, until the spread of liberalism created pressure for change in the later nineteenth century.

There is no convenient source from which to calculate Murdoch's professional income after the mid-1830s. All that can be said is that it probably continued to rise throughout the 1840s, especially after Murdoch began an active practice in Vice-Admiralty in 1836. His fees for eight cases in which he appeared in that court in the years 1836–9 amounted to an estimated £90, almost his entire annual income of a decade earlier. As well, Murdoch probably had more time to devote to his practice after the mid-1830s. His career in the House of Assembly had taken up a fair amount of his time in the years 1826–30, after which he plunged into the writing of his four-volume *Epitome of the Laws of Nova-Scotia* during the years 1830–3. Although he remained very active in voluntary societies and public affairs, Murdoch would still have had more time to devote to clients' affairs after the publication of the *Epitome*. The 1850s were probably Murdoch's most prosperous decade, when he was able to combine his £200 salary as city recorder with a still active practice.

An Expanding Suite of Services

The variety of legal services undertaken by Murdoch as his career matured poses a striking contrast with his earlier letter book, so preoccupied with routine matters of debt. Some of these services were the result of new economic activities being carried on in the province. In early 1836 Murdoch was involved in a flurry of activity regarding a proposed 'Marine Slip or Railway ... as will enable Owners of Ships or Vessels to obtain the repair thereof with dispatch and convenience.'[12] His mandate included drafting a petition to the legislature, agreements between the promoters on the one hand and the patent holder and the builders on the other, a partnership indenture between the promoters, and the preparation of a long lease for the opinion of the attorney general. Twelve years later, he advised John Ross in his negotiations with the Londonderry Mining company and on several points relating to its act of incorporation. He also began to do insurance work, both for and against the American insurance companies that started to offer their services in the province in the 1830s. Murdoch did not expand into the world of insurance agency, however, as William Young and a number of other lawyers did, and there were few local business corporations of any size established before Confederation.

The vast bulk of Murdoch's billings continued to be made for the kinds of transactions and litigation that had been familiar in the province for almost a century. The advertisement inserted by Halifax lawyer Charles E.W. Schmidt in the *Novascotian* in 1836 could just as well have been Murdoch's; Schmidt promised to 'bestow prompt attention to the Collection of Debts, Agencies, and Searches of Titles to Real Estate; and [to] draw ... Deeds, Mortgages, Bonds, Wills, Powers of Attorney, Indentures Agreements and Instruments of all descriptions.'[13] Most of these were based on the precedents copied out so laboriously by clerks during the early years of their apprenticeship. Drafting such documents and advising parties about their consequences formed the backbone of Murdoch's law practice. Such arrangements depend on 'facilitative law,' principally the laws of contract, agency, partnership, trust, wills, and property, which allow parties to order their affairs as seems best to them. As Halifax's middle class grew in numbers, self-consciousness, and prosperity, it created more of a demand for such mechanisms to assist both in business planning and in the transmission of familial assets to the next generation. Such tasks were not glamorous but they were necessary and valued, and provide an important counterweight to the expressions of anti-lawyer sentiment often found in colonial-era newspapers.

Dispute resolution, principally but not exclusively in the courts, formed the second major part of Murdoch's practice. Debt collection remained part of his litigation practice but declined as a proportion of it. Murdoch actually appeared in fewer debt actions in 1835 than he had in 1827, but those in which he appeared mostly involved much higher amounts (in the hundreds of pounds rather than tens) sought by higher-status clients such as Benjamin Wier, Dunbar Douglass Stewart, and the estate of Stewart's father, James Stewart, late of the Supreme Court of Nova Scotia.[14] Beyond the Supreme Court and the Court of Chancery, Murdoch appeared in a dizzying variety of courts and other bodies between 1827 and 1842: the Court of Marriage and Divorce, Vice-Admiralty, Probate Court, the Commissioners' Court, the Inferior Court of Common Pleas, the quarter sessions, the new Mayor's Court created after Halifax's incorporation in 1841, and, on one occasion, a court martial. He also represented clients before City Council, the House of Assembly, the lieutenant governor-in-council, and private arbitrators. Once he carried on a long negotiation with the commissioners of Sable Island with regard to the fate of a ship stranded on that unlucky shore. An examination of Murdoch's activity in the courts of Chancery, Vice-Admiralty, and Marriage and Divorce provides a good overview of both the shifts in his practice over this period and the social and economic context in which this practice was carried on.

Murdoch's practice in Chancery and the two civil law courts (Vice-Admiralty and Marriage and Divorce) got under way only in the 1830s. These three courts were united by a procedural system originating in canon law and continental civil law which was at sharp variance with the common law procedure followed in the Supreme Court and (as a rule) the inferior courts. Common law procedure essentially relied on oral testimony before a jury. The written pleadings that launched a case were largely formulaic and derived from precedents. Once a case got to court, neither the evidence nor the lawyers' arguments were written down, and often the judge's decision was oral as well, or written down very briefly.

Chancery, Vice-Admiralty, and the Court of Marriage and Divorce, by contrast, relied on written testimony heard by a judge with no jury. Pleadings were not formulaic but recounted the promovent's (plaintiff's) tale of woe in lengthy narrative. The impugnant (defendant) replied in kind, and commissioners were then appointed to take the evidence. The witnesses were called to respond to questions drafted by counsel and submitted to the commissioners, who conducted the interrogation. The answers were written down and 'published,' that is, collated in the form of a (frequently sizeable) pamphlet for the perusal of the court. Oral argument was then allowed on points of law. Given this manner of proceeding, it was not surprising that court costs were much higher than in the common law courts, leaving aside entirely the more liberal fee scale that the lawyers were entitled to charge.

Of the three courts, Chancery was the one with which an ordinary citizen would most likely have contact, though more likely as pursued than pursuer. The principal subject of its jurisdiction was the foreclosure of mortgages, which featured in four of the six cases in which Murdoch appeared between 1830 and 1834. Certain remedies such as injunctions and orders for an accounting were available only in Chancery and were sought in the remaining two cases.[15]

The four foreclosure cases were all undefended, with final sale of the property occurring four to six months after the filing of the initial bill of complaint. The time did not vary significantly as between lands inside and outside Halifax: in one case the lands were in Truro and in another in Hants County, with the remaining two in the capital. In two cases, one of the mortgagors was absent from the province, but the standard procedure was simply to order one month's notice in the *Royal Gazette* to the absentee. Failing an answer, the proceedings resumed.[16] Other complicating factors could arise. In *Hugh McDade et ux. v. Mary Hay et al.*, there were interventions by two other parties. First, claimants under an earlier mortgage appeared, seeking to ensure that their claims were not ignored (they were not). Second, the widow of the deceased mortgagee, Michael Leonard, had taken Mr McDade as her second husband, causing the guardians of Leonard's minor children to intervene. Laurence O'Connor Doyle and John Schrage wished to ensure that a portion of the proceeds of sale would be paid into court for the children's benefit (which they were). Despite these complications, Murdoch succeeded in having the property sold and all claims settled in just over four months after the filing of the bill of complaint in November 1833.

The speed of the Chancery in these cases belies the constant criti-

cism about its delay and inefficiency. Chancery could be quick in uncontested cases because there was no need to take written evidence;
contested cases would unfold much more slowly. Whether speed was
a good thing in foreclosure actions depended on one's point of view.
What seemed expeditious to the mortgagee might have seemed unduly
hasty to mortgagors in the process of losing their land. The actions
of the mortgagees in these cases do not seem particularly oppressive
when viewed in context. The mortgage in *McDade*, for example, dated
from 1817, with the principal stated to be payable in one year. Yet the
original mortgagor, Peter Hay, a Halifax mason, had still not paid back
the principal by the time of his death in February 1832. The mortgagee
must have been content to operate on oral renewals as long as Hay
could keep up the interest payments. Hay's death seems to have precipitated the action for foreclosure, since his heirs proved less credit-
worthy than their father. In *John Crowe v. Isaiah Smith*, the mortgagors
had paid not a cent of interest during the four-year term, leaving the
mortgagee little choice but to seek foreclosure. And in *Dunbar Douglass
Stewart v. Halliburton Grant et ux.*, the mortgagor absconded when the
mortgage term expired, again leaving the mortgagee little choice.[17]

Complaints about the oppressive costs of Chancery were closer to
the mark. The total bill of costs (lawyers' fees plus court costs) did not
necessarily vary according to the size of the mortgage debt in question, so that the costs of foreclosure for small mortgage debts could
be disproportionately high. For example, Murdoch acted for Newport
gentleman Dunbar Douglass Stewart (himself a lawyer) in two foreclosure actions in 1834. In one the mortgage debt was for about £150,
in the other over £300, yet the costs in the first were £13 (8.6 per cent of
the debt), in the second £14 (4.6 per cent). Both were much higher than
Murdoch's charges for ordinary debt collection, which were 5 per cent
on sums less than £100 and 2.5 per cent on larger sums.[18] Aside from
the actual costs, Chancery seemed oppressive in another way, in that
only cash sales of foreclosed property were allowed.[19] In a cash-poor
society, this practice not only depressed the sale price but ensured that
the mortgagee was likely to acquire it, as happened in *McDade*.

Many thought of Chancery as oppressive simply because its proceedings exposed the deep economic inequalities of Nova Scotian society. All the mortgagees for whom Murdoch acted were described as
'Esquire' (Stewart) or 'gentleman' (Crowe, Leonard). Stewart was the
son of an assistant judge of the Supreme Court, James Stewart, and the
nephew of another, Brenton Halliburton, who became chief justice in

1833. He had been called to the bar in 1816 but appears to have preferred the life of a county squire at Newport. In the Rhalves proceeding, it was recounted that Frederick Rhalves had taken out mortgages on various properties with not only Simon Robie but also prominent Halifax merchants James and Michael Tobin, Samuel Cunard, and Henry Yeomans. Those being foreclosed against were yeoman Isaiah Smith and his wife, Lydia, grocer Halliburton Grant and his wife, Mary Ann, the family of mason Peter Hay, and farmers Robert and Anna Kent of Truro. Murdoch's developing Chancery practice assisted his professional bottom line, but it also represented a significant shift in his clientele, towards the holders of wealth and status in provincial society.

Proceedings in the Vice-Admiralty Court, to which Murdoch was admitted as a proctor and advocate (equivalent to solicitor and barrister, respectively) by 1836, did not reveal the inequalities of Nova Scotian society in the same stark way that Chancery did.[20] In some ways, it allowed the tables to be turned, as sailors and disgruntled passengers used the court's pre-trial procedures to arrest captains and shipowners in order to answer claims for unpaid wages and breach of contract. In *Enoch Sears v. Nicholas Moran*, for example, Murdoch defended Captain Moran against an action by the ship's cook for £6 15s in wages alleged to be due. Moran was arrested on 8 October to prevent him from leaving port until the action could be heard, which was the usual procedure in Vice-Admiralty. When judgment went against him five weeks later, he became liable for the cook's costs in the amount of £36 15s 10d, not to mention the sums he would have had to pay his own lawyers. Two years later, Murdoch unsuccessfully defended the captain of the brig *Ann* against a claim for unjust dismissal. This time the sailor was entitled to £55 damages plus costs, being seven months' wages and return travel expenses to Halifax from Pernambuco (Brazil), where he had been put off the ship.[21] These vignettes accord with Judith Fingard's interpretation of pre-1845 sailors' wage litigation in Vice-Admiralty, 'where residual mercantilist notions made the judge the special protector of the transient, vulnerable seafarer.'[22]

Murdoch had more success in defending the four actions brought against George Barker, captain of the ship *Panther*, in 1837.[23] In these, as in the two wage cases, he acted as advocate, with lawyer William Sutherland (his cousin by marriage) appearing as proctor. The *Panther* litigation involved an American ship which had accepted £5 each from a group of passengers for a passage from County Sligo to New York in the summer of 1837. The ship was damaged in a storm during the crossing and put into Halifax for repairs and provisions, at which time the passengers instituted their claims for breach of contract. Barker was arrested at the end of August and remained in jail until Murdoch and Sutherland secured his release by a writ of habeas corpus obtained from the Supreme Court in October. The court decided that Vice-Admiralty possessed no jurisdiction over the contracts of passage since they were made on land in Ireland. The judges not only released Barker but issued a writ of prohibition to Vice-Admiralty judge Charles Rufus Fairbanks, forbidding him from proceeding any further with the case.

The affair escalated into a cause célèbre when Fairbanks refused to recognize the writ and proceeded with the case, upon which Sutherland wrote him a private letter indicating his client's intention to pursue legal action against the judge. Fairbanks chose to treat this act as a contempt of court, fined Sutherland £20, and prohibited him from practice.[24] When Sutherland refused to pay, Fairbanks had him committed to jail on 19 December. The same day, Murdoch sought his release by a writ of habeas corpus from the Supreme Court, which was granted two days later on the basis that the Vice-Admiralty Court had, at most, power to fine or imprison for contempt in open court, which was not the case here.[25] The contretemps illustrates once again Murdoch's refusal to tolerate abuse of authority, even at a time in his life when he was coming to be identified more closely with the very 'establishment' he had so often challenged in the past.

The late 1830s saw Murdoch involved in two other Admiralty cases, both involving salvage. His work for the salvors of the ship *Ajax* netted him an estimated £20.[26] In the case of the ship *Scio*, he worked as proctor for Captain John K. Lane, master of the fishing schooner *Franklin* out of Gloucester, Massachusetts. Murdoch's application for salvage compensation illustrated the drama, danger, and courage that characterized the age of sail. The crew of the *Scio* had abandoned ship on 16 May 1838 when the vessel was totally surrounded by ice and fog off the east coast of Nova Scotia. Adrift in a small boat, they were rescued thirteen hours later and brought to Halifax. Captain Lane found the unoccupied ship drifting off Liscomb Harbour three days later, and had it brought to port. His crew unloaded its cargo of lumber and repaired the vessel, intending to sail it back to the United States. On the return voyage, a storm off Halifax forced the abandonment of the *Scio* when it began to leak badly. It drifted to shore and was eventually sold under authority of the court. Its sale price of £194 was awarded half to the owners of the *Franklin* and the salvage crew, and half to the owners of the *Scio* and her cargo, but the latter share of £97 had to bear the full legal costs of £64, including Murdoch's fee for £22.[27]

Murdoch's Admiralty work accurately reflected his place in Halifax society. His clients were not, with a few exceptions, members of the Halifax mercantile elite but rather sea captains and most often American sea captains at that. That 'outsiders' would seek him out as counsel comes as no surprise, and demonstrates his perceived independence. His appointment as surrogate judge in Chancery in 1838 is more of a mystery. Given the well-known irascibility and egotism of Charles Rufus Fairbanks, it is not clear why he would confer this privilege on a lawyer who had just embarrassed him publicly a few months earlier by achieving Sutherland's release from prison. The office afforded only trifling fees but nonetheless carried some prestige, and Murdoch would have been honoured by the appointment. S.G.W. Archibald renewed the appointment when he became master of the rolls in 1841, but Alexander Stewart did not when he succeeded Archibald in 1846.

Murdoch's practice in the Court of Marriage and Divorce was not large in absolute numbers, but in view of the court's very small caseload he was its most experienced lawyer in the 1830s and 1840s. A lifelong bachelor, Murdoch may seem an unlikely champion of women's rights. Yet he represented women in four of the five cases that he pleaded before the court between 1831 and 1850, and in three of these he put the application on the ground of cruelty. He was successful only in the first case, probably because he advised Catherine Laffin to seek just a judicial separation rather than a full divorce.[28] There was much reluctance to terminate a marriage for anything less than adultery, not merely on the part of the judges and executive councillors but among Nova Scotians in general. Cruelty had been a cause of divorce in the province since at least the statute of 1761 which formally constituted the court, and had been pleaded on occasion. Unfortunately, the sketchiness of the records before the 1830s makes it impossible to know whether the plea succeeded.[29]

The first recorded instances of divorces being granted on the ground of cruelty occurred in 1834 and 1835, while Murdoch had obtained Catherine Laffin's judicial separation in 1832 or 1833.[30] The 1830s would remain the high-water mark of indulgence to the plea of cruelty for decades: not until 1879 was it again successfully invoked. Murdoch's efforts on behalf of Eliza Parker in 1841–2 were probably unsuccessful, in spite of the fact that her husband, Joseph, did not appear.[31] His efforts on behalf of Patricia Carey, who also sought a divorce on the basis of cruelty, came to nought when her 1842 petition was not pursued.

A Career Consolidated

By the early 1840s, Murdoch's reputation as a lawyer was well established, as demonstrated by the fact that wealthy clients such as Enos Collins now sought out his services. The economic insecurity of the early years had been overcome, and Murdoch was now able to live comfortably if not opulently. In 1839 he sold his combined office and living quarters on busy Barrington Street and moved to a quieter residential area on Brunswick Street, although his office remained on Barrington Street in other premises. The accumulation of wealth had always been secondary to other goals for Murdoch, but his larger aspirations in the political and cultural fields had been largely frustrated. His *Epitome* did not win the accolades he thought it deserved, nor secure him any professional advancement beyond nomination to some fairly minor offices. Having invested so much in the old order, however, Murdoch was reluctant to throw in his lot with those who wished to embark on a quite different relationship with the mother country. Thus, in spite of being an exemplar of liberal reform in the social and legal fields, he would remain a defender of the 'mixed and balanced' constitution during the struggle for responsible government in the 1830s and 1840s.

If Murdoch's stubborn political independence cost him a place in the House of Assembly and disentitled him to government patronage, it seems not to have harmed his legal career unduly. Perhaps it even enhanced his reputation as a staunch advocate who would plead his client's cause without regard to personal consequences. While attaining some prominence as a barrister, as evidenced by his briefs in Vice-Admiralty and Chancery and his defamation and other suits in the Supreme Court on Wier's behalf, Murdoch did not neglect the solicitorial side of his practice. Through it he moved closer to the heart of the mercantile and business world than he had been in the early years of his practice, and distanced himself somewhat, albeit not totally, from the 'menu peuple' who had initially formed the backbone of his clientele, though the precise rationale for and trajectory of this evolution is unclear. Murdoch's career provides a good example of the way in which the combination of the roles of barrister and solicitor by North American lawyers resulted in their being involved in all aspects of community life. They did not keep members of their communities at arm's length, as English barristers did, nor did they confine themselves to a narrow range of traditional and 'respectable' lawyerly services, as English solicitors seem to have done. Even though most of Murdoch's services could be characterized as traditional, his varied activities on the marine slip project and in connection with Londonderry Mining show that he had no objection to acting as lobbyist, broker, promoter, and business adviser in addition to his usual work. Much as he embraced the idea of the independence of the bar, Murdoch did not hesitate to engage in such services when the opportunity presented itself.

Murdoch's career also permits us to see how the status of North American lawyers was derived mostly from their perceived utility, leadership roles, and broader cultural contributions rather than their class backgrounds or their clientele as such. Through his hard work, patient acquisition of experience and expertise, deep learning, and literary and philanthropic endeavours, Murdoch was able to overcome a highly embarrassing and problematic familial heritage, as well as a lack of effective male patrons, to join the ranks of both the respectable and the successful in mid-Victorian Halifax. Small wonder that the legal profession became perceived as a sure ticket to middle-class status by many upwardly mobile young men at mid-century.

7

The Politics of a Colonial Lawyer: Murdoch, Howe, and Responsible Government

Given Beamish Murdoch's intense interest in the welfare of his community, it is not surprising that early in life he set his sights on a seat in the House of Assembly. More surprising is that the freeholders of Halifax acceded to the twenty-five-year-old Murdoch's desires the first time he offered himself as a candidate, in the election of May 1826. That struggle had an air of David and Goliath about it, as Murdoch competed against two well-established incumbents, lawyer Charles Rufus Fairbanks and merchant John Albro. Faced with such opponents, Murdoch managed to transform his apparent disadvantages into positive attributes. To those humbler freeholders demanding more of a voice in provincial affairs, Murdoch's lack of influential connections bespoke an independence from elite control, which his role in the recent imbroglio at St Paul's seemed to confirm. His youth and idealism suggested that his mind would not be closed to change, though Murdoch did not explicitly present himself as a 'reform candidate'; such a label had little meaning until a decade later. Halifax was a two-member constituency, and when the polls closed, Fairbanks had 486 votes, Murdoch 391, and Albro 359. After this upset victory, the successful candidates were hoisted aloft by their supporters in chairs 'gaily and tastefully decorated by parti-coloured ribbons' and carried first to Fairbanks's residence, where he was set down. 'Mr. Murdoch was then carried through nearly the whole town, amid the huzzas and congratulations of a large proportion of the Inhabitants' – a heady beginning indeed to Murdoch's political career.[1]

This early success was not to be repeated. As noted in the previous chapter, Murdoch was ousted from his seat in the notorious Brandy Election of 1830 through the efforts of the mercantile elite whom he had offended. He was to be unsuccessful in the 1836 election and again in 1840, when he ran for a Halifax County seat. After 1835 he distanced himself from the nascent reform movement, of which his erstwhile friend Joseph Howe became the leader. He and Howe fought on opposite sides of the electoral fence in the 1836 election, and their relationship degenerated into rancorous epistolary battles carried on through the newspapers in the early 1840s. As Howe's star ascended, Murdoch's declined. The year 1843 marked the nadir of his political career. Although not a candidate in the election held that year, Murdoch took an active and vocal role in the public meetings at which the candidates presented their views.[2] After losing one of the Halifax seats to Conservative Andrew Mitchell Uniacke in that election, Reform supporters vented their wrath on Murdoch.[3] An effigy of him was paraded about the city before being publicly burnt – a painful counterpoint to Murdoch's triumphal progress through the streets of Halifax seventeen years before.[4] A study of Murdoch's descent from polestar to pariah provides an opportunity to reassess the debate over the shift to responsible government in British North America.[5]

If at one time a major theme in the study of the emergence of reform in the British North American colonies was the dominance of interests over ideas, such a description is no longer accurate after Jeffrey McNairn's masterful study of the political debates of the era as seen through Upper Canada's newspapers.[6] McNairn has argued convincingly that the spread of newspapers and the debate over political reform gave rise to a Habermasian public sphere in which government by the people as expressed through 'public opinion' supplanted the older idea of the mixed and balanced British constitution. McNairn takes seriously the ideas of both the reformers and the supporters of the status quo, arguing that their debate was lively, rich, and sophisticated; and that the decision of the authorities to abide by the results of the debate – rather than resort to state-sanctioned violence, which had been common in the 1820s and 1830s in Upper Canada – was highly significant for the future of parliamentary democracy in the colony and, by extension, elsewhere in British North America.[7]

This chapter will argue that Beamish Murdoch's role in the political debates of the 1830s and 1840s can be understood only in relation to his ideas about British and Nova Scotian constitutional law, which drew heavily on the Country tradition in British political thought. Murdoch's own self-interest had little effect on his political views. He could not expect much in the way of patronage from the Conservatives if they succeeded in stopping the movement for responsible government, while he stood possibly to gain some kind of office if the Reformers came to power. Reformers were puzzled by Murdoch's behaviour precisely because his public statements and political behaviour seemed to be at odds with his self-interest. If he had only continued loyal to Howe, he might well have secured a place on the Supreme Court in the 1850s. Instead, Murdoch remained for some time a steadfast exponent of traditional British ideas about the mixed and balanced constitution, and the necessity of independent thought and action rather than submission to party as the best way of serving the public good. He stood somewhat aloof from both the Conservative and the Reform groupings as they gradually coalesced in the 1840s, and in this he resembled some more familiar Upper Canadian figures such as Egerton Ryerson and, perhaps to a lesser extent, Allan MacNab, who proclaimed his independence from all parties in 1836. Rather than a conservative, we may perhaps label Murdoch a constitutionalist, someone who was opposed not to incremental changes in the constitution but to major alterations. By the 1860s, though, as we shall see, Murdoch had come to accept the new dispensation and, in effect, to admit that his worst fears had not been realized.

The Mixed and Balanced Constitution

Standard eighteenth-century ideas about the British constitution, familiar also in the pre-Revolutionary American colonies, were based on the classic tension between power and liberty and the necessity for political and constitutional theory to address this fundamental premise.[8] 'Power,' said aspiring assemblyman Jotham Blanchard to the electors in 1830, has 'a natural propensity ... to fortify and enlarge itself – and hence arises all kinds of encroachments.'[9] To prevent these possible encroachments, the British constitution had evolved a series of checks. The glory of the British constitution was that it was both *mixed* and *balanced*. It represented the three principal orders of society, monarch, aristocracy, and commonalty, in such a way ('mixed') as to create checks on the powers of each ('balanced'). The balance among the One, the Few, and the Many was crucial to ensure the optimal amount of liberty consistent with peace, order, and security of property. If any of the three orders engrossed more than its just share of power, disaster in the form of tyranny (royal excess), oligarchy (aristocratic excess), or anarchy (democratic excess) was sure to result.

Within this set of ideas, different emphases were possible. In eighteenth-century England, two schools of thought existed, generally referred to as Court and Country. Country ideology stressed the independence of members of Parliament and frowned on the acceptance by them of any office or emolument in the gift of the crown. Possessed of sufficient income from landed property to afford them the leisure needed to deliberate over national affairs, Country members were to keep an anxious watch on the measures proposed by the ministers of the crown, lest they trench on the liberties of the people. The Court party was more centralist, more supportive of the crown's efforts to manage Parliament in the interests of effective government, and less concerned about the effects of crown patronage. As the British state became ever more powerful during the eighteenth century, Country ideology declined in actual influence, but it retained a certain rhetorical vigour well into the nineteenth century. In the Thirteen Colonies it took on a new lease on life and is recognized as a principal strand in the ideological origins of the American Revolution.[10]

Constantly exposed to these ideas during his apprenticeship and through his reading, Murdoch expressed them in public fora using nautical and architectural metaphors. The rights of the people, he explained, 'were never safer than when the rights of the Crown, and of the aristocracy were also respected, – and produced a balance to the influence of the Commons. If all were reduced to the same body, the vessel of the State might get a ... lurch, as might a ship at sea.' In the same campaign speech, he noted that the 'strongest form of building was that of the pyramid, having a broad base, and narrowing as it increased in height.' Thus, the British constitution, 'consisting of a King or Queen, a House of Lords, and a Commons, gave an apt illustration in politics.' Lawyers, he thought, had a particular role to play in maintaining the constitution: 'they were not disposed to sacrifice the balance of power that their wise Saxon ancestors had established.'[11]

These constitutional nostrums were of course highly idealized representations of political practice in Britain itself. The checks and balances so important to constitutional theory hardly operated there, and if they had operated with their full rigour, it is difficult to see how government could have been carried on. The eighteenth-century political system functioned reasonably well in Britain because the ministers of

the crown were able to secure a parliamentary majority for their measures through the techniques of 'Old Corruption.' Rotten boroughs, the
vast patronage at the disposal of the crown, and outright bribery were
all means of ensuring the support of theoretically independent MPs.
Awareness of these practices in the old colonies caused a tide of indig-
nation that assisted in the delegitimation of British rule, as American
colonists feared that their governors were replicating corrupt British
practices in their own bailiwicks.[12]

In fact, colonial governors seldom posed a serious threat to the polity
on this side of the Atlantic. With few exceptions, neither in the Thirteen
Colonies before the Revolution nor in the loyal colonies thereafter did
the governors possess sufficient power or patronage to manage the assemblies through favouring loyal members. Ironically, the balance so
beloved of constitutional commentators was more present in America
than in Britain itself, with the result that governmental impasse was
often reached. The governors' power was essentially negative – that of
refusing assent to legislation passed by the popular branch. They had
no power to create and implement a governmental program, whether
for economic development, education, or any other end. In both the
old colonies and the new, the weakness rather than the strength of the
executive power would give rise to problems of effective governance.[13]

The American Revolution posed a major challenge to the concept of
the balanced constitution. After much soul-searching, the revolutionar-
ies had come to the conclusion that there was no social element in the
new states corresponding to the House of Lords. A new focus on popular sovereignty emerged to replace the concept of monarchical sovereignty, suggesting that all power flowed from a unitary people. This
approach created new difficulties with regard to the cardinal necessity
of checking excesses of power, but eventually the notion of separation
of powers came to play in the United States roughly the role that a separation of orders had played in British constitutional theory.

Neither those pressing for responsible government in the British
North American colonies nor their opponents were enamoured of the
politico-constitutional model presented by the republic to the south.
Both groups were committed to a monarchical society, and both felt
that the American constitution had become unbalanced and exces-
sively democratic. By 1825, all but three states recognized adult white
male suffrage, but British North Americans still insisted on a property
qualification, however small, as a prerequisite to political representation. Reformers and Conservatives both believed that property and

wealth deserved some form of political recognition, though they disagreed about the exact means of achieving that end. Neither group believed that the elective principle, and thus the popular element, should govern appointment to all important offices. After a brief flirtation with the concept of an elective legislative council in 1836, the reformers dropped the idea, which did not resurface until the 1850s (this time in the hands of the Conservatives). Nor were calls for an elected judiciary made, though occasional petitions for elected justices of the peace can be found.

If the reformers and their opponents were largely agreed on the role of the Many in the constitution, they disagreed over the roles of the One and the Few. Beamish Murdoch and others bitterly resisted the reformers' views on two major issues: that heads of government departments should sit in the Assembly, and that patronage should be dispensed according to the wishes of the party with a majority in the Assembly. Taken together, these practices would reduce the crown's role in the province to that of a spectre, and would concentrate power in the hands of a small executive accountable for its actions only once every four years. This was a truly alarming prospect for those steeped in traditional constitutional lore. 'If such a system were in vogue,' opined the editor of the *Times*, 'we ought to have annual parliaments – but even that would be an inefficient remedy for the corruptible practices that would be resorted to, in order to retain office and emolument.'[14]

For Murdoch, the retention by the governor of some scope for independent action was necessary to check the possibility of overreaching on the part of the Assembly, and the existence of some tension between crown and people was inevitable but healthy. It was understood that the governor was always to strive for harmonious relations with the Assembly, and would normally take into account its wishes in the distribution of patronage and the enactment of important measures. In general, thought Murdoch, the crown had exercised its power wisely in the province. The people of Nova Scotia had acquired 'by the concessions of the crown, a fair and legitimate share of power – commensurate at least with the progress of wealth and population,' and fortunately this had occurred 'without the convulsions which took place among our ancestors in Europe.'[15] They shared in the benefits of 1688 without having to depose a king. In the end, though, it was imperative for the governor to retain some independence, even if it were seldom exercised. What was required was 'a fair responsibility – that which shall not prejudice the Royal prerogative, nor give it dangerous privileges.'[16]

To the reformers' argument that they only wished to implement in Nova Scotia constitutional innovations already adopted in Britain, their opponents replied that whatever the effect of cabinet government in Britain, it was not suited to Nova Scotia. The colony had relatively limited resources and a small population, and the leadership class was correspondingly small. Responsibility on the Howe model would allow a small group to dominate provincial politics and, through its control of patronage, to entrench itself in power indefinitely. It was still necessary for the crown to exert some independent influence in provincial affairs in order to exercise a countervailing influence to the democratic branch and to assist in the preservation of the British connection, even if the crown was becoming a less active agent of the constitution in Britain itself since the passage of the first Reform Bill and the accession of Queen Victoria.[17]

The role of the Legislative Council was also conceived in terms of the mixed and balanced constitution. Lord Stanley stated as late as 1845 that the Legislative Council was supposed 'to arbitrate between the opposite tendencies of the Monarchical and the Democratic Branches of the Constitution, and when necessary, to control and harmonize both.'[18] The Legislative Council had been created in 1838, along with a separate Executive Council, out of the old Council of Twelve, which had come under increasing criticism for its combination of legislative, executive, and judicial roles. Its members comprised the principal officeholders of the colony, plus some of the most important merchants. Service on the council was unpaid; since its members held 'the best situations in the colony, and as the rank of counsellors gives them influence and precedency, and the title of honorable, it has not been found necessary to give pay for their legislative attendance.'[19] This description of the council quickly became out of date after 1830, when a dispatch from London ordained that neither salaried officials nor puisne judges were to be appointed in future; by 1840, the Legislative Council would be composed mainly of merchants.[20]

After Howe and his brethren abandoned their flirtation with an elective council, they did not propose any major change to the mandate of the Legislative Council. It would still serve as an upper house which could initiate legislation or, more usually, scrutinize, reject, or suggest amendments to bills passed by the Assembly. The change envisaged by the Reformers related to the appointment process. Although the council's members would continue to be appointed, it would be brought within the principle of responsibility because future appointments would be made by the governor only on the advice of the party with a majority in the Assembly. Over time a majority of the council would come from the same political party as that found in the Assembly, and they would work in harness. In essence, this change would render the Legislative Council an extension of the Assembly rather than an independent branch of the legislature.

Howe's opponents were disturbed by what they saw as the emasculation of the upper chamber. Under the responsible model, the Legislative Council could not operate as the constitutional equivalent of its ostensible icon, the House of Lords, which acted as the bulwark of wealth against potential radicalism in the Commons. The roles of the One and the Few would virtually disappear under the responsible dispensation, and all would be at the mercy of the Many. Yet it was not clear that the existing system was very satisfactory either. By the 1840s, even opponents of the responsible model agreed that there did 'not appear to be materials in the country to make [the Legislative Council] an independent branch of Legislature ... for many of its members are as unable to attend their duties without being paid as Members of Assembly.'[21] Without sufficient men of means and leisure, the Legislative Council could never truly replicate the House of Lords.

Faced with this difficulty, the opponents of responsibility first tried to articulate a defence of the propertied class and to place members in the Assembly who would uphold its legitimate interests. Later, in the 1850s, they advocated (albeit briefly) an elected Legislative Council. This second strategy need not concern us beyond noting that it was a logical response to the fear of turning legislative councillors into partisan placemen. If voters returned majorities of the same party to each body, the result might not be that different from the responsible system, but voters would not necessarily do so. The interaction of two elected bodies might well restore some of that balance of interests allegedly missing from the Howe constitutional model.

Beamish Murdoch was very much part of the first strategy. When he stood for a seat in the Assembly in 1836 and 1840, he emphasized that if the provincial economy were to flourish, the mercantile interest of Halifax would have to be well represented. Halifax produced nine-tenths of the provincial revenue, yet nine-tenths was expended in the rest of Nova Scotia. 'A large growing town like Halifax [needed] a larger share of the representation ... [and] the want of if caused the collision that now existed.'[22] For Murdoch, Halifax merchants were the engine of provincial prosperity, and Nova Scotia risked ignoring their interests at its peril. How, it might be asked, did Murdoch decide to speak for the mercantile section of the community when that very group had engineered his defeat in the election of 1830? A number of explanations have been suggested by historians, all of them relating to self-interest.[23] Another explanation is possible, given Murdoch's constitutional ideas. In order to explore this avenue, the circumstances surrounding his break with Howe in 1835 must be examined, and this in turn requires an understanding of the importance of 'independence' in Murdoch's political lexicon.

'Independence' and the Break with Howe

In March 1835 Joseph Howe was tried for seditious libel for publishing an article in his newspaper imputing corrupt behaviour to some of the magistrates of Halifax. When all the lawyers he consulted told him he had no case, he resolved to act on his own behalf and was acquitted.[24] Although Beamish Murdoch did not represent Howe formally, he acted informally on Howe's behalf at the trial. After Howe's rambling six-hour address to the jury, Chief Justice Halliburton wished to adjourn for the day. Murdoch remonstrated with him that this would seriously prejudice Howe, since he had abridged his defence in order that the matter could be dealt with in one day.[25] Later, when a group of expatriate Haligonians in New York wished to congratulate Howe on his victory by presenting him with a silver pitcher, Beamish Murdoch was chosen by them as one of the members of the presentation committee, a trust that he 'cheerfully accepted.'[26]

Yet, when one of the Halifax seats was vacated in 1835 after the promotion of Charles Rufus Fairbanks to the bench, leading to an autumn by-election, Murdoch declined to run. He refused even after Howe sought him out and declared that he (Murdoch) had a prior claim on the reformers to any other candidate, having suffered so much in 1830 in defence of popular rights.[27] After the 1836 election, 'the likes of which Nova Scotia had never before seen,' the advocates of reform 'had become a full-blown Reform party and Reformers almost overnight' and won a clear majority in the Assembly.[28] Had Murdoch presented himself as a candidate with Howe's blessing, he would very likely have found himself elected. Why did he not avail himself of this opportunity to stand for a cause with which he was apparently in such sympathy? Why did he oppose Reform on the hustings in the general elections of both 1836 and 1840? Answering these questions requires understanding how Murdoch conceived of the role of independent statesmen within the British constitution.

The concept of independence was 'central to English conceptions of manliness, political virtue and constitutional legitimacy by the mid-eighteenth century' and it was easily translated to the colonies; Phillip Buckner has remarked that 'the most popular word in the vocabulary of colonial legislators was the term "independent."'[29] Not only were members of Parliament ideally independent of the crown, but they were required to be independent of each other. Within this world view, any campaign aimed at creating a group who would collectively propose or defeat particular measures was considered illicit. Most of the nouns describing collective action had a pejorative connotation: faction, cabal, combination, conspiracy. For their part, independent members 'did not see themselves as the nucleus of an alternative government.'[30] Rather, they celebrated and defended their right and duty to scrutinize each legislative measure unencumbered by previous political commitments.

In the British North American colonies, this version of Country ideology remained the dominant conception of the assemblyman's role until the mid-1830s. A perusal of the notices of candidates and their nomination speeches in any Nova Scotia election before that of 1836 will show that candidates appealed primarily to their reputation for independence.[31] Even after Reform candidates began to make public their proposals for specific changes, Beamish Murdoch continued to rely on his 'past conduct in public and private [as] the best criterion of [his] principles.'[32] He insisted that his decision to come forward in 1836 was his own 'spontaneous act,' done 'without the knowledge or concurrence of any party in the town of Halifax.'[33] In 1840 he again relied primarily on his personal qualities, pointing out that he had 'no influence except any that his talents and character might have earned,' although he did put himself forward in a very general way as an advocate of proper representation for the mercantile class of Halifax. Even this step he justified in Country terms. The exclusion of the mercantile element from the Assembly was wrong because the 'principle of the British Constitution was not that any party should so triumph as to be the sole governors of the land. There ought to be a healthy opposition.' He did not mean by this an opposition *party*, but opposition 'directed against extravagance; because parties in power, whatever were the principles by which they obtained it, required controul.'[34]

Murdoch did not give any credit to the institutionalized opposition that emerged with party government. Where there were disagreements

about government policies, Murdoch believed that the best way to re-
solve them was through an ongoing and sustained dialogue. Once the
merits and demerits of particular measures had been fully aired, the
appropriate solution would reveal itself. Throughout the period of reform agitation, Murdoch continued to believe in a unitary public good
ascertainable through the exercise of reason. He disliked the American
system because politics functioned as a marketplace where narrow sec-
tional interests made deals and trade-offs that might work against the
public interest. Responsible government he opposed because, in his
view, it provided for no effective opposition or dialogue. Murdoch's
ideal government would have been a ministry of all the talents where
men of different views and backgrounds (not different parties) could
debate measures of public utility.[35]

Such an ideal was not unattainable. As the colonial office tried to ap-
pease the Reformers after their election victories in 1836 and 1840, it
first directed the division of the old Council into distinct executive and
legislative councils in 1838 and then directed the governor to choose
councillors reflecting both parties in the assembly. Lord Falkland did so
after his appointment as lieutenant governor in 1840 and his 'coalition'
ministry worked through a remarkable agenda of legislative reform between 1841 and 1843, when bills authorizing the incorporation of Halifax, the abolition of the Inferior Court of Common Pleas, a thorough
reform of the criminal law, and a more active system for the supervision
of education in the province were all passed.[36] Although Murdoch was
publicly critical of the partisan basis of this 'mongrel government,' it
nevertheless showed what could be done. Yet it soon became obvious
that the Reformers would not countenance the lieutenant governor's
power to control the make-up of the Executive Council, and further coa-
litions became a political impossibility.

It was Murdoch's intense opposition to party government, the corol-
lary of his commitment to the ideal of independent political representation, that prevented him from subscribing to the Reform cause. He
agreed with some of the changes sought by Howe but could never sacrifice his independence of judgment to join a party of whatever stripe, a
position he expressed using a mathematical analogy: 'Like the asymp-
totes of a parabola, in mathematics, however nearly at times they might
seem to approach, they [i.e., he and Howe] never could unite.'[37] If Murdoch eventually came to be labelled a Conservative, it was because provincial politics by the 1840s did not permit loose fish any more: if one
was not with Reform, one was against it, and therefore a Conservative.
In Murdoch's own mind, he was still independent, and those who had

asked him to come forward in 1840 stated 'that no political pledges were required' of him.[38] Murdoch's withdrawal from the formal arena of provincial politics after 1840 may be attributed to simple discouragement after a decade of rejection, but he may also have felt that he no longer had any useful role to play in the new era of party politics.[39] An observation by Blackstone's biographer, apropos of his subject's discomfort while serving in the House of Commons, might just as well apply to Murdoch: 'It cannot have added to his political appeal or effectiveness that this unclubbable man was so sensitive to apparent slights, while painfully anxious to preserve "independence" by steadfastly following his own convictions, whatever the views and interests of his friends and patrons.'[40]

Independence was always linked with manliness in Georgian and early Victorian political thought, and here Murdoch, a lifelong bachelor of less than robust health raised in an all-female household, was vulnerable to personal attacks that sought to undermine his political credibility. In 1842 Howe called him 'the pale student with the delicate frame of constitution.' Murdoch was 'feeble in body and mind – his stomach don't appear to digest what he has eaten, nor his brain what he has read, and he has lived so much among old women that he has become very much like an old woman himself.'[41] In responding to this insult, Murdoch sought to emphasize his respectability but only succeeded in further demonstrating the distance between his own habits and prevailing ideas of masculine bonhomie: 'Those who know anything of my habits and pursuits are aware that social boards and festive circles have taken up little of my time. I never dined at a public festival but once, and that was with the Irish Society in 1827 or 1828. I never dined at St. George's. And in private life, the position I have for many years held in the Halifax Temperance Society, evinces my disconnection with the pleasures of the table, as they are termed.'[42] The persona of the uxorious, outspoken, and physically vigorous Howe, who had taken on the Halifax establishment virtually single-handed and won in 1835, was particularly appealing at this mid-century moment of masculinist triumph, and Murdoch undoubtedly suffered by the comparison. Murdoch, too, had 'spoken truth to power' on a number of occasions, such as during the St Paul's controversy, the Brandy Election, the challenge via habeas corpus to Justice Fairbanks's imprisonment of a professional colleague, and the trial of Howe himself. But his claim to independence was undercut by his failure to conform to a certain template of masculinity and able-bodiedness.

A number of scholars have noted how the period leading up to responsible government was characterized by 'the rigidification of gender distinctions and the institutionalization of a near-monopoly, on the part of men, not only of political power but of other forms of power ... sanctioned by the state,' evident in the formal exclusion of women from the franchise, among other measures.[43] But this masculinization of the public sphere also had negative repercussions for some men – those who did not conform to a set of idealized male qualities – as well as for women. In addition, Murdoch espoused views that one might call proto-feminist. When discussing the franchise in his *Epitome of the Laws of Nova-Scotia*, for example, he noted that propertied women voted on occasion in Lower Canada (in fact, there were also some instances in Nova Scotia in 1793 and 1806), but expressed no principled view as to the appropriateness of female suffrage; he merely remarked that 'it has not been agitated [in Nova Scotia] whether females may vote or sit.'[44] The mere conjecture that women might actually sit in the Assembly marks Murdoch as someone rather out of step with the mid-century trend in this regard. For men belonging to the nascent reform movement, the possibility that women might 'vote or sit' was ludicrous, a mere legal loophole that had to be – and was – closed at the earliest possible opportunity.[45]

Murdoch's break with Howe and his failure to support what emerged as the Reform cause after 1835 have not been well received by posterity. These actions, it is said, betrayed his earlier commitment to the fearless defence of popular rights. This judgment is misconceived. As stated earlier, Murdoch was not diametrically opposed to all Reform ideas. He agreed with Howe on a number of issues, including the central tenet that a government that had lost the confidence of the House should resign. In the best Country tradition, Murdoch was opposed to the idea of a manifesto and to the necessity of deferring to a party leader in case of a difference of opinion. Murdoch summed up his views on Howe as follows: 'I will not pin my faith to his sleeve, I will exercise my own opinion.'[46] Where the two disagreed, it was because Murdoch remained true to his Country principles, not because he abandoned them.

There were several principal areas of friction between Howe and Murdoch. Murdoch genuinely feared the personality cult that mushroomed around Howe after the libel trial. He knew that someone with Howe's gifts for oratory and journalism could quickly attract considerable political support. On principle, Murdoch feared the creation of large political blocs, which he still viewed with eighteenth-century lenses. It also became apparent early on that Howe would attempt to mobilize these blocs and have them put forward candidates subscribing to their views. Through the summer and fall of 1835, Howe outlined his ideas for electoral reform in the pages of the *Novascotian*, which J.M. Beck has summarized as follows: 'Instead of letting half-a-dozen [elite] candidates ... throw themselves upon the constituency at the last moment, the freeholders should assemble well in advance of the elections, choose suitable candidates, and indicate to them that they had been chosen because of their principles and would be replaced if these were deserted.'[47]

Howe's views are so much in accord with modern views of how party candidates should be selected that it is difficult to appreciate how heretical they seemed to people, such as Murdoch, steeped in Country ideas about independence. When Howe approached Murdoch in the fall of 1835 about running in the by-election under his banner, Murdoch could not have acceded to such a request even if he had agreed completely with Howe's platform. Such a commitment would have been totally inconsistent with his views on the very nature of politics. Murdoch's refusal to pledge himself to particular causes can be seen again in the general election of 1836. The town meeting called to nominate candidates was the first to require pledges of candidates to support particular reforms if elected – in this case, abolition of judges' fees – and it resolved that 'those candidates who will not make these pledges ... shall not have the voice, interest and support, of this meeting.'[48] Aware no doubt of the way matters would unfold, Murdoch did not attend the meeting and simply issued his election card a week later.[49]

Murdoch did not turn against popular rights in 1836. Rather, he acted consistently with his views on the balanced constitution and the need for independent judgment. As Marie Peters observed some time ago, 'independence [was] the only behaviour truly consistent with the theory of the mixed balanced constitution.'[50] These views obliged Murdoch to exert himself against what he saw as threats to the constitution, whether they proceeded from the crown, the aristocratic interest, *or* the popular interest. As a member of the Assembly in the 1820s, Murdoch perceived the main threats to be to the popular interest, especially the attempt by the crown to recommence collection of the long-dormant quit-rents. During the 1830 election it was the pretensions of the upper branch that he opposed, and he drafted the resolutions critical of the Council which were adopted by the Assembly, bringing to a head the 'Brandy Dispute.' With the appearance of new notions of party government and popular responsibility in the mid-1830s, a different threat arose. Murdoch was alarmed by what he saw as an attempt to alter permanently the shape of the constitution by essentially dispensing with the crown and the upper branch as independent interests. Implementation of the full system of responsibility would not ultimately be in the popular interest, in Murdoch's view, because a small executive would be able to manipulate the Assembly and the people through its complete control over patronage. These anxieties, which formed an important strand of Country ideology and were shared by many throughout British North America, were not illegitimate and retain some currency today. Murdoch saw confirmation of his fears in the acceptance by Howe in 1841 of the office of speaker while remaining a member of the Executive Council. For Murdoch, these two offices were totally incompatible, the speaker being responsible to maintain the independence of the House while a member of cabinet was obliged to support governmental measures.[51] William Young and several other Reformers voted against Howe in the election for speaker for this reason, and even Howe's biographer is critical of his combining the two offices.[52]

Locating unchecked power in the Assembly also threatened the position of Halifax as the colony's economic engine, in Murdoch's view, and it was this possibility that compelled him to speak out on behalf of the capital's merchant class even though it had destroyed his political career. From his time as an assemblyman, Murdoch knew how jealously his fellow representatives from the countryside guarded the interests of their localities. Without the counterweight of an appointed Legislative Council with substantial representation from Halifax merchants, Murdoch feared that a majority of rural assemblyman could gang up on Halifax and either milk its revenues for their own purposes or prevent it from flourishing by promoting the interests of their own constituencies. Here, however, he was perhaps unaware of the extent to which the Halifax merchants exerted influence throughout the province through their business and family connections with local oligarchies.[53]

It was perhaps their differing conceptions of government office that most separated Howe and Murdoch. Murdoch accepted the traditional view of government office as a species of property, held normally for life unless gross corruption or startling incompetence could be proved. Such offices should be bestowed only on those who could demonstrate superior talents and education or long service and loyalty to their country. Country ideology demanded that office and government be kept separate, lest the former become the plaything of the latter. Officials typically hired deputies to perform the more routine aspects of their work and provided very little supervision or active direction. The main form of accountability for such officers was financial rather than political; they normally had to supply a bond or sureties for their good behaviour.

In fact, while the old regime was not entirely devoid of meritocratic tendencies, nepotism was pervasive and government offices were widely seen as being the preserve of a small and tightly interrelated official coterie. Trumpeting the call of 'careers open to talents,' Howe argued that the tenure of government officers had to be precarious. New administrations had to have the power to replace officials, and thereby open up the civil service to a wider range of applicants and provide rewards for political supporters. In addition, uniting office and government would provide better opportunities for checking and directing their activities. A sterling example of the need for better accountability was presented to the Reformers in 1845, when it was revealed that the provincial treasurer, Charles Hill Wallace, had been suspended from office as a result of suspected embezzlement. He was found to owe the province some £5,000.[54] It is not known how Murdoch responded to this incident, but it is likely that he would have argued for tightening existing modes of supervision rather than adopting Howe's conception of office. He might also have pointed out that Wallace or his sureties did make good the losses. With the benefit of hindsight, one may criticize both Murdoch's and Howe's positions. Murdoch was perhaps too ready to defend a nepotistic system with little room for newcomers, while Howe's embrace of 'careers open to talents' rapidly evolved into a spoils system that was soon perceived as neither efficient nor fair.

Another charge levelled at Murdoch by posterity is that he was just another of the lawyers who flirted with the cause of Reform only to scuttle back to the safety of conformity when opportunities for advancement appeared. With some justice, Simon Bradstreet Robie, S.G.W. Archibald, Alexander Stewart, and Thomas Chandler Haliburton have all been consigned to this category. If historians have been cynical about the gap between the professed independence of these men and their subsequent actions, it is a cynicism displayed by contemporaries. These examples present clear evidence that personal advancement was more important than ideas in explaining conduct in some cases – though it should be noted that even Country ideology did not prevent an 'independent' member from ultimately accepting a government post such as a judgeship as a reward for long public service. Robie and Archibald may be seen as belonging to this category, while Stewart and Haliburton may be more legitimately charged with paying mere lip service to the popular cause while remaining dyed-in-the-wool Tories.

The obvious contrast between Murdoch and these four men is that they all received lucrative judicial posts and he did not: three became masters of the rolls, while Haliburton inherited his father's place on the Inferior Court of Common Pleas and acceded to a Supreme Court judgeship when the lower court was abolished. They all benefited from the kind of 'connexional' patronage that was typical of the old regime, which nonetheless is generally conceded to have produced a judiciary of fairly high quality. Although QCs were rarely conferred before 1850, promotion to the bench tended to follow the English model whereby acknowledged leaders of the bar received promotion to the bench. All of that changed after responsible government, when the QC designation became widely available as a political reward and judicial posts were generally awarded based on partisan considerations. The link between professional reputation and promotion to the bench, so crucial in England, was broken in British North America, with long-term consequences for the quality and public perception of the Canadian bench. Murdoch thus refused to pledge his faith to Reform just at the time when it might have been able to reward him. As he himself said in 1842, comparing the loss of his seat in 1830 with his current situation, 'if I were actuated by low and grovelling ambition for place, I would have worshipped the Rising Sun and allied myself with Mr. Howe and his party as soon as they appeared [to be] getting into power.'[55] Murdoch's professed commitment to principle appears to be borne out by the facts.

In the late 1830s the ultimate success of a Reform party government was not totally assured, and as late as the end of 1843 Murdoch was predicting that 'the Party Government cannot stand.'[56] Possibly Murdoch calculated that his only chance for preferment lay with the Conservatives, whom he fully expected to triumph in the end. But this seems highly unlikely. As of 1835–6 Murdoch was associated with the defence of popular interests, and not with the official party. Even after the elections of 1836 and 1840, he was still seen as possible Reform material, illustrating both the nuanced nature of Murdoch's convictions and the somewhat inchoate nature of the emergent party groupings. After his 1840 defeat the *Acadian Recorder* was of the view that he would have been solicited again by Reform if he had not come forward in association with the Conservatives.[57] In 1843, after their extremely acrimonious public battles, Howe could still say that Murdoch had 'tried to make himself a tory ... [but] in this attempt he had not been successful yet.'[58] Murdoch had none of the connections of wealth or family that might have endeared him to the Conservatives, and he could not have expected much in the way of reward had he succeeded at the polls. When the Conservatives were in power under J.W. Johnston in 1843–8 and 1857–60, Murdoch received no offices or honours. It was the coalition ministry under Lord Falkland that saw him appointed to the newly created Central Board of Education in 1841, and it was the Howe government that finally conferred the honour of Queen's Counsel on Murdoch on May Day, 1863, just weeks before its crushing defeat at the polls. Not much is known about Murdoch's relations with the Conservatives in the 1850s, but it is possible that he became estranged even from them as they became a more disciplined political party on the Reform (now Liberal) model. If Murdoch ran more or less under the Conservative banner in 1840, it was only because they had not demanded any ironclad commitment from him, which allowed him to be true to his principles.

A final word may be said here about the nature of Murdoch's political views before proceeding to a critique of them. It may seem contradictory to characterize Murdoch as influenced by the Country strand in British political thought when it has been identified as the dominant element in the ideology of those supporting the American Revolution, which Murdoch most definitely did not support. This seeming contradiction can be reconciled by relying on a distinction pointed out by Michel Ducharme, between classical or republican liberty and modern liberty. The former was based on notions of popular sovereignty and political participation by a virtuous, frugal, and equal citizenry, while the latter understood liberty as exercised within a context of parliamentary supremacy, where individuals were free to accumulate wealth but might see their rights curbed in the public interest. The slogan of the former, 'liberty, equality and fraternity,' thus contrasted with that of the latter, 'life, liberty and property.' The American Revolution married Country ideology to republican liberty, while in Britain, Ducharme argues, both Court and Country – aside from a few radical figures – operated within the context of modern liberty and existing institutions; neither sought to replace the British state with one based on popular sovereignty. Murdoch's invocation of Country rhetoric, then, should be understood as relating to the British, non-revolutionary version of that set of ideas.[59]

Beamish Murdoch, Country Ideology, and Responsible Government

Murdoch based his political career on a principled defence of the old representative system, but it is legitimate to ask what relevance these principles had in the Nova Scotian environment of the 1830s and 1840s. Did Murdoch stubbornly adhere to views that no longer had anything to offer contemporaries in their search for more effective government?

In retrospect, Murdoch's concern over a lack of accountability, though valid in some respects, was too much focused on the formal mechanics of government and not enough on informal mechanisms. He thought that government by majority would mean government without an opposition, which he saw as the ultimate threat to liberty and property. In this his fears were those of the lawyer rather than the social scientist. The fact that a government has the power to pass a particular measure does not mean that it will necessarily do so in the face of strong public antipathy mobilized by a 'loyal opposition.' In spite of his own extensive involvement with journalism, Murdoch did not give enough credit to the power of public opinion as manifested through the press.

Nor did Murdoch have a satisfactory solution for the problems posed by the ancien régime's proprietorial concept of office, which raised issues of both accountability and access. The Charles Hill Wallace affair had shown that bonds and sureties were not effective tools for the ongoing supervision of government business. The old concept of office provided little opportunity for the active direction of incumbents. It was adequate for a slow-moving society where policy makers faced few challenges, but not for one where change was continuous. Here Murdoch's fears blinded him to the potential for positive change. With regard to access to office, it is unclear how he thought men of talent outside the official cliques could ever be appointed, given the relative paucity of offices and their tendency to heritability. In his *Epitome* Murdoch expressed the view that 'offices are held at the pleasure of the crown, or are otherwise regulated by acts of assembly, so that an office seems not to be a hereditament [i.e., not inheritable] in Nova Scotia,' but this formal statement of law ignored the frequent bestowal by government of a father's office on his son at the former's demise.[60] Ironically, it was only through the abolition of the proprietorial concept of the recorder's office that Murdoch was allowed to run for, and eventually win, it, as we will see in chapter 8. It may be, however, that Murdoch's de-politicized and non-partisan concept of office, ideally held during good behaviour, was more in line with the eventual emergence of a professional civil service than Howe's spoils system.[61]

Some of Murdoch's concerns were justified, especially his fears about unaccountability where a small executive commanding a majority in the legislature wielded power in a party system. Recent scholarship has noted that, while responsible government did provide a mechanism for the orderly transfer of power between groups with different visions of the public good, it provided few formal restraints on the successful party. Paul Romney concludes that responsible government gave Canadians the worst of both worlds, a political order lacking 'both British self-restraint and American institutional checks,' while Jeffrey McNairn laments the rise of the 'shadow' of responsible government over its 'substance.' [62] Indeed, over-concentration of power in the hands of the executive is still identified as a central problem with Canadian political structures today, even after the adoption of an entrenched Charter of Rights that imposes some restraints on government action. As an example of the legitimacy of Murdoch's concern, it is interesting to contrast the extraordinary public debt that the government of Nova Scotia was prepared to assume in the 1850s with the situation south of the border, where constitutional amendments in a number of states in the 1840s ordained strict limits on public borrowing. Under the old order in Nova Scotia, it is highly unlikely that the Assembly would have authorized borrowing on such a scale. Under party government, however, there was no real check once the proponents of a public railway gained the upper hand. The best example of this problem was the refusal of the government to call an election on the issue of Confederation in 1866–7, an election it well knew it would lose.

The example of the railway points out another problem with Murdoch's approach to politics in the rapidly changing environment at mid-century. Technological advances and political change within Britain meant that decisions about economic policy were more complex than in the past. Under the old model of politics, where every member might scrutinize government measures by his own criteria, the bias was towards inertia and stasis. The existence of vested interests meant that any new measures of economic development (favouring railways over canals, for example) were likely to be voted down. Such actions might protect 'liberty' in some abstract way but might also provide poor government. There was no easy resolution to the tension between providing effective and responsive government and ensuring that state power did not exceed its proper bounds. If the Reformers erred too much in the first direction, those of the Country persuasion arguably erred too much in the latter.

Murdoch was certainly aware of the tension between achieving effective government and respecting citizens' rights. In spite of his fears of an excessive concentration of state power, he was no apologist for minimalist government. He believed that government should actively seek to promote the advancement and welfare of its people through positive measures such as the extension of education, the provision of subsidies to the fishing and agricultural sectors in certain cases, and the support of a police force. Murdoch's *Epitome* is infused with the spirit of eighteenth-century paternal government and devotes several chapters to the contemporary equivalent of social-welfare law.[63] It is important to appreciate how Murdoch could reconcile his obsessive concern over the protection of civil and religious liberties with his views about the legitimacy and necessity of state intervention.

Murdoch's tenure on the Central Board of Education (1841–5) shows how he put these ideas into practice. This body, like the newly incorporated city of Halifax itself, was a product of Lord Falkland's coalition administration. It was created by statute in 1841 to supervise the commissioners appointed in each county to spend the money allotted to them under the 1832 Act for the Encouragement of Schools. The members, two Reformers, two Tories, and Murdoch, selected him as secretary, testimony to his continuing ability to mediate between the two groups. Murdoch quickly drafted a set of rules and regulations for the supervision of the county commissioners of education, and prepared the annual reports of the board, which were crammed with statistics and useful information. He clearly saw the diffusion of education as a valid state responsibility and a crucial pillar of societal improvement. When the act was allowed to expire in 1845, however, an early effort to develop educational policy came to nought, and no attempt would be made again for twenty years, until the reforms of the Charles Tupper administration.[64]

Murdoch's tenure as recorder of the city of Halifax is also notable in this context. During the 1850s the city moved ahead quickly with a broad program of civic amelioration, making it a quite different place at Confederation than it had been in the 1830s. City politics by the 1850s were carried on pursuant to a bipartisan model at odds with the partisan competition dominant in provincial politics. A kind of cooperative model of politics, distinct from both the status quo and the party-majority style offered by the Reformers, was thus possible at least at the

local level. While it is undeniable that Reform was attracting much electoral support in the 1840s, there was still considerable confusion about
and opposition to party government among the populace. A number
of candidates labelled themselves as independents in the elections of
1836 and 1840, wishing to affiliate with neither group. The fact that all
Reform's victories between 1848 and 1857 were fairly narrow also suggests that Nova Scotians were not overwhelming supporters of responsible government, at least in the short term.

The kind of partisan acrimony that accompanied the shift to responsible government directly contradicted earlier ideals of political harmony which encouraged the sublimation of differences in a spirit of
gentlemanly accord.[65] This desire for cooperation, which did not disappear, found other outlets for its expression, notably in the social sphere.
Two moments stand out in the 1840s, one at the beginning and one at
the end. In May 1840 the province enthusiastically feted the marriage
of Queen Victoria and Prince Albert, and in Halifax all the fraternal
societies organized balls, suppers, and processions to honour the event.
The Nova Scotia Philanthropic Society selected members Joseph Howe
and Beamish Murdoch to carry the banner of Acadia at the head of their
procession, a moment to which Murdoch later referred in a humorous
way in an attempt to defuse tensions that had arisen within the organization.[66] Nine years later, Halifax celebrated the centenary of its founding, and once again Joseph Howe and Beamish Murdoch were the two
principal public figures called upon to give meaning to this event. The
scholar Murdoch delivered a centenary oration on a historical theme
to the assembled crowd on 8 June 1849, while the populist Howe composed a widely distributed 'Song for the Centenary.'[67] The symbolism
of these two political opponents uniting in support of a broader pa-
triotic cause went against the philosophy of responsible government,
which stressed the right of winners at the polls to rule rather than cooperation with the losers. We may see in these events some longing
within civil society for cooperation by political opponents, which could
not be satisfied under existing arrangements. Indeed, one may wonder
whether the enormous popularity of voluntary societies in Halifax in
the 1840s represented in part a reaction against the rapid creation of
party blocs.[68]

Yet ultimately Murdoch came to accept and, reluctantly, even to approve of responsible government. By the time he sat down to write his
History of Nova-Scotia, or Acadie in the mid-1860s, he had been able to

observe the workings of the new political order for nearly two decades. He concluded that it had proved itself in practice:

We must not be surprised to find that, in representative governments, tumults, passion and party views occasionally disturb the working of the machinery – that popular excitements and restless demagogues sometimes induce doubts in the reflective mind of the real blessings of liberty; while on the other hand, influence, private ambition and pitiful subserviency may give to a country with a free constitution the aspect of servility, sycophancy and slavery. But all these oscillations proceed from the people themselves and not from any defect in the principles of free government. They are also short-lived evils, and rarely last long enough to inflict a permanent injury on the constitution.[69]

Gone is the language of the One, the Few, and the Many. The steady state of the balanced constitution has been replaced by a more turbulent polity which will experience 'oscillations': excesses of liberty and attempts to capture the state for private gain. Yet in the end these are only epiphenomena and do not indicate 'any defect in the principles of free government.' Here Murdoch expressed himself in a fashion remarkably similar to John Rolph, a Grit member of the Hincks-Morin government in Canada, who observed in 1853 that under the new constitution, popular excitement was the product of 'those commotions of the public mind springing from freedom itself; from the free and independent expression of opinion upon all great concerns of the country; [and] from the conflict of opposing views in the arena of free discussion.'[70] The steady-state Georgian constitution had indeed been replaced by a more responsive one, where the debate over what measures constituted the public good had been opened to a wider range of voices, carried on not just in legislative chambers but throughout the province via the medium of the provincial press.

8

Law and Politics in the Colonial City: Murdoch as Recorder of Halifax, 1850–60

The 1840s were a time of transition for Beamish Murdoch. His aspirations in the field of cultural and political leadership remained largely unfulfilled. The political terrain shifted in a direction Murdoch did not favour, frustrating his ambitions for provincial political office. Nor had his *Epitome of the Laws of Nova-Scotia* achieved the recognition he sought. As he contemplated the debts he had incurred on that score, he must have felt a pang at seeing John George Marshall's *Justice of the Peace, and County and Township Officer* published at provincial expense in 1837.[1] These setbacks led Murdoch to reorder his priorities: he devoted himself more to his law practice, which flourished, and to private study,[2] while channelling his leadership ambitions into the fields of educational and social reform. Murdoch served as commissioner and clerk of the Central Board of Education (1841–5), as we have seen, and also as president of the Halifax Temperance Society from 1837 to 1846. Under Murdoch's leadership, the society's activities were focused, as the city's historians have noted, on 'building a new civic order, one being weaned from strife and degradation by the power of moral persuasion.'[3]

From there it was but a small step to participating directly in the creation of a 'new civic order' by being part of city government, and by the late 1840s Murdoch had set his sights on becoming recorder of the city. The recorder, in effect the city solicitor, had to be a barrister of at least three years' standing (raised to five in 1851) and was responsi-

ble for drafting legislation and by-laws for the city, representing it in
litigation, and assisting the mayor and aldermen in the Mayor's Court
and Police Court. He also had to attend all council meetings, which
were normally held weekly. The salary was a respectable £200 – only
the mayor's at £250 and the city clerk's at £300 were higher – and both
the mayor and recorder had to be approved by the governor-in-council
in addition to securing election. As of 1848, the aldermen elected the
recorder on an annual basis.[4] The legislation did not specify that the
recorder had to devote himself exclusively to his labours for the city,
and Murdoch's account books indicate that he maintained his private
practice during his decade's service as recorder, mostly as a solicitor
but occasionally as a barrister.[5]

Incorporating the City

The incorporation of the city in 1841 had been an early victory of Howe's
reform movement, but by no means a resounding one. True, the appointed magistracy had been replaced by an elected mayor and council,
but a heavy property qualification restricted the franchise to the most
affluent 10 per cent of the population, and the council was composed of
six aldermen and twelve common councillors with differing property
qualifications, of whom only the aldermen were eligible to be selected
as mayor.[6] When the movement for responsible government achieved
success in the late 1840s, the impact on Halifax's municipal government was immediate and far-reaching. In 1848 the city's 1841 legislative charter was repealed and a new one proclaimed, but it was to be
in force for only a year. The 1849 act replacing it contained profound
changes. Where in 1848 the aldermen and mayor had to own property
worth £1,000 and own or lease a house worth at least £50 a year, in 1849
the distinction between aldermen and councillors was abolished and
the property qualification reduced to £500. Electors in 1848 had to be
assessed rates on £50 worth of property or pay rent of £5 pounds a year,
and could exercise their franchise only through open voting. In 1849 the
franchise was extended to include all adult males who were assessed
rates of any amount and had actually paid them in the previous year,
and the secret ballot was adopted – more than twenty years ahead of
the province itself, which authorized it only in 1870.[7]

Once the genie of responsible government was out of the bottle, it
continued to exercise a democratizing influence at the municipal level.
In 1850 the mayor was to be chosen by direct election – a first in Brit-

ish North America – and as a result no longer had to be approved by the governor-in-council.[8] The sovereignty of the urban electorate was thus recognized in form as well as substance. In 1854 the requirement that mayoral candidates had to have served at least one year as alderman was done away with and re-election of the mayor to a maximum of three years was permitted (though he could re-offer after sitting out for at least a year, as several mayors did in the nineteenth century).[9] The franchise was further extended in 1857 to include those who were not assessed rates but had paid the road tax of five shillings in the year preceding the election in question.[10]

A wider franchise and the secret ballot did not immediately attract more widespread participation by mechanics and the less well-off: voter turnout for the 1850 election was estimated at less than 25 per cent.[11] But the identity of the city's first directly elected mayor spoke of a fundamental shift from the rule of local notables to the self-made man. William Caldwell, well known for his role in the city's fire brigades, was a ship's blacksmith 'without the benefit of a liberal education,' as one newspaper delicately put it, who out-polled two prominent merchants for the post.[12] His obituary a few years later eulogized a man who 'by steady industry, unflinching integrity, and boundless benevolence, won his way to competence, without exciting the envy of his compeers,' and flags throughout the city flew at half-mast.[13] When his son Samuel, also a blacksmith, ran for mayor in 1859, he defeated a lawyer as well as a merchant in an election which saw much higher voter turnout than in previous years.[14] Although some were dismissive of his qualifications and class background, Caldwell had earned the right to welcome the Prince of Wales to Halifax when he arrived in July 1860.[15]

Changes in the office of recorder also provide a good illustration of the impact of responsible government in the municipal sphere. The 1841 act was influenced by the proprietorial notion of office, stating that once the first recorder was selected by the councillors, he was to hold office during good behaviour, initially for a period of five years. The first recorder was William Q. Sawers, a well-connected representative of the old regime and sworn enemy of the Reformers, who had just lost his job as a judge of the Inferior Court of Common Pleas when it was abolished in 1841.[16] The legislation abolishing the court provided him a pension of £300 but stated that it would cease if he accepted another office under government of equal or greater value.[17] As the recorder's salary was under £300, it did not trigger forfeiture of the pension, such

that Sawers was drawing a cool £500 from provincial and city taxpayers. In 1846 his tenure was extended by statute but in 1848, acting under
new statutory authority, City Council removed all municipal officers
from office as of 11 October and declared their posts 'open to competition.'[18] Incumbents had to apply in writing for their old positions by
the 16th and had no special advantage should other candidates apply.
Council would fill the positions for one year and from year to year
thereafter. Such were the winds of change sweeping the city in 1848
that a motion was made to dispense with the position of recorder for
the coming year, but it was lost by a vote of 15 to 3. George Blanchard,
a lawyer identified with the Reform cause, applied for the recordership
along with Sawers, and won it by a vote of 10 to 8.[19]

When Murdoch decided to vie for the post of recorder in 1849, he was
probably counting on benefiting from the high public profile he had established during the city's centenary celebrations in June. However, the
partisan rivalries unleashed in the struggle for responsible government
also manifested themselves at the municipal level. The city election in
the fall of 1849 was portrayed in the press as a struggle between Tories
and Reformers for control of City Council, with the Tories reportedly
disappointed when their expected sweep of council did not material-
ize.[20] Well-known Tory Henry Pryor was selected as mayor by council,
but Murdoch lost a three-way contest for the recordership to the incumbent Blanchard, with Sawers securing only one vote. Fortunately,
Murdoch did not let his disappointment prevent him from re-offering
in 1850. This year the atmosphere was entirely different: the partisan
spirit had waned noticeably and although Blanchard re-offered, Murdoch defeated him handily 12 to 4. In 1851 Blanchard applied but then
withdrew and Murdoch was re-elected (three aldermen voted against
him even though he was the only candidate). For the next eight years he
was unchallenged and unanimously elected by council each year, until
he resigned the position in May 1860.[21]

Of at least equal importance with this formal democratization of
civic governance was the growing practice of transparent and accountable civic administration. City Council debates and the city's annual
accounts were reported in the newspapers, and all business had to
be transacted in public: when the question was raised in 1855 as to
whether council could meet in camera, Murdoch's opinion as recorder
was in the negative.[22] Council even debated hiring a reporter to record
its debates but decided against it on the ground of economy: it was

the newspapers' job to hire reporters.[23] In 1858 Mayor Henry Pryor published the city government's first annual report, noting that he had been greatly assisted 'by the learned Recorder, whose long acquaintance with our municipal affairs has made him thoroughly conversant with most of its details.'[24] The next annual report was not issued until 1862, but the practice became the norm thereafter.

The ethical standards observed by the city administration are hard to judge. There were occasional complaints of vote buying, but at least there appear to have been no major scandals in city politics in the 1850s, unlike, for example, the 'ten-thousand-pound job' in Toronto where the mayor's pocketing of a large secret commission on railway debentures gave rise to debate and protracted litigation going all the way to the Privy Council.[25] That was at least partly due, however, to the fact that Halifax's less robust economy provided fewer opportunities for illicit gain than the rapidly growing capital of Canada West. The requirement that the mayor and aldermen function as a Police Court, discussed below, may have provided the opportunity for favouritism and low-level corruption. In 1860 Murdoch was asked to provide an opinion about the legality of aldermen releasing Police Court prisoners before the expiry of their sentences. The discussion on this occasion revealed that prisoners were in fact released early by certain aldermen for 'good behaviour,' while others strenuously opposed the practice.[26] The text of the opinion Murdoch rendered to council is not available but it is likely that he believed the practice illegal.[27] In general, the civic administration seems to have been carried on in the 1850s without startling corruption, and Murdoch's reputation as a pillar of integrity may have discouraged any tendencies to the unethical exploitation of civic office.

After the turbulence of 1848–9, the role of party politics in urban affairs declined but did not disappear. Unlike the 'spoils system' that was evolving in provincial politics, city officials tended to be re-elected to their positions by council each year whether a majority of aldermen were Conservative or Reform. Editorial opinion approved: 'We believe the deliberate judgment of three-fourths of our citizens is in favor of selecting the best men for Municipal honors without reference to class or party.'[28] Murdoch had seen his ideals of government by men rather than party shattered at the provincial level with the shift to responsible government, but they survived in municipal governance and provided a more congenial atmosphere for the exercise of his talents and his devotion to the culture of 'improvement.'

Drafting a City Charter

Unlike Saint John, New Brunswick, but like most other urban centres in British North America, Halifax did not have a royal charter but was a creature of provincial legislation.[29] The city of Halifax was a legal person, a corporation that depended on valid statutory authority for its every action, and the Act concerning the City of Halifax was its constitution. Where the magistrates had personified the town in an organic way appropriate to a more static society, the corporate city of Halifax was meant to shape the physical city, providing services of an extent and quality appropriate to a civilized urban polity, regulating in a direct and active way the lives of its citizens, and settling their everyday disputes. The city's constituent act had to provide an appropriate range of powers if these goals were to be achieved, and the city had to exercise effectively its own power to make by-laws if it were going to carry out its mandate. In addition, these laws had to be publicized adequately if they were to have any legitimacy.

To this end, Murdoch arranged in 1851 for the publication under his name of *The Charter and Ordinances of the City of Halifax, in the Province of Nova Scotia, with Provincial Acts concerning the City, Collated and Revised by Authority of the City Council*.[30] This publication united for the first time all the legislation dealing with the city, as well as the entire set of city by-laws, in one convenient volume. It was far from a mere compilation of existing laws. Murdoch redrafted the entire act and added to it chapters dealing with most matters which had been left to other legislation in the incorporation acts of 1841 and 1848. Only provisions relating to commissioners of streets, statute labour, and firewards remained in provincial legislation outside the new city act. The Act concerning the City of Halifax was passed by the legislature in March 1851 and repealed previous acts. The new act had eight chapters dealing with the structure of city government, assessments, the poor asylum, the bridewell, the common, the cemetery, the track of steamers in the harbour, and the licensing of auctioneers. In organization and style it was clearly influenced by the flirtation with codification which characterized both common law and civil law jurisdictions in mid-century North America, and represented a considerable improvement over traditional common law techniques of legislative drafting. The new act can be read from beginning to end in almost narrative fashion; each section flows logically into the next, forming a coherent whole.

In redrafting the city's constituent acts, Murdoch put into the practice the ideals of simplicity and elegance he had claimed for provincial law in his *Epitome of the Laws of Nova-Scotia*, condensing here and clarifying there. Take, for example, the following clause:

III. And be it enacted, That the Inhabitants of the said Town of Halifax, and their Successors, Inhabitants of the same, within the limits hereinafter mentioned, shall be, and they are hereby constituted a Body Corporate and Politic in fact and in name, by and under the name, style, and title of 'the City of Halifax,' and as such shall have perpetual succession and a Common Seal, with power to break, renew, change, and alter the same at pleasure, and shall be capable of suing and being sued, and of impleading and being impleaded, in all Courts of Law and Equity, and other places, in all manner of Actions, Causes, and matters whatsoever, and of accepting, taking, purchasing and holding Goods and Chattels, Lands and Tenements, Real and Personal, Moveable and Immoveable Estates; and of granting, selling, alienating, assigning, demising, and conveying the same, and of entering into and becoming a party to Contracts, and of granting and accepting any Bills, Bonds, Judgments, or other Instruments or Securities, for the payment or securing of the payment of any Money borrowed or lent, or for the performance or securing the performance of any other duty, matter or thing whatever; and to do and execute all acts, and possess and enjoy all powers and immunities incident to such a Corporation, or which may be for the benefit and advantage thereof, subject to the regulations and provisions hereinafter appointed.

This became, in Murdoch's streamlined version:

1. The inhabitants of the town and peninsula of Halifax are constituted a body politic and corporate, by the name of the City of Halifax.
2. They shall, as a Corporation, have perpetual succession, and a common seal, changeable at pleasure, shall be capable of suing and being sued in all courts of justice, and of acquiring, holding and conveying any description of property, real, personal, or mixt.

To take another example, the section of the 1841 act describing the qualifications of electors had run to forty-four closely set lines of type, while Murdoch's new section contained just two clear and succinct sentences.[31]

Murdoch also prepared two supplements to the 1851 volume, published in 1854 and 1856, which contained subsequent by-laws and later amendments to the incorporating act and other relevant provincial legislation.[32] No significant disputes seem to have arisen over the interpretation of the city's legislation or by-laws while Murdoch was recorder.[33] By contrast, Chief Justice Young characterized as 'confused and inconsistent' amending acts passed in 1861, 1862, and 1864, which were presumably drafted by Murdoch's successor, William Sutherland.[34]

Murdoch's preoccupation with simplicity and clarity was not just based on aesthetic grounds but also embodied a political ideal, one appropriate for a free and independent citizenry entitled to fully comprehensible laws. The four commissioners who produced the province's first statute revision in 1851 shared Murdoch's concerns; they criticized the prolixity and obscurity of previous provincial laws, and aimed at the same simplicity and clarity of expression which they found in recent statutory revisions in New York and Massachusetts. 'The language throughout is plain and intelligible,' they reported, and 'expressions of a doubtful meaning and of a technical character, not familiar to the whole people, are avoided, – and the result is, a body of law which any man of ordinary good sense can easily understand.'[35] The Revised Statutes of Nova Scotia of 1851 combine a structure of Augustan sobriety characteristic of the 1820s with the simple, direct, and economical language favoured by legislators after the achievement of responsible government. They have been described as 'an elegant and innovative work that made the whole of the public statute law accessible to all [, with] a modern, functional appearance and a clear, concise, and uniform style' – an accolade that might be shared by Murdoch's version of the Halifax charter.[36] Later revisions, unfortunately, did not maintain these high standards.

Financing the City

Incorporation of the city in 1841 had given rise to a more active urban administration, such that an editorialist could reflect in 1849 with some complacency upon what had been achieved: citizens owed 'a deep and lasting debt of gratitude to the members of the existing Council' for improvements in the streets, sewers, water, gas lighting, and policing.[37] Once the taste for more services and amenities had been acquired, it proved difficult to satisfy. In 1841 the city had been given power to raise £5,000 via assessment for ordinary purposes, with provision for an extra £2,000 on application to cabinet; but, as Henry Pryor remarked in 1858, by then £12,000 was as much required for ordinary purposes as £5,000 had been in 1841.[38] And that amount covered only recurring expenses such as the salaries of city officials and constables (aldermen were unpaid), the operation of city hall, and the provision of a few services such as gas lighting. Road maintenance and repair was taken care of by an additional assessment (£2,700 in 1857–8) and by the appropriation of the citizens' own efforts in the form of statute labour.

The city had been expressly forbidden from borrowing money in its 1841 charter, but in the 1850s it repeatedly requested and was granted legislative permission to borrow set amounts for specific purposes.[39] Thus, it borrowed money to build a new market, hospital, and prison, to improve the common, and to complete an accurate survey of city streets, while planning to take over the provision of water in the city by purchasing the assets of the Halifax Water Company; the sale, costing taxpayers some £52,000, was approved by council in January 1860. The city fathers could not be accused of favouring their own comfort, however. The civic administration continued to be carried on in the old courthouse building (dating from at least 1810), known as 'a circumscribed, uncomfortable, dirty hole.'[40] A new city hall would not be completed until 1890, a large, functional, and attractive Second Empire building that continues to play its historic role for the much larger and more complex Halifax Regional Municipality.

A more active urban government was bound to create situations causing harm to individuals; the limits of a municipal corporation's legal liability were thus a much-debated topic in the early Victorian world. Existing scholarship suggests that Anglo-American authority adopted a rule of immunity for negligent acts by the city or its agents unless liability was permitted by statute until some U.S. states began to be more receptive to municipal liability later in the nineteenth century, and that Nova Scotia by and large followed the earlier and more restrictive position.[41] This scholarship is based on reported cases and does not look at the actual practice of municipal corporations, which appears to have been more generous than the cases would lead one to expect. When merchant William Murdoch (no relation) sought compensation from the city for the allegedly negligent breaking of his shop windows by some of the firewards, Beamish Murdoch's advice was as follows:

The general principle makes corporate bodies responsible civilly in damages for the acts and neglect of their servants and agents done in the course of and within the scope of their authority in the same way and to the same extent that private persons are liable; applying this principle, I find the firewards etc. are appointed by the corporation from whom they receive their funds and that they form in effect a branch or department of it. Assuming then that the mischief was done to Messrs. Murdoch's property by an accident which with more care might have been averted I conceive the City liable to make it good.[42]

This is essentially the modern rule, and city records contain various examples where Murdoch advised council to pay for harm caused by the negligent acts of city employees.[43]

Murdoch's opinion may seem difficult to square with his views in other cases where individuals sued the city for property damage or physical injury suffered as a result of allegedly negligent repairs to streets. In these cases he said that the city would be liable only if there were an abuse of power (acting beyond its jurisdiction), a 'departure from common justice,' or gross negligence – a significantly higher burden for a plaintiff.[44] Here, however, there was a statute to be reckoned with, one that created the office of superintendent of streets and set out that official's powers and duties.[45] Murdoch (and Nova Scotia courts) regarded this statutory authority as recognizing, if not complete immunity, a less onerous standard of care upon such officials. It also appears that the independence of the superintendent of streets was such that his acts did not automatically engage the city's liability vicariously; Murdoch successfully defended a suit against the city for some actions of the superintendent by arguing in essence that the defendant should sue that official and not the city.[46] Reforms of the early 1860s rationalized this system and made the lines of accountability clearer.[47]

Regulating the City

City Council's devotion to 'improvement' did not limit itself to bricks and mortar issues. It was given the authority to pass by-laws for the 'good rule, peace, welfare, and government' of the city, and exercised the power expansively in the 1850s to deal with both the moral and material hazards of city life, as did cities across North America.[48] Respectable behaviour was encouraged through the prohibition of profane language and lewd or lascivious conduct on city streets and sidewalks, obstructing the free passage of sidewalks, and openly challenging people to fight. The city's ongoing struggle to contain the rowdy behaviour of its soldiers, sailors, and underclass, including a large prostitute population, is neatly limned in these ordinances.[49] The 1850s also saw restrictions on the liberties of animal owners: horses, cows, swine, and goats were not suffered to go at large in the streets as of 1853 while the keeping of swine within the heart of the city was forbidden altogether.[50] After the disastrous New Year's Day fire of 1857, City Council mandated the use of stone or brick in the construction of all new buildings above twenty-six feet; after yet another major fire in 1859, this was reduced to ten feet. All of these measures were of a piece with those collected in the first book of Murdoch's *Epitome*, entitled 'Of Government,' where he devoted chapters to laws connected with agriculture, trade, religion, morals, charity and education, and health and amusement.

Alongside their legislative and executive authority, the mayor and council also possessed judicial authority. The Mayor's Court created under the charter of 1841 and continued in the 1851 revision could hear civil cases to a maximum of £10 for debts and £5 for other matters (assaults, slander, and the like) and had the power to commit for debt. It comprised the mayor, an alderman, and the recorder, and sat on the second and fourth Tuesday of every month. It was basically a small-debts court, useful for the city itself to recover small amounts of taxes and licence fees owing, as well as for private individuals. These courts, based on English precedents, were a feature of the urban landscape in several British North American cities in the middle decades of the century.[51] They appear to have been popular and accessible: in 1852, for example, 1,304 actions were begun in the Mayor's Court, while, in 1857–8, 978 actions were commenced, 370 judgments were obtained to a total value of £1,171 and 66 debtors were imprisoned.[52]

In addition to this civil jurisdiction, the charter required that the mayor and aldermen (who were ex officio justices of the peace) take turns being available as a Police Court for minor offences every day between 10 a.m. and 3 p.m. except Sunday, replacing the former stipendiary police magistrate who was pensioned off. While the statute required only the mayor or one alderman to sit, in practice some combination of the mayor, an alderman, and the recorder was usually present.[53] The 1841 charter had allowed both civil and penal actions to be tried with a jury of three on request of the plaintiff or defendant, but this option was omitted from Murdoch's 1851 revision. The decade showed an enhanced attention to issues of public order, as the police establishment grew from three constables plus the night watch in the 1840s to twelve constables plus the watch by 1861, while the city also built a larger and more intimidating prison at Rockhead Farm in the north end.[54] The number of prosecutions before the Police Court also increased substantially, virtually doubling from 1,283 in 1857–8 to 2,435 in 1861–2; the amount of fines paid into the city treasury also doubled, from $1,052 in the former year to $2,191 in the latter.[55] Prosecutions for drunkenness nearly tripled during this period, from 458 to 1,282, reflecting the relative success of the temperance movement in imposing its moral vision on the city.[56]

The pressure of numbers, the lure of professionalization, and the need to create useful patronage appointments helped to undermine these courts. As early as 1857 the city planned to seek legislation authorizing the appointment of a stipendiary, legally trained magistrate to handle both civil and criminal matters.[57] Several more attempts would be made in the 1860s but the city and province remained at loggerheads over who would have the power of appointment.[58] The city argued, not unreasonably, that it should appoint the candidate, subject to provincial approval, if he were paid with city funds. The province refused to relent and in 1867 passed an act abolishing the Mayor's Court and vesting its jurisdiction in a stipendiary magistrate, to be a barrister of at least five years' standing. The first appointee was Henry Pryor, five-time mayor of the city and a long-time friend of the Conservative administration then in power.[59]

Defending the City

Much of the business that preoccupied the City Council and the recorder was of a routine nature. But on three occasions in the 1850s the city was forced to respond to significant threats: one economic, involving a provincial tax grab; one legal, relating to its authority over the common; and one physical, when the city-owned powder magazine blew up in August 1857, in what may be called the first Halifax Explosion. How the city dealt with these challenges tells us much about the nature of law and authority in mid-century British North America.

The first threat began with an 1854 statute providing for the construction of a provincial railway that would eventually connect Nova Scotia to the other parts of British North America. Initially the city was enthusiastic, believing that the railway would enable it to extend its commercial hegemony over a wider area. In 1851 council had even arranged for banners with slogans proclaiming the city's desire for a railway to be hung on the courthouse.[60] The city agreed to subscribe 100,000 pounds sterling worth of railway stock and to levy an assessment on its citizens to pay the interest on that sum.[61] When delays and cost overruns impeded progress on construction, council came to rue its earlier enthusiasm. By 1858, the railway had still reached only Truro and Windsor and plans for a continuation to New Brunswick and a branch to Pictou had been shelved indefinitely.

The city did not in fact levy the tax contemplated by the 1854 statute and in 1858 the province passed another law requiring it to do so, with provision for amercement (imposition of a fine) by the Supreme Court if it did not comply.[62] The mayor remonstrated with the Legislative Council before the law's passage, while afterwards Murdoch, at council's request, drafted a petition to the queen urging her to refuse assent to the act – all to no avail.[63] A year later the city had still taken no steps to comply with the act, leading Premier and Attorney General J.W. Johnston to write council a blistering letter demanding compliance. At first council was split, and a motion by the mayor to authorize the levy garnered some support, but in the end council kept up its resistance.[64] This it successfully maintained until the matter was finally resolved in the city's favour in 1866. When the Intercolonial Railway arrangements were renegotiated in the run-up to Confederation, Halifax's participation was no longer required; the city would be, in the proud words of Mayor Matthew Richey, 'forever relieved of the long-threatened imposition of the tax in aid of the provincial railways ... the non-attainment of which object formed the true and legitimate ground of our refusal to levy the assessment.'[65]

The second threat to the city's authority arose from a conflict with the military over the use of a portion of the common. Much of the north common was in 'a very rough and unimproved state, of little or no use for pasturage, and from its barren and rugged appearance ... a deformity to the city' until the city drained and improved it at considerable expense in the mid-1850s.[66] No sooner had it done so than the garrison claimed rights to drill troops over most of the area pursuant to an agreement allegedly authorized by the town magistrates in 1800. This erupted into a major controversy in 1859, at which point the city asked Murdoch to prepare a report. He concluded that the town magistrates had had the authority only to regulate and not alienate parts of the common, and that the alleged agreement was ultra vires. Subsequent statutes had authorized the erection of fences on the common by the city under certain circumstances, although Murdoch conceded that this power had been omitted through (his own) oversight in the 1851 redrafting of the city charter. A second opinion solicited from William Young was to the same effect. He advised either an address to the queen or a trespass action or both, and suggested that council erect a symbolic fence on the disputed area and invite the military to pull it down in order to crystallize the issue. The military duly complied and Murdoch then prepared the petition to the queen, of which 500 copies were printed. The language of the petition reflects the intimate connection with the monarch that many still assumed to exist, and also shows that Murdoch was not above a little flattery in order to hold her attention. The petitioners expected 'that colonists here will receive from your majesty a measure of justice and protection, not inferior to that enjoyed by those who live in the more immediate proximity of the throne. On this occasion they cannot omit to mention that the warm interest in the welfare of Halifax and of Nova-Scotia, evinced by your illustrious father while resident here, is among the facts of our civic history, best remembered at our firesides and most deeply appreciated in our hearts.'[67] In spite of this attempt to shore up support from the citizenry, public opinion did not seem as outraged by the military's action as council was. The newspapers found the conflict unseemly and urged the parties to settle, and the first jury trial in the city's trespass action resulted in an equal division and dismissal of the case. The city could have sought a new trial but in view of tepid public support decided to pursue a negotiated settlement. The military gave up its claims to part of the common while having its drilling rights recognized over the remainder without prejudice to public rights of pasturage and access.[68]

The third challenge faced by the city during the 1850s was the explosion at the city-owned powder magazine. In the days before dynamite was available, gunpowder was a widely used explosive. Unlike dynamite, it had to be used in large quantities and was highly flammable, leading to the creation of public facilities for its storage and distribution. In Halifax the magazine was built in the far north end of the city, close to the harbour. When it exploded in the early hours of 14 August 1857, the blast killed at least one person, seriously injured several others, and destroyed a large amount of property. Only quick fire-fighting action prevented the military and naval magazines, a mere fifty yards distant, from also igniting.

It was believed from the outset that the explosion was 'the willful and malicious act of some person or persons unknown,' owing to the discovery nearby of a stone coated in powder with a candle wick attached. The provincial government and the city each issued a proclamation offering a reward of £500 for information leading to the identification of the culprit. The very day of the tragedy, City Council struck a committee of three aldermen to inquire into the circumstances and requested the recorder to be present at all its meetings. After interviewing thirty-one witnesses over six days, the committee reported to the public that the blast was indeed the work of an unknown perpetrator, and that the keeper of the magazine was not at fault. It recommended that City Council alleviate the distress of several poor families living nearby who had lost everything.[69] One thousand copies of the report were printed but the perpetrator was never officially identified. Some merchants whose powder was lost sued the city and lost, but others who were able to show that powder of theirs was removed without a proper signed order were reimbursed £150 by the city; the city in turn held the keeper and his sureties liable for this sum.[70]

In spite of the official silence, suspicion fell heavily on the last person to have taken a load of powder from the magazine, a day and a half before it exploded. This was Alexander 'Sandy' Keith, nephew of Halifax's now iconic brewer who had been mayor of the city in 1852–3. Sandy Keith was a businessman who would be involved in blockade-running and other dubious activities during the American Civil War, and a swindler who was obliged to exit the city in 1864 when some of his victims threatened to catch up with him. The truth about his connection to the magazine explosion came out only decades later in the course of an in-depth investigation by the Pinkerton's detective agency into a much greater tragedy: the Bremerhaven disaster of 1875, in which eighty-one people were killed by the premature detonation of a hidden dynamite bomb as it was being loaded on to a ship in the German port. The goal of the bomber, who turned out to be Sandy Keith, had been for the device to go off at sea, destroying the ship and allowing him to collect certain insurance monies. A 'prominent Halifax banker' told a Pinkerton's agent that Keith had also engineered the 1857 explosion in order to cover up his involvement in a fraudulent scheme regarding the sale of gunpowder from the magazine.[71] Indeed, Keith's testimony to the committee of aldermen should have aroused suspicion. He tried to suggest that the explosion was accidental, a result of the keeper's failure to maintain the magazine in a proper state, while several other witnesses denied that there was anything untoward about its condition.

The amateurish and somewhat laconic response by the city and province to this disaster may seem surprising, but it must be recalled that police investigative techniques were still in their infancy; Halifax's constables were in no way equipped or expected to undertake such activities. Pinkerton's detective agency was established only in the early 1850s and its early clients were mainly private companies rather than governments. Its first Canadian business appears to have arisen in 1866, when the attorney general of Canada West, John A. Macdonald, consulted the agency in connection with the Fenian raids.[72] But even granted the limitations of forensic techniques, one cannot escape the impression that Haligonians did not really want to know the truth. The newspapers did not pay much attention to the affair after the initial shock was over, and denied that Keith could be the Bremerhaven bomber when that allegation surfaced years later.[73] Once City Council had pointed to intentional human agency as the cause of the explosion, it could do no more, but there was a lack of political will at the provincial level to bring the culprit to justice. Alexander Keith, Sr was identified with the Conservatives, who were in power in 1857, but the impulse to turn a blind eye to Sandy Keith's possible involvement went beyond partisan loyalties and arguably represented a kind of collective denial that a member of the local elite could be responsible for such a reprehensible act. Halifax breathed a sigh of relief that the city had escaped more extensive destruction, and moved on.

Halifax city government in the 1850s provides an interesting and somewhat neglected lens through which to observe the logic of responsible government working itself through the polity. With the extension of the franchise, direct mayoral election, the secret ballot, and annual elections, the city could claim to be the most democratic and accountable level of government. It rapidly embraced popular sovereignty as the touchstone of legitimacy but without adopting the political-party model that was emerging in provincial politics. This is not to say that City Council was a paragon of harmony and cooperation, but it did manage to move ahead with an impressive agenda of new physical infrastructure and amenities while dealing with a variety of external threats and problems. In all of this, law was crucial in defining and structuring the relations of authority, in providing legitimacy to municipal action, and in providing a focus and vocabulary for resistance to unpopular measures from other bodies which had an impact on city life.

Responsible government altered the relationship between the city, the province, and even the imperial government in unforeseen ways. On paper the plenary power of the House of Assembly was sufficient to make the city bend to its will. But the very success of a more democratic and responsive civic administration meant that it could resist with impunity provincial attempts to impose a railway tax. The city also tried to do an end run around the province on at least two occasions by appealing to the queen not to approve provincial legislation, while also appealing to her to rein in her military establishment. It must have seemed strange to officials in London that, after years of colonial requests for the imperial government to stay out of local affairs, it was now being asked by one colonial political body to intervene against another in the same colony. It is not clear whether Murdoch or the City Council believed that the imperial government would take any interest in their petitions, or whether they engaged in them mostly for public- relations purposes. It may be significant that, in the course of the dispute over the use of the common, the city quickly backed down when it discerned a lack of public support for a more aggressive stance against the military. The appeal to the throne could also provide a thin but useful legal figleaf to cover what would otherwise have been naked – revolutionary? – resistance to a law perceived to be unjust, as in the case of the railway tax. On another level, the process is significant for what it reveals about the independent role – the standing, as it were – that emerging colonial cities saw themselves as possessing within the Empire.

Resignation

In the spring of 1860 Murdoch was half-way through his tenth year as recorder. Whether he was planning to offer again in the fall will never be known, because an unfortunate series of events led to his premature resignation on 11 May. There had been some bad blood between alderman William Evans (or Evens) and his fellow aldermen during his first term in office (1853–5), when council was on the verge of censuring him for some untoward behaviour during a meeting.[74] Outspoken and insensitive, Evans also had an annoying habit of constantly asking for reconsideration of motions which had passed over his objections, a tactic seldom used by other aldermen. Once again elected to council in the fall of 1859, Evans was soon up to his old tricks. In February 1860, after making allegations of forgery against the city clerk and some councillors that were found to be groundless, Evans was censured by council – the first time it had ever taken such action. Next it was his turn to run athwart Murdoch, who unwisely responded to some provocative accusations, the nature of which remains obscure, made by Evans and alderman John Nash. Murdoch seems to have accused the two aldermen of lying, a charge that council could not allow to pass unnoticed. When council censured him, the recorder tendered his resignation in spite of a conciliatory amendment to the motion of censure – voted against by both Evans and Nash – 'recognizing the extreme provocation under which he spoke.'[75] Murdoch's punctilious sense of honour would have afforded him no other option.

In spite of the abrupt ending to his career as recorder, Murdoch could look back with some satisfaction on his decade in the office, which had allowed him to indulge his passion for improvement and his need to demonstrate independence. His compilation and redrafting of the city's constituent legislation and ordinances was an important landmark in its evolution as a legal and governmental entity exercising its powers in a transparent fashion in the public interest. With the recorder's aid and guidance, the city became a more active body, providing ever more services and amenities with the goal of making it a safer, healthier, and more pleasant place to live, even as it adopted in some respects a more repressive stance vis-à-vis its underclass. Murdoch's position on municipal liability tried to strike a just balance between protecting city taxpayers from excessive claims and recognizing that at least abusive or startlingly negligent action by city employees should give rise to compensation. He tried to use the weapons at his disposal, including litigation and royal petitions, to defend the city from provincial and imperial depredations that he and council considered unwarranted; but his success here was mixed, with the exception of the railway-tax controversy, where the best weapon proved to be continued intransigence.

9

Law, Identity, and Improvement: Murdoch as Cultural Producer

We have seen that the reading of aspirant lawyers was not confined to the narrow realm of black-letter law and private dispute resolution. Rather, lawyers were expected to be familiar with social and political organization in historical and comparative context and to have some acquaintance with English and classical literature. As part of the British diaspora, they were also inheritors of a tradition that explicitly linked 'the rights of Englishmen' and the common law to British exceptionalism and imperial success.[1] Connections between law, culture, and national identity came easily to the lawyers of nineteenth-century British North America.

It is not surprising, then, that in addition to writing treatises and pamphlets destined primarily for their legal peers, lawyers took it upon themselves to make cultural contributions aimed at a broader audience. Through these works they sought to provide shape and guidance to their young societies in the form of history, journalism, and belles-lettres, but some went beyond these standard forms to become early folklorists and anthropologists. The latter interests were a natural outgrowth of lawyers' interests in custom and social ordering and were often stimulated by contact with the First Nations. Examples of lawyer-authors can be found throughout British North America but this chapter will focus on Murdoch's cultural production, using Thomas Chandler Haliburton and Joseph Howe as foils to highlight the specificity of his contributions.

By the 1820s, after nearly seven decades of almost constant war, Nova Scotia found itself at peace. The Pax Britannica provided some space for introspection and reflection, and three writers in particular, lawyers Beamish Murdoch and Thomas Chandler Haliburton and non-lawyer Joseph Howe, devoted sustained attention to the question of Nova Scotian identity during this period. They did so for three different reasons: Murdoch to celebrate and conserve Nova Scotia's past, Haliburton to deplore the colony's present, and Howe to predict its future. This chapter will explore Murdoch's substantial cultural output with principal reference to his early literary efforts, which culminated in his editorship of British North America's first literary periodical, the *Acadian Magazine* (1826–8), and to his *Epitome of the Laws of Nova-Scotia* (1832–3). Another work, Murdoch's *History of Nova-Scotia, or Acadie* (1865–7), has been studied by many scholars, and it will be analysed briefly and selectively here for its contribution to the 'identity' question and for what it reveals about Murdoch's anthropological interests. In addition to these better-known works, Murdoch's writing ranges over virtually every literary form except the novel and short story, including poetry, ballads, literary editing, law-reform pamphlets, essays, newspaper journalism, legislation, and unpublished Mi'kmaq-English and Gaelic-English dictionaries. His library included works in French, Italian, Spanish, Latin, Greek, and German, and in subject matter ranged far beyond law, literature, and the classics. Awareness of the full breadth of Murdoch's work and interests is necessary to appreciate his roles both as cultural producer and as lawyer-scholar.[2]

Existing scholarship treats the literary efforts of Haliburton, Murdoch, and Howe under the rubric of the 'intellectual awakening of Nova Scotia,' which is said to have characterized the years between 1815 and responsible government.[3] Setting their oeuvre in the context of recent work on the evolution of nationalism, in which the idea of nations as 'imagined communities' has been explored, allows a somewhat different approach to this literature. It is widely accepted that the concept of national identity has been actively and selectively constituted by authors and promoters who purport only to discover and expose pre-existing traits of their particular national group.[4] In New World societies, the definition of 'national' identity was a particularly pressing and delicate issue because of the high degree of religious and ethnic heterogeneity.[5] J.M. Bumsted has stated that the Maritimes in the early nineteenth century were societies of 'almost unimaginable cultural diversity.'[6] Acadian, Mi'kmaq, African, and Gael shared the terrain of

Nova Scotia with New England Planters and with people of Germanic, English, and Anglo-Irish origin. Anglicans, dissenters, and Catholics jostled each other. How was the colony to rise above its situation as a congeries of isolated and particularistic settlements? An identity would have to be invented, shared values and common ties would have to be stressed. The English language, the domesticated common law, and a shared history and territory would be the three principal means by which Murdoch sought to create a Nova Scotian identity. This chapter is thus divided into three parts, the first dealing with Murdoch's early literary efforts, the second with his principal legal work, the *Epitome of the Laws of Nova-Scotia*, and the third with his *History of Nova-Scotia, or Acadie*.

A Provincial Creole Printman

Although today the word 'creole' is used to denote a person or language of mixed racial origins, in its original meaning it signified a 'person of (at least theoretically) pure European descent but born in the Americas.'[7] Thus, Benedict Anderson can identify Benjamin Franklin as a 'creole nationalist.' In explaining the evolution of nationalism in the New World, Anderson points to the role of the newspaper as central in defining the perimeters of a particular imagined community. Thus, while acknowledging the key roles played by economic factors, liberalism, and the Enlightenment in stimulating New World nationalism, he concludes that the 'provincial creole printmen played the decisive historic role' in shaping each nation's idea of itself.[8] Beamish Murdoch and Joseph Howe are both good examples of this phenomenon.

Even as a young man, Murdoch was fully aware of the power of print. Writing to the *Acadian Recorder* as 'Brutus' in 1820, he marvelled that 'I can [from the extensive circulation of this paper] enter into the closet of every man in the province, tell him his failings with the confidence of a friend, reward his good conduct with unbought praise, and excite him to deeds of virtue by pointing out their advantages.'[9] The hortatory tone is striking. The young would-be lawyer spoke as a kind of secular priest, using the newspaper as a pulpit, from which platform he sought to act as an arbiter of taste and behaviour. A past indifference to literary achievement in the province was, in Murdoch's opinion, 'rapidly disappearing ... in a great measure through the medium of newspapers, the talents for composition in which would not disgrace any country.'

From the beginning, Murdoch's message was that the New World in general, and Nova Scotia in particular, was different from the Old. Some of these differences were salutary. The pursuit of freedom and wealth in North America allowed its people to 'surmount those obstacles to ... civil union that exist in differences of language, country and religion.' Emigrants from Europe, he observed optimistically, left 'all national jealousies to sink in the Atlantic' during their voyage. Other features of the New World were more problematic and prevented the kind of cultural flowering that Murdoch advocated. One was simply the less developed state of society in the province, compared to the 'endless diversity of occupations' in Britain. In Nova Scotia there were fewer role models, and 'from a want of competition the thirst for knowledge is slaked.' Another obstacle was the insidious 'maxim that money is the summit of felicity.' Even when the immigrant generation had achieved economic security, its members often restricted the education of their sons to 'writing, reading and arithmetic, because every other science is trifling when compared with the Science of multiplying Dollars.' In colonial societies this tendency was reinforced by 'numberless instances of men of genius rising to the highest offices and obtaining a universal applause without much aid from education.'

If education was conceded to be a poor investment in a young society, then what exactly *was* Murdoch's point in prodding his compatriots to respect learning and contribute to the production of a provincial literature? His goals were twofold. First, learning and literature were essential to humanity's moral progress. If one possessed literary talent, one had a duty to society to express it, but people needed to be constantly encouraged to do so: 'Man is so far from enquiring what his duty is that he requires to be incessantly reminded of the most important obligations. The duty of self improvement can never be well understood without indefatigable research and unwearied attention and we pursue it not in proportion to the benefits we might derive from it but in proportion to the stimuli (spurs as they are emphatically named) that excite our energy and activity.' With the aid of modern techniques of publishing and distribution, Nova Scotians could participate in the worldwide march of civilization as easily as anyone else.

Murdoch's second goal was more precise. A provincial literature was necessary to create a Nova Scotian identity. It was Murdoch's fondest hope that one day Nova Scotia might be 'classed among those countries that have reared and produced the benefactors of the human race.' To do so, it would first have to generate a sense of itself, which was best done through the process of literary production. At the age of twenty, Murdoch had thus already formulated his role in provincial society: a spur to cultural excellence, a goad to his fellow citizens to be aware of their talents and of their duty to exploit them. For the next dozen years, he pursued this role with 'unwearied attention.'[10]

These goals animated 'The Literary Forum' (also known to contemporaries as a debating society) which appeared in 1820 in Halifax. Its members were fourteen young men, including Murdoch, all but one of them with links to the law. Their constitution stated that the club aimed at the 'improvement of its Members in general Knowledge and in the art of speaking' through weekly discussions of 'History, Morals, the comparative merit of eminent men, and occasionally points of mere speculation and Law.' It was hoped by its founders that these activities would 'sharpen the intellects and create the habit of classifying the ideas and of accurate thinking.'[11] These goals seem entirely innocuous to modern eyes. Yet the literary/debating club was the subject of much criticism by the older generation, including the parents of some prospective members. Judge Brenton Halliburton refused to serve as patron to the Literary Forum, and S.G.W. Archibald and other prominent citizens were averse to it. Their objections reveal the extent to which conformity of opinion was believed to be necessary for social cohesion by Halifax's conservative elders. They also betray a fear that such groups might provide an undeserved platform for men of the 'wrong' social origins. 'Tullus Hostilius' thundered in the pages of the *Acadian Recorder* that a debating society would 'throw open the door to every flippant cox-combical blockhead to self-constitute himself a second Cicero or Demosthenes,' and that the proponents might better spend their time in more serious pursuits.[12] Even though politics and religion were to be prohibited as topics of discussion, the worthy patriarchs of Halifax were apprehensive of 'anything that may have but the appearance of an opening to the propagation of sentiments opposed to morality or religion and consequently to the peace and happiness of society.'[13] The older generation of notables considered that any discussion of the nature of provincial society might undermine their own role at its apex. The Literary Forum was stillborn.

It was the misfortune of the club's promoters to commence their endeavours at the very time when their contemporary William Wilkie caused 'a tempest in the Halifax teacup' with the publication of *A Letter to the People of Halifax*. This 'incendiary pamphlet' contained stinging critiques of virtually every court and legal official in the province except the lieutenant governor, and merited its author a trial for seditious libel at Easter term 1820. Wilkie was convicted and sentenced to 'Two Years' Imprisonment in the House of Correction ... at hard labor,' but his sentence appears to have been commuted, provided he agreed to leave the province. It is no surprise that the same official clique who sought to purge the body politic of the malcontent Wilkie would view a debating society as the thin edge of a dissentient wedge which could not be tolerated.[14]

One should not, however, make too much of this episode. The fiasco of the Literary Forum illustrated that dependence on the patronage of community notables might frustrate the goals of its members, but a number of them circumvented the disapproval of their elders through direct involvement in journalism. George Renny Young founded the *Novascotian* in 1824 and three years later sold 'the best all-round paper in the province' to Joseph Howe in order to prepare for the legal profession.[15] Murdoch, too, became actively involved in journalism, assisting Philip J. Holland with editorial work at the *Acadian Recorder*.[16] The acquittal of Howe after his libel trial fifteen years after the folding of the Literary Forum indicated that there was an appetite for free speech that could not be staunched by authorities anxious to preserve the status quo.

In 1825 a local disaster provided Murdoch with another occasion to explore the question of local identity. He combined his interests in journalism, history, and poetry in a forty-eight-page pamphlet entitled *A Narrative of the Late Fires at Miramichi, New-Brunswick* ..., published by P.J. Holland in December of that year. The extensive forest fire ravaged the Miramichi valley in early October, left hundreds dead, and caused enormous damage. Murdoch's immediate goal in composing this pamphlet was to provide a poignant account of the tragedy which would inspire readers to contribute to relief efforts. Much of the pamphlet is taken up with an account of the philanthropic response to the event in British North America and New England, alongside a description of 'Remarkable Instances of Suffering.' Murdoch the historian was already at work, however, as he contextualized his story with some description of the history and topography of Northumberland County. Much of the writing, like his *History of Nova-Scotia, or Acadie* forty years later, consists of extracts from original sources (primarily newspapers) spliced with bits of narrative.

Appended to this account of the fire is a two-page poem entitled 'The Conflagration' in which Murdoch meditated on the larger meaning of the disaster. He did not interpret it as evidence of God's displeasure, as a Puritan divine of the previous century might have done, nor as a random act of nature. Rather, the fire is part of God's plan for the universe, foreshadowing the final apocalypse of the End of Days. It is God's way of reminding His people of His awesome power and of the purpose of human existence. In his narrative of the event, Murdoch noted at one point that some survivors thought the Last Day had indeed come, a theme that recurs in the poem:

> The trembling earth appears
> To shake from pole to pole
> As when the trump shall call
> To its last dawn, each soul.

At a more prosaic level, the poem is also about the meaning of community and the need for mutual aid:

> Thro all Columbia speeds the tale
> And showing tears all eyes overflow
> 'Quick man the bark and spread the sail,
> And bear relief to soothe their woe.'

There follow several stanzas describing the response to the disaster in Quebec, Upper Canada, Boston, New York, and the other Maritime provinces, thus affirming the importance of the human bonds that defy geography in this vast portion of the continent.

The significance of this poem lies not in its purely literary value, which is unremarkable, but in Murdoch's attempt to invest a local event with transcendent meaning. It was this dual aspect that defined cultural production for Murdoch: regional writers should attempt to interpret local events for both internal and external audiences. While preserving local idiom and colouration, they should be alert to those elements of universal significance that would allow their work to add to the cumulative cultural achievement of Western civilization. Murdoch's description of the fire early on in his narrative illustrates this process: 'The proximity of immense forests parched up to tinder by the summer's heat, and now in one universal conflagration, caused an ocean of fire that we may conclude to be unparalleled in the history of forest countries, and perhaps not surpassed in horrific sublimity by any natural calamity from this element, that has ever been recorded.'

The distinctively local elements – vast forests, extreme summer heat, the 'ocean of fire' – combine to create an event of 'horrific sublimity,' a key term in eighteenth-century aesthetics. An experience was 'sublime' if it exceeded the usual frontiers of human appreciation, leaving one awestruck by an encounter with great beauty, terror, or complexity.[17] In presenting the Miramichi fire in this way, Murdoch tried to demonstrate that regional writers might have something of value to say to a broader audience, even when treating local events.

Although he continued to write poetry for his own pleasure, 'The Conflagration' remained Murdoch's only published poem, and it appeared anonymously. A long ballad on a historical theme also remained unpublished.[18] In spite of his claims to cultural leadership, Murdoch was not one to overestimate the value of his own work. Like Blackstone, who also forsook poetry for the law, Murdoch rightly concluded that his talents lay in other literary forms and pursued them assiduously, while remaining a staunch advocate of poetry as the highest form of literary expression and collecting a wide range of poetic works for his own library.

Murdoch's role as cultural impresario and promoter of a Nova Scotian identity is also illustrated by his superintendence of the *Acadian Magazine*, a literary periodical published at Halifax between July 1826 and January 1828. The magazine's editorials were unsigned, and it was not until the late 1970s that Murdoch's identity as editor was discovered. Even Murdoch's friend Joseph Howe did not know of his involvement, initially at least, although he did know that the magazine was 'to be conducted ... by some of the Lawyers,' revealing the reflexive connection between law and letters made by contemporaries.[19]

In creating the *Acadian Magazine*, Murdoch wished to further the goals of both internal improvement and external promotion. In the preface to the first number, he expressed the hope that the success of the venture would 'advance the literary standing of the Country, and tend to efface the impression which has been far too prevalent abroad, and particularly in the Mother Country, that we were comparatively ignorant and barbarous.' Within Nova Scotia, Murdoch sought to 'promote the extension or diffusion of science, and the improvement of morals, or [to] afford amusement ... without violating propriety and decorum.' With the advance of schools and public libraries in the province and with 'the general spirit of improvement now in full operation,' the magazine could assist young people 'to improve in all useful branches of literature.'

Whether external audiences were much aware of the *Acadian Magazine* may be doubted, but within Nova Scotia its appearance marked an important milestone in the evolution of provincial literature. In nineteen issues comprising 768 double-columned pages, the *Acadian Magazine* contains dozens of articles on a wide variety of subjects: travel, current events at home and abroad, science, philosophy, biography, history, architecture. Poetry, short fiction, criticism, and essays are also well represented. Most contributors remained anonymous, but authors are known to have resided at Saint John, Pictou, Truro, Windsor, Annapolis Royal, and in Cape Breton as well as Halifax, revealing the journal's broad regional appeal. In fact, over three-quarters of all contributions were locally written, and the January 1827 issue contained solely the work of local authors.[20]

Murdoch had proved that provincial authors were capable of generating sufficient material, at least in terms of quantity, to fill a literary review. With respect to literary merit, the most extensive examination to date of the *Acadian Magazine*'s content has provided a balanced but generally positive assessment, noting the 'skill and competence displayed' in a number of the poems. In general, the periodical catered to a conservative and somewhat sentimental taste, but the most talented contributors show 'evidence of the creative and critical skills of the many writers in the province who have been overshadowed and forgotten because of the reputations of Howe, Haliburton and Goldsmith.'[21] In addition to providing a training ground for such authors, the non-specialized format of the *Acadian Magazine* established the pattern for regional periodicals in the 1830s and 1840s.

Running a law practice, launching a political career, working with various philanthropic societies, and managing a monthly literary journal were enough to tax even Murdoch's energies. At some point in mid-1827, the direction of the *Acadian Magazine* passed to another lawyer, Murdoch's friend J. Scott Tremain, but Murdoch likely continued to play a supporting role until publication ceased early in 1828. Competition from newspapers, which also published locally authored fiction, poetry, and essays, dictated that Maritime literary periodicals of the nineteenth century would lead short lives. Dissatisfaction with the loss of focus on indigenous writing that occurred after Murdoch's departure may also have played a role in the magazine's demise.

Murdoch's endeavours in the latter part of the decade shifted away from the purely literary and towards the kind of historical and legal writing that would make up the bulk of his output in future decades.

The one exception was his possible contribution to the papers of 'the Club,' a group of friends who had their satirical sketches on provincial life published in Joseph Howe's *Novascotian* between May 1828 and October 1831. Tradition associates Murdoch's name with the Club, but there is no proof that he was part of the circle.[22] The lawyer figure of Frank Halliday has more in common with T.C. Haliburton or Laurence O'Connor Doyle than Murdoch. The atmosphere of cigars-and-brandy male camaraderie celebrated in the Club papers strikes one as uncongenial to the abstemious Murdoch, who would soon become active in the temperance cause. It is possible, however, that the image of Murdoch as a paragon of rather dull respectability relates more to his later years, and that he was more convivial in his youth. For the moment, Murdoch's participation in the Club must remain an open question.

Murdoch's shift away from belles-lettres and towards historical and legal writing coincided with his election to the House of Assembly in 1826. The following year he circulated among his colleagues a pamphlet on a topic with special meaning for him: imprisonment for debt. When his efforts to change the law proved fruitless, Murdoch issued a second enlarged edition addressed to the public in 1831. The pamphlet contains a twenty-page essay by Murdoch, followed by a forty-page appendix of extracts from legislative debates on the subject in Upper Canada and the United States and other supporting documents. The essay shows Murdoch at his best as a prose stylist.

Murdoch voiced his objections to imprisonment for debt eloquently and with conviction, and refuted contrary arguments in a clear and convincing manner. His opposition to imprisonment for debt was based not on economics but rather on constitutional and moral grounds. The institution allowed property to be valued above human liberty, put 'arbitrary ... power into hands the most likely to abuse it,' and was incompatible with the requirements of Christianity and civilization. Imprisonment for debt meant that the creditor took no responsibility for extending credit in doubtful cases, and provided no way of distinguishing the genuinely feckless debtor from those who were honest but unfortunate. It served no real deterrent function in an economy where the need for credit was a fact of everyday life. Moreover, 'a jail may teach or foster vicious habits, but it is a poor seminary for improvement of the human character' – a clear reference to his father's unhappy encounter with debtors' prison.

In Murdoch's view, law reform and literature were both part of the *mission civilisatrice* that professional men were bound to foster in this post-war period of peace and relative prosperity.[23] Both were based, ideally, on a sense of shared values and identity. By 1830, Murdoch appears to have resigned himself to the fact that his contribution to belles-lettres would be slight. Other forms of literature beckoned, through which he might better explore the contours of a Nova Scotian identity.

Law as Literature: *An Epitome of the Laws of Nova-Scotia*

As the Jewish proverb states, 'When one door closes, another opens.' Although bitterly disappointed by his defeat at the polls in 1830, Beamish Murdoch was too full of ideas and ambition to remain in a state of depressive inactivity for long. Within months he had turned his energies to his most ambitious project to date: a multi-volume treatise on the law of Nova Scotia. In February 1831 Joseph Howe was pleased to observe that Murdoch was not moping after his defeat but devoting himself to a worthwhile purpose.[24] The prospectus of the work stated that its object was 'to give a brief and clear outline of the elements of English law as it is at present in force in this colony; and to arrange the statute law of the province in methodical order.' In addition to its appeal to professional men, Murdoch hoped the work would be of utility to 'members of the Legislature, magistrates and militia officers ... as well as [to] those who wish to form an idea of the laws by which they are governed.' At a time when articling students were expected to wade through Blackstone's *Commentaries*, Tidd's *Practice*, and other weighty tomes on English law, Murdoch also hoped that his proposed work 'might be useful as an introduction to the study of provincial law.'[25]

In addition to these earnest and public-spirited motivations, Murdoch undoubtedly had more personal considerations in mind as well. A clue to these is provided in the dedication of the work: 'To the Hon. S.S. Blowers, Chief Justice, and President of H.M. Council, this essay on the laws of a colony, over whose tribunals he has long presided, is by his kind permission, inscribed, in token of respect and veneration for his public services, high judicial qualities, and inflexible integrity, which are interwoven with the author's earliest recollections.'[26] Murdoch had good reason to be thankful to Blowers, whose decision in the Market Wharf litigation was a crucial turning point in the history of the Beamish family fortunes. Hope for the chief justice's intercession with regard to some future appointment, possibly even a judgeship, was undoubtedly mingled with gratitude in inspiring this fulsome dedication. While kinship ties counted heavily under the oligarchy, the regime had some meritocratic elements. Had the advent of responsible government not shaken the province's political order, it is possible that Murdoch might eventually have received some official appointment in recognition of his legal and political services.[27] Joseph Howe, even in the midst of his political disagreements with Murdoch, could state in 1840 that the *Epitome* 'ought, long since, to have entitled the author to some especial mark of approbation from the local Government.'[28]

The prospectus for the *Epitome* stated that the work would be published as soon as a sufficient number of subscribers had been found. Having suffered a large loss with his publication of Haliburton's *History*, Joseph Howe was not about to take such a risk again. He agreed to publish the *Epitome* on a contractual basis only, with Murdoch assuming all the risk. In November 1831 Howe announced that 'a number of Subscribers adequate to the expenses of the Work having been obtained, Mr. Murdoch's Epitome of the Laws will go to Press immediately.'[29] The number must not have been 'adequate,' however, since the *Epitome* carried no list of subscribers when it was published, and there were substantial publishing expenses for which Murdoch remained personally responsible. He was able to persuade Howe to take a note for a large part of the cost, which was not ultimately settled by Murdoch for many years. Allowing debts to go unpaid over a long period was not unusual at the time, but the subsequent political antagonisms between Murdoch and Howe probably contributed to the delay in payment in this case.[30]

Howe likely printed about 500 sets of the *Epitome*. Murdoch's record of his account with bookbinder George Phillips refers to 2,071 'copies' – presumably individual volumes – which would yield 518 four-volume sets.[31] The prospectus anticipated that each volume would contain about 200 pages, but they exceeded that mark by a fair margin, containing 239, 300, 244, and 251 pages respectively, for a total of 1,034 pages.[32] The volumes were handsomely produced, well-indexed, contained very few errors, and were small enough in size to be easily handled and transported. The cost to subscribers was to be 8s per volume 'half bound' (i.e., in calf) or 6s 6d in boards, and the work could be obtained through agents in Windsor, Pictou, Annapolis, Sydney, Lunenburg, Kentville, and Truro, as well as in Halifax. How many copies were actually sold is not known, but there is reason to believe the *Epitome* was never a bestseller. The underwhelming response to the appeal for subscribers is one clue. Another is that C.H. Belcher was still advertising the *Epitome* for sale in Halifax in 1842, a decade after the first volume appeared.[33]

Some observers saw the work as part of an emergent provincial literature. The author of a letter to the *Novascotian* responded to the prospectus with the observation that 'every attempt of this kind which adds to
the small pile of our native productions should be liberally encouraged
[to] give a noble spur to our native literati to exert themselves.'[34] Treating the *Epitome* as a contribution to local literature is entirely appropriate, since it is not just a dry compilation of provincial laws (though it
is that at some points) but also an attempt to articulate both a Nova
Scotian legal culture and a provincial identity.

As Benedict Anderson has said, in explaining the rise of nationalism
in the republics of Latin America, 'administrative organizations create
meaning.'[35] He might have added 'legal systems,' and it is rather puzzling that Anderson did not look more closely at local legal orders in
developing his analysis. At a time when law was seen as imbricated
within daily life, and legal regimes considered illustrative of national
characteristics, Murdoch's extrapolation of a provincial identity from
Nova Scotia's legal order was uncontroversial. Modern assumptions
about law as an autonomous domain of inquiry separate from the humanities and social sciences have led historians to ignore legal texts
from the colonial era, as well as the contribution of lawyers to the culture, broadly defined, of that era. Insofar as law and history were 'the
most important sources of metaphor and example' through which British North Americans understood themselves,[36] the study of legal texts
can contribute to a better understanding of cultural, political, and intellectual history of any period.[37]

I have analysed elsewhere the main themes in the *Epitome*.[38] In this
context, it is the work's treatment of the distinctiveness of the Nova
Scotia legal tradition that deserves consideration, for it provides a fine
example of Nova Scotia as an 'imagined community.' An initial comparison of the *Epitome* with Joseph Howe's *Western and Eastern Rambles:
Travel Sketches of Nova Scotia*[39] and with Thomas Chandler Haliburton's
The Old Judge; or, Life in a Colony[40] reveals three different views on Nova
Scotian identity. Haliburton's thesis is that Nova Scotians, lacking the
stabilizing elements of a landed aristocracy and established church,
had become as individualistic and democratic as the Americans – but
without the same initiative and resourcefulness. Nova Scotians' allergy
to hierarchy was a principal cause of the province's decline, a state of
affairs, Haliburton predicted, that would only accelerate with responsible government. This acerbic view is leavened only by reference to
the survival of various folk traditions among farmers and fishermen,

as portrayed in the ghost stories and tall tales that punctuate *The Old Judge*.[41] Howe's judgment of his compatriots is much less severe. He finds them sturdy and independent, mostly hard-working but able to enjoy life too. If they are committed to equality, it is to the British variety (equality before the law) rather than the Jacksonian (one man, one vote).

Murdoch's view of the provincial character in the *Epitome* has much more in common with that of Howe than that of Haliburton and in fact provides some answers to the critiques made by Haliburton in later decades. Murdoch saw liberty and equality as the principal features of provincial law and as fundamental Nova Scotian values. He argued in the *Epitome* that Nova Scotian law improved upon English law in its more rigorous commitment to civil equality in the sphere of private law. Murdoch was no more enamoured of American-style democracy than Haliburton, but he could accept the individualism of Nova Scotians because it had to be exercised within recognized legal bounds. For Murdoch, the response to Haliburton's lament that Nova Scotians had no English-style stabilizing institutions was to point to the law. Law afforded the key to distinguishing between liberty and anarchy, and could also provide a sense of shared values in a diverse population. Understanding Nova Scotia's legal culture, then, illuminated its identity. Law, perhaps even more than newspapers or market relations, was an integrative force within the province, its web of institutions, procedures, and personnel bringing together people of different backgrounds and beliefs. Curiously, Mr Justice Haliburton had relatively little to say about the law as an institution of social order and was content to adopt a kind of populist anti-lawyer sentiment in *The Old Judge*.[42]

It is in Murdoch's discussion of the question of the reception of English law that he began to make his case for a distinct provincial legal tradition. The first step in his argument was to restrict the process of reception: 'The common and statute law of England,' Murdoch asserted, 'are not, as a whole, suited to our situation as a colony.'[43] Murdoch made it clear that much of the common and statute law was inappropriate for Nova Scotia because local conditions were different, not necessarily simpler. In addition, much of the English law was frankly undesirable on its merits: thus, Nova Scotia was spared the 'unnecessary and artificial distinctions between real and personal property,' 'the unjust rules of primogeniture,' and the 'arbitrary legislation' that shackled marriage in the mother country.[44]

According to Murdoch, an English statute could not be deemed suitable unless it had already been incorporated into provincial law through express re-enactment or statutory recognition, a local judicial decision, or 'the general usage of the people at large.'[45] This restrictive attitude to the question of reception served both professional and philosophical ends. On the one hand, it prevented 'dormant' British statutes from suddenly being declared in force, to the possible chagrin of local lawyers and their clients. More generally, this stance reinforced the 'Nova Scotia-ness' of Nova Scotian law and retained the primary responsibility for its promulgation in the Assembly rather than the courts.[46]

This emphasis on the local legislature as the main regulator of the reception of English law was consistent with Murdoch's views on legislative supremacy. Nonetheless, he made a distinction between public and private law in this context. He was well aware that most of the British public or constitutional law had not been specifically re-enacted in Nova Scotia or declared in force by judicial decision. 'Yet,' he declared, 'what are generally esteemed the most valuable portions of British law, have been transplanted into our land, – the Habeas Corpus, – the freedom of the Press – the trial by Jury – the Representative Branch of legislature, – the viva voce examination of witnesses; all those branches of public law ... we possess.'[47] Re-enactment of these statutes on public liberty was unnecessary because of the nature of the original compact between the crown and the early inhabitants: 'The national faith and royal authority pledged to the first settlers [are considered] to have confirmed them in the indisputable possession of that portion of the laws of England.'[48] Murdoch's admiration for British constitutional law exceeded even his respect for legislative supremacy. In effect, he was proposing a kind of federalism, where fundamental rights would be 'entrenched' at the imperial level while the regulation of 'property and civil rights' would remain within the legislative purview of the local government.

For Murdoch, the distinctiveness of Nova Scotia law thus lay in private, not public, law. Murdoch echoed many writers in English and American circles in lamenting the fact that feudalism had been overthrown in the sphere of English public law but lingered in its private law, especially in the law of real property. The beauty of Nova Scotian law was that it breathed the spirit of the free British constitution into the private law. Nova Scotia had the best of both worlds, possessing the British constitution but 'freed from many [laws] that have formed the subject of constant objection in the mother country.'[49] The game laws and tithe laws, representing the privilege of class and church respectively, were unknown. So was the 'expensive and unnecessary variety of Courts' found in England. 'The comparative simplicity of our legal forms, in conveyancing and in law suits, would astonish an English practitioner,' asserted Murdoch, as would 'the cheapness of [our] law proceedings.' Equal division of an intestate's property among his or her children was preferable to primogeniture, while Nova Scotia's liberal divorce law was preferable to the English parliamentary divorce, a 'system [that] seems to favor the wealthy by holding out ... a remedy from which all in middle or humble life are debarred.'[50]

Murdoch's main purpose in the *Epitome* was to inspire pride and confidence in local rather than imperial traditions. This he did by praising the ingenuity of previous generations in erecting a distinctive provincial code admirably suited to local conditions: 'I may refer to every chapter of this book to show, that having an opportunity of establishing a Provincial Code with the benefit of the experience and philosophy of older countries, our forefathers have not failed in their duty; but have transmitted to us a system simple and concise, founded on the best principles, and that, except on a few points, they have left little to their successors beyond the duty of preserving, polishing and throwing light upon, the useful result of their labour.'[51] Just as the pioneering generations had conquered the wilderness, replacing it with the rudiments of civilization, so had they pruned the tangled undergrowth of the English common law into the 'simple and elegant structure of laws which long experience has rendered an object of public attachment.'[52] Loyalty to the British constitution and loyalty to provincial law were like Chinese boxes, nestling comfortably one inside the other. If matters of municipal regulation occasionally required rejecting the British model, that was understood never to put in question the overarching constitutional bond.

If the provincial code was a book in which the Nova Scotian character might be read, what did it reveal? Some of Murdoch's key words have already been referred to – 'simple,' 'elegant,' 'free' – but their nuances need to be explored. The word 'simple' in particular is apt to mislead. Murdoch did not mean that Nova Scotians were a rustic lot with only rudimentary legal needs; the 'pioneer days' were long over in Nova Scotia by the time Murdoch sat down to write in 1830. By 1830, the provincial population was 120,000, well over double the figure at Murdoch's birth, and Halifax sheltered some 15,000 souls. While not large by the standards of cities in the United States, Halifax compared favourably with York (Toronto), Saint John, and Quebec. From about the time of Murdoch's birth, Halifax had been adding stately stone structures to its original complement of wooden buildings, leaving at least some visitors with an impression of solidity, refinement, and even grandeur. Visiting Halifax in the summer of Waterloo, Bishop Joseph-Octave Plessis of Quebec found that the city's buildings vied with each other in 'the beauty of their situation and the variety of their structure,' though his account of appalling conditions of poverty elsewhere in the region makes for grim reading.[53] For Murdoch, such conditions of inequality (which existed in Halifax as well) did not affect his perception that most of the province had been 'civilized' for as long as he could remember.

And so, when Murdoch spoke of a 'simple' code of provincial law, he did not mean 'primitive' or 'underdeveloped.' Rather, he used the word with both an aesthetic and a political connotation. A simple code avoids unnecessary technicalities and distinctions, thereby allowing an immediate grasp of the basic principles at work. Thus, the Nova Scotia law of property provided the minimum number of distinctions between realty and personalty, and the law of succession treated all of a deceased's property as a fund to be shared among his or her heirs, contrary to the complexities of English law. What appealed to Murdoch here was not only the justice of the Nova Scotian solution, but its aesthetics.

Blackstone and Murdoch were at one in believing that the common law had an aesthetic appeal. Daniel Boorstin has shown how Blackstone encompassed two somewhat contradictory conceptions in eighteenth-century aesthetics: the 'beautiful,' which emphasized order, symmetry, and rationality; and the 'sublime,' associated with disorder, grandeur, and irrationality.[54] We have already seen that Murdoch's aesthetic reflected this dichotomy, associating beauty with the built environment and sublimity with the natural environment. His ideals of beauty might best be captured in architectural terms, as Georgian classicism in its rather austere Palladian incarnation. Throughout the *Epitome*, Murdoch tried to reflect this aesthetic by explaining terms of art, translating Latin and law-French maxims, and writing in a direct and unadorned style.[55]

In his devotion to these ideals, Murdoch was by no means alone. Joseph Howe, with his constant classical allusions, was to the political world what Murdoch was to the legal. Indeed, some have argued that the canons of eighteenth-century classicism still dominate the aesthetics of Maritime literature.[56] Murdoch would have imbibed these values at the Halifax Grammar School, and he had only to look around him to see them everywhere manifest in architecture. His friend T.C. Haliburton's Clifton estate at Windsor, his mentor's summer home at Mount Uniacke, the graceful Town Clock surmounting the Citadel, his own place of worship, St George's Round Church, all radiated the stately confidence in symmetry and proportion of the Georgian aesthetic ideal. It was probably Murdoch himself who remarked of the newly opened Province House that a 'uniformity and neatness pervades the outside of the building, [which] ... is said by strangers, in correctness of proportion, to exceed any edifice in America' – a judgment confirmed, incidentally, by posterity.[57] For Murdoch, it was no coincidence that this Palladian building should generate a legal order of Palladian simplicity and elegance.

Nova Scotians had a 'simple' code for a 'free' people. All Nova Scotians were equally free in the eyes of the law, including Roman Catholics and blacks. At its most basic level, freedom meant freedom from enslavement: 'This was fully recognized by the decision given many years ago at Annapolis, when the doctrine was acted upon that slaves brought into this country became free ipso facto upon landing.'[58] In fact, the decision of Chief Justice Blowers was not quite this bold, but Murdoch was prepared to see it as illustrative of the broader principle.[59] It is unlikely that Murdoch accepted blacks as social equals, but he did accord them legal equality. There is also no evidence that he shared the overtly racist ideas of Haliburton or Chancellor James Kent who, while mildly anti-slavery, considered 'the African race ... essentially a degraded caste, of inferior rank and condition in society.'[60] Murdoch's insistence that there was now 'no religious distinction remaining in our Provincial code' described an important aspect of his attempt to shape a distinct provincial character.[61] The British national character was inextricably bound up with Protestantism, in spite of the recent 'toleration' of Roman Catholics, and Murdoch's effort to distance Nova Scotia from that tradition was a significant contribution to the debate over the provincial identity.

Murdoch's emphasis on equality did not extend to the acceptance of the Mi'kmaq as full members of provincial society. Nova Scotia was a self-consciously New World society, but its original inhabitants were to have only the most marginal place within it. One fact especially put them beyond the pale: they 'had [no] idea of property (of an exclusive nature) in the soil, before their intercourse with Europeans.' Murdoch's views on the Mi'kmaq would change over the ensuing decades, but in 1832 he portrayed them as barely distinguishable from beasts at the time of European contact. While they might have grievances, said Murdoch, these were now 'matter for the historian, rather than for the jurist.'[62]

Murdoch believed that the commitment of the legal order to simplicity and freedom reflected the Nova Scotian character, epitomized in the yeoman ideal that informed his legal, political, and historical vision. Provincial literature of the period celebrated the 'humble and vigorous' Nova Scotian, contrasting images of an aged and decadent mother country with those of colonial youth and virtue, in a striking parallel to American imagery of the Revolutionary period.[63] In insisting upon the quiet and sturdy virtue of the Nova Scotian character, Murdoch and his contemporaries sought to discountenance the earlier aristocratic norms disseminated from Halifax's garrison culture, norms that involved conspicuous consumption, public drunkenness, and licentiousness from the governor and his lady on down.[64]

A sober and respectable representative of the middle classes, Murdoch sought to reconstitute the provincial identity in his own image. His project, whether he was fully conscious of it or not, was to claim for the useful and industrious middle classes the virtue that the eighteenth century had seen as reposing in the landed gentry. Yet the distinction between the 'gentry' and the 'middle classes' was not so sharp in Murdoch's mind. He himself always tried to project a gentlemanly image, seeking to demonstrate a cultural affinity with certain aristocratic values even as he tried to distance himself from others.

Murdoch found an organizing principle for the innovations of provincial law in 'the civil law of Rome [, which] has a greater share in the composition of our laws than it has in those of the mother country ... [and to which] we must often look for aid as an interpreter.'[65] In his affection for the civil law, Murdoch followed in the footsteps of his mentor Crofton Uniacke, as we saw in chapter 3. Murdoch did not mean just that Nova Scotia law, like the English, had recourse to the substantive principles of Roman law in certain specific fields such as admiralty law. Rather, he invoked the idea of Roman law as the *jus commune* of all Europe and its diaspora, as a reservoir of timeless legal wisdom that could be referred to in order to supplement or clarify the rules and principles of any municipal law. Its manner of organizing the law, as revealed in Justinian's *Digest* and the *Institutes* of Gaius, also appealed to Murdoch as he faced the seeming jumble of English law, so preoccupied with questions of jurisdiction and remedies and so little with the principles of substantive law. He would rely on civilian concepts of codification and legislative expression when it came to redrafting the Halifax city charter, as we saw in the previous chapter. As M.H. Hoeflich has written, 'the Roman and civil law systems in the Anglo-American legal world [served as] sources of jurisprudential inspiration, as models of intellectual elegance, and as a comparative basis for law reform efforts.'[66]

The appeal of the Roman law is described in these terms in a text that Murdoch (certainly) and Kent (probably) both relied upon: Arthur Browne's *A Compendious View of the Civil Law, being the Substance of a Course of Lectures Read in the University of Dublin* (London, 1797–9).[67] This appeal of civil law was always subject to one caveat. Browne's second lecture, 'On the Comparative Excellence of the Civil and Common Laws,' restated the common wisdom among English-speaking writers, to the effect that the civil law was preferable in matters of private law while the common law was preferable in public law. The civil law was thought to contain an arbitrary spirit in matters pertaining to the liberty of the subject, in contrast to the panoply of rights and privileges afforded to English citizens.

Murdoch dissented radically from these views, presenting the whole period of European control of Acadia as a unity. 'From the earliest settlements of the French in 1603 to the present time,' he stated, 'all inhabitants of the colony have enjoyed all essential civil and political liberties.'[68] Murdoch did not portray the conquest of Acadia as representing the triumph of superior British law over the reactionary regime of the French.

There were probably two reasons for Murdoch's more generous approach. First, it shows him as a consistent proponent of the environmentalist explanation of cultural change.[69] To explain the high value afforded liberty in the provincial context, Murdoch pointed to the necessity of coping with a bracing climate and, originally, a virgin wilderness. What was sauce for the British goose would have to be sauce for the Acadian gander. This environmentalism happily provided a formula for harmonious relations between the two 'founding peoples,' which could be applied not only in Nova Scotia but also in Canada. Decades later, Murdoch would write to Henry Morgan that the strife between English and French Canadians 'must by and by be merged in the common love of the land of their birth or adopted residence.'[70] Murdoch's lifelong preoccupation with the Acadian question meant that he also followed events in Canada with great interest, since he correctly saw Anglo-French tensions as one of the mainsprings of Canadian history.[71]

In addition to his environmentalism, it was the necessity for the two 'races' to live in harmony that caused Murdoch to adopt an organic approach to provincial legal history. He knew that the Acadians would never be able to forget the events of 1755; his respect for their history made the adoption of a triumphalist interpretation of the British presence impossible.[72] In his brief political career, Murdoch did what he could to bring the Acadians more into the mainstream of provincial political life by championing the cause of Catholic relief and by appealing in French to potential Acadian constituents.[73]

The quality that distinguishes the *Epitome* from most other works of the period is the nature of its intended audience. Many of Murdoch's contemporaries wrote with one eye on a British audience, actual or virtual – one thinks of Haliburton especially in this context. Whether to raise the profile of Nova Scotia in England, to create a larger market for their product, or to demonstrate their cultural loyalty, these writers tried to communicate with their own fellow citizens in a way that would also be understood and accepted by British readers. This fact inevitably shaped their writing, sometimes subtly, sometimes in more important ways.

In reading the *Epitome*, one does not feel the presence of a British audience. The work is addressed to Nova Scotians, in Nova Scotian terms. No doubt Murdoch would have been highly gratified to know that the work was read in Britain, but that was not his goal. For someone who followed the colonial tradition of referring to Britain as 'home,' he seems to have been interested in Britain solely as a cultural phenomenon, not as an actual place. He never visited the mother country, for example. This exclusive focus on a local audience illustrates a respect for his compatriots and a commitment to place that is seldom matched in the literature of the period. A third-generation Nova Scotian, Murdoch was 'at home' in Nova Scotia in a way that Haliburton perhaps never was; only of Joseph Howe could the same be said.

Although Murdoch came to be called 'Nova Scotia's Blackstone' by subsequent generations, his debt to Blackstone was fairly small.[74] Murdoch used the word *Epitome* to describe his work, not *Commentaries*, and the similarity between the two works exists only at a very general level in that both are comprehensive institutional works on the common law, aimed at a literate public as well as legal professionals. Murdoch did not follow Blackstone's organization (or Kent's for that matter) nor copy much of his content except for the book on real property, where there was not much point to reinventing the wheel. The *Epitome* was more likely to criticize Blackstone than to praise him. Murdoch was clearly uncomfortable with Blackstone's apparently Court-centred political views and probably disliked the high Anglican stance that led Blackstone to state that Protestant dissent, not to mention the practice of Roman Catholicism, was still probably a crime in spite of the Toleration Act 1689 – a position totally at variance with Murdoch's more ecumenical views. In short, the *Epitome* is a truly indigenous work of legal literature from first to last.[75]

It has become an article of faith in the postmodern world that all identities are constructed rather than inherent. In spite of his commitment to a certain environmental determinism, common to legal historians since Jean Bodin in the sixteenth century, Murdoch would probably have agreed that, at some level, identity in a New World society like Nova Scotia was a matter of selection. This selection can be questioned. Was Murdoch's vision of Nova Scotians accurate? Self-serving? Was his Nova Scotian identity 'imaginary' rather than 'imagined?' In her description of Haliburton's Windsor, Gwendolyn Davies has exposed the contrast between the town's appearance, as 'genteel and pretty as one of Jane Austen's Regency English villages,' and the 'debt, death, murder, illness, scandal, racism, arrogance, misogyny, [and] class ostracization ... [that] lurk[ed] beneath the surface.'[76] How does one reconcile the optimistic Enlightenment humanism of the *Epitome* with the underlying reality which, as in Windsor, lurked beneath the surface of provincial life?

The answer lies in the role that law and identity are supposed to play. The law is a human institution that has measurable effects on individuals and on society. It must come to terms with many unpleasant human situations: debt, murder, scandal, racism, and so on. It can do so only if it is animated by a clear set of values in its principles and rules, in the minds of its personnel, and in the minds of the public who are subject to it and who look to it for protection. In a free society there will always be debate about some of the law's principles; others, like the proscription of murder, will command wide allegiance. In a general treatment of Nova Scotia law, we should not expect to find an exhaustive catalogue of social failings, because these are more or less taken for granted. The fallibility of human beings is why law exists in the first place. It is appropriate for such a work to focus on the ideals that animate the law, rather than the instances where those ideals may have been subverted or ignored. The more widely the ideals are diffused among the population, Murdoch would have said, the more likely they will be respected and enforced.

With regard to the issue of identity, it is perhaps more legitimate to criticize Murdoch for glossing over the defects in provincial society. Any identity will be composed of negative and positive traits, and Murdoch accentuates the latter almost to the point of excluding the former. He lauds Nova Scotians' commitment to freedom without any recognition that this 'freedom' was differentially experienced by women, the poor, blacks, Acadians, the Mi'kmaq, and non-Anglicans. Arguably, when Murdoch spoke of the qualities of simplicity and freedom that he saw in the provincial character, he was creating an identity of aspiration rather than one that actually reflected Nova Scotian society. In contrast to Haliburton, for example, Murdoch attempted to create an identity for Nova Scotians in which all religions[77] and racial and ethnic groups, with the glaring exception of the Mi'kmaq, could participate. The identity proposed by Murdoch is recognizably British, but in an inclusive rather than exclusive sense. The qualities of tolerance and ecumenism that Murdoch purported to find in the provincial character did have some basis in fact, even if they were not universally observed, and religious freedom was legislatively embraced early on throughout British North America.[78]

Provincial Historian

By 1860, Murdoch was ready to devote himself to a project he had begun forty years earlier: a history of his native province.[79] His retirement from the recordership in 1860, followed by his gradual withdrawal from law practice, freed him to devote himself virtually full time to research and writing. The death of his father in 1855, for whose support he was completely responsible, had removed a major drain on his finances and perhaps too a certain emotional burden. With no dependants (his aunt had her own income from her share of the Market Wharf) and relatively modest needs, Murdoch was able to live comfortably on the income from his realty, supplemented by his savings.

The time was right not only for Murdoch but for Nova Scotia as well. Whether one approved or disapproved of the change, the achievement of responsible government signalled a new era, which allowed the previous period to be seen more clearly as a unity. A whole generation had grown up since the publication of Haliburton's *History* in 1829, and

Haliburton himself had long since retired and moved to England. A more numerous, assertive, and discerning middle class was ready for a new and comprehensive look at the province's past, as revealed by the commercial success of Murdoch's *History*.[80] On the substantive and methodological side, the discovery of many important documents permitted a fresh look at key events in Nova Scotian history, especially the deportation of the Acadians. The emergence of the Acadian question as a focus of international controversy in the 1850s after the publication of Longfellow's *Evangeline* also spurred Murdoch to explore the issue as thoroughly as possible.

Murdoch's treatment of the Acadians and the role of his *History* in Canadian historiography have attracted the interest of a number of historians in recent years, and it is not the purpose of this chapter to revisit those questions.[81] The *History* is here examined as Murdoch's final and most extensive work of literature, the final expression of his Nova Scotian patriotism. In thematic terms it presents a continuation of Murdoch's ideas about the efflorescence of British civilization in Nova Scotia, based on what Patrick Clarke has called 'his *idées-fixes* of liberty, loyalty, and progress.'[82] Within this general pattern of continuity, however, Murdoch shifted his views on two topics, the effect of responsible government and the role of the Mi'kmaq in provincial history.

Murdoch devoted his entire *soixantaine* to his work on the *History*. In the preface to Volume III, penned in January 1867, he states that he began work on the project eight years earlier. Volume III of the *History* appeared in the spring of 1867, but Murdoch continued to work on a projected fourth volume until early 1869 at least, when he wrote to the Maine historian John Edwards Godfrey that he had completed Volume IV down to 1842 (Volume III had ended at 1827) and hoped to take events down to 1866 'if spared.'[83] As with the projected but never-completed fifth volume of the *Epitome*, Murdoch's energy could not measure up to his initial enthusiasm.

The non-appearance of Volume IV of the *History*, however, may have reflected more than a dearth of energy on Murdoch's part. He had, after all, completed the manuscript down to 1842. Dealing with the period from 1842 to 1866 would have forced Murdoch to revisit the most painful episodes of his political life and to deal with his troubled relationship with Joseph Howe. Given Murdoch's penchant for circumspection, the fact that he managed to deal with these matters even in manuscript form occasions some surprise. The manuscript has unfortunately not survived, depriving us of a valuable perspective on one of the most important periods in Nova Scotia's political life. One can only suspect that Murdoch found it impossible to deal with the period without causing offence to some persons still living, and rather than risk reopening old wounds, he decided to follow his usual instincts and refrain from publication.

Although Volume IV is lost to us, Murdoch does provide a kind of retrospective on responsible government in Volume II, in which he grudgingly admitted that his fears had not come to pass. While 'passion and party views [might] occasionally disturb the working' of governmental machinery, such 'oscilliations proceed[ed] from the people themselves' and did not reflect any deficiency of constitutional principle.[84] As noted in chapter 7, the steady state of the mixed and balanced constitution has been replaced by the doctrine of popular sovereignty, which had been anathema to him two decades earlier. Having seen that responsible government seemed only to increase the attachment of Nova Scotians to the monarchy, rather than the reverse – witness the spectacular success of the Prince of Wales's visit in 1860 – Murdoch must have been reassured that the changes of 1848 had not imperilled the colony's relationship with the crown.[85]

Murdoch was not one to change his views lightly, but the *History* contained a public examination of conscience – if not a full confession – with regard to his views on the aboriginal inhabitants of Nova Scotia.[86] It will be recalled that in his *Epitome* Murdoch, normally a paragon of restraint, had permitted himself to characterize the Mi'kmaq in an overtly racist fashion, by appearing to deny their very humanity and refusing to admit that they might be 'civilized.' It is worth quoting the passage in full to contrast it with Murdoch's later views:

I will not enter into any inquiry as to the justice of the invasion of the agricultural and comparatively civilized countries of the southern continent by the Spanish and Portuguese nations, but confine myself to the case of these Northern regions, where our own nation and that of France took possession of an uncultivated soil which was before filled with wild animals and hunters almost as wild. It might with almost as much justice be said that the land belonged to the bears and wild cats, the moose or the carriboo, that ranged over it in quest of food, as to the thin and scattered tribes of men, who were alternately destroying each other or attacking the beasts of the forest. But the course of events has nearly extirpated them from the soil; and the subject of their wrongs, for many they had to complain of, is now matter for the historian, rather than for the jurist. I do not think that they themselves had any idea of property (of an exclusive nature) in the soil, before their intercourse with Europeans. Much injustice however was done to those simple creatures by those who communicated to them the artificial vices of civilized society.[87]

The treatment of the Mi'kmaq in the *History* was, on the surface, diametrically opposed to that in the *Epitome*. The reader is advised that the Mi'kmaq 'have usually been honest, frank, brave and humane, and they exhibited these qualities as well before as since their conversion to the Christian faith.' Further, it should not be 'supposed that the Indians ... were the ignorant, naked savages some persons may have imagined.' In fact their material culture was advanced and appropriate for their needs, and Murdoch singled out for special praise their canoes, wigwams, moccasins, baskets, and snowshoes. Finally, he bestowed the ultimate accolade: the language of the Mi'kmaq was 'so complete ... so musical and refined, as to lead to the inference that they had long been a *civilized* and thinking race of people.'[88]

Murdoch proceeded to give some analysis of what might be called the legal culture of the Mi'kmaq. After the initial conflicts with the English in the post-1749 period, Murdoch found that the native people 'adher[ed] most strictly to their engagements, [and were] most scrupulous and attentive to abstain from doing the slightest injury to the white people or to abstract the value of one penny of their cattle or goods, showing that they deeply respected and well understood the rights of property.' Far from being savage brutes, the Mi'kmaq understood the fundamental concepts of contract and property. 'The only difference of opinion that remained,' continued Murdoch, 'was, that the Indian believed he had a clear right to cut down or bark a tree in the unfenced and uncultivated wilderness – while those who held a written grant or deed, in some rare instances grudged him this privilege, and considered him a trespasser.'[89] Further, in a display of cultural relativism that many Nova Scotians must have found shocking, Murdoch opined that Governor Charles Lawrence's bounty on Indian scalps was much worse than the Mi'kmaq practice of scalping, which was simply part of their war customs and justified by their own laws under certain circumstances.[90] No such justification could be advanced by Lawrence, according to Murdoch.

What can explain this apparent volte-face? The answer appears to be: additional research, more extensive contact with the Mi'kmaq themselves, and Mi'kmaq demographics. When Murdoch wrote the impugned passages in the *Epitome* in the early 1830s, he merely parroted the prejudices of his society, and little literature was available to refute such ideas. In a long footnote to the passage quoted above, Murdoch cited Kent's *Commentaries* as being in agreement with his views, and noted that Kent based his opinion on Vattel's *Le Droit des Gens, ou Principes de la Loi Naturelle* ... (1758). Murdoch's passage is pure Vattel in two respects: the distinction between the conquest of the 'civilized empires of Peru and Mexico,' which Vattel regarded as a 'notorious usurpation,' and the North American situation; and the clear inference that agriculturalists can legitimately displace hunter-gatherer societies in order to enhance productivity and feed the earth's population. Hunter-gatherers, said Vattel, 'usurp more extensive territories than, with a reasonable share of labour, they would have occasion for, and have ... no reason to complain, if other nations, more industrious and too closely confined come to take possession of a part of those lands.' The tribes of the extensive tracts of North America 'rather ranged through than inhabited them,' an expression that Murdoch mimics with reference to the fauna of Nova Scotia.[91]

Murdoch failed to note, however, that Kent regarded Vattel's position as highly theoretical in New England, where in practice 'the colonists were not satisfied ... to settle the country without the consent of the aborigines, procured by fair purchase, under the sanction of the civil authorities ... The prior Indian right to the soil of the country was generally, if not uniformly recognised and respected by the New-England Puritans.'[92] Kent also discussed the seminal decision of Chief Justice John Marshall in *Johnson v. McIntosh* (1823),[93] where 'the natives were admitted to be the rightful occupants of the soil, with a legal as well as just claim to retain possession of it.'[94] Concerned no doubt about upsetting land titles in the province, Murdoch wished to avoid characterizing Mi'kmaq land rights as justiciable.

The beginnings of what we might call Murdoch's anthropological research seem to have begun fairly soon after the publication of the *Epitome*. In 1837 he joined the Nova Scotia Philanthropic Society, an association modelled on the fraternal societies for the English, Scottish, and Irish which were such an important part of Halifax life. Membership was restricted to those born in Nova Scotia and the society aimed to dispense charity to its members who had fallen on hard times and to non-members if funds permitted. Its inclusive approach to the Nova Scotian identity is worth remarking: the group's founders highlighted the 'vast fund of good they might be the means of producing, as well to the remnant of Aboriginee, as to the rising generations of coloured and white inhabitants.'[95] At its 1838 annual meeting, the society named a committee, which included Murdoch and merchant Thomas Forrester, 'to ascertain the numbers, tribes, situation and present condition of the aborigines of this Province; with a view to some effective system of relief' and to report at the next meeting.[96]

This task may or may not have involved personal meetings with Mi'kmaq individuals, but another of Murdoch's associational ties undoubtedly did. The Old Nova Scotia Society arranged for the participation of Mi'kmaq representatives in all important public ceremonies in early and mid-Victorian Halifax. During the celebrations attendant upon Queen Victoria's marriage in 1840, for example, Mi'kmaq men, women, and children marched in a procession organized by the society, and two Mi'kmaq youths carried the society's banner. Afterwards, they were treated to a 'great repast' of fish dishes (it being a Friday) on the Grand Parade.[97] Further meetings with the Mi'kmaq must have ensued, since Murdoch had completed a 200-page Mi'kmaq-English dictionary, including a ten-page account of the rules of Mi'kmaq grammar, by March 1864.[98] Language of course holds the key to the *mentalité* of a people: conversation with Mi'kmaq people would have provided a window on their culture and history, one Murdoch lacked when he wrote the *Epitome*.

In addition to his own researches, Murdoch could rely on an increasing number of publications in the 1840s and 1850s which provided valuable new information and insights about the region's native peoples. Foremost among these were works by Murdoch's good friend, the New Brunswick lawyer and natural historian Moses Perley, and by the Reverend Silas Tertius Rand, linguist, missionary, and pioneer anthropologist.[99] Perley travelled extensively among the Mi'kmaq and Maliseet and published a number of detailed reports on the reserves in the 1840s in his capacity as commissioner of Indian affairs for New Brunswick. Sharply critical of the government's Indian policy, he was removed from his post in 1848.[100] Joseph Howe's reports as commissioner of Indian affairs for Nova Scotia also made available more reliable information about the Mi'kmaq in the 1840s. Then came Rand's 1849 lectures on behalf of the Micmac Missionary Society[101] and his later lectures on 'The Claims and Prospects of the Indians' given at Halifax on 17 and 24 October 1854. Rand presented Nova Scotia's European population with the fullest and most sympathetic account of Mi'kmaq culture ever to appear in the province to that date, and spoke in terms of plunder and compensation. Murdoch referred to Rand's work in the preface to Volume III of his *History*, but once again cir-cumspection prevailed; he neither considered the issue of possible compensation nor discussed ongoing Mi'kmaq complaints about en-croachment on reserve lands.[102]

Demographic change might also have urged Murdoch to study the Mi'kmaq more closely. When he wrote the *Epitome*, the last of the Beo-thuk in Newfoundland, Shawnadithit, had just died in 1829, and the disappearance of the Mi'kmaq was thought to be a distinct possibility. In the passage from the *Epitome* quoted above, Murdoch stated that the native people had been 'nearly extirpated ... from the soil.' Subsequent references to the Mi'kmaq are all in the past tense, as if they had already disappeared. It may be that Murdoch referred to Mi'kmaq grievances as 'matter for the historian, rather than for the jurist' because he ex-pected the imminent extinction of the race to make their claims aca-demic in law. A decade after the *Epitome*, Joseph Howe had predicted the extinction of the Mi'kmaq within forty years if present trends con-tinued. By the 1860s, however, it was clear that they were not going to die out and that a role would have to be found for them in provincial society. Murdoch noted in his *History* that a recent census had revealed 1,407 Mi'kmaq in the province, a figure that, while not large, precluded any thought of extinction in the foreseeable future.[103]

A cynical interpretation of Murdoch's account of the Mi'kmaq in the *History* might stress that, at bottom, his position remained the same as in the *Epitome*. Aside from Lawrence's bounty, Murdoch still did not suggest that there was anything questionable in the treatment of the Mi'kmaq by the British crown or the Nova Scotia government. He stated that, after about 1770, the Mi'kmaq were satisfied with their re-lationship with the crown, when he must have known of at least some of the various petitions to the crown and to the region's legislatures complaining of illegal dispossession.[104] Murdoch criticized the individ-ual settler who might begrudge an Indian the right to cut down a tree on undeveloped private land, without referring to possible Mi'kmaq claims against unsettled crown land. And, although Murdoch was aware of the Royal Proclamation of 1763, he did not address the issue of how settlement was allowed to proceed after that date without any attempt to deal with the claims of the indigenous people.

In Murdoch's defence, it might be said that, at this particular junc-ture in provincial history, the humanization of the Mi'kmaq in the eyes of the settler population was a necessary prelude to any discussion of legal claims. Education would have to precede activism. Murdoch's own attitude was perhaps the best illustration of this process. Having once applied his mind to the question, he was prepared to abandon the prejudices he had displayed in the *Epitome* and to adopt a much more sympathetic attitude to Nova Scotia's native people. He and Silas Rand were two of the few intellectuals in mid-century Nova Scotia to advocate more respectful and humane treatment of the Mi'kmaq.

In erudition the *History* probably surpasses the *Epitome*, but in originality and in its treatment of the Nova Scotia identity it must be said that the *Epitome* is the superior work. While the strain of covering simultaneously his literary, sociological, and legal bases is all too evident in the *Epitome*, Murdoch returns to his key themes often enough to sustain interest. The relative simplicity and informality of its style contrast favourably with the plodding chronometricity of the *History*, while the circumspection and obliqueness that are so pronounced in the *History* are much less evident in the *Epitome*. As a perspective on the Nova Scotia identity as seen through its legal culture, the *Epitome*'s account, while idealistic and prettified, contains nonetheless a good deal that is convincing.

The principal defect of the work, and one of the probable reasons for its failure to thrive by means of subsequent editions, was its somewhat backward-looking nature even as it was published in 1832. Although at times critical of English law 'at home,' the *Epitome* gave few signs of being aware of criticisms of the operation of particular laws or courts in Nova Scotia. It did state that the division between the courts of common law and the Court of Chancery 'produces much practical evil,' and advocated the fusion of the two which ultimately came to pass in 1855, after the achievement of responsible government.[105] On such a highly charged topic as imprisonment for debt, however, on which Murdoch's reform views were well known from other writings, he made only the mildest of critiques.[106] Murdoch was too astute an observer not to see that provincial society was on the cusp of a period of escalating change, generated by increased immigration, freer trade, and the passage of the first Reform Bill in England, and manifested in the stirrings of reform in Nova Scotia itself. Perhaps he thought that anchoring provincial law solidly in the past was all the more necessary in such a period of flux. If so, he was mistaken. The Georgian verities of the *Epitome* would soon mark it as belonging to a vanished era, as the early Victorian lawyer reached for the latest edition of Kent's *Commentaries on American Law*, brought in by steamship from New York or Boston.[107] But, in its exhaustive treatment of the constitution and laws of a British North American colony prior to responsible government, the *Epitome* provides historians and legal scholars with a uniquely valuable window on the legal culture of a settler colony.

10

Epilogue

In the fall of 1863, the *Acadian Recorder* began a series entitled 'Sketches of Our Bar' with a profile of Beamish Murdoch. 'Max,' who confessed himself to be 'something of a physiognomist,' provided the following portrait of Beamish Murdoch as he approached the final decade of his life:

[A] long life of generous sentiments has given to Beamish Murdoch the soft-toned, almost girlish sweetness of expression which draws you to the man in spite of yourself ... He keeps so quiet in these feverish, democratic times that he might soon sink out of sight ... I should think he likes to live well. Here he stands in the Court this autumn day with a heavy great coat and a huge scarf wrapped with slovenly carelessness about his throat ... [He is now] walking, as is his custom, erect, and how tenderly using his stick as he uses all things animate and inanimate ... May he go gently down the street we are all going, to the inevitable gate.[1]

Courteous, gentle, quiet, proud, careful of his health, a little careless of his appearance, as a Victorian bachelor might be, Murdoch was no doubt instantly recognized as he tapped his way cautiously about the streets of Halifax. The reference to him sinking out of sight was surely a reference to his public career, not his physical presence. A contemporary photograph confirms the physical impression left by 'Max': the subject is balding, with a high forehead, mutton-chop whiskers, wispy beard, and pedant's paunch. He sits stiffly erect but still gives an impression of frailty. The eyes are small and indistinct; the years of study and copying have taken their toll.[2]

The *Acadian Recorder*'s tribute confirmed that the year 1863 had been an *annus mirabilis* for Beamish Murdoch, during which he was showered with honours and accolades by his professional peers and juniors, his government, and his fellow citizens. The legal profession welcomed him once again, making him vice-president of the Barristers' Society in 1863–4 after a hiatus of nearly four decades.[3] Murdoch's role as a kind of elder statesman was also acknowledged by the younger generation of articled clerks, who invited him to give a lecture, 'On the Origins and Sources of Nova Scotia Law,' on 29 August 1863.[4] In a magnanimous gesture, the government of Joseph Howe in its dying days conferred the distinction of Queen's Counsel on Beamish Murdoch, on 1 May 1863.[5] The wounds caused by partisan strife during the struggle for responsible government had finally begun to heal, albeit just in time for new ones to be inflicted in the run-up to Confederation. A few years later, this list of honours would be completed with an honorary DCL, awarded by King's College in June 1867 as a tribute to the author of *A History of Nova-Scotia, or Acadie*. For Murdoch, who had not been able to attend university, this was a signal tribute, to which he responded 'in a Latin speech of some length.'[6]

Murdoch had moved by the 1860s from Brunswick Street to the more salubrious precinct of Spring Garden Road, where he could take the air in the Public Gardens. The Supreme Court had followed a similar migration away from the busy port area, moving into its splendid new quarters in 1860 during the visit of the Prince of Wales.[7] The city over which Murdoch had presided as recorder was evolving, physically and socially, in ways he must have found gratifying. To be sure, poverty was by no means abolished, and class and sectarian antagonisms at times boiled to the surface. Earlier in 1863, citizens and soldiers had come to blows in one of the periodic bouts of rioting that was the price of having a British garrison. Gradually, though, the raffishness of old Halifax with its drunken soldiers, brawling sailors, and upper-class rakes was giving way to the middle-class regimen of order, sobriety, and respectability. New gas lighting, a better water supply, improved streets and sidewalks, the laying out of the Public Gardens and the spacious new Camp Hill Cemetery all made the city a more attractive and, to some extent at least, a safer and more agreeable place by mid-century than it had been two or three decades earlier.

By 1863, Murdoch was effectively the head of the Beamish family. His uncle Thomas Ott Beamish had died in 1860, as had Aunt Sarah. Maria had died in 1851, leaving Aunt Harriette Ott Beamish as the last survivor of her generation. Aside from his cousin Thomas Beamish Akins, with whom he continued to share many interests, Murdoch's closest contacts were with his cousin Charles Ott Beamish, partly because of their joint ownership of the Market Wharf. Each of the aunts had groomed one of her numerous nephews as heir. Maria had chosen Charles, the eldest son of her eldest brother, to whom she left her interest in the Market Wharf property. Harriette of course had chosen (or been 'assigned') Beamish, and Sarah had left her share in the Market Wharf to Akins.[8]

Charles was much more at home in the 'feverish, democratic times' of the 1860s than his relative. Something of an entrepreneur, and connected with coal mining and various investment schemes, he had married well in 1853. His wife, Sarah, was the daughter of T.W. James, the deputy provincial secretary. They had five children, but only a daughter, Maria Theresa, born in 1858, survived to adulthood. Beamish Murdoch planned to follow family tradition by selecting Charles as his sole heir, rather than sharing his estate among his numerous cousins. Cousin Francis Stephen Beamish, who had articled with Murdoch and been called to the bar in 1847, might have seemed a more obvious choice, but he had left Halifax for Cleveland, Ohio, in the 1850s and bounced back and forth between the two cities before finally retiring in Halifax. For Murdoch, who had never ventured farther than Saint John, such gadding about must have been difficult to understand, but his cousin was not alone. British North American lawyers began to explore work and educational opportunities in the United States in greater and greater numbers from the 1850s onward. One might wonder why Murdoch did not sell his practice to Francis Beamish, but such ideas were foreign to pre-Confederation lawyers, even those as permeated with capitalist ideals as Montreal's St James Street lawyers.[9] Law practices were not yet seen as independent businesses possessing goodwill, possibly because client loyalties were considered insufficiently stable to constitute property.

Murdoch did indeed 'sink out of sight' during the Confederation era. Although he no doubt followed the debates, his major preoccupation throughout the decade was the completion of his *History*. By 1870, Murdoch had abandoned any plans to publish his fourth volume, and he could finally begin to make arrangements for a true 'retirement.' He planned to retire to Lunenburg but was not able to depart until Aunt Harriette expired, aged eighty-two, on 8 April 1872. If all had gone as planned, Harriette should have left her 5/28 interest in the Market Wharf, valued at $12,000 at her death, to Beamish. Indeed, she did so in a will dated 25 May 1854. The will survives, in her hand but not witnessed (and therefore legally invalid), with the pencilled notation '29 April 1872. Found this. BM.' Murdoch must have been highly annoyed at this turn of events, this seeming act of negligence or pique by a woman to whom he had been as a son for many years. Harriette's death intestate meant that her interest in the wharf would be shared among a dozen nieces and nephews.[10]

Soon after Harriette's death, Murdoch moved to Lunenburg, where he purchased a home from his friend Senator Henry Adolphus Newman Kaulbach. The source of their friendship is obscure, and on the surface it was an unlikely one. Kaulbach was thirty years Murdoch's junior and 'one of the largest land proprietors and shipowners in Lunenburg County ... [with] a reputation for unsympathetic, unfair and sharp dealing.'[11] The Kaulbachs had been one of the leading families in Lunenburg since the Creation, and H.A.N. Kaulbach was one of the first aspirant lawyers in the province to attend Harvard Law School. Elected to the House of Assembly in 1863, Kaulbach was defeated in 1867 because of his support of Confederation, but he received his reward with a Senate appointment in March 1872.[12] Soon after Murdoch died, Kaulbach would erect the 'ostentatious yet elegant' Medway Hall, 'the most splendid residence ever built in Lunenburg.'[13]

In the summer of 1872, the Kaulbachs had five children, ranging in age from fourteen years to a few months. Murdoch particularly enjoyed the company of the senator's wife, Eunice Sophia, and began to spend a considerable amount of time at the Kaulbach residence. The presence of a somewhat eccentric old bachelor amid this bustling family must have caused some difficulties. A falling-out with the Kaulbachs ensued, upon which Murdoch sold his house in the spring of 1874 and returned to Halifax to live with Charles Beamish. Murdoch stayed long enough to dispose of the Market Wharf in August for $53,200, of which his share was about $11,500.[14] By the fall, however, he had quarrelled with Charles Beamish and returned to Lunenburg, where he purchased a second house from Kaulbach. From this point on, Murdoch was inseparable from the Kaulbachs and appears to have greatly enjoyed this exposure to the kind of family life he had never had. In July 1875, when the Kaulbachs' house was destroyed by fire, Murdoch insisted they come to live with him, which they did.

Murdoch's physical health declined rapidly in the fall of 1875, but he continued to attend to most of his own business and receive visitors. He was plagued by a series of strokes, but soldiered on. His last postcard, dated 13 January 1876 and addressed to Maria Beamish, was ominous but strangely cheery. Murdoch wrote that he had 'barely escaped death from paralysis of the brain' but was now on the mend. He died less than a.month later, on 9 February, at the age of seventy-six.

From the summer of 1874, the final two years of Murdoch's life had begun to take on a surreal air. According to several sources, this pillar of Victorian propriety seems to have lost his moorings, finally succumbing to the demons of sex and alcohol which he had resisted, with at least apparent success, for his entire life. Whether the causes of these behavioural changes were physiological (some form of senile dementia) or psychological (disorientation after leaving his lifelong home at Halifax) can never be known. Whether the extent and nature of this new behaviour was exaggerated for the purposes of litigation also cannot be known. The major sources for this unlikely transformation are the 300-page transcript of evidence taken in the litigation arising out of a challenge by Charles Beamish to his cousin's last will, and the reasons for judgment of the Nova Scotia Supreme Court in the cause.[15]

Charles Beamish reported that, while Murdoch lived with him briefly in Halifax in 1874, he proposed to Henrietta James, a young kinswoman of Charles's wife. During the litigation over his cousin's will, Charles Beamish alleged that Murdoch had become possessed of 'a diseased and insane passion for the wife of [H.A.N. Kaulbach].' Something odd did seem to be going on: even a poem Murdoch wrote for little Rupert Kaulbach in 1874, 'On seeing my little friend Rupert Kaulbach nestling on the bosom of a young lady,' had an unusually erotic flavour:

> He is but five, but he's all alive
> To female beauty's charms;
> She may be fifteen, but she is his queen
> While she folds him in her arms.[16]

There were also various reports of attempted sexual improprieties with housekeeping staff in Halifax and Lunenburg, though no solid evidence emerged to substantiate them.

Then there was the alcohol problem. Mr Justice Alexander James found as a fact that the Kaulbachs supplied Murdoch with two gallons of whisky per week, besides champagne, sherry, and claret. This portrait of a former temperance advocate spending his last days soaked in

alcohol makes one pause. It is difficult to believe that in a small community such as Halifax, where few vices remained private for long,
Murdoch could have been a temperance leader and closet alcoholic.
The evidence points rather to the onset of the problem late in life. Given
the strong and recurring hints of problems with alcohol on the part of
Murdoch's father and grandfather, the possibility of a genetic predis-
position cannot be excluded.[17]

Further evidence of uncharacteristic behaviour came from neighbour
Edmund Tobin at the trial. Tobin recounted an October 1875 conversation in which Murdoch told him that he 'had had a grand conflagration, and burnt up a lot of his papers a few days previous.'[18] Possibly
Murdoch felt the need to be liberated from the mountains of paper with
which he had surrounded himself for much of his life, but such a need
would have been highly novel for him. It is difficult to understand how
Murdoch the historian could commit such an act without giving his
cousin Akins at least the chance to rescue items of value for posterity.
The symbolism of the bonfire – a literal burning of bridges – in dissoci-
ating Murdoch from his past, however, cannot be denied.

The real story of Murdoch's last days will remain forever unknow-
able, since the trial transcript is full of diametrically opposed testimony
given by witnesses who were either interested in the outcome or related through friendship, blood, or affinity to the principal parties to
the suit. One fact stands out, however, and that is the growing influence of the Kaulbachs over their friend. The five wills made by Beamish
Murdoch during the last ten months of his life tell the story clearly. The
first, dated April 1875, left roughly half his estate to 'my best and tried
friend, my cousin' Charles Beamish, appointed him executor, and gave
the other half to Charles in trust for Eunice Kaulbach for her separate
use. In this will Murdoch left all his books to Akins. The second will,
dated June 1875, was made at New Ross while attending a wedding
with Mrs Kaulbach. She now received three-quarters of Murdoch's estate, Charles Beamish one-quarter. Two wills made in August were not
substantially different. By this point, the Kaulbachs were living with
Murdoch after the loss of their house.

When will five was made on 15 November 1875, the Kaulbachs were
still living with Murdoch. Charles Beamish was totally excluded, and
Senator Kaulbach and lawyer William Owen were appointed executors. Thomas Beamish Akins was allowed to select only twenty books
from Murdoch's large library. Eunice Kaulbach was to have a life interest in the residue of Murdoch's estate, with remainder to her children.

This will was eventually upheld by the Nova Scotia Supreme Court, but not without a struggle.[19]

Charles Beamish was granted probate of the April 1875 will by the Halifax County Court of Probate and challenged the November 1875 will on the basis of undue influence and incapacity when Kaulbach presented it for probate at Lunenburg.[20] The probate judge, George Thesiger Solomon, had apprenticed alongside Murdoch in the Uniacke law office sixty years before. It probably did not hurt the Kaulbach cause that Solomon's son, Edward H. Solomon, was a witness to the impugned November 1875 will. The validity of the will was upheld by Solomon after witnesses were examined for three tedious weeks during the summer of 1876.

Charles Beamish then appealed to the Supreme Court of Nova Scotia, where the judges had to sift through evidence 'in the last degree contradictory and irreconcilable.'[21] The majority judgment of Chief Justice William Young, with whom Justices William Frederick Desbarres and Henry W. Smith concurred, did not really attempt to reconcile the evidence, and at least the first two judges appear to have relied more on their own personal impressions of Murdoch than on the evidence. Desbarres stated that he had known Murdoch 'from early boyhood, and, from what I know of him, I do not think he was likely to be swayed or influenced by any person in the disposition of his property.' He added that, of course, he had decided the case only on the basis of the evidence.[22] In the end, Young was content to rely on the testimony of a Dr Jacobs, who testified that Murdoch was of sound mind on the 15th of November, and on that of a number of clergymen who stated they had never seen Murdoch under the influence of spirits or in any way disoriented. With regard to Murdoch's 'insane passion' for Eunice Kaulbach, Young opined that it was 'doing injustice to [Murdoch's] memory to infer from some rash or thoughtless expressions a criminal and insane desire, and a deliberate purpose to disturb the domestic peace of those whom he regarded as his best friends.'[23]

Justice Alexander James agreed in the result but came very close to dissenting. He went into the evidence much more thoroughly than Young and purported to reconcile it by proposing that Murdoch 'used the liquor as DeQuincy used opium, to bring himself up to a standard of intelligence and mental activity.' Murdoch 'was at his best when he had consumed a large quantity of ardent spirits,' and those witnesses who described him as 'dejected, weak, tottering, dirty and imbecile' had seen him when he was not under the stimulus of drink, but rather going through withdrawal.[24] James was troubled by the fact that Kaulbach was Murdoch's solicitor in fact and was closely involved in the preparation of his last three wills. However, he was unable to find that Kaulbach had actually kindled or exploited the imaginary grievances against Charles Beamish which led Murdoch to exclude him from his bounty. Kaulbach's conduct came close to the line, but in the end Murdoch had acted as a free agent. As Chief Justice Young said, 'a will, however capricious or harsh, cannot be set aside if it be the act of a volition free and untrammelled.'[25]

In spite of all the evidence of uncharacteristic behaviour, the case for Murdoch's alleged testamentary incapacity is unconvincing. Letters written by him as late as three weeks before his death are entirely cogent and go into financial matters in some detail. On its face, the charge of undue influence looked more compelling, but the legal test at the time was extremely stringent. Unlike the case of *inter vivos* gifts, where a pre-existing fiduciary relationship (such as solicitor-client) between donor and donee was sufficient to raise a presumption of undue influence, no such presumption existed in the testamentary context. The whole onus lay on Charles Beamish to show that any influence exercised by Kaulbach 'amount[ed] to force and coercion destroying free agency,' an almost insuperable evidentiary burden.[26]

A final appeal to the Supreme Court of Canada followed, but it was quashed because the Supreme and Exchequer Court Act allowed appeals to the highest court only from decisions originating in superior courts (the probate court was considered an inferior court).[27] It was a pyrrhic victory in one sense, since Eunice Kaulbach died the same year.[28] Her husband remarried the next year, and the funds from Murdoch's estate were presumably given to the Kaulbach children as they came of age. Ultimately, almost the sole asset of Murdoch's estate (aside from his library) remained what he had inherited early in life: the sale price of his interest in the Market Wharf. His professional income had supported him in comfort all his life, and covered his political and publishing ventures, but had resulted in no visible savings.

Little Rupert Creighton Sawyer Kaulbach, who had so charmed Murdoch as a child, followed in the paternal footsteps. He is a perfect example of a pattern that emerged clearly in the later nineteenth century, whereby scions of old 'gentry' families acquired professional qualifications from universities in order to solidify and legitimate the influence they exerted in their home communities.[29] Rupert Kaulbach attended Harvard Law School in 1891–4 (though without graduating) and acquired BA, MA, and LLB degrees from Dalhousie before returning to Lunenburg to practise law for the rest of his life. He was also a good example of the growing emphasis on sport which evolved to provide a masculine image for the new professionalism; Kaulbach's 1956 obituary was more intent on describing his exploits in cricket, hockey, football, figure skating, and golf than in the legal arena.[30]

Our principal interest in Rupert Kaulbach is to trace the fate of Beamish Murdoch's library, which seems to have remained in the possession of Senator Kaulbach until his death in 1896.[31] Many books currently held by Dalhousie University libraries contain Beamish Murdoch's signature or stamp, followed by the inscription 'to H.A.N. Kaulbach' in the latter's handwriting. Rupert was called to the bar in 1898 and presumably took possession of the library or part of it at some point thereafter. In 1926 Rupert Kaulbach, KC, 'generously presented to the [Dalhousie] Arts Library 107 volumes, containing an interesting very old edition of Euripides; and to the Law Library 110 volumes, mostly dealing with French Law. These books are from the library of Beamish Murdoch, historian of Nova Scotia and are of special value on that account.'[32] The donation was not catalogued for many years, and was then mingled with other large collections, making it very difficult to reconstitute this substantial fragment of Murdoch's library. Whether Kaulbach retained the remainder of Murdoch's library or disposed of it is unknown. Fortunately, the library of Murdoch's contemporary William Young is much better known and has been the subject of scholarly analysis.[33] In 1835, after less than a decade in practice, Young's library already held some 600 volumes (representing 300 titles). In its multilingual nature, its coverage of civil law and American law in addition to British legal sources, and its inclusion of non-legal material, Young's library likely had many parallels to Murdoch's. Both demonstrated the breadth and depth of intellectual engagement displayed by the more ambitious of this generation of colonial lawyers.

11

Conclusion

Two interrelated themes have been woven through this book: the nature of British North America's legal professionalism and its legal culture. In this chapter I will link each of these themes to broader debates recently conducted by historians. First, I will examine how what we have learned about British North American professionalism fits with Michael Burrage's impressive comparative study of the impact of revolutions on the legal profession.[1] Second, I will suggest that the study of nineteenth-century legal culture requires us to modify the notion of Canada as a liberal empire founded on 'the primacy of the individual and the inviolability of certain individual rights,' as powerfully argued in the work of Ian McKay.[2]

In the generation after Murdoch's death, a number of changes occurred in professional organization, preparation, and practice. The Maritimes caught up to Ontario and Quebec by enacting legislation obliging all members of the legal profession to belong to a statutorily empowered provincial barristers' society and stripping the judges of most of their disciplinary powers. University legal education, pioneered in Quebec, became available in Nova Scotia and New Brunswick and spread to western Canada in the early twentieth century, while the Law Society of Upper Canada created its own law school at Osgoode Hall. Business corporations became much more active and their demands for legal services called into existence the modern multi-partner law firm in the larger cities. Lawyers began to organize on a pan-Canadian basis, first, abortively, in the 1890s, then definitively in 1914 with the founding of the Canadian Bar Association, and a new discourse on legal ethics began to emerge, partly in response to a sense that law was becoming more of a business than a profession. By 1900, the barriers to entry for women, Jews, and non-whites had been breached, however tentatively. With these changes the modern Canadian legal profession emerges in a reassuringly familiar form, seemingly discontinuous with the colonial legal profession that preceded it.

I argue the contrary: that these changes of the fin de siècle, while significant in their own right, all emerged in an organic way in essential continuity with the colonial legal profession. The theme of continuity is not itself a new one: both Christopher Moore's study of the Law Society of Upper Canada and R.D. Gidney and W.P.J. Millar's examination of the professions in nineteenth-century Ontario stress the continuities between the expansive Georgian professionalism of Murdoch's youth and the more hard-edged, increasingly university-based professionalism of the later nineteenth century. Yet neither work analyses in any detail why this should have been so. I argue that the deep taproot of the North American legal profession was the decision to unite the roles of barrister and solicitor in a single profession, typically called 'attorney' in the United States and 'lawyer' in Canada. This development set the North American legal profession on a rather different track from its English ancestors. In England, the energies of the legal professions were largely spent in skirmishes with each other, as barristers sought to distance themselves from solicitors while solicitors sought to model themselves on barristers in a Sisyphean quest for respectability. English scholars tend to work on either barristers or solicitors but not both, with the result that this dynamic has been ignored or under-appreciated. Michael Burrage has performed a signal service in restoring it to view. He may overstate the extent to which English solicitors withdrew from business opportunities in the nineteenth century, but he is surely correct to say that, in any relative sense, English solicitors were far less directly involved in the inner life of corporations than their American (and, I would argue, Canadian) cousins; his argument that this occurred because solicitors wished to ape the independence of the barrister is plausible although the circumstantial nature of the evidence precludes any conclusive interpretation.[3]

The North American lawyer was largely liberated from this dynamic, and from much else that accompanied the traditions of the English legal professions. The lawyers of Upper Canada long remained the most anglophile of all Canadian lawyers, but even there we have often not distinguished adequately between words and actions. A rhetorical affiliation with the English bar did not prevent British North American lawyers in Upper Canada or elsewhere from structuring their professional lives in ways very different from English barristers and solicitors. For the Canadian lawyer, an active role at the pulsing heart of corporate life – as opposed to the provision of a narrowly defined suite of legal services – eventually became a logical extension of the wide-ranging and client-centred role lawyers had played in their communities since colonial times. The mid-century Montreal lawyers studied by G. Blaine Baker, who led the way in this regard,

were all actively involved in their clients' enterprises in ways that exceeded the momentary provision of technical advice. They often became effective partners of those clients, with directness that makes the identification of divisions between legal and other types of business labour difficult ... [As a result,] law and the economy became less rather than more distinguishable from each other [as] lawyers became joint venturers in transportation, financial, mercantile, manufacturing, and resource-extraction businesses instead of pinpoint providers of state-sanctioned, problem-solving skills.[4]

These men did not pause to ask themselves whether such activities were appropriate for lawyers, nor did they seem particularly concerned about their own professional autonomy: they just forged ahead. The economic precocity of Toronto and Montreal in the middle decades of the nineteenth century meant that such behaviour was largely confined to those cities at that time, but lawyers in other centres such as Halifax and Winnipeg followed suit when large financial and industrial concerns came their way later in the century.[5]

In the colonial capitals, elite lawyers such as William Blowers Bliss might dream about living the life of an English barrister and keeping the riff-raff out of the local bar, but he at least had the wit to realize that such ideas were indeed fantasies. The colonial lawyer could not be too choosy about what clients he represented or what services he would perform for them. He was not likely to turn down work because it or the client was not 'respectable.' His life was a constant search for more clients and more services that could provide more diverse sources of revenue, and he was always competing both with other lawyers and with non-legally-trained personnel who could perform many solicitorial functions. The colonial lawyer did not benefit from the English solicitor's comfortable monopoly on conveyancing, as noted earlier. We have seen that Murdoch's clientele changed almost completely between the 1820s and 1830s even as it increased in volume: acquiring clients was no guarantee of keeping them. Murdoch's indifferent health prevented him from riding the circuits, but many others did in an effort to gain exposure and clients. Even lawyers as successful as William Young continued to travel the circuit until late in their careers.

As the numbers of lawyers increased rapidly in British North America in the decades after the end of the Napoleonic Wars, the resulting competition encouraged a steady movement of lawyers out of the capitals and into the countryside in search of fresh markets, as we saw in chapter 4. In this competitive context, it seems likely that the successful lawyer would be the one who responded with the most creativity and facilitative zeal to his clients' needs – as Baker's Montreal lawyers clearly did – not the one who sat aloof from clients or from business concerns in the manner of the English barrister. Baker studied primarily anglophone lawyers but the careers of some francophones such as George-Étienne Cartier were not that dissimilar.[6] Massachusetts lawyer Warren Dutton captured this 'can-do' spirit well in an 1819 observation, echoing Murdoch's own description of the role of lawyers in the British colonies: 'In this country, there is little or no division of labour in the profession. All are attornies, conveyancers, proctors, barristers and counselors ... It is this habit of practical labour, this general knowledge of business, which connects the professional man in this country with all classes of the community, and gives him an influence, which pervades all.'[7] Lawyers had a choice: they could be responsive to clients' demands, or they could look for another profession. They were not judges in training, as English barristers were; responsiveness, not detachment, was their motto.

The blurring of the line between business and profession, then, was not a phenomenon that emerged with the rise of North American corporate capitalism. The line had been blurred long before – let us recall Murdoch's observation in 1832 that the colonial lawyer was 'emphatically ... a man of business,' and his enthusiastic advocacy on behalf of Halifax's mercantile community in the 1840s. What was different later in the nineteenth century was the increasing angst about the blurring of the line between business and profession with the emergence of the large urban 'law factories' and the rise of corporate law. Neither of those threats to lawyerly independence had existed before mid-century, when the prevalence of sole practitioners with long client lists seemed an adequate barrier against the capture of the legal profession by special interests.[8]

The union of barrister and solicitor also made the idea of university legal education more feasible in North America. In nineteenth-century England, 'while there was some support within both professions for educational reform,' the inns of court and the solicitorial profession effectively resisted public pressure for some kind of university training in law. They were successful partly because of endless jockeying around the issue of whether there would be one or two streams of such education, and partly because Oxford and Cambridge had no interest in teaching law, seeing it as essentially technical and unsuited to scholarly exposition.[9] There needed to be only one program of legal education in North America, where cash-poor universities were more than willing to teach whatever might bring in students; in the United States, the demise of apprenticeship in the 1830s and 1840s fortuitously swelled the potential market for university legal education. Abraham Lincoln may have had virtually no formal education of any kind, but a generation later things were very different: his son studied law at Harvard and Chicago and also served a year-long, voluntary apprenticeship in a Chicago law office in the 1850s.[10] As Burrage notes, when the bar associations re-emerged at the end of the nineteenth century, they would have preferred to reinstitute some kind of apprenticeship as a prerequisite to practice but were not able to combat the now-entrenched 'degree privilege' of the universities.[11]

In Canada, everywhere outside Ontario the bar societies were behind the move to create university legal education. They did not plan to surrender control over admission to the bar or give up apprenticeship, but they were prepared to participate in a partnership with the universities and long retained significant control over the content of the curriculum and the general ethos of the law faculties.[12] The universities, for their part, did not have anything like the same clout as their U.S. counterparts and were delighted to add prestigious law faculties to their institutions. There did not have to be triangular negotiations with two professions, as in England, and the provincial barristers' societies readily cooperated with the universities, again, everywhere except Ontario.[13]

This portrayal of an essentially North American legal profession distinguished from the English by its historic decision to be one profession rather than two essentially contradicts Burrage's argument about the determinative impact of the American Revolution on the U.S. legal profession. Revolutionary effects cannot be the prime factor moulding the

U.S. legal profession if its behaviour is in important respects mirrored in non-revolutionary Canada. My argument would be even more persuasive if I could show that the ethical choices made by the pre-Confederation bar were similar to those of U.S. lawyers, since a distinction in ethical codes is one of the key areas in which Burrage portrays U.S. and English lawyers as making very different choices; unfortunately, there is insufficient evidence of the behaviour of British North American lawyers on some key ethical questions: the use of contingency fees, for example, or the use of creative forms of agency and partnership relations. When such evidence does become available, in the post-Confederation period, it supports my argument that the choices made reflected U.S. more than English influences, but further exploration of this theme would take us too far afield and will have to await further research.[14]

Burrage is undoubtedly correct on one thing, however: revolutions do have an impact on governance, and it is in their governance patterns that we see the most significant and lasting differences between the American and Canadian legal professions. As Burrage demonstrates, the demise of the bar associations in United States in the 1830s and 1840s forever changed the shape of American lawyers' governance. When bar associations re-emerged after the Civil War, they were voluntary associations with restrictive memberships (whether on the basis of social class, practice area, gender, race, ethnicity, or religion) that tended to be seen as elitist by non-members, the public, and legislatures. Disciplinary powers remained with the courts. When legislation creating 'integrated bars'– that is, those that could demand compulsory membership and in some cases exercise disciplinary powers, similar to Canadian bar societies – appeared in the twentieth century in some states, it was not at the request of lawyers, many of whom preferred the ability to conduct their profession with a maximum of freedom. And, while some thirty-two states had integrated bars by 1995, many do not exercise disciplinary powers, which are mostly vested in the courts and statutory tribunals; moreover, the presence of integrated bars has not prevented the proliferation of competing voluntary associations, including those that Burrage calls 'anti-bar associations,' which contest the right of official bar councils to speak for the profession. Burrage's conclusion is bleak: 'It is difficult to think of a legal profession in any other country … that has had such a turbulent history of co-existing and alternative forms of government, or such a record of self-confessed failure.'[15]

The contrast with the Canadian scene is obvious. Strong forms of statutory autonomy for the bar were recognized early on in Upper and

Lower Canada, and spread to the Maritimes and the rest of Canada by the early twentieth century, as noted in chapter 4. The authority of such bodies long remained largely unchallenged internally or externally, in spite of fairly significant stratification among lawyers based on income, client type, and so on. The close relationship between provincial legislatures and the bar societies cannot be explained simply by reference to the presence of lawyers in the legislature, since lawyers were also present in U.S. state legislatures, sometimes in greater numbers than in Canada, and they were often hostile to measures sought by 'official' representatives of the state bars. The first major public challenge to the authority of the Law Society of Upper Canada in 150 years, according to Christopher Moore, came in the one area where it was so out of step with public opinion in Ontario and elsewhere: the struggle over legal education launched by the resignation of the academic staff of its own Osgoode Hall Law School in 1949.[16] After 1970 the Law Society was increasingly forced to negotiate its authority with the state and other bodies: 'the principle of self-government endured, but authority over the legal profession was becoming permanently subdivided.'[17] Even so, provincial bar societies (with modest lay representation on their councils) remain at the very heart of professional regulation in Canada, to an extent probably unequalled in any other common law jurisdiction. Internal dissent has generally been handled by the election of members with new ideas to bar councils and subsequent negotiation, not by the secession of discontented groups.[18] Using A.O. Hirschman's famous trilogy of exit, voice, and loyalty, Canadian lawyers mostly sought voice over the alternatives when they were dissatisfied with their bar councils.[19]

Given the common roots of the Canadian and American legal professions in colonial British America, the unitary nature of the profession, and the similar nature of the day-to-day practice of law in the United States and Canada, such different historic choices about governance must plausibly be traced to some larger ideas about law, authority, and social ordering. Burrage does not consider the Canadian example except on isolated points, but where governance is concerned his argument about the influence of revolutions has considerable explanatory power. Where the antebellum U.S. legal profession was characterized by the dismantling of barriers to entry, governance by common law and the market, and a hostile relationship with state legislators, by 1867 a state-sanctioned model of governance by autonomous bar councils in Ontario and Quebec was normative and would soon spread to the other provinces, and three- or four-year apprenticeships remained pre-requisites for entry to the profession, shrinking to one year only after the advent of university legal education.

Where Burrage and some U.S. scholars have gone astray is in con-sidering that, if the Thirteen Colonies had not revolted, the American legal profession would have gone on to become more and more like the English legal professions: divided, class-conscious, and oriented to the state and social elites. Thus, Burrage observes that 'there is no reason to suppose that the [pre-Revolutionary] American lawyers were delib-erately rejecting the principle of a divided bar in favour of some new form of legal practice that they had themselves invented.' Rather, they were, he asserts, 'moving towards an English form of professional self-government, with similar corporate institutions and similar corporate goals.'[20] For his part, Stephen Botein speculates that, if not for the train of events generated by the Stamp Act, 'the colonial legal profession at mid-century may have been destined to achieve standing as a kind of provincial mandarinate, defined by and responsive to cues from White-hall.'[21]

It is puzzling why scholars pondering such counter-factuals do not cast their eyes north of the border, where a non-revolutionary America was indeed established. Burrage is at least partly right, in that the Brit-ish North American legal profession did have similar corporate goals to the English legal professions, but to achieve them by means of a leg-islatively fused profession rather than a divided one was decidedly un-English. If any group might have been expected to replicate the caste distinction between barristers and attorneys, it was the Loyalist law-yers of New Brunswick and Nova Scotia. Yet, as we have seen, in nei-ther colony was a divided bar attempted and steps were taken both in Nova Scotia and in Ontario to ensure that immigrant English barristers could never do so. In Upper Canada, with much higher British immi-gration and many more lawyers trained or born in England, the lure of the divided profession did resurface at times; on several occasions in the 1830s, attempts were made to prevent barristers from practis-ing as attorneys but all failed, and the unified profession triumphed.[22] As for Botein's prediction, it confuses aspiration with reality, and the situation of a small cadre of well-connected lawyers with all the rest. Few lawyers in colonial British North America became mandarins serv-ing the state or wealthy through their connections to it. They could not afford to languish in the colonial capitals awaiting the dropping of a few crumbs of imperial patronage; rather, as we saw in chapter 4, they fled over-serviced colonial capitals for better prospects in the under-serviced countryside, where they worked hard in a competitive environment to earn their living.

Only in Upper Canada can one find anything remotely resembling an inn of court, but again appearances can be deceiving. As Baker has argued, the Law Society 'was essentially a hybrid whose English parentage was somewhat recessive ... While the structural similarities are superficially compelling, substantive counterparts are limited,' especially in the field of education, to which the Law Society of Upper Canada devoted considerable attention in its early decades.[23] With its requirements of term-keeping at Osgoode Hall (four terms from 1828 to 1857, two from 1858 to 1871, when the requirement was abolished), the education and socialization of lawyers was more centralized in Upper Canada than in the other colonies, but once lawyers were called to the bar they spread throughout the countryside and became deeply embedded in their communities.

A brief comparison with Australia may shed further light on the significance of having a unified profession or not. If my argument seems to suggest that a divided profession was economically unviable in a New World setting of low population density, how, it may be asked, did New South Wales, and thereafter most Australian states, end up with a divided profession very much on the English model? The answer seems to be that they almost did not, and in any case economic exigencies drove them largely to ignore the traditional division of labour outside major cities. The original convict population had included some attorneys who, after attaining their freedom, set up legal practices which included pleading in the courts, thus combining the roles of barrister and solicitor. The Third Charter of Justice for New South Wales, promulgated in 1823, expressly permitted the Supreme Court to admit qualified candidates to practise both as barristers and as attorneys, and Chief Justice Francis Forbes seemed to favour a fused profession on the ground that it was more suitable to the circumstances of a young colony. A number of English expatriate barristers then sought to ban the 'convict lawyers' from pleading in the courts and pressed hard for a division of the bar. Forbes reluctantly acquiesced in his colleagues' desire to divide the profession, and the court published a draft rule to this effect in 1829. After confirmation of this rule in London in 1834, New South Wales recognized a formally divided profession that English and Irish barristers were able to dominate; before long, they had exerted their influence so as to reshape the entire legal order in a more English-style configuration, and when in due course they were promoted to the bench, they controlled the judiciary as well. Had Chief Justice Forbes put up more resistance to the English barristers' argument – his action was controversial at the time and he was later said to have greatly regretted it – the Australian legal profession may well have evolved in a manner more akin to that in North America, with the roles of barrister and solicitor united in one person.[24]

This comparison reveals the crucial importance of the nascent indigenous bar and of the steps taken by the legislatures in Upper Canada and Nova Scotia to force English barristers to conform to local professional norms. In all three jurisdictions, Upper Canada, Nova Scotia, and New South Wales, expatriate English barristers sought to impose their vision of a profession divided largely along lines of class or status with them on top. In the British North American colonies, they were legislatively precluded from doing so; the Third Charter of Justice of New South Wales, being only permissive with regard to a unified profession and not prohibitive of a divided one, gave the English barristers sufficient wiggle room to make a deal with the judges, themselves all trained as English barristers. The indigenous lawyers who opposed this move had no representative assembly to which they could appeal, the Legislative Council of the colony being a purely appointive body until 1842. That a divided profession actually worked against the interests of the public and all but a small coterie of urban barristers is suggested by evidence from the colony/state of Victoria, which also recognized a divided profession when it separated from New South Wales in 1851. Rob MacQueen's work on the fusion debate in Victoria shows that the two-professions model was as uneconomic outside Melbourne as it was in British North America. In the second half of the nineteenth century, outside the capital Victorian barristers and solicitors practised 'as if the profession was already amalgamated,' the only clear rule being that solicitors could not plead cases before the Supreme Court.[25]

This look at the U.S. and Canadian legal professions, then, provides an example of a pattern familiar to students of comparative United States-Canada studies: with regard to the economy and the conduct of daily life, there are many similarities, but as soon as one enters the field of politics, institutions, and attitudes to authority, differences begin to be more marked. Beamish Murdoch could recommend Baltimore lawyer David Hoffman's *Course of Legal Study* (ahead of Blackstone!) to law students in Nova Scotia as 'the best [introductory treatise] I have met with, [which] should be read carefully by every student,' even as he abhorred the republican system of government.[26] Canadian lawyers may have mimicked to some extent the corporate activities and organizations of their English brethren, but in the way they earned their daily bread, the breadth of clientele they served, and their deep involvement in community and business life, they shared in a distinctive North American pattern of lawyering with deep roots in the colonial period.

Turning to our second theme, Murdoch's written oeuvre and his career point to some important characteristics of British North American legal culture: its response to diversity and the role of native peoples and its understanding of liberty. Murdoch tried to portray Nova Scotia law as having eradicated any legal distinctions between Protestant and Catholic, black and white, and those of Acadian and British ancestry. He was overly enthusiastic in this regard in the sense that racially segregated education would later emerge along with the public school system itself. But in general the British North American colonies recognized few legal distinctions among non-aboriginals based on racial identity or religious affiliation before Confederation; they did not, for example, replicate any of the anti-miscegenation laws that spread across most of the United States during the antebellum period,[27] and they preferred a model of equality rather than tolerance for dealing with religious differences. Social discrimination, and its impact on the actual administration of the law, was a different problem, one that would take much longer to recognize and eradicate.

If at first Murdoch was reticent to include the Mi'kmaq as equal members of provincial society, he made up for this to some extent later on in life when he had become more familiar with their situation. But this concession had little impact on the central questions facing the British North American colonies vis-à-vis their aboriginal inhabitants. What was the nature and extent of their legal rights, if any, over their traditional territories, which had now been mostly settled by Europeans? And what role would they play in colonial society? Murdoch seemed to assume that the Mi'kmaq would continue to follow their traditional way of life apart from the mainstream of colonial society and did not advocate their becoming agriculturalists, but this reckoned without the depletion of game and disruption of traditional hunting patterns caused by European settlement, and the constant whittling away of reserve lands by European squatting. Without, for the most part, a secure land base or significant compensation in lieu, the First Nations of British North America were condemned to an uncertain limbo between traditional and European ways of life, a state to which the residential schools of the twentieth century seemed the perfect solution. Murdoch and later legal writers seemed to regard the First Nations question as someone else's problem, and took little responsibility for its resolution.

Murdoch's work also demonstrates the openness of British North American legal culture to legal as well as social diversity: he embraced Roman law, civilian techniques of codification, and American innovations to flesh out the common law of Nova Scotia, while also rejecting aspects of the English inheritance he found unsuitable. Others have noted this theme of 'polyjurality' in the evolution of Quebec law, but its presence in Murdoch's work shows that it had a wider British North American resonance.[28] Such 'legal pantheism' was also present in the early national United States but disappeared fairly quickly after about 1840.[29] In England, meanwhile, the influence of the civil law as a whole was fast fading with the abolition of the civil law courts in the mid-Victorian overhaul of the administration of justice and the resulting disappearance of the civilian lawyers as a distinct profession, although discrete aspects of civilian jurisprudence, such as French contract law, remained attractive to English jurists.

And what of Murdoch and liberty? With the renaissance of historical interest in Canada as a liberal society, it is appropriate to ask whether this study of Murdoch can shed any light on past understandings of liberalism and liberty.[30] Murdoch was a zealous defender of traditional civil and political liberties, liberties that he saw as having been enjoyed by the Acadians as well as the British. He certainly supported private property, a competitive economy, and, more generally, the commercial interests that he saw as the backbone of the provincial economy. But one does not get the impression that the right to property trumped all other liberties in his world view. The occasions when Murdoch came to public notice through involvement in some legal or political controversy typically involved traditional civil-liberties concerns: the unjust imprisonment of lawyer William Sutherland, the dispute over the selection of the new rector at St Paul's, the trial of Joseph Howe. His attempts to protect the inhabitants of Halifax from the dreaded railway levy were made on behalf of all ratepayers, small and large. The *Epitome* devotes a good deal of space to the doctrines of property law, but primarily the land law and not the emergent law of commercial property. More important, it contains almost an entire volume dealing with provincial regulatory laws covering trade, agriculture, and social welfare; this choice has no counterpart in Kent's *Commentaries*, which are devoted to private law and constitutional law and offer very little coverage of the exercise of state police power. Nor does Murdoch express any disapproval of this extensive regulation of the provincial economy, quite the contrary.

Murdoch's conception of liberty has more in common with what Michel Ducharme has labelled 'modern liberty' than with the classical liberty that underlay the American and French revolutions as well as the Canadian rebellions of 1837–8.[31] Modern liberty, as Ducharme explains, emphasizes that individual rights to life, liberty, and property, while fundamental, are not pre-political. They exist within an institutional context that includes a representative parliament which can override or tailor these rights in the public interest. Change within this system comes about through the election of new representatives and the circulation of new ideas through a free press, not through overthrowing the entire state edifice. Classical liberty, by contrast, emphasizes direct political participation by a virtuous citizenry whose natural rights exist prior to the state. If those rights are imperilled, the response is to overthrow the state and impose a new regime, or at the very least, as many state constitutional conventions did in the nineteenth century, adopt a new constitution. Modern liberty aims to protect the rights of the individual, but those rights are seen as existing within a social, political, and institutional context, giving rise to a creative tension between the rights and interests of the individual and those of the community or broader society. Those tensions ultimately must be mediated by a representative body of some kind, hence the importance for Murdoch of serving in the Assembly. This version of liberty can have its own liberal and conservative variants (for example, Whigs and Tories in England), but it is not reactionary or counter-revolutionary just because it does not fuel revolutions. As Ducharme notes, the constitutions established for the Canadas in 1791 (similar to those already existing in the Maritimes) were permeated with Enlightenment ideas and represented a major step forward in self-governance; it is unhelpful as well as inaccurate to label them counter-revolutionary.[32]

Ducharme's portrayal of modern liberty seems to me to capture much better the ideas that motivated Murdoch and many of his British North American contemporaries than the definition of liberalism initially put forward by Ian McKay in his article proposing the 'liberal order framework' as a unifying concept for the writing of Canadian history.[33] McKay's insistence that liberalism favours 'the epistemological and ontological primacy of the category "individual"' and the protection and accumulation of property as its highest goal seems to ignore the role of political, legal, and other institutions in both nurturing and limiting individual rights. In his focus on an exaggerated version of individualism, McKay overlooks one of the key factors distinguishing Canadian from American history: the constant conjugation of individual liberty with order (or public welfare) and pluralism in Canada as opposed to its embrace as a free-standing natural right.[34] The contrasting developments in the governance of the legal profession analysed in chapter 4 provide a perfect example of this dichotomy. Where American states abolished barriers to entering the legal profession in the name of individual freedom and effectively abolished professional self-governance at the same time, the British North American colonies continued to insist on lengthy apprenticeships, obligatory observation of court proceedings, and an increasingly stringent series of entrance and exit exams as a form of *encadrement* for aspiring lawyers. Once called to the bar, these lawyers were obliged to belong to a professional body corporate in the Canadas (and later, in the Maritimes as well) and to participate in its governance; moreover, these bodies proved to be remarkably durable over time, not fragmenting, shattering, or withering away. Ducharme's distinction between modern and classical liberty explains these differences in a satisfying way; McKay's possessive individualism cannot.

The legal culture of British North America, then, certainly valued individual liberty and sought to protect the rights of individuals. It did not see this as the sole goal of the law, however, and recognized that rights exist in a historical and institutional context that may require their modification over time as new exigencies arise. For adherents of modern liberty, the highest form of liberty was not the absence of restraint but the right to participate in free institutions, a trope that would be played on to great effect by provincial premiers later in the century. In treating rights as, in a sense, defeasible, modern liberty may be accused of delaying the development of a 'rights culture' in Canada, a phenomenon that is often said to have emerged only after the Second World War.[35] I would suggest, rather, that a relatively robust rights culture in the pre-Confederation period, anchored in the heritage of the Glorious Revolution, exemplified by Murdoch and evident in the struggles for responsible government, became gradually weakened with the rise of the federal and provincial states and the concomitant entrenchment of legal positivism and modern professionalism, all of which were hostile to culturally or historically grounded notions of rights. Any further exploration of the emergence of Canada's 'rights culture' must give due weight to both legal culture and political culture, which overlap but are not identical.

Appendix
Bibliography of Published and Manuscript Works by Beamish Murdoch

Published

A Narrative of the Late Fires at Miramichi, New Brunswick: with an Appendix Containing the Statements of Many of the Sufferers, and a Variety of Interesting Occurrences; together with a Poem, Entitled 'The Conflagration.' Halifax: P.J. Holland, 1825.

The Acadian Magazine. Halifax, July 1826–July 1827.

An Essay on the Mischievous Tendency of Imprisoning for Debt, and in other Civil Cases. 2d ed. Halifax: J.S. Cunnabell 1831.

An Epitome of the Laws of Nova-Scotia. 4 vols. Halifax: Joseph Howe 1832–3.

An Epitome of the Laws of Nova-Scotia. 4 vols. Holmes Beach, Fla.: Wm. W. Gaunt and Sons, 1971 [photo-reproduction edition].

'Oration.' *Celebration of the Centenary Anniversary of the Settlement of the City of Halifax. June 8th, 1849.* Halifax, n.p., 1850.

The Charter and Ordinances of the City of Halifax, in the Province of Nova Scotia, with the Provincial Acts Concerning the City, Collated and Revised by Authority of the City Council. Halifax: Wm. Gossip 1851.

A Supplement Containing the Ordinances of the City of Halifax, Nova Scotia Passed since 1851 and the Recent Provincial Acts Concerning the City. Halifax: English and Blackadar 1854.

A Second Supplement Containing Ordinances of the City of Halifax, Nova Scotia Passed in 1854, 1855 and 1856; Several Provincial Acts Concerning the City, Passed in 1855 and 1856; and Extracts from the Revised Statutes. Halifax: J. and W. Compton 1856.

A History of Nova-Scotia, or Acadie. 3 vols. Halifax: James Barnes 1865–7.

Unpublished

'Forms of the Supreme Court' (c. 1815–21). Manuscript commonplace book
  held by Rare Books Collection, Sir James Dunn Law Library, Dalhousie University.
'Historical Memoirs of the British North American Provinces since His Present Majesty's Accession' (c. 1829). NSARM, Beamish Murdoch Papers, MG
  1, vol. 726.
Gaelic-English dictionary (1848). NSARM, Beamish Murdoch Papers, MG 1,
  vol. 727A, no. 2.
Micmac-English dictionary (1864). NSARM, Beamish Murdoch Papers, MG 1,
  vol. 727A, no. 1.

Notes

1: Introduction

1 Kenneth Pryke, 'Murdoch, Beamish,' *Dictionary of Canadian Biography* (*DCB*) 10.
2 R.D. Gidney and W.P.J. Millar, *Professional Gentlemen: The Professions in Nineteenth-Century Ontario* (Toronto: University of Toronto Press 1994); Christopher Moore, *The Law Society of Upper Canada and Ontario's Lawyers, 1797–1997* (Toronto: University of Toronto Press 1997); G. Blaine Baker, 'Legal Education in Upper Canada, 1785–1889: The Law Society as Educator,' in David H. Flaherty, ed., *Essays in the History of Canadian Law, Vol. II* (Toronto: University of Toronto Press for the Osgoode Society 1983); G. Blaine Baker, 'Law, Practice and Statecraft in Mid-Nineteenth-Century Montreal: The Torrance-Morris Firm, 1848–1868,' in Carol Wilton, ed., *Beyond the Law: Lawyers and Business in Canada, 1830–1930* (Toronto: University of Toronto Press for the Osgoode Society 1990); G. Blaine Baker, 'Ordering the Urban Canadian Law Office and Its Entrepreneurial Hinterland, 1825–1875,' *University of Toronto Law Journal*, 48 (1998): 175; D.G. Bell, *Legal Education in New Brunswick: A History* (Fredericton: University of New Brunswick 1992); Christine Veilleux, 'Les Gens de Justice à Québec, 1760–1867' (PhD thesis, Université Laval, 1990); Christine Veilleux, *Aux Origines du Barreau Québécois, 1779–1849* (Sillery, Que.: Septentrion 1997); Sylvio Normand, 'La transformation de la profession d'avocat au Québec, 1840–1900,' in Claire Dolan, ed., *Entre Justice et Justiciables: Les Auxiliaires de*

la Justice du Moyen Âge au XXe Siècle (Quebec: Les Presses de l'Université Laval 2005); Jean-Philippe Garneau, 'Une culture de l'amalgame au prétoire: les avocats de Québec et l'élaboration d'un langage juridique commun au tournant des XVIIIe et XIXe siècles,' *Canadian Historical Review*, 88 (2007): 113; D.G. Bell, 'Maritime Legal Institutions under the Ancien Regime, 1710–1850,' *Manitoba Law Journal*, 23 (1995): 103; Philip Girard, 'The Maritime Provinces, 1850–1939,' *Manitoba Law Journal*, 23 (1995): 380; Philip Girard, 'The Roots of a Professional Renaissance: Lawyers in Nova Scotia, 1850–1910,' *Manitoba Law Journal*, 20 (1991): 148.

3 References to the literature on this point can be found in chapter 7.

4 '"So Elegant a Web": Providential Order and the Rule of Secular Law in Early Nineteenth-Century Upper Canada,' *University of Toronto Law Journal*, 38 (1988): 184–205; 'Law, Practice and Statecraft'; 'Strategic Benthamism: Rehabilitating United Canada's Bar through Criminal Law Codification, 1847–54,' in Jim Phillips, R. Roy McMurtry, and John T. Saywell, eds., *Essays in the History of Canadian Law, Vol. X, A Tribute to Peter N. Oliver* (Toronto: University of Toronto Press for the Osgoode Society 2008).

5 *Revolution and the Making of the Contemporary Legal Profession in England, France, and the United States* (New York: Oxford University Press 2006).

6 W. Wesley Pue and David Sugarman, eds., *Lawyers and Vampires: Cultural Histories of Legal Professions* (Oxford and Portland, Ore.: Hart Publishing 2003), 13. David Lemmings's important work on the English bar in the seventeenth and eighteenth centuries is another good example of scholarship on the cultural history of lawyers: *Gentlemen and Barristers: The Inns of Court and the English Bar, 1680–1730* (New York: Oxford University Press 1990), and *Professors of the Law: Barristers and English Legal Culture in the Eighteenth Century* (New York: Oxford University Press 2000).

7 Pue and Sugarman, *Lawyers and Vampires*, 6.

8 Lawrence Friedman, 'The Concept of Legal Culture: A Reply,' in David Nelken, ed., *Comparing Legal Cultures* (Aldershot, U.K.: Dartmouth 1997), 34.

9 See the debate between Roger Cotterell and Lawrence Friedman in Nelken, eds., *Comparing Legal Cultures*. Garneau, 'Une culture de l'amalgame au prétoire,' also has a good discussion of the utility of the concept of legal culture.

10 Ann Fidler, '"A Dry and Revolting Study": The Life and Labours of Antebellum Law Students,' in Pue and Sugarman, eds., *Lawyers and Vampires*, 67. Fidler is paraphrasing Michael Grossberg, '"Fighting Faiths" and the Challenges of Legal History,' *Journal of Social History*, 25 (1991): 195–6.

11 Dominique Marquis, 'Une élite mal connue: les avocats dans la société

montréalaise au tournant du XXe siècle,' *Recherches sociographiques*, 36 (1995): 307–25.

12 Bell, 'Maritime Legal Institutions,' 124.

13 See generally Philip Girard, 'Themes and Variations in Early Canadian Legal Culture: Beamish Murdoch and his *Epitome of the Laws of Nova-Scotia*,' *Law and History Review*, 11 (1993): 101–44.

14 This is not to say that these phrases and the world view subtending them cannot usefully be explored. See Greg Marquis, 'Doing Justice to "British Justice": Law, Ideology and Canadian Historiography,' in W. Wesley Pue and Barry Wright, eds., *Canadian Perspectives on Law and Society: Issues in Legal History* (Ottawa: Carleton University Press 1988), 43–69, and his 'In Defence of Liberty: 17th-Century England and 19th-Century Maritime Political Culture,' *University of New Brunswick Law Journal*, 42 (1993): 69–94; Philip Girard, 'British Justice, English Law, and Canadian Legal Culture,' in Phillip Buckner, ed., *Canada and the British Empire* (Oxford: Oxford University Press 2008).

15 Historians to date have focused more on the economic aspects of 'improvement' as opposed to its moral and cultural dimensions, which were of more interest to Murdoch: Daniel Samson, *The Spirit of Industry and Improvement: Liberal Government and Rural-Industrial Society, Nova Scotia, 1790–1862* (Montreal and Kingston: McGill-Queen's University Press 2008); Ian McKay, 'Canada as a Long Liberal Revolution: On Writing the History of Actually Existing Canadian Liberalisms, 1840s–1940s,' in Jean-François Constant and Michel Ducharme, *Liberalism and Hegemony: Debating the Canadian Liberal Revolution* (Toronto: University of Toronto Press 2009), 350–1.

16 Bell, 'Maritime Legal Institutions,' 125.

17 Brian Young, *The Politics of Codification: The Lower Canadian Civil Code of 1866* (Montreal and Kingtson: McGill-Queen's University Press 1994).

18 These will be referred to in due course but it should be noted that a study of William Young's legal career based on his extensive legal papers has recently been completed: William Laurence, '"A Literary Man and a Merchant": The Legal Career of Sir William Young' (PhD thesis, Dalhousie University, 2009).

19 'Law, Practice and Statecraft'; 'Ordering the Urban Canadian Law Office.'

20 Gidney and Millar, *Professional Gentlemen*, begin serious quantitative study only in 1851, when the first census reports become available. Veilleux, 'Les Gens de Justice à Québec,' 134–5, uses bar-admission records and other sources to track the numbers of advocates and notaries practising both in Quebec City and in the province as a whole from the Conquest to Confed-

eration, but does not explore their geographic mobility. Elizabeth Bloom-field, 'Lawyers as Members of Urban Business Elites in Southern Ontario, 1860–1920,' in Wilton, ed., *Beyond the Law*, explores the geographic diffu-sion of lawyers in Ontario at a later period but does not track the move-ments of individual lawyers.

21 On the changing concept of independence, see Philip Girard, 'The Inde-pendence of the Bar in Historical Perspective: Comforting Myths, Trou-bling Realities,' in *In the Public Interest: The Report and Research Papers of the Law Society of Upper Canada's Task Force on the Rule of Law and the Indepen-dence of the Bar* (Toronto: Irwin Law 2007).

22 There is a large literature on the new professionalism but for a Canadian overview see Girard, 'Roots of a Professional Renaissance.'

2: Antecedents

1 This is the date traditionally given, probably because it is inscribed on Murdoch's tombstone in Hillcrest Cemetery, Lunenburg, but there is no documentary proof for it. The St Paul's baptismal records at Nova Scotia Archives and Records Management (NSARM), mfm. reel 11553, show the baptism of Benjamin Salter Beamish Murdoch on 14 February 1802, with the marginal notation: '1 yr old.' A more authoritative piece of evidence for a birth date of late July or early August is Murdoch's admission as an attorney of the Supreme Court of Nova Scotia on 22 July 1821. By statute, one could be admitted an attorney only on reaching majority. Murdoch completed his apprenticeship in November 1819, and it was only the at-taining of his majority that delayed his admission as an attorney by nearly two years. So scrupulously observed was the requirement of majority that it is doubtful whether Murdoch would have been admitted even ten days before his twenty-first birthday. However, such a slight relaxation of the rule, perhaps to accommodate a judicial vacation, is possible.

2 *Royal Gazette and Nova Scotia Advertiser*, 5 Nov. 1799.

3 L.M. Cullen, 'The Irish Diaspora of the Seventeenth and Eighteenth Cen-turies,' in Nicholas Canny, ed. *Europeans on the Move: Studies on European Migration, 1500–1800* (Oxford: Clarendon Press 1994), 144–6.

4 Much of what is known about the Murdoch family in Ireland comes from two principal sources: the writings of Eliza Frame (1820–1904), a great-niece of the Reverend James Murdoch and amateur historian, and a published compilation of family lore distilled by W.J. Stairs and his wife, Susan, and published posthumously by their family. Susan Stairs

was Murdoch's great-granddaughter, who learned much of the family tradition from her grandmother, Susannah (Murdoch) Duffus. See [Eliza Frame], *Descriptive Sketches of Nova Scotia, in Prose and Verse, by a Nova Scotian* (Halifax: A. and W. McKinlay 1864); 'Rev. James Murdoch. 1767–1799,' *Nova Scotia Historical Society Collections*, 2 (1881): 100; W.J. and Susan Stairs, comps., *Family History. Stairs, Morrow* (Halifax: McAlpine Publishing 1906). On Frame, see Janet Guildford, 'Frame, Elizabeth Murdoch,' *DCB* 13. These sources must be used with some caution since they are based on oral traditions which in many cases cannot be authenticated by written documents. Where they can be so authenticated, they have proved to be generally accurate.

5 The record of his matriculation in 1759 is held at the University of Edinburgh Archives, but records for the 1760s have not survived. It was not usual for candidates for the ministry to graduate from the university, and Murdoch did not do so (personal communication from the assistant librarian, 17 Sept. 1996).

6 See generally James Robertson, *History of the Mission of the Secession Church to Nova Scotia and Prince Edward Island from Its Commencement in 1765* (Edinburgh: John Johnstone 1847), 20.

7 Frame, *Descriptive Sketches*, 243. Frame gives a detailed account of Murdoch's ordination, based on original documents made available to her by one of Murdoch's granddaughters but apparently no longer extant: *Family History. Stairs, Morrow*, 231.

8 Although no direct proof of a connection exists, it may be that the Murdochs were enticed by an advertisement in the *Belfast Newsletter* of April 1768 inviting settlers to board 'the good ship Nancy,' bound for 'the Fertile and Flourishing Province of Nova-Scotia, in America.' All who paid for their passage in Belfast were promised one hundred acres for every head of family, fifty acres for each wife and child, and one hundred acres for every single man, free of rent for the first five years and subject only to a charge of £10 for each 100 acres payable over ten years. I thank Nancy O'Brien for this reference.

9 Information on the marriage and progeny of the Reverend James Murdoch and Abigail (Salter) Murdoch is derived from entries in their family Bible reproduced in *Family History. Stairs, Morrow*, 229. The original Bible, published at Edinburgh in 1766, is held at NSARM, MG 8, vol. 22. All manuscript group (MG) and record group (RG) citations below involve documents found at NSARM, unless otherwise indicated.

10 J.M. Bumsted, 'Alline, Henry,' *DCB* 4.

11 Frame, *Descriptive Sketches*, 44–5. For the background to Alline's movement, see Gordon T. Stewart, *Documents Relating to the Great Awakening in
Nova Scotia 1760–1791* (Toronto: Champlain Society 1982).

12 On Salter's political troubles, see Barry Cahill, 'The Treason of the Merchants: Dissent and Repression in Halifax in the Era of the American Revolution,' *Acadiensis*, 26, no. 1 (1996): 52–70.

13 The only contemporary evidence is that of the Reverend John Wiswall, the
Society for the Propagation of the Gospel (SPG) missionary at Cornwallis, who managed to oust Murdoch from enjoyment of the glebe revenues
by legal action in 1785: Wiswall to William Morice, 6 Aug. 1786, NSARM
Micro-Biography, Rev. John Wiswall, mfm. reel 11153, 77. He refers to
Murdoch's 'dismissal' by his congregation, but this word can refer to either a voluntary or involuntary departure in this context. Wiswall does not
elaborate on the circumstances of the 'dismissal.'

14 Debra Anne McNabb, 'Land and Families in Horton Township, N.S. 1760–
1830' (MA thesis, University of British Columbia, 1986), 52–5.

15 Eliza Frame gives an account of his travels in the 1790s based on fragments
of his diary she found during a trip to Musquodoboit in the 1860s: *Descriptive Sketches*, 33–50.

16 *Royal Gazette and Nova Scotia Advertiser*, 3 Dec. 1799.

17 Murdoch's life and career are treated at greater length in Philip Girard,
'Preacher to Planter to Pariah: The Vicissitudes of the Reverend James
Murdoch,' in Margaret Conrad and Barry Moody, eds., *Planter Links: Community and Culture in Colonial Nova Scotia* (Fredericton: Acadiensis Press
2001), 105–18.

18 Benjamin Salter's daybook for June–October 1799, MG 3, vol. 1838c,
records numerous payments to Andrew Murdoch in cash and in kind.

19 D.C. Harvey, ed., *The Diary of Simeon Perkins* (Toronto: Champlain Society
1978), vol. 4 (1797–1803), 164. See also entries at 163, 167.

20 Ibid., 162.

21 The estate papers of Benjamin Salter, RG 48 (Halifax County Court of Probate), S1, mfm. reel 19421.

22 *Brook Watson, William Goodal and John Turner v. Susannah Salter, John and
Thomas Fillis, and Andrew Murdoch, administrators of Benjamin Salter* (1802),
and *Brook Watson, William Goodal and John Turner v. Andrew Murdoch*
(1802), RG 39C (Halifax), box 84. Watson had also been the most pressing of Malachi Salter's creditors in the 1770s, according to Susan Buggey,
'Salter, Malachi,' *DCB* 4. In his petition to the House of Assembly in 1806,
Murdoch admitted to owing Watson the £3,000: MG 100, vol. 193, no. 44
(typescript transcription of petition dated 18 Nov. 1806).

23 *Andrew Murdoch v. Charles Chipman* (1802), RG 39 C (Halifax), box 84.

24 Endorsed on the writ of execution issued in *Brook Watson et al. v. Andrew Murdoch.*

25 In his 1805 petition to the House of Assembly, Murdoch noted that more than 130 persons had been committed to debtors' prison at Halifax in the preceding two years: RG 5 A, vol. 12. Most would have been released after a fairly brief stay if their debts were under £100.

26 On the development of debtor-creditor law, see generally Philip Girard, 'Married Women's Property, Chancery Abolition and Insolvency Law: Law Reform in Nova Scotia, 1820–1867,' in Philip Girard and Jim Phillips, eds., *Essays in the History of Canadian Law, Vol. III* (Toronto: University of Toronto Press for the Osgoode Society 1990).

27 RG 5 U, vol. 4 (1804–12).

28 In August 1814 Murdoch petitioned the Council for a land grant, stating that he had 'resided for these last six years constantly in the said Province': RG 20 A (1814). This is a curious statement given that Murdoch had lived his whole life in the province. It makes more sense if the six years is taken to refer to his release from prison, which would place that event in 1808. Although recommended for 250 acres, it seems Murdoch ultimately did not receive any land since his name does not appear in the Crown Land Grants index. On Watson, see the entry in *DCB* 5 by L.F.S. Upton.

29 Thomas Chandler Haliburton, *The Old Judge; or, Life in a Colony* (Ottawa: Tecumseh Press 1978), 128.

30 MG 1, vol. 187, no. 81; RG 1, vol. 173 at 343.

31 Philip Girard, 'Taking Litigation Seriously: The Market Wharf Controversy at Halifax, 1785–1820,' in G. Blaine Baker and Jim Phillips, *Essays in the History of Canadian Law, Vol. VIII, In Honour of R.C.B. Risk* (Toronto: University of Toronto Press for the Osgoode Society 1999), 213–40.

32 Halifax County Registry of Deeds, RG 47, vol. 48, 232, deed from Andrew Murdoch to Beamish Murdoch dated 8 July 1825; vol. 49, p. 364, deed from Beamish Murdoch to Andrew Murdoch dated 9 July 1825. The purchase price in both transactions was stated to be £300, so in substance the parties were effecting an exchange of the properties.

33 RG 47, vol. 80, 270, release from Andrew McGrigor to Beamish Murdoch, 17 May 1845. The document recites that Beamish Murdoch requested Mc-Grigor to pay off the holders of two mortgages made by Andrew Murdoch in May 1843 in the amount of £145, and now that Beamish Murdoch had repaid McGrigor in full, McGrigor conveyed to him all Andrew Murdoch's former interest in the property in question.

34 MG 3, vol. 1836a, f.41; MG 3, vol. 1837, f.45 is a draft letter by Beamish

Murdoch, dated 24 March 1860, to Dewis regarding final payment of his 'late father's account.' Andrew Murdoch died at Parrsboro on 30 Oct. 1855 at the age of 78: *Presbyterian Witness*, 10 Nov. 1855, 179.

35 *Family History. Stairs, Morrow*, 236.

36 Ibid., 237.

37 Eliza Frame, 'Rev. James Murdoch,' 108–9. Another, more curious, void in the Murdoch family history is the fate of Andrew's mother, Abigail Murdoch. Widowed in 1799 and left with several of her ten surviving children still at home and no apparent source of income, Abigail found herself in a position that was far from enviable. She remarried at St Paul's in 1803, to Henry King, 'bachelor,' a much older man who died at Boston in 1817. She herself died in Halifax in 1833: *Acadian Recorder*, 31 May 1817; 21 Dec. 1833. The absence of any reference to her life post-1799 in Eliza Frame's or Susan Stairs's accounts suggests some estrangement from the Murdoch clan, possibly as a result of the second marriage.

38 References to Beamish Murdoch as 'Salter' include: RG 20 A (1814) (petition of Andrew Murdoch for land grant referring to son 'Salter Beamish Murdoch'); Dale McClare, ed., *Louisa's Diary: Journal of a Farmer's Daughter, Dartmouth, 1815* [Louisa Collins, future wife of Murdoch's uncle Thomas Ott Beamish] (Halifax: Nova Scotia Museum 1989), 26, entry for 1 Oct. 1815; will of Frederick Ott Beamish, dated 9 June 1817, which names as executor 'Salter Murdoch, my nephew': Halifax County Court of Probate, RG 48, B32, mfm. reel 19397. Murdoch signed as 'Beamish Murdoch' when witnessing this will, however. There are no references to Murdoch as 'Salter' after 1821 in any documents seen by the author.

39 Michael MacCarthy-Morrogh, *The Munster Plantation: English Migration to Southern Ireland 1583–1641* (Oxford: Clarendon Press 1986). C.T.M. Beamish, *Beamish: A Genealogical Study of a Family in County Cork and Elsewhere* (London: privately published 1950), 9. The following account of the Beamish family in Ireland is based largely on this source, itself based on primary sources.

40 *Beamish Genealogical Study*, 144–9.

41 Ibid., 150–2. A generation after their emigration, a collateral branch of the family responded to this same problem by deciding to focus on a product that could be consumed at home. The Beamish and Crawford Brewery, established in 1792, has survived for two centuries in Cork and now exports Beamish Ale to the international market.

42 Information on the Beamish family in Nova Scotia is derived largely from Terrence M. Punch, 'Beamish of Kilvurra and Halifax,' *Nova Scotia Historical Quarterly*, 9 (1979): 269–78. Thomas's brother Richard Beamish

emigrated to North America but not to Nova Scotia, and nothing more is known of him. Their sister Elizabeth Beamish either accompanied or followed Thomas to Halifax, where she remained, unmarried, until her death in 1826.

43 Halifax Assessments 1775–6, RG 1, vol. 411, doc. 7.

44 Will of Frederick Ott Beamish, 1 June 1780, Halifax County Court of Probate, no. 022.

45 This incident was recounted by Thomas Beamish Akins, who lived with Sarah Ott Beamish much of her life, to John Thomas Bulmer, who recorded it in his obituary notice of Akins in the *Canadian Voice*, 9 May 1891.

46 She moved to separate quarters in 1804, wherein she opened a school for young children, but remained very much part of the family: *Royal Gazette*, 31 May 1804.

47 Wilfrid Prest, *William Blackstone: Law and Letters in the Eighteenth Century* (Oxford: Oxford University Press 2009), 13–27, 55–6.

3: Apprenticeship

1 '"A Dry and Revolting Study": The Life and Labours of Antebellum Law Students,' in W. Wesley Pue and David Sugarman, eds., *Lawyers and Vampires: Cultural Histories of Legal Professions* (Oxford and Portland, Ore.: Hart Publishing 2003), 66.

2 This approach, which examines in a detailed way Old World and New World linkages within a specific cultural group over time, has been used with some success by social historians: see, for example, Ian Ross Robertson, 'Highlanders, Irishmen, and the Land Question in Nineteenth-Century Prince Edward Island,' in L.M. Cullen and T.C. Smout, eds., *Comparative Aspects of Scottish and Irish Economic and Social History, 1600–1900* (Edinburgh: Donald 1977); Rusty Bittermann, 'Agrarian Protest and Cultural Transfer: Irish Immigrants and the Escheat Movement on Prince Edward Island,' in Thomas P. Power, ed., *The Irish in Atlantic Canada 1780–1900* (Fredericton: New Ireland Press 1991).

3 Christopher W. Brooks, *Lawyers, Litigation and English Society since 1450* (London: Hambledon Press 1998), 149.

4 Aside from Blackstone's lectures, Oxford and Cambridge taught only canon law and civil (Roman) law until the nineteenth century.

5 On the development of the bar in England, see Wilfrid Prest, ed., *Lawyers in Early Modern Europe and America* (New York: Holmes and Meier 1981); Brooks, *Lawyers, Litigation and English Society*; Raymond Cocks, *Foundations of the Modern Bar* (London: Sweet and Maxwell 1983); Daniel Duman,

The English and Colonial Bars in the Nineteenth Century (London: Croom Helm 1983); David Lemmings, *Gentlemen and Barristers: The Inns of Court and the English Bar, 1680–1730* (Oxford: Oxford University Press 1990), and its sequel, *Professors of the Law: Barristers and English Legal Culture in the Eighteenth Century* (Oxford: Oxford University Press 2000). On attorneys, see Robert Robson, *The Attorney in Eighteenth-Century England* (Cambridge: Cambridge University Press 1959); Brooks, *Lawyers, Litigation and English Society*, and his earlier study, *Pettyfoggers and Vipers of the Commonwealth: The 'Lower Branch' of the Legal Profession in Early Modern England* (Cambridge: Cambridge University Press 1986). On solicitors, see Harry Kirk, *Portrait of a Profession: A History of the Solicitor's Profession, 1100 to the Present Day* (London: Oyez 1976). There is an enormous literature on Blackstone and his *Commentaries*. The most convenient way to approach it is via Wilfrid Prest's recent biography, *William Blackstone: Law and Letters in the Eighteenth Century* (Oxford: Oxford University Press 2009).

6   Michael Miles, '"A Haven for the Privileged": Recruitment into the Profession of Attorney in England, 1709–1792,' *Social History*, 11 (1986): 197–208. Miles argues that the increase in professional status was influenced by the influx of men from relatively privileged backgrounds into attorneys' offices. See as well David Sugarman, 'Bourgeois Collectivism, Professional Power and the Boundaries of the State: The Private and Public Life of the Law Society, 1825 to 1914,' *International Journal of the Legal Profession*, 3, no. 1 (1996): 81–135, which also deals in some detail with the regulation of the lower branch in the eighteenth century.

7   On England, see Robson, *The Attorney*, 20. The association was called the Society of Gentlemen Practisers in the Courts of Law and Equity. Its Irish counterpart has not been commented on in the literature, but its existence is known from the writings of G.E. Howard, on whom see below, text accompanying notes 44–7.

8   2 Geo. II, c. 23. Brooks, *Lawyers, Litigation and Society*, 155, argues that 'the statute had more to do with using formal proof of apprenticeship as a way of collecting government revenue in the form of stamp duties than with reforming legal training.'

9   13 & 14 Geo. III, c. 23 (Ire.).

10 *Revolution and the Making of the Contemporary Legal Profession: England, France, and the United States* (New York: Oxford University Press 2006), 447.

11 Ibid., 455.

12 Ibid., 526–7.

13 A Metropolitan and Provincial Law Association arose in 1847 to represent provincial solicitors but it merged with the Incorporated Law Society in

1873 and from that time the latter's hegemony was not seriously challenged from within: Sugarman, 'Bourgeois Collectivism,' 102–4.

14 Burrage, *Revolution*.

15 Even when county bar associations began to emerge in the 1750s, their
efforts to persuade local courts to restrict practice to regularly sworn attorneys were unsuccessful: Gerald W. Gawalt, *The Promise of Power: The Emergence of the Legal Profession in Massachusetts 1760–1840* (Westport, Conn.:
Greenwood Press 1979), 15.

16 Virginia, for example, required that prospective attorneys be examined by
a board of General Court attorneys appointed by the governor and coun-
cil before being licensed to practice; A.G. Roeber, *Faithful Magistrates and
Republican Lawyers: Creators of Virginia Legal Culture, 1680–1810* (Chapel
Hill: University of North Carolina Press 1981), 108–9. For a brief but useful
overview of the legal profession in the colonial period, see Lawrence
M. Friedman, *A History of American Law*, 3d ed. (New York: Simon and
Schuster 2005), 53–9.

17 J.M. Murrin, 'The Legal Transformation: The Bench and Bar of Eighteenth-
Century Massachusetts,' in S.N. Katz, ed., *Colonial America: Essays in Politics and Social Development* (Boston: Little Brown 1971).

18 Anton-Hermann Chroust, *The Rise of the Legal Profession in America*, 2 vols.
(Norman: University of Oklahoma Press 1965), 1: 107.

19 Roeber, *Faithful Magistrates*, 110.

20 Frank L. Dewey, *Thomas Jefferson, Lawyer* (Charlottesville: University Press
of Virginia 1986). Jefferson gave up after eight years of practice at the bar
of the General Court, the superior court of Virginia.

21 Statutes of Upper Canada, 1797, c. 20.

22 The role of the 1811 Act for the Better Regulation of Attornies, Solicitors
and Proctors in effecting this fusion will be discussed in chapter 5.

23 Wood, *Radicalism of the American Revolution*, 74–7.

24 Uniacke had also served as principal to Voster Lombard, whose parents
had sent him from County Cork to Halifax in 1783 expressly to apprentice
with their countryman: D.G. Bell, 'Richard John Uniacke's Advice to a
Young Lawyer, 1797,' *Nova Scotia Historical Review*, 8, no. 2 (1988): 138.

25 Biographical information on the Uniackes used in this chapter is drawn
from the following sources unless otherwise stated: Brian Cuthbertson, *The
Old Attorney General: A Biography of Richard John Uniacke* (Halifax: Nimbus
1980); *DCB* entries on Richard John Uniacke (vol. 6), Norman Fitzgerald
Uniacke (vol. 7), Richard John Uniacke, Jr (vol. 6), Robert Fitzgerald Uniacke (vol. 9), and James Boyle Uniacke (vol. 8). See also Brian Cuthbertson,
ed., 'Fatherly Advice in Post-Loyalist Nova Scotia: Richard John Uniacke

to His Son Norman,' *Acadiensis*, 9, no. 2 (1980): 78; Bell, 'Richard John Uni-acke's Advice to a Young Lawyer, 1797'; [Barry Cahill], 'Attorney-General Uniacke's Advice to a Young Lawyer, 1798,' *Nova Scotia Historical Review*, 15, no. 1 (1995): 127.

26 Charles R. McKirdy, 'The Lawyer as Apprentice: Legal Education in Eighteenth Century Massachusetts,' *Journal of Legal Education*, 28 (1976): 124. Chroust's *Rise of the Legal Profession in America*, although a classic work on the history of the legal profession in the United States, virtually ignores apprenticeship as a key element in professional formation during the antebellum period, while over-emphasizing the contribution of general and specifically legal university education during the same period. G. Blaine Baker, 'Legal Education in Upper Canada,' 79, makes a similar point in the Canadian context.

27 A.R. Chase to Salmon P. Chase, 4 Nov. 1825, as cited in Fidler, '"A Dry and Revolting Study,"' 71.

28 D.G. Bell, *Legal Education in New Brunswick: A History* (Fredericton: University of New Brunswick 1992); 'Paths to the Law in the Maritimes, 1810–1825: The Bliss Brothers and Their Circle,' *Nova Scotia Historical Review*, 8, no. 2 (1988): 6; William Laurence, '"A Literary Man and a Merchant": The Legal Career of Sir William Young' (PhD thesis, Dalhousie University, 2009), 85–107.

29 Baker, 'Legal Education in Upper Canada.'

30 The Acadian legal culture was not evident at a professional level but had been acknowledged by the Annapolis regime and survived at a popular level, even after the deportation. See Jacques Vanderlinden, 'À la rencontre de l'histoire du droit en Acadie,' *Revue de l'Université de Moncton*, 28 (1994): 47, and the remarkable constitution drafted for the Acadians of Cape Sable by the Abbé Jean-Mandé Sigogne in 1799, reproduced in H. Leander d'Entremont, 'Father Jean Mandé Sigogne, 1799–1844,' Nova Scotia Historical Society *Collections*, 23 (1936): 105–10; Thomas G. Barnes, '"The Dayly Cry for Justice": The Juridical Failure of the Annapolis Royal Regime, 1713–1749,' in Philip Girard and Jim Phillips, eds., *Essays in the History of Canadian Law, Vol. III, Nova Scotia* (Toronto: University of Toronto Press for the Osgoode Society 1990). The survival of continental legal traditions among the German and French-speaking populations on Nova Scotia's South Shore has been as little studied as their juridical acculturation, although a beginning is made in Kenneth Paulsen, 'Land, Family and Inheritance in Lunenburg Township, Nova Scotia, 1760–1800,' in Margaret Conrad, ed., *Intimate Relations: Family and Community in Planter Nova Scotia, 1759–1800* (Fredericton: Acadiensis Press 1995).

31 Laurence, 'A Literary Man & a Merchant,' 100–2.
32 Belcher (1710 –76) and Bulkeley (1717–1800) can both be found in *DCB* 4.
 Bulkeley's role as master of the rolls is treated in some detail in Barry Cahill, 'From Imperium to Colony: Reinventing a Metropolitan Legal Institution in Late Eighteenth-Century Nova Scotia,' in Donald W. Nichol et al.,
 eds., *TransAtlantic Crossings: Eighteenth-Century Explorations* (St John's: Me-
 morial University of Newfoundland 1995). On Finucane, see Barry Cahill,
 '"Fide et Fortitudine Vivo": The Career of Chief Justice Bryan Finucane,'
 Nova Scotia Historical Society *Collections*, 42 (1986): 153.
33 Under the English form of foreclosure, the creditor could either sue the
 debtor on the mortgage covenant and leave the debtor with the land, or
 take the land itself in satisfaction of the debt. Under Irish practice, the
 creditor could arrange for a sale by auction of the debtor's interest in the
 land, and sue the debtor for any deficiency if the sale did not produce
 enough to satisfy the mortgage debt. See generally Law Reform Commission of Nova Scotia, *Discussion Paper: Mortgage Foreclosure and Sale* (Halifax: The Commission 1997).
34 Irish influences on the political and legal culture of early Upper Canada
 are discussed in Baker, 'Legal Education in Upper Canada,' 67 (similarities
 between King's Inns of Ireland and Law Society of Upper Canada); John
 McLaren, 'The King, the People, and the Law … and the Constitution:
 Justice Robert Thorpe and the Roots of Irish Whig Ideology in Early Upper
 Canada,' in Jonathan Swainger and Constance Backhouse, eds., *People and
 Place: Historical Influences on Legal Culture* (Vancouver: UBC Press 2003);
 and McLaren's 'Reflections on the Rule of Law: The Georgian Colonies of
 New South Wales and Upper Canada, 1788–1837,' in Diane Kirkby and
 Catharine Colborne, eds., *Law, History, Colonialism: The Reach of Empire*
 (Manchester: Manchester University Press 2001).
35 No comprehensive Irish legal history has yet appeared, but to date the le-
 gal profession has garnered most attention. See generally J.F. McEldowney
 and Paul O'Higgins, *The Common Law Tradition: Essays in Irish Legal History*
 (Dublin: Irish Academic Press 1990); Daire Hogan and W.N. Osborough,
 eds., *Brehons, Serjeants and Attorneys: Studies in the History of the Irish Legal
 Profession* (Dublin: Irish Academic Press 1990); Colum Kenny, *King's Inns
 and the Kingdom of Ireland: The Irish 'Inn of Court,' 1541–1800* (Dublin: Irish
 Academic Press 1992); Daire Hogan, *The Legal Profession in Ireland, 1789–
 1922* (Dublin: Incorporated Law Society of Ireland 1986); Brian Henry,
 *Dublin Hanged: Crime, Law Enforcement and Punishment in Late Eighteenth-
 Century Dublin* (Dublin: Irish Academic Press 1994); W.N. Osborough, ed.,
 Explorations in Law and History (Dublin: Irish Academic Press 1995).

36 See generally James Kelly, *Poyning's Law and the Making of Law in Ireland, 1660–1800* (Dublin: Four Courts Press 2007).

37 Robert Bickersteth, 'The Garde Family,' *Journal of the Cork Historical and Archaeological Society*, 5 (1899): 200.

38 North American indentures could be more precise on this point. A 1742 indenture not only prohibited William Livingston (later governor of New Jersey) from contracting matrimony, but specified that 'he shall not Comitt fornication'; cited in McKirdy, 'Lawyer as Apprentice,' 126.

39 The original indenture does not survive but was extant as late as 1890. Lawrence G. Power reproduced it in his biographical sketch 'Richard John Uniacke,' Nova Scotia Historical Society *Collections*, 7 (1889–91): 78. Murdoch's indenture does not survive, but it was probably similar to Uniacke's. Voster Lombard's 1783 indenture with Uniacke reproduced it almost verbatim: RG 39, ser. J, vol. 117. George Pyke's 1787 indenture was also very similar, except that Uniacke covenanted to 'use his best Endevours to Instruct and Learn him ... the Business and Profession of an Attorney,' as well as to secure him admission at the end of the term. Pyke promised to arrange for himself 'competent Cloathing Dyet Lodging and Washing and Necessarys of every Kind': MG 100, vol. 211, no. 11. Neither mentions any sum of money paid to Uniacke.

40 The figure is derived from *Wilson's Dublin Directory for the Year 1769*, which showed 720 attorneys in Dublin. The record of the admission of Richard John Uniacke as an attorney in Trinity term 1779 is found in the manuscript volume of admissions of attorneys, 1752–92, held at King's Inns Library, Dublin.

41 Elizabeth Bowen, *Bowen's Court*, 2d ed. (London: Longmans 1964), 175–6.

42 Walter Gordon Wheeler, 'Libraries in Ireland before 1855: A Bibliographical Essay' (typescript ms., 1957), held at the Department of Early Printed Books, Trinity College, Dublin. This essay contains at 160–216 a list of catalogues of library auctions which appeared in Irish newspapers in the later eighteenth and nineteenth centuries. A number of barristers' collections appear, but not a single collection is identified as having belonged to an attorney.

43 Toby Barnard, 'Howard, Gorges Edmond (1715–1786),' *Oxford Dictionary of National Biography*, http://www.oxforddnb.com/view/article/13903 (accessed 4 Sept. 2009).

44 Understood as the English-derived law as introduced and applied in Ireland, rather than the original Gaelic law.

45 Howard's other major legal works included: *A Treatise on the Rules and Practice of the Equity Side of the Exchequer in Ireland ...* (Dublin: Oli. Nelson

1760); *The Rules and Practice of the High Court of Chancery in Ireland, with the Several Statutes relative thereto* (Dublin: E. Lynch 1772); *A Supplement to the Rules and Practice of the High Court of Chancery in Ireland* (Dublin: E. Lynch 1774); *An Abstract and Commonplace of all the Irish, British, and English Statutes relative to the Revenue of Ireland* ... (Dublin: Executors of David Hay 1779). Two important pamphlets are his *Queries, relative to ... Defects and Grievances in Some of the Present Laws of Ireland* (Dublin: Oli. Nelson 1761), and *Some Questions upon the Legislative Constitution of Ireland* (Dublin: S. Powell 1770) [published under the pseudonym Poblicola].

46 On Uniacke's library, see MG 1, vol. 1769, no. 42, 'List of Books Belonging to late Hon. R.J. Uniacke to be Sold Monday at 11 a.m. by W.M. Allan.' His library contained approximately 1,000 volumes, about half of which were law books.

47 An Act for the Better Regulation of the Admission and Practice of Attornies, 13 & 14 Geo. III, c. 23 (1773). W.N. Osborough declared the second requirement to be 'of singular importance' in years to come: 'The Regulation of the Admission of Attorneys and Solicitors in Ireland, 1600–1866,' in Hogan and Osborough, eds., *Brehons, Serjeants and Attorneys*, 120. See below, chapter 4, for a discussion of the adoption of a similar provision in the Nova Scotia statute of 1811, which is arguably derived from the Irish statute of 1773.

48 On the 'popery' laws, see W.N. Osborough, 'Catholics, Land, and the Popery Acts of Anne,' in Thomas P. Power and Kevin Whelan, eds., *Endurance and Emergence: Catholics in Ireland in the Eighteenth Century* (Dublin: Irish Academic Press 1990); and on the constitutional developments, see Kelly, *Poynings' Law*.

49 This manuscript volume is held in the Rare Books collection of the Sir James Dunn Law Library at Dalhousie University, where it is catalogued under the title 'Forms of the Supreme Court,' the title that appears on its cover. This title no longer describes accurately the contents of the volume, but it will be used here to avoid confusion. The volume has entries on every page, but there is continuous pagination only from pages 1 to 33. Thereafter, only the right-hand side is paginated to page 151, but entries were inserted later on the left-hand side. These will be referred to as 'facing x.'

50 'Forms of the Supreme Court,' 43.

51 Ibid., 38.

52 Ibid., 39, 41, 42.

53 Beamish Murdoch, *Epitome of the Laws of Nova-Scotia*, 4 vols. (Halifax: Joseph Howe 1832–3), 1: 3–4.

54 'Forms of the Supreme Court,' facing 74.

55 Ibid., facing 35.
56 *Epitome*, 1: 7–10.
57 *Epitome*, 1: 8–9.
58 *Acadian Recorder*, 20 Sept. 1820, letter by 'Brutus.'
59 *Epitome*, 1: 8.
60 Laurence, 'A Literary Man & a Merchant,' 95–107. Young did peruse Hoffman to at least some extent according to Laurence (106).
61 *Epitome*, 1: 10.
62 Fidler, '"A Dry and Revolting Study,"' 86–7. For a recent overview of Blackstone's influence in the United States, see Michael Hoeflich, 'American Blackstones,' in Wilfrid Prest, ed., *Blackstone and His* Commentaries: *Biography, Law, History* (Oxford and Portland, Ore.: Hart Publishing 2009).
63 *Epitome*, 1: 14.
64 Laurence, 'A Literary Man & a Merchant,' 95.
65 *The Law Society of Upper Canada and Ontario's Lawyers, 1797–1997* (Toronto: University of Toronto Press 1997). The quote from Robinson is from Patrick Brode, *Sir John Beverley Robinson: Bone and Sinew of the Compact* (Toronto: University of Toronto Press for the Osgoode Society 1984), 9.
66 Hoeflich, 'American Blackstones.'
67 Alexander Leith, *Commentaries on the Laws of England Applicable to Real Property by William Blackstone, Adapted to the Present State of the Law in Upper Canada* (Toronto: W.C. Chewett 1864). A second edition by James Frederick Smith appeared in 1880, and this was in turn reworked by Edward Douglas Armour as *A Treatise on the Law of Real Property Founded on Leith & Smith's Edition of Blackstone's Commentaries on the Rights of Things* in 1901, with a second edition in 1916.
68 Dr Alexander Croke, appointed judge of the Vice-Admiralty Court at Halifax in 1801, was a qualified civilian advocate as well as a member of the English bar. Many of his decisions are collected in James Stewart, ed., *Reports of Cases Argued and Determined in the Court of Vice-Admiralty at Halifax, in Nova-Scotia ...* (London, 1814), and a number of them cite the civilian writers on international and admiralty law such as Voet, Vattel, and Grotius. According to these reports, Crofton appeared along with his father as early as 1812. On the English civilian lawyers and their eventual demise, see Stephen Waddams, *Law, Politics and the Church of England: The Career of Stephen Lushington 1782–1873* (Cambridge and New York: Cambridge University Press 1992).
69 Joseph C. Sweeney, 'The Admiralty Law of Arthur Browne,' *Journal of Maritime Law and Commerce*, 26, no. 1 (1995): 59–132. The demand for the work is indicated by its republication in London in 1802–3 and a posthu-

mous republication in New York in 1840. Browne was a third-generation
New Englander who went to Ireland at the age of sixteen to study at Trinity College and never returned to the United States.

70 Philip Girard, 'Themes and Variations in Early Canadian Legal Culture:
Beamish Murdoch and his *Epitome of the Laws of Nova-Scotia*,' *Law and History Review*, 11, no. 1 (1993): 101. Murdoch recommended Browne as part
of his reading list to legal apprentices: *Epitome*, 1: 14.

71 His father's library contained a copy, as did that of his brother Norman.
The Sir James Dunn Law Library at Dalhousie University holds a copy of
the five-volume second Paris edition of this work, published in 1695–7,
containing the bookplate of 'Norman F[itz]Gerald Uniacke, Lincoln's Inn
1805.' An English translation by William Strahan of Doctors' Commons
(the home of the civilian lawyers) noted that Domat had omitted 'such
Parts of the Civil Law as are not at present of general Use, and select[ed]
all the Fundamental Maxims of Law and Equity, which must be the same
in all Countries, and appl[ied] them to the most common Affairs of Human Life, in a plain and easy Method, and in their Natural Order.' *The
Civil Law in Its Natural Order: Together with the Public Law* (London 1722),
ix–x.

72 *The New Jury Law: Forming a Title of the Code of Legal Proceedings according
to the Plan Proposed for the Statute Law of the Realm* (London: J. and W.T.
Clarke 1825); Samuel Bealey Harrison, *Evidence: Forming a Title of the Code
of Legal Proceedings, according to the Plan Proposed by Crofton Uniacke, Esq.*
(London: Butterworth 1825). Harrison, an English barrister and treatise
writer, emigrated to Upper Canada in 1837, where he played an important
political role in the movement for responsible government. Considerably
younger than Uniacke, he seems to have been an acolyte of his during the
1820s. See George Metcalf, 'Harrison, Samuel Bealey,' *DCB* 10.

73 See chapter 8.

74 The American edition was published by Hilliard, Gray, Little, and Wilkins.
On the campaign for codification of the law in the United States, see C.M.
Cook, *The American Codification Movement* (Westport, Conn.: Greenwood
Press 1981).

75 Harrison, *Evidence*, ix–x (emphasis in original).

76 The phrase is that of Sir William Jones, in the preface to his learned *Essay
on the Law of Bailments* (2d ed., London, 1798). It is a sad commentary on
the continuance of this state of affairs that four Uniacke brothers (three
lawyer/officeholder/politicians and a clergyman) have a place in the
DCB, while Crofton, the only brother to leave an engaging and substantial
corpus of published work, has been left out.

77 Girard, 'Themes and Variations,' 130–44.
78 *The Statutes at Large, Passed in the Several General Assemblies Held in His Majesty's Province of Nova-Scotia* ... (Halifax: John Howe and Son 1805), v–x. Cf. Donald Desserud, 'Nova Scotia and the American Revolution: A Study of Neutrality and Moderation in the Eighteenth Century,' in Margaret Conrad, ed., *Making Adjustments: Change and Continuity in Planter Nova Scotia, 1759–1800* (Fredericton: Acadiensis Press 1991), 110–12, who provides a more nuanced interpretation of the preface.
79 It is worth recalling that Uniacke was present in Ireland during the run-up to the constitutional change of 1782 which saw Westminster recognize the supremacy of the Irish Parliament in all domestic matters; it seems that he sympathized with the liberal nationalist wing of the Ascendancy on this matter: Cuthbertson, *Old Attorney General*, 3–4.
80 These were published as *Letters to the King, First Published in the True Briton, by the Stranger* (London: printed for J.J. Stockdale 1820). Crofton had established himself in London in 1819 but was not called to the English bar until 1825. He petitioned to have the normal quota of terms reduced in view of his Nova Scotia experience, but was refused; Lincoln's Inn Black Books, XX, 12 and 27 Feb. 1822.
81 D.G. Bell, 'Slavery and the Judges of Loyalist New Brunswick,' *University of New Brunswick Law Journal*, 31 (1981): 9.
82 See in particular Barry Cahill, 'Slavery and the Judges of Loyalist Nova Scotia,' *University of New Brunswick Law Journal*, 43 (1994): 73.
83 Barry Cahill, '*Habeas Corpus* and Slavery in Nova Scotia: *R. v. Hecht, ex parte Rachel*, 1798,' *University of New Brunswick Law Journal*, 44 (1995): 179.
84 *Epitome*, 1: 43; Girard, 'Themes and Variations,' 122–4.
85 Rhode Island native Arthur Browne, whose career we have noted earlier, provides an example of New England's religious insularity. In later life he said that he 'had never seen a Roman Catholic until he was seventeen years old, and he then soon considered him a prodigy; but he had since by interviews with many respectable men of that sect got rid of his prejudices'; cited in Sweeney, 'The Admiralty Law of Arthur Browne,' 65n.16. A work quite similar to Murdoch's *Epitome* in form, scope, and purpose, Zephaniah Swift's *A System of the Laws of Connecticut* (1795) is nonetheless distinguished from it by its evident anti-Catholicism. One might also mention in this context the dramatic works of New Brunswick Loyalist lawyer Henry Bliss. Between 1838 and 1866, the London-based Bliss wrote a half-dozen plays on historical themes, all based on a dramatic opposition between English liberty and Mediterranean Catholic tyranny.
86 Barry Moody, 'Growing up in Granville Township, 1760–1800,' in Mar-

garet Conrad, ed., *Intimate Relations: Family and Community Life in Planter Nova Scotia, 1759–1800* (Fredericton: Acadiensis Press 1995). Moody argues that the ideal of Anglo-Protestant homogeneity that characterized New England settlements was unattainable amid the cultural diversity of later eighteenth-century Nova Scotia.

87 Philip Girard, 'Married Women's Property, Chancery Abolition, and Insolvency Law: Law Reform in Nova Scotia, 1820–1867,' in Girard and Phillips, eds., *Essays in the History of Canadian Law, Vol. III.*

4: The Legal Profession in Nova Scotia: Organization and Mobility

1 An Act for the Better Regulation of Attornies, Solicitors and Proctors, Practising in the Courts of Law and Equity in this Province, Statutes of Nova Scotia (SNS) 1811, c. 3.

2 Michael Burrage, *Revolution and the Making of the Contemporary Legal Profession: England, France, and the United States* (New York: Oxford University Press 2006), 22–41.

3 G. Blaine Baker, 'Legal Education in Upper Canada, 1785–1889: The Law Society as Educator,' in David H. Flaherty, ed., *Essays in the History of Canadian Law, Volume II* (Toronto: University of Toronto Press 1983), 58–67. Christopher Moore, *The Law Society of Upper Canada and Ontario's Lawyers, 1797–1997* (Toronto: University of Toronto Press 1997), 17–34, suggests less lofty purposes behind the creation of the Law Society of Upper Canada: protection of existing practitioners and support for their mutual improvement. He agrees that the society's role began to be more important after the close of the War of 1812.

4 D.G. Bell, *Legal Education in New Brunswick: A History* (Fredericton: University of New Brunswick 1992), 2–9.

5 While advocates were banned in New France, it should be noted that notaries were not, and indeed were encouraged and supported by the royal administration in all French colonies as indispensable to the legal needs of family and economic life.

6 The governor had admitted them previously, qua president of the Supreme Court's predecessor, the short-lived General Court. The early history of the legal profession in Nova Scotia is analysed in some detail in Barry Cahill, 'The Origin and Evolution of the Attorney and Solicitor in the Legal Profession of Nova Scotia,' *Dalhousie Law Journal*, 14 (1991): 277.

7 Murdoch also did not believe that any of the English legislation on attorneys, including the act of 1729, was in force in Nova Scotia: *Epitome*, 3: 116. Cahill, 'Attorney and Solicitor,' 279–80, states that the English act

of 1729 was considered to be in force in Nova Scotia as of 1760, but this seems doubtful. The English act specified an apprenticeship period of five years, but the actual length of service in Nova Scotia varied widely around that mean. Further, it seems unlikely that the Supreme Court would have specified a period of service of four years in 1799 if an English act mandating a five-year period were already considered to be in force.

8 Cahill, 'Attorney and Solicitor,' 285n.35.

9 Baker, 'Legal Education,' 86–91.

10 On the 1804 statute, see David Sugarman, 'Bourgeois Collectivism, Professional Power and the Boundaries of the State: The Private and Public Life of the Law Society, 1825 to 1914,' *International Journal of the Legal Profession*, 3 (1996): 89.

11 W.B. Bliss to Henry Bliss, 13 April 1818, Bliss Papers, MG 1, vol. 1598, no. 221. Bliss's experience was remarkably similar, and indeed may have been more rigorous, than that of English attorney William Hickey in 1775. As Christopher Brooks summarizes the account, 'Hickey's father had arranged for him to be examined by a friend of his, Justice Yates. Hickey had breakfast with Yates while the judge's clerk dealt with the paperwork. To Hickey's own astonishment, the questioning extended no further than polite inquiries about whether or not he "liked the law"'; *Lawyers, Litigation and English Society since 1450* (London: Hambledon Press 1998), 157.

12 The act was not limited to oral pleading in court; it reserved for attorneys the ability to 'sue out any Writ or Process ... to commence, carry on, solicit or defend, any action or actions, or any other proceedings, either before or after judgment ... in the name or names of any person or persons in any of His Majesty's Courts of this Province,' but did not prevent lay persons such as justices of the peace and notaries public from engaging in the solicitorial aspects of legal work, such as conveyancing, drafting wills and agreements, and the like. The *Novascotian*, 4 Dec. 1828, carried an advertisement from notary public William Romans of Pictou, who advised that he was 'ready to draw Leases, Deeds, Mortgages, Protests, and agreements of every description, in a neat and correct style.' Nova Scotian lawyers do not seem to have made any attempts to monopolize this business in the nineteenth century.

13 Moore, *Law Society*, 30–1: 'After 1797 the immigrant lawyer was required to have his authority to practice ratified by the Law Society of Upper Canada – and had thereby to acknowledge its members' standing as equivalent to his own ... Hence, the act neatly removed the risk that some proud barrister might persuade the chief justice that the underqualified locals were an affront to his dignity and to the court's' – exactly the risk that

materialized in New South Wales, resulting in a divided profession on the Antipodean frontier. This point is developed further in chapter 11, below.

14 Thomas Chandler Haliburton, *The Old Judge; or, Life in a Colony* (Ottawa: Tecumseh Press 1978), 188.

15 Alexander Winniett was admitted an attorney in 1827 and never signed the barristers' roll but was listed in *Belcher's Farmers' Almanack* as practising in the Annapolis area until at least 1858. William Chandler was admitted as an attorney in 1836, practised at Amherst until 1843, then disappeared from *Belcher's* until 1852. Curiously, he was admitted to the bar in 1851 and began to practise at Arichat, where he remained for some years. One William Buckerfield practised for many years at Amherst after his admission as an attorney in 1845, and was never called to the bar. These were the only locally born men known to have practised as attorneys without being called to the bar between 1811 and 1850. For the few immigrant lawyers who practised without being called to the bar locally, see below, note 52 and accompanying text.

16 R.D. Gidney and W.P.J. Millar, *Professional Gentlemen: The Professions in Nineteenth-Century Ontario* (Toronto: University of Toronto Press 1994), 77; Moore, *Law Society*, 86–8.

17 Bliss to Henry Bliss, 17 June 1823, Bliss Papers, MG 1, vol. 1598, no. 239.

18 An Act for the Better Regulation of Barristers, Advocates, Attornies, Solicitors and Proctors, Practising in the Courts of this Province, SNS 1836, c. 89. The act of 1811 expired in 1818 and was replaced by acts of 1818 and 1824; on the expiry of the latter two acts, the 1811 act was largely re-enacted by the act of 1836. The 1836 act was to be in force for ten years, was renewed by SNS 1846, c. 42, for a further ten years, and was then made perpetual by its inclusion in the Revised Statutes of Nova Scotia (RSNS) of 1851, as the statute Of Barristers and Attornies, c. 132. In 1864 the one-year wait was abolished and one was called simultaneously as a barrister and attorney: RSNS 1864, c. 130, s. 10.

19 SNS 1836, c. 89, s. 18.

20 Bell, *Legal Education*, 12–18.

21 G. Édouard Rinfret, *Histoire du Barreau de Montréal* (Cowansville, Que.: Yvon Blais 1989), 31–3. A facsimile reproduction of the rules of the Library Society is found at 207–13. The Brothers-in-Law Club was a dining club. See also G. Blaine Baker, 'Public Frivolity and Patrician Confidence: Lower Canada's "Brothers-in-Law," 1827 to 1833,' in *Mélanges Paul-André Crépeau* (Montreal: Quebec Research Centre of Private and Comparative Law 1997).

22 *Novascotian*, 2 Feb. 1825.

23 *Epitome*, 3: 117.
24 The Law Society of Upper Canada had adopted the same expedient in its early years, making all existing members 'benchers' in 1799: Moore, *Law Society*, 45.
25 Nova Scotia Barristers' Society Fonds, MG 20, vol. 1015, no. 2 (1834–6).
26 *Novascotian*, 10 Feb. 1830, 2 Feb. 1846, 10 Jan. 1848; *Acadian Recorder*, 16 Oct. 1830, 1 March 1834, 9 Sept. 1848.
27 After an apparently agreeable dinner held in 1827, reported in the *Novascotian* (22 March 1827), there are no reports of subsequent dinners.
28 *Journals and Proceedings of the House of Assembly of the Province of Nova Scotia* (1844) (Halifax: Queen's Printer 1844), 29 March 1844. It is not clear that there was much significance attached to the question of the society's incorporation. It seems to have been sought for largely utilitarian reasons such as facilitating the holding of property; Moore, *Law Society*, 62, argues that this was the case in Upper Canada in 1821. See, however, Jean-Marie Fecteau, 'État et associationnisme au XIXe siècle québécois: éléments pour une problématique des rapports État/société dans la transition au capitalisme,' in Allan Greer and Ian Radforth, eds., *Colonial Leviathan: State Formation in Mid-Nineteenth-Century Canada* (Toronto: University of Toronto Press 1992), for the suggestion that there may have been more at stake here than mere convenience.
29 Bell, *Legal Education*, 21–2.
30 The incident can be followed through the records of the Court of Vice-Admiralty, RG 40, vol. 11, nos. 1–4; MG 2, vol. 732, no. 210. See also Arthur Stone, 'The Admiralty Court in Colonial Nova Scotia,' *Dalhousie Law Journal*, 17 (1994): 407–9.
31 A note on editorial practice. I have lower cased the terms 'reform' and 'reformers' when discussing Nova Scotia politics prior to the 1840s, since in that early period the reform movement had not yet coalesced into a distinct political force; for the 1840s and afterwards, the greater maturity of 'Reform' and 'Reformers' warrants the upper case.
32 *Novascotian*, 22 March 1847. The controversies involving the judges are examined in greater length by Jim Phillips and Bradley Miller, '"Too Many Courts and Too Much Law": The Politics of Judicial Reform in Nova Scotia, 1830–1841,' *Law & History Review*, 29 (forthcoming 2011).
33 Gidney and Millar, *Professional Gentlemen*, 60–7; see also Moore, *Law Society*, 110–11.
34 SNS 1850, c. 13.
35 Of Barristers and Attornies, RSNS 1864, c. 130.
36 Bell, *Legal Education*, 36.

37 W. Wesley Pue, 'Rebels at the Bar: English Barristers and the County Courts in the 1850s,' *Anglo-American Law Review*, 16 (1987): 303–52.

38 Cited by Moore, *Law Society*, 101.

39 Cited by Bell, *Legal Education*, 38.

40 An Act to Incorporate the Nova Scotia Barristers' Society, SNS 1858, c. 85. Section 2 of the act declared that the personal property of the former society was vested in the new corporation.

41 NSARM, *Bye-Laws of the Nova Scotia Barristers' Society* (Halifax: James Bowes and Sons 1861), V/F vol. 131, no. 27. Although adopted by the society in February 1860 and approved by the provincial cabinet in March, the rules were not published until 1861.

42 Philip Girard, 'The Roots of a Professional Renaissance,' *Manitoba Law Journal*, 20 (1991): 154–5.

43 *Acadian Recorder*, 4 Feb. 1860. It should be noted that the editor, Hugh Blackadar, was not a lawyer.

44 Of Barristers and Attornies, RSNS 1864, c. 130, s. 6.

45 Both Haliburton and Archibald have entries in the *DCB*; see Bonnie Husksins's entry on Haliburton in *DCB* 13 and Kenneth Pryke's on Archibald in *DCB* 12.

46 The reference to democracy is qualified because, in spite of the provisions about elections, the turnover on the elected council was very low in the 1850s through 1870s: Girard, 'Professional Renaissance,' 155.

47 The only reasonably reliable census figures for Nova Scotia's population during this period come from 1827 (123,000) and 1838 (202,500). I have used a figure of 100,000 for the population in 1820. Comparison with Massachusetts reveals a not dissimilar profile, with significant growth in the profession there coming about two decades earlier. The ratio of lawyers to population doubled from 1:2900 in 1800 to 1:1400 in 1810 and then remained at about 1:1100 throughout the period 1820–40; Gerald W. Gawalt, *The Promise of Power: The Emergence of the Legal Profession in Massachusetts 1760–1840* (Westport, Conn.: Greenwood Press 1979), 14. By comparison, Ontario was underserviced by lawyers, following Nova Scotia's 1:2600 to 1:1800 trajectory only decades later, in the period 1851–71; Gidney and Millar, *Professional Gentlemen*, 398, Table 4.

48 This phenomenon has not been much commented on, but see Brian Cuthbertson, *Johnny Bluenose at the Polls: Epic Nova Scotia Election Battles 1758–1848* (Halifax: Formac 1994), 11–13. Cuthbertson also notes the importance of marriage ties in cementing alliances between lawyers and the families of local notables. On the Halifax/non-Halifax statistics, see Philip Girard and Jeffrey Haylock, 'Stratification, Economic Adversity, and Diversity in an

Urban Bar: Halifax, Nova Scotia, 1900–1950,' in Constance Backhouse and
W. Wesley Pue, *The Promise and Perils of Law: Lawyers in Canadian History*
(Toronto: Irwin Law 2009), 78.

49 A.W.H. Eaton, *History of King's County* (Salem, Mass.: Salem Press 1910),
443.

50 RG 5, ser. P, vol. 41, no. 5; RG 1, vol. 226, no. 16. Such examples are admittedly rare in this period, but they serve nonetheless to demonstrate
that lawyers' services were not considered indispensable even in cases
involving the death penalty. William Lee was convicted of murder and
sentenced to death in the Guysborough case. His 'counsel,' the clerk of the
peace, was the brother of John George Marshall, whom Lee had wished
to defend him. Marshall was unable to attend and sent his brother some
notes and precedents he had made when he was involved with the case at
an earlier stage.

51 J. Alphonse Deveau, ed., *Diary of a Frenchman* (Halifax: Nimbus 1990), 73.

52 Metonicus's almanac of 1794 and previous almanacs contain no listing
of lawyers. The first available almanac to contain such a listing is Ward's
(1820).

53 Information on mobility is derived from *Belcher's Farmers' Almanack* which,
from 1824, provides on an annual basis the name and location of every
lawyer in the province considered to be a member of the practising bar.
For a brief period in the 1830s, the almanacs even note the number of apprentices being instructed by each lawyer in the province.

54 Document, 'The Autobiography of Chief Justice Sir William Young, *aet.*
21,' *Nova Scotia Historical Review*, 12, no. 2 (1992): 130.

55 J.L. MacDougall, *History of Inverness County Nova Scotia* (Belleville, Ont.:
Mika Publishing 1972 [Truro, 1922]), 82, refers to 'James Turnbull, a Low-
lander who had been educated and had studied law in the Old Country.'
Turnbull was never called to the bar in Nova Scotia and is likely to have
been a Scottish solicitor. He is erroneously referred to as a barrister in Shir-
ley Elliott, *The Legislative Assembly of Nova Scotia: A Biographical Directory*
(Halifax: Province of Nova Scotia 1984). The other four Scots were Alexander Primrose, b. c. 1790 in Banffshire, arrived Halifax by 1816, called to the
bar 1823; William Young, b. 1799 in Falkirk, arrived Halifax 1814, called
to the bar 1826; his brother George Young, b. 1802 in Falkirk, arrived Halifax 1814, called to the bar 1834; and James Fogo, b. at Glasgow, arrived
in Pictou as a boy, called to the bar 1838. James R. Smith was the father
of a future justice of the Supreme Court of Nova Scotia, Henry W. Smith
(1875–90), born at St Kitts, West Indies, in 1826.

56 Gidney and Millar, *Professional Gentlemen*, 196. Based on the fact that 47

per cent of the province's lawyers were born in Ontario, the authors claim somewhat curiously that the legal profession was exceptionally 'Canadianized' in that province. It may have been so by comparison with medical men and the clergy, but the claim cannot be sustained in any intercolonial context.

57 There are no good studies of the mobility of English attorneys in the nineteenth century, but an eighteenth-century study suggests a contrast with the British North American experience: 'With a strong village and agricultural clientele, and good practices in county towns and mixed counties, many 18th-century attorneys seem to have inhabited an economy of their own, both independent of the manufacturing districts and able to survive the vicissitudes of agricultural boom and slump': Philip Aylett, 'A Profession in the Marketplace: The Distribution of Attorneys in England and Wales 1730–1800,' *Law & History Review*, 4 (1987): 30. Aylett tries to explain the counter-intuitive fact that the geographic distribution of attorneys in England in 1802 was almost identical to that in 1730, as was the absolute number of attorneys (4,600 in 1730 vs. 4,700 in 1802), in spite of high population growth and the emergence of major manufacturing centres.

58 The emigrants were Charles Dickson Archibald (1825), who went first to Newfoundland as registrar of the Supreme Court and then to England, where he remained involved in business activities rather than the law for the rest of his life; George H. Emerson (1828), who emigrated to Newfoundland; and Beamish Murdoch's friend Thomas Forman (1827), who emigrated to New South Wales in 1828 and died there in 1831.

59 The courtship correspondence of Harry King and Halli Fraser makes up the major part (322 out of 543 items) of the King-Stewart Papers, Library and Archives Canada (LAC), MG 24 I 182 (at NSARM see MG 1, King-Stewart Papers, mfm. reel 10367). Of the 322 courtship letters, 174 were penned by King and these have been transcribed with a critical introduction by Alice Terry Marion in 'Harry King's Courtship Letters, 1829–1831' (MA thesis, Acadia University, 1986). References will include the date of the letter and page number of the thesis.

60 Marion, 'Courtship Letters,' 12 Nov. 1829, 72–3.

61 Both George H. and Hugh A. Emerson seem to have landed on their feet in Newfoundland. Each held the office of solicitor general and was appointed to the Legislative Council, Hugh before the achievement of responsible government, which he opposed, and George, a supporter of Reform, thereafter: see entries in the *Encyclopedia of Newfoundland and Labrador*, vol. 1 (St John's: Newfoundland Book Publishers [1967] 1981).

62 Marion, 'Courtship Letters,' 14 Sept. 1829, 59.

63 The act of 1824, which had created the position of first justice for the four districts of the Inferior Court of Common Pleas, prohibited them from practising law or holding any other government office: SNS 1824, c. 38.

64 Marion, 'Courtship Letters,' 14 Sept. 1829, 56.

65 Ibid., 6 Nov. 1830, 283.

66 Ibid., 9 Jan. 1831, 334.

67 Ibid., 13 March 1831, 365.

68 Digby may have been briefly without a lawyer in 1835–42, but there were a number of lawyers in nearby towns. The status of Chester is unclear. The town's sole lawyer, William Greaves, was no longer listed in *Belcher's* after 1834, but he remained in the town, was made a local master in chancery in 1840, and died in Chester in 1853. His position with the Customs Department may have been seen as incompatible with the ongoing practice of law.

69 The lists in *Belcher's* upon which this interpretation is based are quite rigorous in excluding anyone who was not thought to be a member of the 'practising bar.' The compiler seems to have known when lawyers retired, for example, after which their names no longer appeared on the list (perhaps they requested removal of their names?). In a number of cases, practising lawyers disappear from *Belcher's* even though they can be identified as still living in the community with which their practice was associated. These cases seem to involve the acceptance of particular offices or the decision of a lawyer to devote himself principally to non-legal (usually business) interests. There were a few cases where a practising lawyer quit his profession to train for the ministry, and in these cases his name always disappeared from the list (see, e.g., E.A. Crawley, Thomas Maynard, and James J. Ritchie). In brief, lawyers appearing in *Belcher's* can with some confidence be defined as those men identified by contemporaries as devoted principally to the practice of law.

70 Bell, *Legal Education*, 22.

71 Statutes of Canada (SC) 1847, c. 21. These were replaced by a single professional corporation in 1870. See generally André Vachon, *Histoire du notariat canadien 1621–1960* (Quebec: Presses de l'Université Laval 1962), 91–100.

72 Acte pour l'incorporation du barreau du Bas-Canada, SC 1849, c. 46.

73 Dale Gibson and Lee Gibson, *Substantial Justice: Law and Lawyers in Manitoba 1670–1970* (Winnipeg: Peguis Publishers 1972), 77.

74 Cameron Harvey, ed., *The Law Society of Manitoba, 1877–1977* (Winnipeg: Peguis Publishers 1977).

75 Kenneth Pryke, 'Archibald, Adams George,' *DCB* 13.

76 Neil Vallance, 'Separating "The Sheep from the Goats" – the Barristers

from the Solicitors – in the Colony of Vancouver Island,' *The Advocate* (B.C.), 59, no. 4 (2001): 555–60.

77 Alfred Watts, *History of the Law Society of British Columbia, 1869–1973* (n.p., n.d.), 4–5, 28.

78 By 1867, discipline of lawyers was still largely in the hands of the courts rather than lawyers themselves, but instances of discipline were as yet so seldom encountered that the failure to achieve control over it by this point cannot be counted a significant failure on the part of the bar.

5: The Making of a Colonial Lawyer, 1822–7

1 Richard John Eckert, *'The Gentlemen of the Profession': The Emergence of Lawyers in Massachusetts, 1630–1810* (New York: Garland Publishing 1991), p.2 of unpaginated preface. Works such as A.G. Roeber, *Faithful Magistrates and Republican Lawyers: Creators of Virginia Legal Culture, 1680–1810* (Chapel Hill: University of North Carolina Press 1981), tell us little about the actual work of lawyers, and even Eckert's book contains only a few pages on the subject (at 203–8). See, though, Carol Berkin, *Jonathan Sewall: Odyssey of an American Loyalist* (New York: Columbia University Press 1974), chapter 2; and Milton M. Klein, 'The Rise of the New York Bar: The Legal Career of William Livingston,' in David H. Flaherty, ed., *Essays in the History of Early American Law* (Chapel Hill: University of North Carolina Press 1969). With regard to antebellum lawyers, Maurice G. Baxter, *Henry Clay the Lawyer* (Lexington: University Press of Kentucky 2000), is disappointing. Jerome Mushkat and Joseph G. Rayback, *Martin Van Buren: Law, Politics, and the Shaping of Republican Ideology* (DeKalb: Northern Illinois University Press 1997), is considerably better but not able to discuss Van Buren's client base in any detail. By far the best study is Mark Steiner, *An Honest Calling: The Law Practice of Abraham Lincoln* (DeKalb: Northern Illinois University Press 2006).

2 Stephen Botein, 'The Legal Profession in Colonial North America,' in Wilfrid Prest, ed., *Lawyers in Early Modern Europe and America* (New York: Holmes and Meier 1981).

3 Gerald W. Gawalt, *The Promise of Power: The Emergence of the Legal Profession in Massachusetts 1760–1840* (Westport, Conn.: Greenwood Press 1979); Paul D. Carrington, 'Tocqueville's Aristocracy in Minnesota,' *William Mitchell Law Review*, 26 (2000): 485.

4 On the first point, see three works by G. Blaine Baker: 'The Juvenile Advocate Society, 1821–1826: Self-Proclaimed Schoolroom for Upper Canada's Governing Class,' Canadian Historical Association *Historical Papers*, 1985;

'Legal Education in Upper Canada, 1785–1889: The Law Society as Educator,' in David H. Flaherty, ed., *Essays in the History of Canadian Law, Volume II* (Toronto: Osgoode Society 1983); '"So Elegant a Web": Providential Order and Rule of Secular Law in Early Nineteenth Century Upper Canada,' *University of Toronto Law Journal*, 38 (1988): 184; Paul Romney, 'From the Types Riot to the Rebellion: Elite Ideology, Anti-Legal Sentiment, Political Violence, and the Rule of Law in Upper Canada,' *Ontario History*, 79 (1987): 113; D.G. Bell, 'Paths to Law in the Maritimes, 1810–1825: The Bliss Brothers and Their Circle,' *Nova Scotia Historical Review*, 8 (1988): 6; Carol Wilton, '"Lawless Law": Conservative Political Violence in Upper Canada, 1818–1841,' *Law and History Review*, 13, no. 1 (1995): 111–36.

On the second point , see R.D. Gidney and W.P.J. Millar, *Professional Gentlemen: The Professions in Nineteenth-Century Ontario* (Toronto: University of Toronto Press 1994); and Christopher Moore, *The Law Society of Upper Canada and Ontario's Lawyers, 1797–1997* (Toronto: University of Toronto Press 1997).

5 Jean-Philippe Garneau, 'Une culture de l'amalgame au prétoire: Les avocats de Québec et l'élaboration d'un langage juridique commun au tournant des XVIIIe et XIXe siècles,' *Canadian Historical Review*, 88 (2007): 113.

6 An earlier version of these chapters appeared as 'The Making of a Colonial Lawyer: Beamish Murdoch of Halifax, 1822–1842,' in Carol Wilton, ed., *Inside the Law: Canadian Law Firms in Historical Perspective* (Toronto: University of Toronto Press for the Osgoode Society 1996), 57–99.

7 See generally Philip Girard, 'The Independence of the Bar in Historical Perspective: Comforting Myths, Troubling Realities,' in *In the Public Interest: The Report and Research Papers of the Law Society of Upper Canada's Task Force on the Rule of Law and the Independence of the Bar* (Toronto: Irwin Law 2007).

8 His letter book devoted to clients with business in Halifax County has not survived.

9 These are, respectively, MG 3, vols. 1838B, 1836B, 1836A, 1836C, 1835B, 1838A, 1837, and 1835A.

10 RG 39, ser. M.

11 Gordon Bale, *Chief Justice William Johnstone Ritchie: Responsible Government and Judicial Review* (Ottawa: Carleton University Press 1991), 15.

12 A full account of the dispute can be found in Philip Girard, 'Taking Litigation Seriously: The Market Wharf Controversy at Halifax, 1785–1820,' in G. Blaine Baker and Jim Phillips, eds., *Essays in the History of Canadian Law, Volume VIII, In Honour of R.C.B. Risk* (Toronto: University of Toronto Press for the Osgoode Society 1999).

13 Beamish Murdoch, *Epitome of the Laws of Nova-Scotia*, 4 vols. (Halifax: Joseph Howe 1832–3), 1: 12.
14 The one-lawyer towns were Shelburne, Digby, Cornwallis, Windsor, Yarmouth, Amherst, and Truro. 'Pythagoras,' *The Nova Scotia Almanack for Town and Country for the Year of Our Lord 1821* (Halifax: Edmund Ward 1821). Newly annexed Cape Breton was not included in the almanac. The island appears to have had only one resident lawyer in 1820–1, Richard Gibbons, Jr of Sydney. E.M. Dodd would be the second after his call to the bar in 1822.
15 For an overview of the provincial and urban economy during this period, see David Sutherland, 'Halifax Merchants and the Pursuit of Development, 1783–1850,' *Canadian Historical Review*, 59, no. 1 (1978): 1–17; Judith Fingard, Janet Guildford, and David Sutherland, *Halifax: The First 250 Years* (Halifax: Formac 1999); Julian Gwyn, *Excessive Expectations: Maritime Commerce and the Economic Development of Nova Scotia, 1740–1870* (Montreal and Kingston: McGill-Queen's University Press 1998); Daniel Samson, *The Spirit of Industry and Improvement: Liberal Government and Rural-Industrial Society, Nova Scotia, 1790–1862* (Montreal and Kingston: McGill-Queen's University Press 2008).
16 Daniel Duman, *The English and Colonial Bars in the Nineteenth Century* (London: Croom Helm 1983), 202.
17 One study of access to justice in early modern England found that 70 per cent to 80 per cent of litigants appearing in the courts of King's Bench and Common Pleas between 1560 and 1640 came from the ranks of yeoman farmers, merchants, artisans, labourers, and professional men and their widows: Christopher W. Brooks, *Lawyers, Litigation and English Society since 1450* (London: Hambledon Press 1998), chapter 2.
18 Summary Trial of Actions Act, SNS 1822, c. 30 (one JP had jurisdiction for debts up to £3), raised to £10 by SNS 1837, c. 60. Neither Murdoch's account books nor his letter book give any hint that he ever appeared before a justice of the peace in a debt (or any other) matter.
19 Dale Darling, 'Nova Scotia Supreme Court Records, Halifax County, 1830–1832,' (unpublished ms., 1993), on file with the author. These figures include all claims, not just debt claims, but debt cases constituted between 80 per cent and 90 per cent of all Supreme Court litigation during these years. The Supreme Court case files are virtually complete for these years but become much less so in the later 1830s. The 1827 study is mine, based on perusal of RG 39, ser. J, vol. 105 (1821–30), Supreme Court Book of Original Entries for Halifax.
20 Inferior Court of Common Pleas, Halifax County, RG 37 HX, vol. 25.

21 At least, this can be deduced from the rapid decline in the number of judgments rendered in the Inferior Court of Common Pleas for Halifax County
after 1818. From an average of fifty cases per year in the years 1815–18, the
number of judgments declined to three or four annually for the next five
years and to zero in 1824–6, then remained at one or two annually until
1831. A study of the case load of the Commissioners' Court for the period
1827–37 requested by the House of Assembly revealed that the court rendered 435 judgments in 1828 alone. *Journals and Proceedings of the House of
Assembly of the Province of Nova Scotia* (1837), appendix 81. Lawyers did not
have a monopoly on pleading in the Commissioners' Court but the state
of the records does not permit us to determine the extent of their involvement or that of lay pleaders.

22 Supreme Court Book of Original Entries, 1815–30, RG 39, ser. J, vol. 105.

23 MG 3, vol. 1838B. There are eighty-five documents in the letter book, but I
have excluded the last one from consideration since it relates to Murdoch's
personal business. The top right-hand corner of the volume is shorn off,
removing the pagination, but the documents follow in chronological sequence and will be referred to by date.

24 Parrsboro was part of Kings County at this time; it would not become part
of Cumberland County until 1840.

25 RG 39, ser. J., vol. 105, 15 Sept. 1825. A similar train of events occurred
when Murdoch tried to collect a debt from merchant Israel Harding on
behalf of Halifax merchants William and Francis Letson. A summons sent
to the sheriff of Cumberland in January 1826 could not be served on Harding, but by the end of the year Murdoch had found that Harding was living in Yarmouth. He wrote Harding there on 16 November, informing him
that he was now responsible for the expenses of the Cumberland writ (£1
3s 8d) as well as the original debt of £4 12s 7d, and urged him to settle as
soon as possible 'as I have directions to sue for the same and do not wish
to put you to greater expense.'

26 On the difficulties of transportation in Nova Scotia in the first half of the
century, see Robert Mackinnon, 'Roads, Cart Tracks, and Bridle Paths:
Land Transportation and the Domestic Economy of Mid-Nineteenth-Century Eastern British North America,' *Canadian Historical Review*, 84 (2003):
177.

27 The work is known from the second edition, 1831; no copy of the 1827 first
edition appears to have survived.

28 MG 3, vol. 1838B, Murdoch to E.H. Chandler [sic: Cutler], sheriff of Annapolis, 17 Nov. 1826.

29 Ibid., Murdoch to Kenneth McDonald, sheriff of Sydney, 10 Aug. 1825.

30 SNS 1819, c. 22 (first passed in 1763). See generally Philip Girard, 'Married Women's Property, Chancery Abolition, and Insolvency Law: Law Reform in Nova Scotia, 1820–1867,' in Philip Girard and Jim Phillips, eds., *Essays in the History of Canadian Law: Volume III, Nova Scotia* (Toronto: Osgoode Society 1990), 92–100.

31 MG 3, vol. 1838B, Murdoch to Henry Blackadar, 8 June 1828 [*sic*: 8 July].

32 The tale can be followed through the following letters in MG 3, vol. 1838B: 17 Nov., 3 Dec. 1823; 8 March 1824; 7 March 1826. Complaints about Winniett from others dated back to at least 1821: RG 1, vol. 230, docs. 52–4, 86; vol. 231, doc. 44. In other colonies, complaints about the sheriff had more effect. Sir William Blackstone's son Henry emigrated to Lower Canada and became sheriff of the district of Trois-Rivières in 1799. After various complaints about his lack of financial and moral probity, the government decided to make his reappointment conditional on the providing of additional security for all public monies in his hands. When he could not satisfy this condition, he was not reappointed in 1805, although he was then appointed coroner for the district of Quebec, a position he held until his death in 1825; William R. Riddell, 'The Blackstones in Canada,' *Illinois Law Review*, 16 (1921): 255–67.

33 Ibid., Murdoch to Alexander Stewart, 27 May 1828.

34 Ibid., 10 April 1823.

35 Ibid., Murdoch to Ross and William Murray, 23 June 1828. The Murrays had agreed to act as sureties to McLennan.

36 The partnership agreement drafted in 1823 contained such a clause. For a fuller precedent, see 'Charles E.W. Schmidt's Precedent Book 1827,' 39, a manuscript held in the Rare Books collection of the Sir James Dunn Law Library at Dalhousie University.

37 On arbitration generally, see Murdoch's *Epitome*, 4: 36–41. In cases where no more than two partners disputed an amount less than £500, the legislature provided in 1829 that they had to choose arbitration on the model described rather than go to Chancery. If the parties refused to choose arbitrators, the Supreme Court would do so for them: SNS 1829, c. 28. Murdoch supported the bill in the Assembly: *Novascotian*, 12 March 1829.

38 Ibid.

39 Eckert, '*Gentlemen of the Profession*,' 205.

40 Sir William Young Papers, MG 2, vol. 760.

41 *Novascotian*, 13 April 1825, 124–5. The original case file is extant in RG 39, ser. C (Halifax), box 169, but it is framed as a formulaic demand for debt and gives no hint of the context.

42 The case file is no longer extant, but Murdoch gives a brief account of the case in his *Epitome*, 3: 82–3.

43 Admission to the Chancery bar was pro forma for those already admitted to the bar of the Supreme Court, but the exact date of Murdoch's admission is unknown.

44 RG 36, ser. A, box 163, no. 773.

45 *William Sutherland v. Thomas J. Keegan, Beamish Murdoch, Michael Burnet, Bartholomew Hackett, David Fletcher, and John Albro*, RG 39, ser. J, vol. 105, 20 Sept. 1826. Sutherland catered the meal and sued for the agreed price in this action, which he said had not been paid.

46 George Renny Young's *Novascotian* contains satirical coverage, reported in dialect, of disputes between Irishmen in the Commissioners' Court in almost every issue in early 1825.

47 William Laurence, '"A Literary Man and a Merchant": The Legal Career of Sir William Young' (PhD thesis, Dalhousie University, 2009), 174–6.

48 *Acadian Recorder*, 21 Jan. 1826. For the letter to Watts, see MG 3, 1838B, 13 Aug. 1827. Tybo alleged that he had purchased a horse from a vendor and left him in possession; Watts then purchased the horse from Tybo's vendor, knowing that it had already been sold to Tybo.

49 This calculation is not as straightforward as it might seem given the presence of 'collective' clients such as the families of deceased persons. If it was clear that a deceased man had left a widow, the estate was counted as two clients, one male and one female. While somewhat arbitrary, this method allows some generalizations to be made without having to trace the families of each deceased client, and without overstating the presence of women.

50 RG 39, ser. J, vol. 105, 13 Oct. 1825.

51 MG 3, vol. 1838B, Murdoch to Hinshelwood, 14 Aug., 23 Dec., 30 Dec. 1823, 10 Sept. 1824. For a more comprehensive look at women as both creditors and debtors, see Julian Gwyn, 'Women as Litigants before the Supreme Court of Nova Scotia, 1754–1830,' in Philip Girard, Jim Phillips, and Barry Cahill, eds., *The Supreme Court of Nova Scotia, 1754–2004: From Imperial Bastion to Provincial Oracle* (Toronto: University of Toronto Press for the Osgoode Society 2004).

52 This includes the eighteen women identified as widows.

53 MG 3, vol. 1836B, 61–2.

54 Ibid. The account with James Scott at the end of the volume shows that Murdoch was paying £90 per annum in rent for the house at 32 Barrington Street before he purchased it for £1,102 on 27 November 1832, after which he paid annual interest of £66.

Murdoch's total income from other sources is not known. He received £40 per annum from Philip J. Holland for editorial assistance on the *Acadian Recorder* over the period May 1824–September 1826. Murdoch had begun to invest in mortgages by at least 1827: MG 10, vol. 23, no. 47b is the release of the equity of redemption in a Cape Breton property from Thomas Nowlan to Murdoch and J. Scott Tremain, which recites that they had taken a mortgage for £37 on the property in 1827.

55 MG 3, vol. 1838B, Murdoch to Capt. Thomas Hurlow, 7 June 1828.

56 Laurence, '"A Literary Man & a Merchant,"' 189.

57 Bliss Family Fonds, MG 1, vol. 1598, no. 246, W.B. Bliss to Henry Bliss, 29 April 1824.

58 Ibid., no. 274, W.B. Bliss to Henry Bliss, 24 June 1829.

59 Gidney and Millar, *Professional Gentlemen*, note this phenomenon at 140–4. The letters of Nova Scotia lawyer Harry King, referred to in chapter 4, provide colourful evidence of circuit rituals and sociability; see also Jim Phillips and Philip Girard, 'Courts, Communities and Communication: The Nova Scotia Supreme Court on Circuit, 1816–1850,' in Hamar Foster, Benjamin L. Berger, and A.R. Buck, eds., *The Grand Experiment: Law and Legal Culture in British Settler Societies* (Vancouver: UBC Press for the Osgoode Society 2008).

60 Michael Grossberg, 'Institutionalizing Masculinity: The Law as a Masculine Profession,' in Mark C. Carnes and Clyde Griffen, *Meanings for Manhood* (Chicago: University of Chicago Press 1990), 136–7.

61 Matthew McCormack, *The Independent Man: Citizenship and Gender Politics in Georgian England* (Manchester and New York: Manchester University Press 2005). This theme is further explored in chapter 7, below.

62 An indenture of apprenticeship between Murdoch and George Renny Young, dated 1 Nov. 1821, shows that Murdoch was prepared to take on an apprentice just after his own admission as an attorney: Sir William Young Papers, MG 2, vol. 731, no. 42. The indenture is signed and sealed by both parties, but George's father may have objected, since an accompanying document embodying his consent to the arrangement (necessary in view of George's minority) is unsigned. George Young, brother of the future premier and chief justice William Young, postponed his decision to study law and occupied himself with the editorship of the *Novascotian* in the interim. He was called to the bar in 1834.

63 *Novascotian*, 31 May 1832.

64 The precocious industrial development of Montreal led to some early law partnerships there, particularly among the anglophone bar: see G. Blaine Baker, 'Ordering the Urban Canadian Law Office and Its Entrepreneurial

Hinterland, 1825 to 1875,' *University of Toronto Law Journal*, 48 (1998): 175.

65 Brian Cuthbertson, *Johnny Bluenose at the Polls: Epic Nova Scotian Election Battles 1758–1848* (Halifax: Formac 1994), 58, has analysed voting patterns in the 1830 election (which Murdoch lost) and concluded that 'almost all Murdoch's votes were "independent" ones … and came from the middle and humble classes.'

66 It is difficult to assess what 'success' means for an individual lawyer, much less to determine the relative success of a number of lawyers. As a rough index of size of client base, one might take the number of Supreme Court cases in which Murdoch and thirteen other near contemporaries appeared in the year 1827, derived from RG 39, ser. J, vol. 105 (1821–30), Supreme Court Book of Original Entries for Halifax. The top group comprises James Stewart Clarke, William Young, Charles Twining, and J. Scott Tremain, with fifty-seven, fifty-four, twenty-five, and twenty-two cases respectively. Murdoch came next with fifteen, Wentworth Flieger had six, and all the rest had between one and four appearances. This was a low year for Murdoch, since he had had thirty-three, twenty-three, and thirty-two appearances in the previous three years, putting him far ahead of most of his contemporaries.

67 13 April 1825.

68 It is possible that, in a small community such as Halifax in the 1820s, some at least of the jurors would have known the litigants personally or by repute and been able to form opinions about their credibility based on out-of-court experiences.

69 The dispute is explored more fully in Judith Fingard, 'Twining, John Thomas,' *DCB* 8, and her entry on John Inglis in *DCB* 7.

70 Letter by 'Martin Luther,' *Acadian Recorder*, 4 Dec. 1824. Under English ecclesiastical law, the crown could appoint a new rector to an English parish only in the unusual case where the incumbent rector was promoted to a bishopric, as Inglis was.

71 See the letter by 'Juridicus,' *Novascotian*, 27 April 1825, 140–1. The tone and style of the letter are very much that of Murdoch, but there is no clear proof verifying his authorship.

72 *Novascotian*, 4 May 1825.

73 Norah Story, 'The Church and State "Party" in Nova Scotia, 1749–1851,' Nova Scotia Historical Society *Collections*, 27 (1947): 46.

74 Greg Marquis, 'In Defence of Liberty: 17th-Century England and 19th-Century Maritime Political Culture,' *University of New Brunswick Law Journal*, 42 (1993): 69.

75 Cuthbertson, *Johnny Bluenose*, 58.
76 David A. Sutherland, 'Voluntary Societies and the Process of Middle-Class Formation in Early-Victorian Halifax, Nova Scotia,' *Canadian Historical Association Journal*, 1994, 237.
77 G.E. Hart, 'The Halifax Poor Man's Friend Society, 1820–27: An Early Social Experiment,' *Canadian Historical Review*, 34 (1953): 109; NSARM, Halifax Poor Man's Friend Society, *Annual Reports*; Judith Fingard, 'The Relief of the Unemployed Poor in Saint John, Halifax, and St John's, 1815–1860,' *Acadiensis*, 5 (1975): 32. For an overview of the society's activities in light of the movement to establish savings banks for the working classes, see Dan L. Bunbury, 'From Region to Nation: Government Savings Banks in the Maritimes and Canada, 1824–1900' (PhD thesis, Dalhousie University, 1995), 58–87.
78 *Novascotian*, 2 Feb. 1825. As secretary to the society (jointly with fellow lawyer E.A. Crawley), Murdoch probably authored the report on the society's history and current activities which appeared in the 18 Feb. 1825 issue of the *Novascotian*.
79 These are examined in chapter 9, below.
80 Murdoch's political career is examined in chapter 7, below.

6: The Maturing of a Colonial Lawyer, 1828–50

1 David A. Sutherland, 'Deblois, Stephen Wastie,' *DCB* 7. The Brandy Dispute is considered at greater length in J. Murray Beck, *The Politics of Nova Scotia*, vol. 1 (Tantallon, NS: Four East Publications 1985), 103–6; M. Gene Morrison, 'The Brandy Election of 1830,' *Nova Scotia Historical Society Collections*, 30 (1954): 151–83; Brian Cuthbertson, 'Place, Politics and the Brandy Election of 1830,' *Royal Nova Scotia Historical Society Collections*, 41 (1982): 5–19.
2 Murdoch's political ideas are considered more fully in the next chapter.
3 For further analysis see chapter 9, below.
4 Quoted in Sandra Lynn Barry, '"Shades of Vice ... and Moral Glory": The Temperance Movement in Nova Scotia 1828–48' (MA thesis, University of New Brunswick, 1986), 64.
5 William Laurence, '"A Literary Man and a Merchant": The Legal Career of Sir William Young' (PhD thesis, Dalhousie University, 2009), 197–207.
6 King to Fraser, 10 Dec. 1829, as transcribed in Alice Terry Marion, 'Harry King's Courtship Letters, 1829–1831' (MA thesis, Acadia University, 1986), 100.
7 An advertisement in the *Yarmouth Herald*, 7 April 1843, instructed indi-

viduals with claims against the company to direct them to local agents or to their 'standing counsel,' Beamish Murdoch.

8 In 1834 Murdoch was retained by the District of Halifax to assist the clerk of the peace, David Shaw Clarke, in drafting eight bills for the consideration of the legislature, but this is the only such entry in his account books. There are very occasional references to representing clients at trials at Quarter Sessions, and in 1841 Murdoch was paid £36 to prosecute Lieutenant A.B. Parker of the 64th Regiment before a court martial at Halifax.

9 A merchant would 'protest' a bill of exchange or bill of lading if the goods mentioned in it arrived in damaged condition. Bottomry is an agreement whereby a shipowner pledges the vessel in return for a loan to pay the expenses of the voyage.

10 See generally Terrence M. Punch, *Irish Halifax: The Immigrant Generation* (Halifax: International Education Centre, St Mary's University, 1981).

11 While this was a respectable income, it does not mean that Murdoch was necessarily in easy circumstances. Two judgments were obtained against him in the Supreme Court in 1835, the first on a promissory note for £90 given to Joey H. Metzler by Murdoch in February 1834, the second on an 1833 note for £50 given jointly by Murdoch and his uncle Thomas Ott Beamish to Simon Crabbs: RG 39 C (Halifax), box 179. These judgments suggest a liquidity problem, perhaps brought on by the debts incurred by Murdoch in the publication of his *Epitome*.

12 An Act for Securing to John Story, and His Assigns, the Exclusive Right in a Certain Slip or Railway, for the Use of Vessels, SNS 1834–5, c. 23. The act allowed Story exclusive use of this device for ten years, provided it was erected within a year. When it was not, Murdoch lobbied the legislature for an extension to 1 August 1836: SNS 1836, c. 77.

13 *Novascotian*, 17 Aug. 1836.

14 RG 39, ser. J, vol. 107 (1835–46).

15 The cases files are all found in RG 36: *James Black v. James and Andrew Muir* (1830), box 190, no. 917; *John H. Flohr and Sarah Rhalves v. Simon B. Robie et al.* (1830), box 192, no. 924; *John Crowe v. Isaiah Smith* (1830), box 197, no. 951; *Dunbar Douglass Stewart v. Robert Kent et ux.* (1833), box 213, no. 1038; *Hugh McDade et ux. v. Mary Hay et al.* (1833), box 213, no. 1039; *Dunbar Douglass Stewart v. Halliburton Grant et ux.* (1834), box 215, no. 1056. Prior to 1836, a list prepared by the registrar in Chancery provided the name of counsel beside each case. The post-1836 list has disappeared, making it difficult to trace a particular lawyer's profile in the court after that date.

16 They could be reopened within three years upon the return of the debtor, and the foreclosing mortgagee had to provide security to cover the even-

tuality that the foreclosure might be successfully defended within that time.

17 Short mortgage terms of a year or two were the norm during this period. It is likely that the parties contemplated annual renewals provided the interest payments were maintained. Nonetheless, the creditor could insist on total repayment at the end of the term.

18 MG 3, vol. 1838B, Murdoch to the Reverend Alexander Waugh, 20 June 1826.

19 Ibid., Murdoch to Ann Hinshelwood, 10 Sept. 1824.

20 The first reference in Murdoch's own records (MG 3, vol. 1838A) to an 'appearance in V-A Court' is in August 1835, in proceedings taken by the attorney general to declare forfeit the cargo of the American Schooner *Caleb* for violation of the Navigation Acts; the case file is in RG 40, vol. 9, no. 7. Murdoch recorded that he appeared for Joseph Bryant, a merchant from Castine, Maine, who owned the cargo. The earliest trace of Murdoch in the minute book of the court is in the October 1836 case of *Enoch Sears v. Nicholas Moran*, RG 40, vol. 9, no. 15. For an overview of the development of the Court of Vice-Admiralty in Nova Scotia, see Arthur J. Stone, 'The Admiralty Court in Colonial Nova Scotia,' *Dalhousie Law Journal*, 17 (1994): 363–429.

21 RG 40, vol. 12, no. 2.

22 Judith Fingard, *Jack in Port: Sailortowns of Eastern Canada* (Toronto: University of Toronto Press 1982), 187.

23 RG 40, vol. 11, nos. 1–4. See also Stone, 'Admiralty Court,' 407–9, for a treatment of what follows.

24 Such techniques remained in use thirty years later, when the Nova Scotia Supreme Court chose to treat an allegation of bias against Chief Justice William Young, made in a private letter to him from Halifax lawyer T.J. Wallace, as a contempt of court, and struck Wallace from the barristers' roll. This time it took the Judicial Committee of the Privy Council to undo the precipitous act: *In re T.J. Wallace* (1865), 5 N.S.R. 654. Such actions ultimately resulted in the removal of much of the judges' disciplinary power over the bar during the professional reform campaign of the 1880s.

25 *In re William Sutherland's Application for Habeas Corpus* (1837), RG 39, ser. C, box 180. *Novascotian*, 6 Dec. 1837, 386, 20 Dec. 1837, 403, 27 Dec. 1837, 410.

26 RG 40, vol. 13, no. 1. The file does not show the costs awarded to Murdoch. The estimate is based on his fees in *The Scio*, which amounted to £25 in all. The court file in *The Ajax* is even more voluminous, so the £20 estimate is a conservative one.

27 RG 40, vol. 12, no. 12. The file is substantial and obviously involved a good

deal of work on Murdoch's part. He charged Lane £3 for 'extra work' above the costs he received from the court.

28 This case is known only through oblique references, since no case file has survived. On 17 October 1831 Murdoch wrote to the court secretary, Sir Rupert George, to set a date for the hearing of the case: RG 1, vol. 238, no. 72 1/2. His account books show Catherine Laffin as a client, and in 1838 he was obliged to sue the surviving executor of her husband to recover his fees in the action, which Mr Laffin had failed to pay during his lifetime: *Murdoch v. Cassedy*, RG 39 C (Halifax), box 181. Murdoch alleged that he successfully obtained a decree of judicial separation and an order for alimony on Mrs Laffin's behalf. This case is also the first one in which Murdoch is known to have appeared before the Court of Marriage and Divorce; he was presumably admitted as a proctor and advocate by mid-1831 at the latest.

29 Kimberley Smith Maynard, 'Divorce in Nova Scotia, 1750–1890,' in Philip Girard and Jim Phillips, eds., *Essays in the History of Canadian Law, Volume III, Nova Scotia* (Toronto: University of Toronto Press for the Osgoode Society 1990), 249.

30 The 1835 divorce of Charlotte Hynes was obtained in the usual way through the Court of Marriage and Divorce. The 1834 divorce of Anne Kidston was obtained via a private act of the House of Assembly, the only such divorce in Nova Scotia history. She remarried shortly after, her new husband being Mr Justice William Hill of the Supreme Court of Nova Scotia; see Maynard, 'Divorce in Nova Scotia,' 237–8.

31 All the evidence was taken, but the last document in the file is the petition for its publication. There may have been a final decree which is no longer in the file.

7: The Politics of a Colonial Lawyer: Murdoch, Howe, and Responsible Government

1 *Novascotian*, 10 May 1826.

2 *Times* (Halifax), 31 Oct. 1843, *Morning Post*, 9 Nov. 1843. All future references to the *Times* refer to the Halifax newspaper of that name.

3 Reform candidates had won all four Halifax seats – two each in the county and the town – in the watershed 1836 election, and had retained them in 1840. Thus, Uniacke's victory in regaining one of these seats for the Conservative cause in 1843 was bitterly resented by the Reformers.

4 *Times*, 28 Nov. 1843; *Novascotian*, 4 Dec. 1843.

5 A useful starting place to enter this literature is the bibliographical essay

contained in Phillip A. Buckner, *The Transition to Responsible Government: British Policy in British North America, 1815–1850* (Westport, Conn.: Greenwood Press 1985), 341–4. More recent work includes Buckner's 'Whatever Happened to the British Empire?' *Journal of the Canadian Historical Association,* 4 (1993): 3–32; J. Murray Beck, *Joseph Howe,* 2 vols. (Montreal and Kingston: McGill-Queen's University Press 1982–3); Paul Romney, 'From the Rule of Law to Responsible Government: Ontario Political Culture and the Origins of Canadian Statism,' Canadian Historical Association *Historical Papers,* 1988, 86–119, and his 'From Constitutionalism to Legalism: Trial by Jury, Responsible Government, and the Rule of Law in the Canadian Political Culture,' *Law and History Review,* 7 (1989): 121–74; Allan Greer and Ian Radforth, eds., *Colonial Leviathan: State Formation in Mid-Nineteenth-Century Canada* (Toronto: University of Toronto Press 1992); Jeffrey L. McNairn, *The Capacity to Judge: Public Opinion and Deliberative Democracy in Upper Canada, 1791–1854* (Toronto: University of Toronto Press 2000); R. Blake Brown, *A Trying Question: The Jury in Nineteenth-Century Canada* (Toronto: University of Toronto Press for the Osgoode Society 2009); Michel Ducharme, *Le Concept de Liberté au Canada à l'Époque des Révolutions Atlantiques 1776–1838* (Montreal and Kingston: McGill-Queen's University Press 2010).

   On the relationship of responsible government to legal and judicial developments in the Maritimes, see Philip Girard, 'Married Women's Property, Chancery Abolition, and Insolvency Law: Law Reform in Nova Scotia, 1820–1867,' in Philip Girard and Jim Phillips, eds., *Essays in the History of Canadian Law, Volume III, Nova Scotia* (Toronto: University of Toronto Press for the Osgoode Society 1990); idem, 'The Supreme Court of Nova Scotia, Responsible Government, and the Quest for Legitimacy, 1850–1920,' *Dalhousie Law Journal,* 17, no. 2 (1994): 430–57; idem, 'The Maritime Provinces, 1850–1939: Lawyers and Legal Institutions,' *Manitoba Law Journal,* 23 (1995): 380–405; D.G. Bell, 'Judicial Crisis in Post-Confederation New Brunswick,' *Manitoba Law Journal,* 20 (1991): 181–95; idem, 'Maritime Legal Institutions under the *Ancien Régime,* 1710–1850,' *Manitoba Law Journal,* 23 (1995): 103–31.

6 McNairn, *Capacity to Judge.*
7 On state-sponsored violence, see Carol Wilton, *Popular Politics: Political Culture in Upper Canada, 1800–1850* (Montreal and Kingston: McGill-Queen's University Press 2000).
8 Gordon S. Wood, *The Creation of the American Republic, 1776–1787* (New York: Norton 1972), 18–28. These ideas have also been thoroughly explored by Bernard Bailyn, *The Ideological Origins of the American Revolution,*

enl. ed. (Cambridge, Mass.: Belknap Press 1992); and J.G.A. Pocock, *The Machiavellian Moment: Florentine Political Thought and the Atlantic Republican Tradition* (Princeton, N.J.: Princeton University Press 1975). In the Canadian context, see Gordon T. Stewart, *The Origins of Canadian Politics: A Comparative Approach* (Vancouver: University of British Columbia Press 1986). One of the few attempts to look at these ideas in the Maritime context can be found in Donald Desserud, 'Nova Scotia and the American Revolution: A Study of Neutrality and Moderation in the Eighteenth Century,' in Margaret Conrad, ed., *Making Adjustments: Change and Continuity in Planter Nova Scotia, 1759–1800* (Fredericton: Acadiensis Press 1991), especially 105–12.

9 *Novascotian*, 15 Sept. 1830.

10 Bailyn, *Ideological Origins*.

11 *Novascotian*, 29 Oct. 1840.

12 Wood, *American Republic*, 145–6; Bailyn, *Ideological Origins*, 122–30.

13 Buckner, *Transition to Responsible Government*, 50–7. Stewart's argument in *The Origins of Canadian Politics*, that the 1790–1850 period saw the entrenchment of a state-oriented 'Court' approach to government and politics which the Reformers simply continued in a new guise, cannot be sustained. He confuses the reach with the grasp of the old regime, and the use of patronage to create a loyal class of officials with its usage to control the Assembly and manage a legislative program. The former was attempted in all the British North American colonies on a wide scale, the latter was not. Stewart's emphasis on the essential continuity in Canadian politics pre- and post-1850 is contradicted by much of his own evidence, which vividly illustrates the impotence of the executive branch before the achievement of responsible government. Cf. Greer and Radforth, *Colonial Leviathan*, and Bell, 'Maritime Legal Institutions,' 117–21, 129–30.

14 15 March 1842.

15 *Epitome*, 1: 58.

16 *Times*, 15 March 1842.

17 These arguments were detailed by J.W. Johnston in two documents drafted in January 1847; Murdoch would undoubtedly have agreed with the substance of both. See Memorandum of Executive Council to Lieutenant Governor John Harvey, 28 Jan. 1847, *Journals and Proceedings of the House of Assembly of the Province of Nova Scotia* (1847), appendix 16, 73–81; memorandum of Executive Council to Harvey for submission to Earl Grey, 30 Jan. 1847, RG 1, vol. 119, 74–80.

18 Stanley to Falkland, 20 Aug. 1845, *Journals and Proceedings of the Legislative Council of the Province of Nova Scotia* (1846), appendix 1.

19 *Epitome*, 1: 63. On the Legislative Council during this period, see J. Murray Beck, *The Government of Nova Scotia* (Toronto: University of Toronto Press 1957), 100–5.

20 Viscount Goderich to Lieutenant Governor Peregrine Maitland, 7 Dec. 1830, reproduced in Frederick Madden, ed., *Imperial Reconstruction, 1763–1840: The Evolution of Alternative Systems of Colonial Government* (New York: Greenwood Press 1987), 588. The Reformers' critique of the role of the chief justice on the Legislative Council is considered in Jim Phillips and Bradley Miller, '"Too Many Courts and Too Much Law": The Politics of Judicial Reform in Nova Scotia, 1830–1841,' *Law & History Review*, 29 (forthcoming 2011).

21 *Times*, 1 Feb. 1842. The Colonial Office constantly rebuffed pleas to pay the councillors for their attendance, and it was not until 1854 that they were paid.

22 *Novascotian*, 29 Oct. 1840.

23 Beck, *Joseph Howe*, 1: 240–2, suggests that Murdoch was one of a group of elite lawyers who felt their positions threatened by the emergence of the Reform movement. B.C. Cuthbertson, *Johnny Bluenose at the Polls: Epic Nova Scotia Election Battles 1758–1848* (Halifax: Formac 1994), although generally sympathetic to Murdoch, suggests at 92 that his politics were 'no doubt influenced by the needs of his legal practice and having such clients as Enos Collins.' While it is true that by the 1840s Murdoch's clientele came less from the artisanal classes and more from those solidly ensconced in the middle class, he never represented the higher echelons of the Halifax merchants to any significant degree. Enos Collins appears as a client in Murdoch's account books for the first time in 1839, and a few times over the 1840s, but always for relatively small matters. Murdoch held no retainer from Collins and charged him no fees higher than £10 in any year until 1847, when Collins paid ten guineas to have his will drafted; MG 3, vol. 1836a, file 2.

24 The classic account of the trial is J. Murray Beck, '"A Fool for a Client": The Trial of Joseph Howe,' *Acadiensis*, 3, no. 2 (1974): 28–44, later revised as chapter 9 of *Joseph Howe*, vol. 1. It should now be read along with Barry Cahill, '*R. v. Howe* for Seditious Libel: A Tale of Twelve Magistrates,' in F. Murray Greenwood and Barry Wright, eds., *Canadian State Trials, Volume I: Law, Politics, and Security Measures, 1608–1837* (Toronto: University of Toronto Press for the Osgoode Society 1996), which complements and in some cases corrects Beck's account; and with Lyndsay M. Campbell, 'Licence to Publish: Joseph Howe's Contribution to Libel Law in Nova Scotia,' *Dalhousie Law Journal*, 29 (2006): 79.

25 The jurors were polled and wished to continue, but in view of the difficulty of keeping order in the court, the trial was finally adjourned until the
next day; *Novascotian*, 12 March 1835.

26 *Times*, 2 June 1835.

27 *Times*, 8 Dec. 1840. Murdoch recounted this visit and Howe's statement in
a letter to the editor, and Howe did not seek to refute it in a reply in the
Novascotian, 10 Dec. 1840, so it seems that Murdoch's statement is accurate.
There appears to be no contemporary newspaper account of this occur-
rence.

28 Beck, *Politics of Nova Scotia*, 1: 110–11.

29 M. McCormack, *The Independent Man: Citizenship and Gender Politics in
Georgian England* (Manchester and New York: Manchester University Press
2005), 80; Buckner, *Responsible Government*, 70.

30 Buckner, *Responsible Government*.

31 E.g., the candidates' speeches made during the election campaign of 1830:
Novascotian, 15 Sept. 1830. Stewart's statement in *The Origins of Canadian
Politics*, 92, that Country ideology 'was only a fringe phenomenon in the
Canadian colonies,' is not accurate for the pre-1850 period, whatever its
truth over the long term may be.

32 *Novascotian*, 17 Nov. 1836.

33 *Novascotian*, 7 Dec. 1836.

34 *Novascotian*, 29 Oct. 1840.

35 David Sutherland has noted a similar predilection on the part of J.W. Johnston: 'J.W. Johnston and the Metamorphosis of Nova Scotia Conservatism'
(MA thesis, Dalhousie University, 1968), 185.

36 See generally Beck, *Politics of Nova Scotia*, 1: 118–24. Beck is unenthusiastic
about the Falkland coalition but does not examine its legislative accom-
plishments.

37 *Times*, 21 Dec. 1841.

38 *Novascotian*, 29 Oct. 1840.

39 Murdoch was publicly encouraged to run in the city by-election made necessary by the death of Thomas Forrester in the fall of 1841, but did not take
up the offer; *Times*, 30 Nov. 1841.

40 Wilfrid Prest, *William Blackstone: Law and Letters in the Eighteenth Century*
(Oxford: Oxford University Press 2009), 204.

41 *Novascotian*, 7 July 1842.

42 *Times*, 12 July 1842.

43 Lykke de la Cour, Cecilia Morgan, and Mariana Valverde, 'Gender Regulation and State Formation in Nineteenth-Century Canada,' in Greer and
Radforth, *Colonial Leviathan*, 164.

44 *Epitome*, 1: 65.
45 Bell, 'Maritime Legal Institutions,' 118, reviews the pre-1850 situation regarding female suffrage.
46 *Novascotian*, 12 Nov. 1840.
47 *Joseph Howe*, 1: 149.
48 *Novascotian*, 17 Nov. 1836.
49 At least, there is no record of Murdoch speaking at the meeting in the extensive report of its proceedings contained in the *Novascotian*, 17 Nov. 1836. If Murdoch had wished merely to oppose the substance of the resolutions, he would have attended the meeting and spoken against them. He objected to being put in the position of having to make a pledge, regardless of its content. The explosive nature of the judges' fees issue in Nova Scotia is explored by Phillips and Miller in '"Too Many Courts and Too Much Law."'
50 Marie Peters, 'The *Monitor* on the Constitution, 1755–65: New Light on the Ideological Origins of English Radicalism,' *English Historical Review*, 86 (1971): 715, as cited in McCormack, *The Independent Man*, 3.
51 *Novascotian*, 12 Nov. 1840.
52 *Joseph Howe*, 1: 224.
53 Cuthbertson, *Johnny Bluenose*, passim, discusses these connections.
54 Dan Bunbury, 'Scandal and Reform: The Treasurer's Office in Nova Scotia, 1845–60,' *Nova Scotia Historical Review*, 15, no. 2 (1995): 43–71.
55 *Times*, 26 July 1842.
56 *Halifax Morning Post*, 9 Nov. 1843.
57 14 Nov. 1840.
58 *Halifax Morning Post*, 9 Nov. 1843.
59 Ducharme, *Le Concept de Liberté*, 5–8. See also Bob Harris, *Politics and the Nation: Britain in the Mid-Eighteenth Century* (Oxford: Oxford University Press 2002), chapter 2, who defends Country thought in Britain as a coherent ideology which managed to include a commercial element over time (stressing 'honest commerce' over stock-jobbing and the like), thus adapting its historic emphasis on frugality to a society characterized by greater wealth and more extensive consumption.
60 *Epitome*, 2: 63.
61 I thank Jeffrey McNairn for this observation.
62 Romney, 'From the Rule of Law to Responsible Government,' 117; McNairn, *Capacity to Judge*, chapter 7.
63 Volume I contains chapters dealing with the law connected with agriculture, trade, religion, morals, charity and education, and health and amusement. See Philip Girard, 'Themes and Variations in Early Canadian Legal

Culture: Beamish Murdoch and His *Epitome of the Laws of Nova-Scotia*,' *Law and History Review*, 11, no. 1 (1993): 129–30.

64 The Reformers on the board were Joseph Howe and Michael Tobin, the Tories J.W. Johnston and Dr Charles Cogswell. Murdoch's rules and annual reports can be found in RG 14, vol. 30. The relevant statutes are SNS 1832, c. 2; SNS 1841, c. 43; and SNS 1845, c. 25, which discontinued the Central Board of Education and returned to the 1832 system of supervision requiring the county commissioners to submit their annual reports to the lieutenant governor.

65 On these earlier ideals and customs, see Cuthbertson, *Johnny Bluenose*, 33–4.

66 *Times*, 21 Dec. 1841.

67 *Novascotian*, 11 June 1849.

68 David A. Sutherland, 'Voluntary Societies and the Process of Middle-Class Formation in Early-Victorian Halifax, Nova Scotia,' *Journal of the Canadian Historical Association*, 1994, 250, refers briefly to the role of fraternalism in bridging ethnic, sectarian, and political differences.

69 *History*, 2: 325–6.

70 As cited in McNairn, *Capacity to Judge*, 319–20.

8: Law and Politics in the Colonial City: Murdoch as Recorder of Halifax, 1850–60

1 See generally Jim Phillips, 'A Low Law Counter Treatise? "Absentees" to "Wreck" in British North America's First JP Manual,' in Angela Fernandez and Markus D. Dubber, eds., *The Legal Treatise in History* (London and Portland, Ore.: Hart Publishing, forthcoming 2012).

2 For example, in 1848 Murdoch completed his manuscript 'Irish Vocabulary' (a Gaelic-English dictionary, with the Irish words written in Gaelic script), which must have involved a prodigious amount of research: Beamish Murdoch Papers, MG 1, vol. 727A, no. 2.

3 Judith Fingard, Janet Guildford, and David Sutherland, *Halifax: The First 250 Years* (Halifax: Nimbus 1999), 65.

4 SNS 1848, c. 39, s. 68.

5 Murdoch appears as counsel for private clients in *Jones v. Williams* (1854), 2 N.S.R. 303; *Dale v. The Ship 'Velocity'* (1855), 2 N.S.R. 390; and *Nash v. Mc-Cartney* (1857), 3 N.S.R. 167.

6 SNS 1841, c. 55.

7 SNS 1848, c. 39; SNS 1849, c. 14; SNS 1870, c. 24.

8 SNS 1850, c. 4. Direct election was adopted in Montreal in 1852, Saint John

in 1854, Charlottetown in 1855, and Toronto in 1859, though the last city reverted to aldermanic selection in the late 1860s before again adopting direct election in 1874: Greg Marquis, 'The Contours of Canadian Urban Justice, 1830–1875,' *Urban History Review*, 15 (1987): 271, 273.

9 SNS 1854, c. 45. This change was largely symbolic since a mayor without council experience was elected only once in the nineteenth century, in 1870, when a Father of Confederation, W.A. Henry, was the people's choice: *Annual Reports of the Several Departments of the Civic Government of Halifax, Nova Scotia for the Civic Year 1904–05* (Halifax: Holloway Bros. 1906), 240. There was nothing to prevent a mayor from serving many periods of three one-year terms provided he sat out one year between them, but in practice no mayor in the nineteenth century served more than two periods of three years each.

10 SNS 1857, c. 32.

11 *Novascotian*, 7 Oct. 1850.

12 Ibid.

13 *Morning Chronicle*, 8 July 1854.

14 *Morning Journal*, 3 Oct. 1859.

15 *Morning Journal*, 23, 26, 28 Sept. 1859.

16 Sawers was named custos rotulorum after nearly the entire town magistracy resigned in the wake of the Howe trial in 1835, and a bitter enmity remained between him and the Howe family: see J.M. Beck, '"A Fool for a Client": The Trial of Joseph Howe,' *Acadiensis*, 3, no. 2 (1974): 40–2.

17 SNS 1841, c. 3, s. 7. It may be noted that Sawers had served only nine years on the court before being pensioned off, and lived another twenty-eight: a prime example of the high cost of the proprietorial notion of office.

18 SNS 1846, c. 57; NSARM, Halifax City Council Minutes, 11 Oct. 1848.

19 City Council Minutes, 16 Oct. 1848. Interestingly, councillors voted by ballot in these elections and those of 1849, but thereafter the selection of city officials was done by open voting within council, presumably on the theory that councillors should be accountable for their choices.

20 *Novascotian*, 29 Oct. 1849.

21 *Novascotian*, 7 Oct. 1850.

22 City Council Minutes, 16 Oct. 1855.

23 City Council Minutes, 4 Nov. 1856. In fact, coverage of municipal issues was very unpredictable; debates on important issues were sometimes ignored while those on ceremonial or minor matters might occupy several columns.

24 *Annual Report of the Several Departments of the City of Halifax 1857–58* (Halifax 1858).

25 Paul Romney, '"The Ten Thousand Pound Job": Political Corruption, Equitable Jurisdiction, and the Public Interest in Upper Canada 1852–6,' in David H. Flaherty, ed., *Essays in the History of Canadian Law, Volume II* (Toronto: University of Toronto Press for the Osgoode Society 1983). The mayor was found to have acted in a legally and ethically impermissible fashion.

26 City Council Minutes, 30 Jan., 30 April 1860; *Morning Journal*, 3 Feb. 1860.

27 There was no support in the city charter for any such power, and Murdoch observed that he 'had felt not a little displeased when he found that the persons at whose trial he had assisted the Court for nearly a whole day, had been set at liberty': *Morning Journal*, 3 Feb. 1860. The practice nonetheless persisted into the 1860s: *Unionist and Halifax Journal*, 22 Sept., 11 and 23 Oct., 4 and 13 Nov., 11 and 13 Dec. 1865.

28 *Morning Chronicle*, 9 Sept. 1854.

29 The distinction was not merely semantic. The Saint John Common Council argued successfully in court on several occasions that provincial legislation could not infringe rights granted by the city's royal charter: T.W. Acheson, *Saint John: The Making of a Colonial Urban Community* (Toronto: University of Toronto Press 1985), 45–7. Halifax, to its regret, benefited from no such immunity.

30 Halifax: William Gossip 1851. 'Charter' is here used in a loose sense, meaning simply the collection of legislation creating and empowering the city at a given point. Murdoch was given additional remuneration for his work in preparing this volume, which went beyond his statutory duties: City Council Minutes, 12 April 1851. Confusingly, the 1851 act was not included in the annual volume of provincial statutes for 1851 although it was included in a consolidation of private and local legislation produced in that year.

31 Murdoch's francophilia may have nourished his interest in codification and simplified legislative drafting, which in this instance went further than even most Quebec legislators were prepared to go: see Pierre Issalys, 'La Loi dans la culture juridique québécoise: sources et cheminement d'une idée,' in Josiane Boulad-Ayoub, Bjarne Melkevik, and Pierre Robert, eds., *L'Amour des lois. La crise de la loi moderne dans les sociétés démocratiques* (Quebec: Presses de l'Université Laval, 1996), especially 313–22.

32 *A Supplement Containing the Ordinances of the City of Halifax, Nova Scotia Passed since 1851 and the Recent Provincial Acts concerning the City* (Halifax: English and Blackadar 1854); *A Second Supplement Containing Ordinances of the City of Halifax, Nova Scotia in 1854, 1855 and 1856; Several Provincial Acts concerning the City, Passed in 1855 and 1856; and Extracts from the Revised Statutes* (Halifax: J. and W. Compton 1856).

33 In one instance an oversight by Murdoch does seem to have exposed the
    city to liability. In 1853 council requested legislation creating a new official
    called the superintendent of streets and intended to abolish the older office
    of overseer of streets. Murdoch failed to expressly abolish the older office
    in the new law, with the result that the old overseer successfully claimed
    half his old salary from council: City Council Minutes, 11 Jan. 1854.

34 *The City of Halifax v. McLearn* (1865), 5 N.S.R. 689. Only three other cases
    involving the city were reported in the *Nova Scotia Reports* before *McLearn*,
    and in none of them was interpretation of the city's constituent legislation
    a major issue: *Evens v. City of Halifax* (1861), 5 N.S.R. 111; *The City of Halifax
    v. The Nova Scotia Electric Telegraph Co.* (1859), 4 N.S.R. 83; *Beamish v. City of
    Halifax* (1857), 3 N.S.R. 227.

35 RSNS 1851, viii.

36 Desmond H. Brown, *The Genesis of the Canadian Criminal Code of 1892* (To-
    ronto: University of Toronto Press 1989), 83.

37 *Novascotian*, 1 Oct. 1849.

38 *Annual Report 1857–58.*

39 SNS 1841, c. 55, s. 79.

40 *Acadian Recorder*, 15 Feb. 1872.

41 Peter Karsten, *Between Law and Custom: 'High' and 'Low' Legal Cultures in
    the Lands of the British Diaspora – the United States, Canada, Australia, and
    New Zealand, 1600–1900* (Cambridge: Cambridge University Press 2002),
    363–88; James Muir, 'Instrumentalism and the Law of Injuries in Nine-
    teenth-Century Nova Scotia,' in Philip Girard, Jim Phillips, and Barry Ca-
    hill, eds., *The Supreme Court of Nova Scotia, 1754–2004: From Imperial Bastion
    to Provincial Oracle* (Toronto: University of Toronto Press for the Osgoode
    Society 2004).

42 City Council Minutes, 26 May 1856.

43 City Council Minutes, 22 Nov. 1853 (horse injured in city pound); 10 May
    1858 (losses resulting from powder-magazine explosion); 21 March 1859
    (plaintiff thrown from sleigh after collision with street obstruction).

44 City Council Minutes, 6 March 1854.

45 While SNS 1853, c. 36, created the office of superintendent of streets and
    said he should be 'under the direction and control of the city council,' it
    also stated that the powers of commissioners of streets, appointed under
    the province's general statute on roads, RSNS 1851, c. 64, 'shall be vested
    in the superintendent, but subject to any order of the City Council.' In
    other words, these powers were vested not in the city, which then chose
    to appoint an official to carry them out, but rather in the official, subject
    to city oversight. This appears to be the true rationale for the decision in
    Evens v. City of Halifax (1861), 5 N.S.R. 111.

46 *Evens v. Halifax* (1861), 5 N.S.R. 111.

47 *Annual Report of the Several Departments of the City of Halifax 1861–62* (Halifax: Compton and Co. 1862), 8.

48 William Novak, *The People's Welfare: Law and Regulation in Nineteenth-Century America* (Chapel Hill and London: University of North Carolina Press 1996).

49 See generally Judith Fingard, *The Dark Side of Life in Victorian Halifax* (Halifax: Pottersfield Press 1989); idem, 'Jailbirds in Mid-Victorian Halifax,' in John Yogis, ed., *Law in a Colonial Society: The Nova Scotia Experience* (Toronto: Carswell 1984); Jim Phillips, 'Poverty, Unemployment and the Administration of the Criminal Law: Vagrancy Laws in Halifax, 1864–1890,' and B. Jane Price, '"Raised in Rockhead. Died in the Poor House": Female Petty Criminals in Halifax, 1864–1890,' both in Philip Girard and Jim Phillips, *Essays in the History of Canadian Law, Volume III, Nova Scotia* (Toronto: University of Toronto Press for the Osgoode Society 1990).

50 Hendrik Hartog, 'Pigs and Positivism,' *Wisconsin Law Review* (1985): 899–935, argues that similar ordinances in New York City were not effective to end the practice, framing the issue as one of conflicting normative orders. On the current state of the evidence, it is impossible to know whether the civic authorities had more success in Halifax.

51 Marquis, 'Canadian Urban Justice, 1830–1875.'

52 Halifax Mayor's Court Records, RG 42B, vol. 7; *Annual Report 1857–58*. One action in 1852 is noted as being brought *in forma pauperis*, suggesting the court could be used even by the disadvantaged.

53 While a member of council had to be available every day to sign documents and the like, the Police Court usually sat two days a week to hear pleas and conduct trials; the court's minute books in RG 42, ser. D, are quite detailed.

54 *Annual Report 1861–62*, 3.

55 Cf. the figures in *Annual Report 1857–58* with those in *Annual Report 1861–62*.

56 For similar patterns of prosecution in Toronto in this period, see Nicholas Rogers, 'Serving Toronto the Good: The Development of the City Police Force 1834–84,' in Victor L. Russell, ed., *Forging a Consensus: Historical Essays on Toronto* (Toronto: University of Toronto Press 1984), 132–3.

57 *Acadian Recorder*, 16 Jan. 1857.

58 *Unionist and Halifax Journal*, 21 Jan. 1866.

59 SNS 1867, c. 82. See Philip Girard, 'Pryor, Henry,' *DCB* 12. Halifax had had a stipendiary police magistrate from 1815 to 1841 but abolished the office at incorporation; Philip Girard, 'The Rise and Fall of Urban Justice in

Halifax, 1815–1886,' *Nova Scotia Historical Review*, 8, no. 2 (1988): 257. Other British North American cities appointed stipendiaries after a flirtation with mayoral courts, such as Hamilton (1846), Kingston (1847), Saint John (1849), Toronto (1851), and Montreal (1852): Marquis, 'Canadian Urban Justice, 1830–1875.'

60 City Council Minutes, 15 Oct. 1851.

61 SNS 1854, c. 2, s. 7. An earlier statute to the same effect could not be implemented after Britain withdrew loan guarantees that had supposedly been promised.

62 SNS 1858, c. 11.

63 City Council Minutes, 22 and 29 March, 19 April, 25 May 1858. Another petition to the queen was also sent at the same time, urging rejection of a private act passed by the province forcing the city to provide compensation to one Stephen Seldon whose house was torn down by the firewards during the New Year's Day conflagration of 1857. The order to do so was given by one fireward and two aldermen when a provincial law, RSNS 1851, c. 99, required three firewards to give the order if compensation was to be provided to the affected landowner. An Act for the Relief of Stephen Seldon, SNS 1858, c. 94, recited that the house was torn down 'by the desire and with the sanction of the then governor of this province' and deemed that it had been done in accordance with the requirements of the 1851 law. The city finally paid Seldon £200: City Council Minutes, 25 Jan., 26 Feb., 5 March, 19 April, 18 June, 13 Aug. 1858, 13 June, 26 and 30 Sept. 1859.

64 City Council Minutes, 22 March, 29 March, 19 April, 25 May 1858.

65 *Annual Report of the Several Departments of the City of Halifax 1866–67* (Halifax 1867).

66 *Petition of the City of Halifax, Nova Scotia, to Her Majesty the Queen, respecting the Interference of the Military Authorities with the Common of Halifax* (Halifax: James Bowes and Sons 1859), 4.

67 Ibid.

68 Ibid., 47–50. In spite of the publication date of 1859, City Council deliberations on the matter down to its resolution in July 1860 are included in the pamphlet. A second edition with additional material may have been issued without changing the cover page.

69 *The Report of the Committee of Aldermen respecting the Recent Explosion of the Gunpowder Magazine, at Halifax with Depositions of the Witnesses Examined by Them on the Subject* (Halifax: s.n. 1857).

70 City Council Minutes, 10 May 1857.

71 The tangled tale is explored in Ann Larabee, *Dynamite Fiend: The Chilling*

Story of Alexander Keith Jr., Nova Scotian Spy, Con-Artist & International Ter-rorist (Halifax: Nimbus 2005). Keith was living under an assumed name in Europe and the Halifax press denied that he was the Bremerhaven bomber when the information was made public, but Larabee's evidence seems convincing. An opera entitled *The Inventor*, based on Keith's life, premiered in Calgary in 2011: www.calgaryopera.com.

72 D.R. Williams, *Call in Pinkerton's: American Detectives at Work for Canada* (Toronto: Dundurn Press 1998), 23, 44–6.

73 When sought out by the police in Bremerhaven, Keith committed suicide, thus taking the secret of his involvement in the Halifax explosion to the grave.

74 City Council Minutes, 16, 19 Oct. 1855.

75 City Council Minutes, 7 and 11 May 1860. The newspapers unfortunately steered clear of the controversy, reporting Murdoch's resignation and the election of his successor William Sutherland but providing no context. One possible source of ill will between Evans and Murdoch was Evans's loss of a suit against the city for negligence. The name of the plaintiff in *Evens v. City of Halifax* (1861), 5 N.S.R. 111, was William Evens (or Evans) (both spellings are used in the case file at NSARM) and there was only one other William Evans in the city directories of the period, one W.L. Evans of Dartmouth. The plaintiff and his wife had been injured when their carriage was overturned after running over a pile of dirt placed in the street under the authority of the commissioner of streets. The accident occurred in June 1859 and Murdoch successfully defended the suit in April 1860, just before the controversy with Evans in council. The reported decision relates to a second trial in the same matter which Evans also lost, and in which Murdoch was not involved. It is not completely certain that the plaintiff in *Evens v. Halifax* was the alderman, but if he was it would provide some additional motivation for the conflict between him and Murdoch.

9: Law, Identity, and Improvement: Murdoch as Cultural Producer

1 J.G.A. Pocock, *The Ancient Constitution and the Feudal Law*, rev. ed. (New York: Cambridge University Press 1987); Linda Colley, *Britons: Forging the Nation, 1707–1832*, 2d ed. (New Haven, Conn., and London: Yale University Press 2005).

2 A complete bibliography of Murdoch's published works is provided in the Appendix. On Murdoch's library, see the next chapter. On the lawyer as man of letters in the U.S. context, see Robert Ferguson, *Law and Letters in American Culture* (Cambridge, Mass.: Harvard University Press 1984);

Arthur Konefsky, 'Law and Culture in Antebellum Boston,' *Stanford Law Review*, 40 (1988): 1132.

3 D.C. Harvey, 'The Intellectual Awakening of Nova Scotia,' *Dalhousie Review*, 13 (1933): 18.

4 A seminal text is Benedict Anderson, *Imagined Communities*, 2d ed. (London: Verso 1991).

5 Anderson's *Imagined Communities* considers this question with particular reference to Latin America, but New England was to some extent an exception in being much less culturally diverse than most other parts of the New World.

6 'The Cultural Landscape of Early Canada,' in Bernard Bailyn and Philip D. Morgan, eds., *Strangers within the Realm: Cultural Margins of the First British Empire* (Chapel Hill: University of North Carolina Press 1991), 363.

7 Anderson, *Imagined Communities*, 47n.1.

8 Ibid., 65. In fact, Anderson argues that modern nationalism originated in the Americas rather than Europe.

9 30 Sept. 1820. The identity of 'Brutus' has been confirmed by the appearance of a draft version of this letter in Beamish Murdoch's 1814–20 commonplace book entitled 'Forms of the Supreme Court,' facing 49–51.

10 The preceding quotations are taken from a draft letter in ibid., facing 49–51, much of which was published in the *Acadian Recorder*, 20 Sept. 1820.

11 Eleven were articled clerks and two others would become lawyers in the early 1830s. 'Rules, Constitution and Correspondence regarding the Literary Forum, 1820,' MG 20, vol. 222, no. 95.

12 *Acadian Recorder*, 20 May 1820.

13 'Rules, Constitution and Correspondence regarding the Literary Forum.'

14 The Wilkie case is exhaustively considered in Barry Cahill, 'Sedition in Nova Scotia: *R. v. Wilkie* and the Incontestable Illegality of Seditious Libel before *R. v. Howe* (1835),' *Dalhousie Law Journal*, 17 (1994): 458. Cahill suggests that Wilkie may have been apprenticed to a lawyer at this time. More details on the rise and fall of the forum may be found in William Laurence, '"A Literary Man and a Merchant": The Legal Career of Sir William Young' (PhD thesis, Dalhousie University, 2009), 111–18.

15 The assessment is that of J. Murray Beck, *Joseph Howe*, vol. 1 (Montreal and Kingston: McGill-Queen's University Press 1984), 43.

16 Murdoch recorded a payment in his account book of £66 13s from Philip J. Holland for editorial services from 18 Sept. 1824 to 26 May 1826, representing a rate of pay of £40 per annum. A later payment shows that he again provided editorial services from September 1835 to June 1836: MG 3, vol. 1836a.

17 Daniel Boorstin, *The Mysterious Science of the Law* (Cambridge, Mass.: Harvard University Press 1941), chapter 4.
18 The untitled ballad is found written in Murdoch's hand in the back of his signed copy of *Jacobite Melodies: A Collection of the Most Popular Legends, Ballads, and Songs of the Adherents of the House of Stuart, from 1640 ... [to] 1746* (Edinburgh: William Aitchison 1823), held by the Legislative Library of Nova Scotia.
19 Joseph Howe to Agnes Burgess, 9 April 1826, Burgess Papers, MG 1, vol. 162a. On Murdoch's role, see Gwendolyn Davies, 'The Editorship of *The Acadian Magazine* July 1826–January 1828,' *Canadian Notes & Queries*, 26 (December 1980): 10.
20 Tom Vincent, 'The Acadian Magazine,' in William Toye and Eugene Benson, eds., *The Oxford Companion to Canadian Literature*, 2d ed. (Toronto: Oxford University Press 1997), 4.
21 Gwendolyn P. Davies, 'A Literary Study of Selected Periodicals from Maritime Canada, 1789–1872' (PhD thesis, York University, 1979), 92.
22 Gwendolyn Davies, 'The Club Papers: Haliburton's Literary Apprenticeship,' in her *Studies in Maritime Literary History, 1760–1930* (Fredericton: Acadiensis Press 1991). See also Carrie MacMillan, 'Colonial Gleanings: "The Club" Papers (1828–31),' *Essays on Canadian Writing*, 31 (1985): 51.
23 Murdoch was appointed along with three other leading lawyers, S.G.W. Archibald, William Hill, and James Boyle Uniacke, to a law reform commission in 1832, when the Assembly determined that it was 'necessary to revise the Civil and Criminal Codes of the Province, and to render the practice of the Courts of Law and Equity more simple and less expensive': SNS 1832, c. 42. They recommended only minor reforms to court structure, but on the substantive law side advocated a consolidation of the criminal statutes, a reduction in the number of capital crimes, and a general statutory consolidation: *Report of the Commissioners into Courts and Law, 1834*, in *Journals of the House of Assembly of the Province of Nova Scotia* (1834), appendix 59. Curiously, the Assembly revoked the commissioners' mandate in 1837, declaring that they had 'not proceeded in the discharge of the duties ... committed to them': SNS 1837, c. 55. All their suggestions were eventually taken up between 1841 (reform of the criminal law) and 1851 (statutory revision).
24 *Novascotian*, 24 Feb. 1831.
25 Ibid. J.G. Marshall, who published a JP manual entitled *The Justice of the Peace and County and Township Office, in the Province of Nova Scotia ...* (Halifax: W. Gossip 1837, 2d ed. 1846), damned the *Epitome* with faint praise in the preface to his own work: 'The work by Mr. Murdoch, although valu-

able and generally useful, has, evidently, not been designed to be one of that description [guide to magistrates]. It is chiefly an exhibition of our Statutes in general. Now, as a very considerable part of the authority and duties of Justices of the Peace arises out of the Common and Statute law of England, such as Precedents and Forms for their use, are of essential importance, it follows, that a work of that nature cannot form a complete and universal guide for the discharge of the almost endless variety of their duties.' While it is true that the *Epitome* was not meant as a manual for justices of the peace, it is much more than 'an exhibition of our Statutes in general' and contains constant references to the 'Common and Statute Law of England.' And one may doubt whether Marshall's intended audience found his alphabetical style of organization as accessible as Murdoch's thematic presentation in providing a real understanding of the law.

26 *Epitome of the Laws of Nova-Scotia*, 4 vols. (Halifax: Joseph Howe, 1832–3), 1: iii.

27 Murdoch's appointment as commissioner and secretary to the Central Board of Education in 1841, discussed in chapter 7, was a step in this direction, but the board expired in 1845. Murdoch's main appointment thereafter was not a provincial one but the municipal office of recorder of the city of Halifax.

28 *Novascotian*, 23 Jan. 1840.

29 *Novascotian*, 30 Nov. 1831.

30 Beck, *Joseph Howe*, 1: 100, states that Howe took notes from Murdoch for £460, upon which he did not receive final payment until 1850.

31 MG 3, vol. 1836A, f.24.

32 A fifth volume, to be devoted to local and private legislation (i.e., laws dealing with the powers of particular local governments or institutions, the incorporation of individual companies or churches, etc.), was promised when Volume IV was issued, but it never appeared: *Novascotian*, 4 Sept. 1833.

33 Advertisement in Halifax *Times*, 5 April 1842.

34 *Novascotian*, 24 March 1831.

35 Anderson, *Imagined Communities*, 53.

36 Greg Marquis, 'In Defence of Liberty: 17th Century England and 19th Century Maritime Political Culture,' *University of New Brunswick Law Journal*, 42 (1993): 42.

37 An increasing body of European, British, and North American scholarship explores this approach. For a particularly good example, see G. Blaine Baker, 'The Reconstitution of Upper Canadian Legal Thought in the Late-Victorian Empire,' *Law and History Review*, 5 (1985): 286. For another

suggestive analysis, see A.W.B. Simpson, 'The Rise and Fall of the Legal
Treatise: Legal Principles and the Forms of Legal Literature,' *University of
Chicago Law Review*, 48 (1981): 632.

38 'Themes and Variations in Early Canadian Legal Culture: Beamish Murdoch and His *Epitome of the Laws of Nova-Scotia*,' *Law & History Review*, 11
(1993): 101.

39 M.G. Parks, ed., *Western and Eastern Rambles: Travel Sketches of Nova Scotia*
(Toronto: University of Toronto Press 1973).

40 First published in 1849, *The Old Judge* is most easily available in the 1978
Tecumseh Press reprint of the 1860 London edition, edited by M.G. Parks.

41 *The Old Judge; or, Life in a Colony* (1849); Colin Boyd, '"The Great American
Mammoth Circus": *The Old Judge* and Democracy in Nova Scotia,' in Richard A. Davies, ed., *The Haliburton Bi-Centenary Chaplet: Papers Presented at
the 1996 Thomas Raddall Symposium* (Wolfville, N.S.: Gaspereau Press 1997),
269. It is true that Haliburton's earlier *Historical and Statistical Account of
Nova Scotia* was more optimistic about the future of the colony and had
more in common with the works of Howe and Murdoch; Richard A. Davies, *Inventing Sam Slick: A Biography of Thomas Chandler Haliburton* (Toronto:
University of Toronto Press 2005), 44, observes that there is 'no simple explanation for this transition.'

42 Barry Cahill, 'The "Old Judge" in *The Old Judge*: Nostalgic Tory-Loyalism
as the Key to Understanding Nova Scotia's Pre-Modern Legal Culture,' in
Davies, ed., *Haliburton Bi-Cententary Chaplet*, 251.

43 Murdoch, *Epitome*, 1: 33.

44 Ibid., 1: 35–6.

45 Ibid., 1: 34.

46 Murdoch's views were echoed in the most important case on reception
to be decided by Nova Scotia courts in the colonial period: *Uniacke v.
Dickson* (1848), 2 N.S.R. 286, which was prosecuted for the crown by the
son of Murdoch's patron. Chief Justice Brenton Halliburton decided that
Tudor statutes imposing a crown lien upon the lands of customs officers
in cases of defalcation could not be considered in force in Nova Scotia in
the absence of re-enactment by the local legislature. On reception generally, see T.G. Barnes, '"As Near as May Be Agreeable to the Laws of This
Kingdom": Legal Birthright and Legal Baggage at Chebucto, 1749,' in P.B.
Waite et al., eds., *Law in a Colonial Society: The Nova Scotia Experience* (Toronto: Carswell 1984); Barry Cahill, '"How Far English Laws Are in Force
Here": Nova Scotia's First Century of Reception Law Jurisprudence,' *University of New Brunswick Law Journal*, 42 (1993): 113.

47 *Epitome*, 1: 35.

48 Ibid., 1: 43.
49 Ibid., 1: 35.
50 Ibid., 1: 23. On divorce generally, see Kimberley Smith Maynard, 'Divorce in Nova Scotia, 1750–1890,' in Philip Girard and Jim Phillips, eds., *Essays in the History of Canadian Law, Volume III, Nova Scotia* (Toronto: University of Toronto Press for the Osgoode Society 1990).
51 *Epitome*, 1: 36. Murdoch was so concerned to emphasize the distinctiveness of Nova Scotia's legal code that he barely referred to the governor's power of suspension and the crown's prerogative of disallowance of colonial legislation: 1: 31.
52 Ibid., 1: 59.
53 Cited in Cyril Byrne, 'The Maritime Visits of Joseph Octave Plessis, Bishop of Quebec,' Nova Scotia Historical Society *Collections*, 39 (1977): 38.
54 Boorstin, *The Mysterious Science of the Law*, chapter 4.
55 His aim seemed to be misunderstood by a Saint John lawyer, who complained that the work had 'an air of extemporaneous speech.' Its informal style he regarded as a drawback rather than an asset: *Halifax Monthly Magazine*, July 1832, 1 (reproducing a review in the Saint John *Courier*). An emphasis on plain speaking and informality was the stylistic hallmark of the literature of the period, as in 'The Club' papers, the work of Thomas Chandler Haliburton, and Thomas McCulloch's *The Letters of Mephibosheth Stepsure* (1821–2, repr. Halifax 1860).
56 Janice Kulyk Keefer, *Under Eastern Eyes: A Critical Reading of Maritime Fiction* (Toronto: University of Toronto Press 1987), 66–7.
57 *The Acadian Magazine*, 1826, quoted in Elizabeth Pacey, *Georgian Halifax* (Hantsport, N.S.: Lancelot Press 1987), 43 ('the best use of a Palladian compositional formula found in Canada').
58 *Epitome*, 1: 43.
59 D.G. Bell, 'Slavery and the Judges of Loyalist New Brunswick,' *University of New Brunswick Law Journal*, 31 (1982): 9.
60 James Kent, *Commentaries on American Law*, 4 vols., 2d ed. (New York: O. Halsted 1832), 1: 464. On Haliburton's racism, see George Elliott Clarke, 'Must We Burn Haliburton?' and Greg Marquis, 'Haliburton, Maritime Intellectuals and "The Problem of Freedom,"' both in Davies, ed. *Haliburton Bi-Centenary Chaplet*.
61 *Epitome*, 1: 65, but see below, note 75.
62 Ibid., 2: 57. Murdoch's changing views on the Mi'kmaq are explored below.
63 See, e.g., *Halifax Monthly Magazine*, March 1831, 397.
64 Brian Cuthbertson, *The Loyalist Governor: A Biography of Sir John Wentworth* (Halifax: Nimbus 1983).

65 *Epitome*, 1: 35. For examples, see Girard, 'Themes and Variations,' 118–19.
66 M.H. Hoeflich, *Roman Law and Civil Law and the Development of Anglo-American Jurisprudence in the Nineteenth Century* (Athens, Ga., and London: University of Georgia Press 1997), 132. The positive approach to the civil law displayed by Murdoch's mentor Crofton Uniacke is explored in chapter 3.
67 Murdoch refers to this work as Browne's 'Civil and Admiralty Law.' A second London edition appeared in 1802–3, and the first United States edition was published in 1840. Browne was born in Rhode Island of Anglo-Irish stock, left North America to study at Trinity College Dublin at the age of sixteen in 1772, and spent the rest of his life in Ireland, where he achieved high legal, political, and academic honours, including appointment as Regius Professor of Civil and Canon Law at Trinity College in 1785: Joseph C. Sweeney, 'The Admiralty Law of Arthur Browne,' *Journal of Maritime Law and Commerce*, 26 (1995): 59. Browne observed that 'much of the civil law ... was incorporated with our own, though by long use the debt is forgotten, and we are apt to consider it as part of our original stock': cited in Seán Patrick Donlan, '"Our Laws Are as Mixed as Our Language": Commentaries on the Laws of England and Ireland, 1704–1804,' *Electronic Journal of Comparative Law*, 12, no. 1 (2008), http://www.ejcl.org/121/art121-6.pdf.
68 *Epitome*, 1: 42.
69 On Haliburton's environmentalism in his *Historical and Statistical Account of Nova-Scotia*, see M. Brook Taylor, *Promoters, Patriots and Partisans: Historiography in Nineteenth-Century English Canada* (Toronto: University of Toronto Press 1989), 49.
70 Beamish Murdoch to H.J. Morgan, 28 Sept. 1865, H.J. Morgan Papers, LAC, MG 29D 61, vol. 47.
71 For Murdoch's private views on the Acadian question, see Alice R. Stewart et al., 'A Nova Scotia-Maine Historical Correspondence, 1869,' *Acadiensis* 14, no. 2 (1985): 108.
72 On pre-1749 attempts by the British administration to come to terms with Acadian civil law, see Thomas G. Barnes, '"The Dayly Cry for Justice": The Juridical Failure of the Annapolis Royal Regime, 1713–1749,' in Girard and Phillips, eds., *Nova Scotia Essays*.
73 An example of his campaign literature from the election of October 1840 survives: 'A Messieurs les Électeurs Français Acadiens du comté d'Halifax, demeurants en Chezetcook,' NSARM Library, Akins Collection.
74 D.C. Harvey, 'Nova Scotia's Blackstone,' *Canadian Bar Review*, 11 (1933): 339.
75 See generally Philip Girard, 'Of Institutes and Treatises: Blackstone's *Com-*

mentaries, Kent's *Commentaries,* and Murdoch's *Epitome of the Laws of Nova-Scotia,'* in Angela Fernandez and Markus D. Dubber, eds., *The Legal Treatise in History* (London and Portland, Ore.: Hart, forthcoming 2012).

76 'Haliburton's Windsor,' in Davies, ed. *Haliburton Bi-Centenary Chaplet,* 76.

77 While Murdoch was correct in noting the general trend towards equal treatment of Anglicans, dissenters, and Catholics, he did not acknowledge that some residual distinctions between Anglicans and others remained in provincial law until 1850; Susan Buggey, 'Churchmen and Dissenters: Religious Toleration in Nova Scotia 1758–1835,' (MA thesis, Dalhousie University, 1981).

78 For a suggestive treatment of the development of tolerance as a response to diversity, see Barry Moody, 'Growing up in Granville Township, 1760–1800,' in Margaret Conrad, ed., *Intimate Relations: Family and Community in Planter Nova Scotia, 1759–1800* (Fredericton: Acadiensis Press 1995). See also Sheldon J. Godfrey and Judith C. Godfrey, *Search out the Land: The Jews and the Growth of Equality in British Colonial America, 1740–1867* (Montreal and Kingston: McGill-Queen's University Press 1995).

79 In the 1820s Murdoch had helped Haliburton with his own history of the province and had begun his own research on the history of the British North American colonies: Beamish Murdoch Papers, MG 1, vol. 726, 'Historical Memoirs of the British North American Provinces since His Present Majesty's Accession.'

80 Three hundred sets were sold on a single day in 1867, and a further three hundred were purchased by the provincial Department of Education to be used as prizes: Anon., 'Friday the Thirteenth,' *Journal of Education,* 15, no. 3 (5th ser.) (1966): 23.

81 Taylor, *Promoters, Patriots, and Partisans,* 187–207; Patrick D. Clarke, 'The Makers of Acadian History in the Nineteenth Century' (PhD dissertation, Université Laval, 1988); idem, 'Beamish Murdoch: Nova Scotia's National Historian,' *Acadiensis,* 21 (1991): 85.

82 Clarke, 'Makers of Acadian History,' 258–9.

83 Murdoch to Godfrey, 22 Feb. 1869, reproduced in Alice R. Stewart, James B. Vickery, and Edward S. Kellogg, eds., 'A Nova Scotia-Maine Historical Correspondence [Document],' *Acadiensis,* 14 (1985): 108.

84 *History,* 2: 325–6.

85 Ian Radforth, *Royal Spectacle: The 1860 Visit of the Prince of Wales to Canada and the United States* (Toronto: University of Toronto Press 2004).

86 For the broader context, see D.G. Bell, 'Was Aboriginal Dispossession Lawful? The Response of 19th-Century Maritime Intellectuals,' *Dalhousie Law Journal,* 23 (2000): 168, and L.F.S. Upton, *Micmacs and Colonists: Indian-*

White Relations in the Maritimes, 1713–1867 (Vancouver: University of British Columbia Press 1979).

87 Murdoch, *Epitome*, 2: 57.

88 *History*, 1: 38–9 (emphasis added).

89 *History*, 2: 430–1. For the incident on which this observation is probably based, see the *Novascotian*, 6 April 1846.

90 *History*, 2: 308–9.

91 Quotes taken from the English translation, *The Law of Nations, or Principles of the Law of Nature* ... (London: G.G. and J. Robinson 1797), 36–7. The copy of this edition in the Sir James Dunn Law Library at Dalhousie University contains two pages of writing in a hand very similar to Murdoch's. The first page lists twenty-three writers on international law. The second contains a number of specific references to Vattel of a mostly laudatory nature, including the notation that Sir William Scott called him 'the most correct ... of modern Professors of Public Law.'

92 James Kent, *Commentaries on American Law*, 2d ed. (New York: O. Halsted 1832), 3: 389.

93 21 *United States Reports* 543.

94 Kent, *Commentaries*, 3: 379. The second edition contains a lengthy discussion of subsequent decisions of the U.S. Supreme Court, *Cherokee Nation v. Georgia* (1831) and *Worcester Nation v. Georgia* (1832), but these would not have been discussed in Volume III of the first edition, which appeared in 1828 and was probably the volume Murdoch used. There is a large literature on the fate of aboriginal sovereignty and land rights after European contact, but for an excellent overview see Michel Morin, *L'Usurpation de la souveraineté autochtone: Le cas des peuples de la Nouvelle-France et des colonies anglaises de l'Amérique du Nord* (Montreal: Boréal 1997).

95 *Constitution, Fundamental Rules, and Byelaws of the Nova-Scotia Philanthropic Society* (Halifax: James Spike 1838). See also D.C. Harvey, 'Nova Scotia Philanthropic Society,' *Dalhousie Review*, 3 (1939): 287.

96 *Novascotian*, 15 Nov. 1838. I thank Lyndsay Campbell for this reference.

97 *Novascotian*, 7 May 1840. Some particulars can also be gleaned from Bonnie Huskins, 'Public Celebrations in Victorian Saint John and Halifax' (PhD thesis, Dalhousie University, 1991).

98 The dictionary is in the Beamish Murdoch Papers, MG 1, vol. 727A, no. 1. Sources for this work are unclear. The only published account of the Mi'kmaq language as of 1860 was Walter Bromley's brief glossary of Mi'kmaq terms, published in Haliburton's *General Description* in 1823. Murdoch may have consulted his friend Moses Perley, who knew the Mi'kmaq well. There must also have been some correspondence between

Dr Silas Rand and Murdoch, but no trace of it survives today: personal communication with Dr Dorothy Lovesey, 30 Nov. 1994. Rand's own dictionary was not published until just before his death: *Dictionary of the Language of the Micmac Indians* (Halifax: Nova Scotia Printing 1888). All of this points to personal interaction with Mi'kmaq speakers as a principal source for Murdoch's dictionary.

99 Dorothy Lovesey, *To Be a Pilgrim: A Biography of Silas Tertius Rand 1810–1889* (Hantsport, N.S.: Lancelot Press 1992). Prior to Rand's publications, the main source of published material in English on the Mi'kmaq was Haliburton's *General Description of Nova Scotia* (Halifax, 1823), 45–61. On early philanthropic work with the Mi'kmaq, see Judith Fingard, 'English Humanitarianism and the Colonial Mind: Walter Bromley in Nova Scotia 1813–25,' *Canadian Historical Review*, 54, no. 2 (1973): 123.

100 W.A. Spray, 'Perley, Moses Henry,' *DCB* 7. Perley and Murdoch were corresponding in 1832–3, and both Murdoch and T.B. Akins visited Perley and his family in Saint John on separate occasions during this time; Perley to Murdoch, 7 Nov. 1832, 23 Feb. 1833, T.B. Akins Papers, MG 1, vol. 8, nos. 22, 23. A letter from Perley to his mother dated 6 Sept. 1833 refers to the recent visit by Akins: 'He is very like Murdoch, and like him, has never been abroad until now'; New Brunswick Museum, Moses Perley Cabinet Document. It is difficult to imagine Perley approving of Murdoch's remarks on the Mi'kmaq in the *Epitome*.

101 *A Short Statement of Facts relating to the History, Manners, Customs, Language and Literature of the Micmac Tribe of Indians, of Nova Scotia and P.E. Island* (Halifax: James Bowes and Son 1850).

102 *History*, 3: vii. Murdoch neither belonged to the Micmac Missionary Society nor contributed money to it, according to the society's published annual reports (1850–63).

103 Estimates are reviewed in Virginia Miller, 'The Decline of Nova Scotia Micmac Population, A.D. 1600–1850,' *Culture*, 2, no. 3 (1982): 107–20. Miller suggests that the nadir occurred about 1840, with definite population increase after 1840. The 1871 Census of Canada recorded 1,666 Mi'kmaq in Nova Scotia.

104 These are reviewed in Jennifer Reid, *Myth, Symbol and Colonial Encounter: British and Mikmaq in Acadia, 1700–1867* (Ottawa: University of Ottawa Press 1995), 78.

105 *Epitome*, 4: 48–9.

106 Ibid., 4: 17.

107 On the disappointing reception that awaited the *Epitome*, and the popularity of Kent's work in Halifax, see Girard, 'Themes and Variations,' 130–5.

268   Notes to pages 183–7

10: Epilogue

1 *Acadian Recorder*, 31 Oct. 1863.
2 The photograph is part of the NSARM photograph collection and is reproduced in Carol Wilton, ed., *Inside the Law: Canadian Law Firms in Historical
  Perspective* (Toronto: University of Toronto Press for the Osgoode Society
  1996), 58.
3 *Belcher's Farmer's Almanack* notes the membership of the executive of the
  society from its inception, and Murdoch appears on the executive committee only in the year 1827, before again appearing in 1863–4.
4 Although apparently not published at the time, the lecture must have circulated in manuscript form. For details of its later publication, see the Appendix.
5 Executive Council Minutes, RG 3, vol. 1, no. 166, 1 May 1863.
6 *Morning Chronicle*, 1 July 1867. It was customary for the citation and the
  candidate's address to be read in Latin.
7 See generally Brian Cuthbertson, 'Halifax Homes of the Nova Scotia Supreme Court,' in Philip Girard, Jim Phillips, and Barry Cahill, eds., *The
  Supreme Court of Nova Scotia, 1754–2004: From Imperial Bastion to Provincial
  Oracle* (Toronto: University of Toronto Press for the Osgoode Society 2004).
8 Will of Maria Ott Beamish, Halifax County Court of Probate, no. 1403; will
  of Sarah Catherine Ott Beamish, no. 1931 (mfm. at NSARM).
9 G. Blaine Baker, 'Ordering the Urban Canadian Law Office and Its Entrepreneurial Hinterland, 1825 to 1875,' *University of Toronto Law Journal*, 48
  (1998): 224–5.
10 For the holograph will, see MG 100, vol. 109, no. 18. Beamish Murdoch
  was appointed administrator of his aunt's estate: Halifax County Court of
  Probate, no. 1924 (mfm. at NSARM).
11 J.M. Beck, 'The Last Days of Beamish Murdoch' (unpublished ms., 1993), 7,
  NSARM, V/F, vol. 376, no. 28.
12 The appointment was handled by Joseph Howe, then secretary of state
  for the provinces: J.M. Beck, *Joseph Howe*, vol. 2 (Montreal and Kingston:
  McGill-Queen's University Press 1983), 278.
13 Beck, 'Last Days,' 19.
14 'Agreement of Sale between Beamish Murdoch, Thomas Beamish Akins
  and Charles Beamish of the First Part and Edward Morrison of the Second
  Part, for the Sale of the Market Wharf,' NSARM, MG 100, vol. 160, no. 11c.
15 The case was eventually appealed to the Supreme Court of Canada, and
  the appeal book was printed as *Appeal from the Supreme Court of Nova
  Scotia. In the Matter of ... the Last Will and Testament of Beamish Murdoch ...*

(Halifax: William MacNab, 1879) (hereafter *Appeal Book*). The decision of
the Supreme Court of Nova Scotia is reported as *In re Beamish Murdoch's
Will*, (1878) 12 N.S.R. 428–56.

16 MG 100, vol. 35, no. 96. There are three other stanzas.

17 I thank Barry Cahill for drawing this possibility to my attention.

18 *Appeal Book*, 28.

19 All the wills are reproduced in the *Appeal Book*.

20 Lunenburg County Court of Probate, Probate Acts, vol. 2, at 93 (NSARM,
mfm. reel 19924).

21 *In re Beamish Murdoch's Will*, 436.

22 Ibid., 445.

23 Ibid., 441.

24 Ibid., 450.

25 Ibid., 442.

26 *Parfitt v. Lawless* (1872) L.R. 2 P. & D. 462 at 470. See also H.S. Theobald,
A Concise Treatise on the Law of Wills, 6th ed. (London: Stevens and Sons
1905), 28.

27 *Charles Beamish et al. v. Kaulbach* (1879), 3 S.C.R. 704.

28 The *Lunenburg Progress*, 7 Oct. 1879, reported her death at age forty-two.

29 On this phenomenon, see Philip Girard, 'The Roots of a Professional Renaissance: Lawyers in Nova Scotia, 1850–1910,' *Manitoba Law Journal*, 20
(1991): 148.

30 *Chronicle-Herald* (Halifax), 13 April 1956. Brian Cuthbertson, *Lunenburg
Then and Now* (Halifax: Formac Publishing 2002), 61, reports that Kaulbach
brought organized ice hockey to Lunenburg in 1898, having learned it at
boarding school in Ontario.

31 As for Murdoch's personal papers, those at NSARM are modest in quantity and quality aside from the records from his law practice and some items
relating to his historical and linguistic researches. Presumably these had
remained, fortuitously, in Akins's or Charles Beamish's custody and thus
escaped the 'grand conflagration' of October 1875, when Murdoch burned
most of his papers.

32 Excerpt from the 1926 Annual Report of Dalhousie University, as communicated by Ms. Karen Smith, special collections librarian, Dalhousie
University, 5 Aug. 1997. I thank Ms. Smith for this information and also
for preparing a list of fourteen volumes in the Killam Library's Rare Books
Collection bearing Beamish Murdoch's signature. The volumes, published
between 1693 and 1832, are on diverse subjects, from forest planting to
travel literature to the *Lettres* of Cardinal Richelieu (Paris, 1695); half are in
Latin or in modern European languages other than English.

33 William Laurence, 'Acquiring the Law: The Personal Law Library of William Young, Halifax, Nova Scotia, 1835,' *Dalhousie Law Journal*, 21 (1998): 490–516.

11: Conclusion

1 *Revolution and the Making of the Contemporary Legal Profession in England, France, and the United States* (New York: Oxford University Press 2006).
2 McKay outlined his argument in 'The Liberal Order Framework: A Prospectus for a Reconnaissance of Canadian History,' *Canadian Historical Review*, 81 (2000): 617–45. The article is reproduced and the thesis debated in Jean-François Constant and Michel Ducharme, eds., *Liberalism and Hegemony: Debating the Canadian Liberal Revolution* (Toronto: University of Toronto Press 2009). The quotation, paraphrasing the thrust of McKay's thesis, is found in the editors' introduction to the latter volume at 7. Michel Ducharme, *Le Concept de Liberté au Canada a l'Époque des Révolutions Atlantiques, 1776–1838* (Montreal and Kingston: McGill-Queen's University Press 2010), provides an alternate analysis of the nature and evolution of Canadian liberty that I find more persuasive, as will be argued subsequently.
3 Burrage relies exclusively on existing secondary literature, which is scant with regard to the lives and practices of provincial solicitors in nineteenth-century England. There are several accounts of London firms of solicitors, but none address the question of what these firms actually did for their clients aside from passing references to traditional lawyerly services such as incorporations, share issues, mergers, litigation, and ordinary conveyancing and contract drafting. See, e.g., Judy Slinn, *Clifford Chance: Its Origins and Development* (London: Granta 1993); *A History of Freshfields* (London: n.p., 1984); *Ashurst Morris Crisp: A Radical Firm* (London: Granta 1997). Andrew Swann Rowley, 'Professions, Class and Society: Solicitors in 19th Century Birmingham' (PhD thesis, University of Aston in Birmingham, 1988), suffers from the same omission. Burrage does not convincingly refute evidence of solicitorial innovation such as the use of contingency fees in railway-passenger litigation provided in Rande Kostal, *Law and English Railway Capitalism 1825–1875* (Oxford: Clarendon Press 1994), but much of Kostal's evidence about solicitors being viewed as enemies rather than friends of the railway industry is broadly consistent with Burrage's interpretation.
4 G. Blaine Baker, 'Ordering the Urban Canadian Law Office and Its Entrepreneurial Hinterland, 1825 to 1875,' *University of Toronto Law Journal*, 48 (1998): 175 at 180.

5 See, e.g., Gregory P. Marchildon, 'International Corporate Law from a
   Maritime Base: The Halifax Firm of Harris, Henry, and Cahan,' in Carol
   Wilton, ed., *Beyond the Law: Lawyers and Business in Canada 1830 to 1930*
   (Toronto: University of Toronto Press for the Osgoode Society 1990); Dale
   Brawn, 'Dominant Professionals: The Role of Large-Firm Lawyers in Man-
   itoba,' in Carol Wilton, ed., *Inside the Law: Canadian Law Firms in Historical
   Perspective* (Toronto: University of Toronto Press for the Osgoode Society
   1996).

6 Brian Young, *George-Étienne Cartier: Montreal Bourgeois* (Montreal and
   Kingston: McGill-Queen's University Press 1981).

7 As cited in Gerald W. Gawalt, *The Promise of Power: The Legal Profession
   in Massachusetts 1760–1840* (Westport, Conn.: Greenwood Press 1979),
   176–7.

8 This analysis supports Norman Spaulding's revisionist account of the development of legal ethics in the United States: 'The Myth of Civic Repub-
   licanism: Interrogating the Ideology of Antebellum Legal Ethics,' *Fordham
   Law Review*, 71 (2003): 1397 (refuting the position that early U.S. lawyers
   observed virtuous ethical canons based on the public interest rather than
   zealous advocacy).

9 Burrage, *Revolution*, 464–5. See also Christopher W. Brooks and Michael
   Lobban, 'Apprenticeship or Academy? The Idea of a Law University,
   1830–1860,' in Jonathan A. Bush and Alain Wijfells, *Learning the Law: Teaching and the Transmission of Law in England 1150–1900* (London: Hambledon
   Press 1999).

10 Mark Steiner, *An Honest Calling: The Law Practice of Abraham Lincoln*
   (DeKalb: Northern Illinois University Press 2006), 53–4.

11 Burrage, *Revolution*, 301–5. For an overview of changes in the nineteenth-
   century U.S. legal profession, see Alfred S. Konefsy, 'The Legal Profession:
   From the Revolution to the Civil War,' in Michael Grossberg and Christopher Tomlins, eds., *The Cambridge History of Law in America, Vol. II* (New
   York: Cambridge University Press 2008). Unfortunately, the decision to
   devote a separate essay in the volume to legal education (Hugh C. Macgill
   and R. Kent Newmyer, 'Legal Education and Legal Thought, 1790–1920')
   means that the link between the decline of the bar associations and the rise
   of university legal education is lost, and with it, much of the distinctiveness of U.S. developments in the nineteenth century.

12 The relative strength of the parties to this partnership varied from province to province: Sylvio Normand, 'La transformation de la profession
   d'avocat au Québec, 1840–1900,' in Claire Dolan, ed., *Entre Justice et Justiciables: Les auxiliaires de la justice du Moyen Âge au XXe siècle* (Sainte-Foy,

Que.: Presses de l'Université Laval 2005), argues that the Quebec law schools long remained as virtual wards ('en tutelle') of the bar.

13 Quebec does not fit as neatly within this argument as common law Canada because of the existence of two legal professions, advocates and notaries. However, the division of labour between the two was not the same as that between barristers and solicitors in England. Quebec advocates functioned as barristers and solicitors in much the same way that lawyers in English Canada did, meeting clients, providing a wide range of advice, and drafting documents as well as pleading in the courts; the only difference with their common law colleagues was that a number of defined transactions such as marriage settlements, wills, and certain kinds of real estate conveyancing remained the monopoly of notaries. When university legal education for lawyers began in nineteenth-century Quebec, it was aimed initially only at future advocates, not at notaries. When post-secondary legal training for notaries developed, however (at the request of the notarial corporation itself), it was offered by the established university law schools and involved their taking essentially the same course as advocates with some add-ons. The formal existence of two legal professions did not prevent their cooperating on the parameters of a largely common university legal education, a situation that was virtually unthinkable in England: André Vachon, *Histoire du notariat canadien 1621–1960* (Quebec: Presses de l'Université Laval 1962), 141–6.

14 I explore this theme in an unpublished paper, 'The Making of the Legal Profession in British North America: Reform vs. Revolution' (2010).

15 Burrage, *Revolution*, 322.

16 Christopher Moore, *The Law Society of Upper Canada and Ontario's Lawyers, 1797–1997* (Toronto: University of Toronto Press 1997), 232. See also C. Ian Kyer and Jerome E. Bickenbach, *The Fiercest Debate: Cecil A. Wright, the Benchers, and Legal Education in Ontario 1923–1957* (Toronto: University of Toronto Press for the Osgoode Society 1987); Philip Girard, *Bora Laskin: Bringing Law to Life* (Toronto: University of Toronto Press for the Osgoode Society 2005), chapter 8. Some might say that the debate over the admission of women to the bar was the first 'major public challenge.' But public opinion was not nearly as united around this issue as the later issue of university legal education. See Barry Cahill, 'Legislative Privilege or Common-Law Right? Provincial State Intervention and the First Women Lawyers in Nova Scotia,' in Janet Guildford and Suzanne Morton, eds., *Making up the State: Women in 20th-Century Atlantic Canada* (Fredericton: Acadiensis Press 2010).

17 Moore, *Law Society*, 294.

18 For a twentieth-century example of challenge and response within the Nova Scotia Barristers' Society, see Philip Girard and Jeffrey Haylock, 'Stratification, Economic Adversity, and Diversity in an Urban Bar: Halifax, Nova Scotia, 1900–1950,' in Constance Backhouse and W. Wesley Pue, eds., *The Promise and Perils of Law: Lawyers in Canadian History* (Toronto: Irwin Law 2009).

19 Albert O. Hirschman, *Exit, Voice, and Loyalty: Responses to Decline in Firms, Organizations, and States* (Cambridge, Mass.: Harvard University Press 1970).

20 Burrage, *Revolution*, 224.

21 'The Legal Profession in Colonial North America,' in Wilfrid Prest, ed., *Lawyers in Early Modern Europe and America* (New York: Holmes and Meier 1981), 130.

22 G. Blaine Baker, 'Legal Education in Upper Canada 1785–1889: The Law Society as Educator,' in David H. Flaherty, ed., *Essays in the History of Canadian Law, Volume II* (Toronto: University of Toronto Press for the Osgoode Society 1983), note 73, states that the Law Society made attempts to separate the profession fully in 1830, 1839, 1840, and 1841.

23 Ibid., 66–7.

24 J.R.S. Forbes, *The Divided Legal Profession in Australia: History, Rationalisation, and Rationale* (Sydney: Law Book Co. 1979); J.M. Bennett, *Sir Francis Forbes, First Chief Justice of New South Wales 1823–1837* (Sydney: Federation Press 2001), 105–9.

25 Rob McQueen, 'Together We Fall, Divided We Stand: The Victorian Legal Profession in Crisis, 1890–1940,' in W. Wesley Pue and David Sugarman, eds., *Lawyers and Vampires: Cultural Histories of Legal Professions* (Oxford and Portland, Ore.: Hart Publishing 2003), 300–2.

26 *Epitome*, 1: 10.

27 Peggy Pascoe, *What Comes Naturally: Miscegenation Law and the Making of Race in America* (New York: Oxford University Press 2009); and see the comparative discussion of these statutes in Philip Girard with Jim Phillips, 'Re-Thinking "the Nation" in National Legal History: A Canadian Perspective,' *Law & History Review*, 29 (2011): 607–26.

28 David Howes, 'From Polyjurality to Monojurality: The Transformation of Quebec Law, 1875–1929,' *McGill Law Journal*, 32 (1987): 523–58.

29 H. Patrick Glenn, 'Persuasive Authority,' *McGill Law Journal*, 32 (1987): 261; Bernard Hibbitts, however, has noted considerable interest by U.S. law reviews in Canadian legal matters down to about 1900: '"Our Arctic Brethren": Canadian Law and Lawyers as Portrayed in American Legal Periodicals, 1829–1911,' in G. Blaine Baker and Jim Phillips, eds., *Essays in*

the History of Canadian Law, Volume VIII, In Honour of R.C.B. Risk (Toronto: University of Toronto Press for the Osgoode Society 1999), 268.

30 See especially Constant and Ducharme, eds., *Liberalism and Hegemony*.

31 'Closing the Last Chapter of the Atlantic Revolution: The 1837–38 Rebellions in Upper and Lower Canada,' *Proceedings of the American Antiquarian Society*, 116 (2006): 411–28.

32 These ideas are elaborated in Ducharme, *Le Concept de liberté*. Jerry Bannister's proposal of a 'loyalist order' in Canada as a counter to McKay's 'liberal order' has much in common with Ducharme and with the views put forward here, but in my view his recourse to the notion of counter-revolution is unhelpful: 'Canada as Counter-Revolution: The Loyalist Order Framework in Canadian History, 1750–1840,' in Constant and Ducharme, eds., *Liberalism and Hegemony*.

33 'The Liberal Order Framework.' McKay responds to his critics and modifies his initial views in 'Canada as a Long Liberal Revolution: On Writing the History of Actually Existing Canadian Liberalisms, 1840s–1940s,' in Constant and Ducharme, eds., *Liberalism and Hegemony*.

34 Philip Girard, 'Liberty, Order and Pluralism: The Canadian Experience,' in Jack P. Greene, ed., *Exclusionary Empire: English Liberty Overseas, 1600–1900* (New York: Cambridge University Press 2009). On the slippage from 'public welfare' to 'order' in Canadian constitutional documents, see John Ralston Saul, *A Fair Country: Telling Truths about Canada* (Toronto: Viking 2008).

35 E.A. Heaman, 'Rights Talk and the Liberal Order Framework,' in Constant and Ducharme, eds., *Liberalism and Hegemony*.

Index

2011   Robert J. Sharpe, *The Lazier Murder: Prince Edward County, 1884*
       Philip Girard, *Lawyers and Legal Culture in British North America: Beamish Murdoch of Halifax*
       John McLaren, *Dewigged, Bothered, and Bewildered: British Colonial Judges on Trial, 1800–1900*
       Lesley Erickson, *Westward Bound: Sex, Violence, the Law, and the Making of a Settler Society*

2010   Judy Fudge and Eric Tucker, eds., *Work on Trial: Canadian Labour Law Struggles*
       Christopher Moore, *The British Columbia Court of Appeal: The First Hundred Years*
       Frederick Vaughan, *Viscount Haldane: 'The Wicked Step-father of the Canadian Constitution'*
       Barrington Walker, *Race on Trial: Black Defendants in Ontario's Criminal Courts, 1858–1958*

2009   William Kaplan, *Canadian Maverick: The Life and Times of Ivan C. Rand*
       R. Blake Brown, *A Trying Question: The Jury in Nineteenth-Century Canada*
       Barry Wright and Susan Binnie, eds., *Canadian State Trials, Volume III: Political Trials and Security Measures, 1840–1914*
       Robert J. Sharpe, *The Last Day, the Last Hour: The Currie Libel Trial* (paperback edition with a new preface)

2008   Constance Backhouse, *Carnal Crimes: Sexual Assault Law in Canada, 1900–1975*
       Jim Phillips, R. Roy McMurtry, and John T. Saywell, eds., *Essays in the History of Canadian Law, Volume X: A Tribute to Peter N. Oliver*
       Greg Taylor, *The Law of the Land: The Advent of the Torrens System in Canada*
       Hamar Foster, Benjamin Berger, and A.R. Buck, eds., *The Grand Experiment: Law and Legal Culture in British Settler Societies*

2007   Robert Sharpe and Patricia McMahon, *The Persons Case: The Origins and Legacy of the Fight for Legal Personhood*
       Lori Chambers, *Misconceptions: Unmarried Motherhood and the Ontario Children of Unmarried Parents Act, 1921–1969*
       Jonathan Swainger, ed., *A History of the Supreme Court of Alberta*
       Martin Friedland, *My Life in Crime and Other Academic Adventures*

2006   Donald Fyson, *Magistrates, Police, and People: Everyday Criminal Justice in Quebec and Lower Canada, 1764–1837*

Dale Brawn, *The Court of Queen's Bench of Manitoba, 1870–1950: A Biographical History*

R.C.B. Risk, *A History of Canadian Legal Thought: Collected Essays*, edited and introduced by G. Blaine Baker and Jim Phillips

2005 Philip Girard, *Bora Laskin: Bringing Law to Life*

Christopher English, ed., *Essays in the History of Canadian Law: Volume IX – Two Islands: Newfoundland and Prince Edward Island*

Fred Kaufman, *Searching for Justice: An Autobiography*

2004 Philip Girard, Jim Phillips, and Barry Cahill, eds., *The Supreme Court of Nova Scotia, 1754–2004: From Imperial Bastion to Provincial Oracle*

Frederick Vaughan, *Aggressive in Pursuit: The Life of Justice Emmett Hall*

John D. Honsberger, *Osgoode Hall: An Illustrated History*

Constance Backhouse and Nancy Backhouse, *The Heiress versus the Establishment: Mrs Campbell's Campaign for Legal Justice*

2003 Robert Sharpe and Kent Roach, *Brian Dickson: A Judge's Journey*

Jerry Bannister, *The Rule of the Admirals: Law, Custom, and Naval Government in Newfoundland, 1699–1832*

George Finlayson, *John J. Robinette, Peerless Mentor: An Appreciation*

Peter Oliver, *The Conventional Man: The Diaries of Ontario Chief Justice Robert A. Harrison, 1856–1878*

2002 John T. Saywell, *The Lawmakers: Judicial Power and the Shaping of Canadian Federalism*

Patrick Brode, *Courted and Abandoned: Seduction in Canadian Law*

David Murray, *Colonial Justice: Justice, Morality, and Crime in the Niagara District, 1791–1849*

F. Murray Greenwood and Barry Wright, eds., *Canadian State Trials, Volume II: Rebellion and Invasion in the Canadas, 1837–1839*

2001 Ellen Anderson, *Judging Bertha Wilson: Law as Large as Life*

Judy Fudge and Eric Tucker, *Labour before the Law: The Regulation of Workers' Collective Action in Canada, 1900–1948*

Laurel Sefton MacDowell, *Renegade Lawyer: The Life of J.L. Cohen*

2000 Barry Cahill, *'The Thousandth Man': A Biography of James McGregor Stewart*

A.B. McKillop, *The Spinster and the Prophet: Florence Deeks, H.G. Wells, and the Mystery of the Purloined Past*

Beverley Boissery and F. Murray Greenwood, *Uncertain Justice: Canadian Women and Capital Punishment*

Bruce Ziff, *Unforeseen Legacies: Reuben Wells Leonard and the Leonard Foundation Trust*

1999   Constance Backhouse, *Colour-Coded: A Legal History of Racism in Canada, 1900–1950*
       G. Blaine Baker and Jim Phillips, eds., *Essays in the History of Canadian Law: Volume VIII – In Honour of R.C.B. Risk*
       Richard W. Pound, *Chief Justice W.R. Jackett: By the Law of the Land*
       David Vanek, *Fulfilment: Memoirs of a Criminal Court Judge*
1998   Sidney Harring, *White Man's Law: Native People in Nineteenth-Century Canadian Jurisprudence*
       Peter Oliver, *'Terror to Evil-Doers': Prisons and Punishments in Nineteenth-Century Ontario*
1997   James W.St.G. Walker, *'Race,' Rights and the Law in the Supreme Court of Canada: Historical Case Studies*
       Lori Chambers, *Married Women and Property Law in Victorian Ontario*
       Patrick Brode, *Casual Slaughters and Accidental Judgments: Canadian War Crimes and Prosecutions, 1944–1948*
       Ian Bushnell, *The Federal Court of Canada: A History, 1875–1992*
1996   Carol Wilton, ed., *Essays in the History of Canadian Law: Volume VII – Inside the Law: Canadian Law Firms in Historical Perspective*
       William Kaplan, *Bad Judgment: The Case of Mr Justice Leo A. Landreville*
       Murray Greenwood and Barry Wright, eds., *Canadian State Trials: Volume I – Law, Politics, and Security Measures, 1608–1837*
1995   David Williams, *Just Lawyers: Seven Portraits*
       Hamar Foster and John McLaren, eds., *Essays in the History of Canadian Law: Volume VI – British Columbia and the Yukon*
       W.H. Morrow, ed., *Northern Justice: The Memoirs of Mr Justice William G. Morrow*
       Beverley Boissery, *A Deep Sense of Wrong: The Treason, Trials, and Transportation to New South Wales of Lower Canadian Rebels after the 1838 Rebellion*
1994   Patrick Boyer, *A Passion for Justice: The Legacy of James Chalmers McRuer*
       Charles Pullen, *The Life and Times of Arthur Maloney: The Last of the Tribunes*
       Jim Phillips, Tina Loo, and Susan Lewthwaite, eds., *Essays in the History of Canadian Law: Volume V – Crime and Criminal Justice*
       Brian Young, *The Politics of Codification: The Lower Canadian Civil Code of 1866*
1993   Greg Marquis, *Policing Canada's Century: A History of the Canadian Association of Chiefs of Police*
       Murray Greenwood, *Legacies of Fear: Law and Politics in Quebec in the Era of the French Revolution*

1992   Brendan O'Brien, *Speedy Justice: The Tragic Last Voyage of His Majesty's Vessel Speedy*
       Robert Fraser, ed., *Provincial Justice: Upper Canadian Legal Portraits from the Dictionary of Canadian Biography*
1991   Constance Backhouse, *Petticoats and Prejudice: Women and Law in Nineteenth-Century Canada*
1990   Philip Girard and Jim Phillips, eds., *Essays in the History of Canadian Law: Volume III – Nova Scotia*
       Carol Wilton, ed., *Essays in the History of Canadian Law: Volume IV – Beyond the Law: Lawyers and Business in Canada, 1830–1930*
1989   Desmond Brown, *The Genesis of the Canadian Criminal Code of 1892*
       Patrick Brode, *The Odyssey of John Anderson*
1988   Robert Sharpe, *The Last Day, the Last Hour: The Currie Libel Trial*
       John D. Arnup, *Middleton: The Beloved Judge*
1987   C. Ian Kyer and Jerome Bickenbach, *The Fiercest Debate: Cecil A. Wright, the Benchers, and Legal Education in Ontario, 1923–1957*
1986   Paul Romney, *Mr Attorney: The Attorney General for Ontario in Court, Cabinet, and Legislature, 1791–1899*
       Martin Friedland, *The Case of Valentine Shortis: A True Story of Crime and Politics in Canada*
1985   James Snell and Frederick Vaughan, *The Supreme Court of Canada: History of the Institution*
1984   Patrick Brode, *Sir John Beverley Robinson: Bone and Sinew of the Compact*
       David Williams, *Duff: A Life in the Law*
1983   David H. Flaherty, ed., *Essays in the History of Canadian Law: Volume II*
1982   Marion MacRae and Anthony Adamson, *Cornerstones of Order: Courthouses and Town Halls of Ontario, 1784–1914*
1981   David H. Flaherty, ed., *Essays in the History of Canadian Law: Volume I*